Asymmetries, Courts, and Comparative Constitutional Law

Studies in Territorial and Cultural Diversity Governance

Series Editors

Francesco Palermo
Joseph Marko
Roberta Medda-Windischer

VOLUME 24

The titles published in this series are listed at *brill.com/tcdg*

Asymmetries, Courts, and Comparative Constitutional Law

A Dynamic Accommodation of Diversity in Divided Multi-tiered Systems

By

Lidia Bonifati

BRILL | NIJHOFF

LEIDEN | BOSTON

This work was supported by BOF Fellowship for Joint PhDs from the University of Antwerp (project ID 46337) and by the "Marco Polo" Programme of the Department of Legal Studies at the University of Bologna.

Library of Congress Cataloging-in-Publication Data

Names: Bonifati, Lidia author
Title: Asymmetries, courts, and comparative constitutional law : a dynamic accommodation of diversity in divided multi-tiered systems / by Lidia Bonifati.
Description: Leiden ; Boston : Brill Academic Publishers, Inc, 2025. | Series: Studies in territorial and cultural diversity governance ; volume 24 | Includes bibliographical references and index.
Identifiers: LCCN 2025029954 | ISBN 9789004736870 hardback | ISBN 9789004739109 epub
Subjects: LCSH: Constitutional law--Political aspects | Constitutional courts | Federal government | Comparative law | Cultural pluralism | Asymmetric synthesis
Classification: LCC K3165 .B667 2025 | DDC 342--DC23/ENG/20250711
LC record available at https://lccn.loc.gov/2025029954

Typeface for the Latin, Greek, and Cyrillic scripts: "Brill". See and download: brill.com/brill-typeface.

ISSN 2213-2570
ISBN 978-90-04-73687-0 (hardback)
ISBN 978-90-04-73910-9 (e-book)
DOI 10.1163/9789004739109

This book is printed on acid-free paper and produced in a sustainable manner.

To my parents, Giovanni and Margherita, and to my brother Michele,
for getting me here
To my wife Chiara, for loving me every step of the way

Contents

PART 2
The Role of Constitutional Courts

Foreword

This book by Lidia Bonifati is innovative, inspiring, and an invaluable contribution to scholarship for many reasons.

One reason is that this book bridges two important strands of literature on compound systems that too often remain isolated: the power-sharing literature and federalism literature.

As a way to accommodate territorially concentrated minorities, constitutional asymmetry is a key concern in power-sharing literature. There, the debate was mostly on the potentially destabilising nature of constitutional asymmetry. Constitutional asymmetry, however, was never measured; thus, it was impossible to determine at what level asymmetry constitutes a potential danger. I introduced the 'constitutional asymmetry score' in my book on *Dynamic Federalism*,[1] and I am extremely happy that Lidia Bonifati took this up to measure, for the first time, constitutional asymmetry in a wide range of multi-tiered multinational systems. It allows us to assess the intensity of constitutional asymmetry and to situate it in each of the three structural dimensions: status, powers, and fiscal arrangements.

By contrast, traditional federal theory – based on a limited set of 'model' federations, mostly Western, homogeneous and coming together – sat uneasily with new systems of dispersed authority and with constitutional asymmetry common to these systems. This book takes an important new step in a burgeoning scholarship on constitutional asymmetry as a feature of multinational federal systems, only a few years after Maja Sahadžić laid the foundations for a federal perspective on constitutional asymmetry.[2] It focuses on federal dynamics rather than (much contested) narrow definitions of federations in traditional federal theory. This way, it can include new systems of dispersed authority as multi-tiered systems in their own right instead of so-called 'quasi-federations' – a popular term in federal theory, but both misleading and derogatory. As Lidia writes in her introduction, integrating constitutional systems in the Global South as fully-fledged systems, away from the implied superiority of traditional theory, is a much-needed decolonial perspective. At the same time, the book examines systems that are widely recognised as 'federations' – Belgium, Canada and India – in a way that takes them

1 Patricia Popelier, *Dynamic Federalism. A New Theory for Cohesion and Regional Autonomy* (London and New York: Routledge, 2021).

2 Maja Sahadžić, *Asymmetry, Multinationalism and Constitutional Law: Managing Legitimacy and Stability in Federalist States* (London and New York: Routledge, 2020).

out of the straitjacket of traditional theory, unfamiliar with multinationalism and how it impacts constitutional design.

Another reason is that the book brings together political science and legal scholarship. In what Erk and Swenden call the "new wave of federalism studies",[3] focused on federal dynamics, political, social, and economic scholars have taken the lead, and legal scholars are lagging behind. This is a loss for this "new wave", as it fails to capture valuable insights on the role of courts and legal procedures in federal dynamics. Lidia Bonifati's book provides irrefutable proof thereof, where she shows how legal along with extra-legal factors explain the different manifestations of constitutional asymmetry, and how courts reshape the degree of these asymmetries. Leading up to the courts' approach to constitutional asymmetry, the book also discusses their role in accommodating diversity. Bringing courts into the study of federalism and asymmetry is a major contribution in itself, especially considering its breadth, including national and supranational courts, as well as quasi-judicial bodies. This builds on what Stefan Graziadei coined "power-sharing courts"[4] and extends it through a comparison with hybrid courts.

With her interdisciplinary background, her scholarly rigour, and the ease with which she penetrates and connects strands of literature, this author is a young talent to follow closely, her book what was needed to fuel the "new wave of federalism studies" across disciplines.

Enjoy the reading!

Patricia Popelier

3 Jan Erk, and Wilfred Swenden, "The New Waves of Federalism Studies," in *New Directions in Federalism Studies*, ed. Jan Erk, and Wilfred Swenden (London and New York: Routledge, 2010), 1–15.

4 Stefan Graziadei, "Power Sharing Courts," *Contemporary Southeastern Europe* 3, no. 2 (2016): 66–105.

Acknowledgements

Writing a book is certainly a group effort, and many people deserve to be thanked. First and foremost, I would like to thank Susanna Mancini and Patricia Popelier for being my constant guide during and after the Ph.D. Their invaluable support made it possible to keep working on my doctoral thesis and exploring new paths of my previous research, which eventually led to this book. I will be forever grateful to Giuseppe de Vergottini for first teaching me about the importance of method in comparative constitutional law. His pioneering work has become the foundation of my research mindset.

I want to express my profound gratitude to Francesco Biagi, Philipp Dann, Elena Ferioli, Justin O. Frosini, Cedric Jenart, Giuseppe Martinico, Leonardo Pierdominici, Maja Sahadžić, Diletta Tega, Arianna Vedaschi, and Jens Woelk, who all contributed with their time and insights on my work. I am also sincerely grateful to Francesco Palermo, who has generously supported the inclusion of this book in the Brill Series on *Studies in Territorial and Cultural Diversity Governance* and has always been ready to discuss my research.

Part of this research has been conducted during my Ph.D., and I want to thank the incredible institutions and research staff that hosted me: the Faculty of Law at the University of Antwerp, the Department of Law at the European University Institute, and the Institute for Comparative Federalism at EURAC Research. The feedback I received during these visiting periods has been among the most important and thought-provoking I ever received. I am also grateful to the University of Bologna and the University of Antwerp for funding my research experience abroad, respectively through the Marco Polo Programme of the Department of Legal Studies and the BOF Fellowship for Joint Ph.D.s of the University of Antwerp.

Thanks to all the friends and colleagues I met along the way in Bologna, Antwerp, and Milan for being part of this journey, especially Pier Francesco Bresciani, Lucrezia Cadamuro, Chiara Graziani, Francesco Lucherini, Alessandro Martinuzzi, Alberto Nicotina, and Micol Pignataro. I would also like to thank Sylvie Armstrong for proofreading this book and patiently reading almost every piece of English-written research I produced.

Special thanks to my lights in the darkness: Francesca Raimondo, Justine Muller, Marco Poli, and Nicolò Paolo Alessi. They are all amazing researchers, and this book would not have been the same without their support and all the time they dedicated to reading and discussing my work with me when I was stuck.

I would also like to thank Ornella and Riccardo for always showering me with love, especially the Summer in Salina when much of this book was written. The endless laughs we shared on their terrace have been a precious gift that made it all easier. This book was written not only in Salina but across multiple cities, each leaving a unique mark on the project's development: Antwerp, Bologna, Bolzano, Florence, Milan, Oxford, and Palermo. Belfast and Sarajevo occupy a particular place in this journey, having nurtured the initial seeds of this research and continuing to provide ongoing inspiration.

I do not have enough words to thank my friends and family, by blood and by choice, who were always ready to celebrate with me and encourage me. Mom, Dad, Michele, and Giulia, this is all for you. Thank you for always being there for me, especially when I needed it the most.

Finally, I am incredibly grateful to my wife, Chiara. She witnessed the very birth of this research and watched it grow into something that neither of us could ever anticipate. I could have never wished for a better partner for this adventure.

Needless to say, I am solely responsible for any errors and omissions in this book, and any opinions expressed are solely my own.

Abbreviations

AC	Autonomous Community
ACHR	American Convention on Human Rights
ACHRP	African Commission on Human and Peoples' Rights
ACtHRP	African Court on Human and Peoples' Rights
AV	Alternative Vote
BiH	Bosnia and Herzegovina
BJP	Bharatiya Janata Party
CCI	Council of Constitutional Inquiry
DPA	Dayton Peace Agreement
EACJ	East African Court of Justice
ECHR	European Convention on Human Rights
ECOWAS	Economic Community of West African States
ECRML	European Charter for Regional or Minority Languages
ECtHR	European Court of Human Rights
FCNM	Framework Convention for the Protection of National Minorities
HCNM	High Commissioner on National Minorities
HJPC	High Judicial and Prosecutorial Council
IACHR	Inter-American Commission on Human Rights
IACtHR	Inter-American Court of Human Rights
ICCPR	International Covenant on Civil and Political Rights
ICESCR	International Covenant on Economic, Social and Cultural Rights
ICR	International Civilian Representative for Kosovo
ICJ	International Court of Justice
ICJR	Institute for Criminal Justice Reform
IGR	Intergovernmental Relations
ILO	International Labour Organisation
JCPC	Judicial Committee of the Privy Council
MTS	Multi-Tiered System
NI	Northern Ireland
OSCE	Organisation for Security and Co-operation in Europe
PR	Proportional Representation
SAA	Stabilisation and Association Agreement
SNE	Subnational entity
STV	Single Transferable Vote
UKSC	Supreme Court of the United Kingdom
UNDRIP	UN Declaration on the Rights of Indigenous Peoples
USSC	Supreme Court of the United States

Case Law

Domestic Jurisprudence

Belgium

Constitutional Court, Judgement No. 25, 26 June 1986.
Constitutional Court, Judgement No. 47, 25 February 1988.
Constitutional Court, Judgement No. 132, 14 July 2004.
Constitutional Court, Judgement No. 172, 22 November 2006.
Constitutional Court, Judgement No. 168, 10 November 2011.

Bosnia-Herzegovina

Constitutional Court, Case U-5/98 III, 1 July 2000 (*Constituent Peoples'* case).
Constitutional Court, Case U-44/01, 27 February 2004 (*Place Names* case).
Constitutional Court, Case U-6/07, 4 October 2008.
Constitutional Court, Case U-9/09, 26 November 2010.
Constitutional Court, Case U-17/09, 27 March 2010.
Constitutional Court, Case U-1/11, 13 July 2012.
Constitutional Court, Case U-3/13, 26 November 2015.
Constitutional Court, Case U-2/22, 16 May 2022.
Constitutional Court, Case U-10/22, 22 September 2022.
Constitutional Court, Case U-5/23, 2 March 2023.

Canada

Canadian Western Bank [2007] 2 SCR 3.
Reference Re Secession of Québec [1998] 2 S.C.R. 217.
Re: Objection by Québec to a Resolution to Amend the Constitution [1982] 2 SCR 793.
Re: Resolution to Amend the Constitution [1981] 1 SCR 733

India

Danial Latifi & Anr v. Union of India [2001] Supp. (3) S.C.R. 419.
Ewalangki-E-Ryambai v. Jaintia Hills District Council (2006) 4 SCC 748.
In Re Article 370 of the Constitution (2023), WP (C) 1013/2019.
Kesavananda Bharati Sripadagalvaru & Ors. v. State of Kerala & Anr. (1973) 4 SCC 225; AIR 1973 SC 1461
Mangal Singh v. Union of India, AIR 1967, SC 944.
Mohd. Ahmed Khan v. Shah Bano Begum [1985] 3 S.C.R. 844.
Mohd. Maqbook Damnoo v. State of Jammu and Kashmir (1972) 1 SCC 536.
Prem Nath Kaul v. State of Jammu and Kashmir AIR 1959 SC 749.

Pu Myllai Hlycho v. State of Mizoram (2005) 2 SCC 92.
RC Poudyal v. Union of India (1994) Supp 1 SCC 324.
Sampath Prakash v. State of Jammu and Kashmir AIR 1970 SC 1118.
State Bank of India v. Santosh Gupta (2017) 2 SCC 538.
State of Sikkim v. Surendra Prasad Sharma (1984), 5 SCC 282.

Indonesia

Constitutional Court, Decision No. 4/PHPU.A-VII/2009 (*Papua DPD* case).
Constitutional Court, Decision No. 14/PHPU.D-XI/2013 (*Papua gubernatorial election* case).

Italy

Constitutional Court, Judgement No. 20, 16 July 1956.
Constitutional Court, Judgement No. 22, 11 May 1961.
Constitutional Court, Judgement No. 1146, 29 December 1988.
Constitutional Court, Judgement No. 366, 23 July 1991.
Constitutional Court, Judgement No. 213, 19 June 1998.
Constitutional Court, Judgement No. 106, 12 April 2002.
Constitutional Court, Judgement No. 274, 24 July 2003.
Constitutional Court, Judgement No. 303, 1 October 2003.
Constitutional Court, Judgement No. 14, 13 January 2004.
Constitutional Court, Judgements Nos. 50 and 51, 28 January 2005.
Constitutional Court, Judgement No. 80, 16 March 2007.
Constitutional Court, Judgement No. 365, 7 November 2007.
Constitutional Court, Judgement No. 102, 15 April 2008.
Constitutional Court, Judgement No. 105, 18 April 2008.
Constitutional Court, Judgement No. 61, 5 March 2009.
Constitutional Court, Judgement No. 10, 15 January 2010.
Constitutional Court, Judgement No. 170, 13 May 2010.
Constitutional Court, Judgements Nos. 198 and 199, 20 July 2012.
Constitutional Court, Judgement No. 251, 25 November 2016.
Constitutional Court, Judgement No. 7, 17 January 2019.
Constitutional Court, Judgement No. 37, 13 March 2021.
Constitutional Court, Judgement No. 192, 3 December 2024.

South Africa

Constitutional Court, Certification of the Constitution of the Republic of South Africa, 1996 (CCT 23/96) [1996] ZACC 26; 1996 (4) SA 744 (CC); 1996 (10) BCLR 1253 (CC) (6 September 1996).

Spain

Spanish Constitutional Tribunal, Judgement No. 4, 2 February 1981.
Spanish Constitutional Tribunal, Judgement No. 76, 5 August 1983.
Spanish Constitutional Tribunal, Judgement No. 247, 17 December 2007.
Spanish Constitutional Tribunal, Judgement No. 103, 11 September 2008.
Spanish Constitutional Tribunal, Judgement No. 31, 28 June 2010.
Spanish Constitutional Tribunal, Judgement No. 42, 25 March 2014.
Spanish Constitutional Tribunal, Judgements Nos. 89 and 90, 2 July 2019.

United Kingdom

R (Miller) v. Secretary of State for Exiting the EU [2017] UKSC 5, [2018] AC 61.

International Jurisprudence

African Commission on Human and Peoples' Rights

Centre for Minority Rights Development (Kenya) and Minority Rights Group (on behalf of Endorois Welfare Council) v. Kenya, Communication No. 276/03 (2010).
Katangese Peoples' Congress v. Zaire, Communication No. 75/92 (1995).

European Court of Human Rights

Baralija v. Bosnia and Herzegovina, Case 30100/28, 29 October 2019.
Kovačević v. Bosnia and Herzegovina, Case No. 43651/22, 29 August 2023.
Mathieu-Mohin and Clerfayt v. Belgium, Case No. 9267/81, 2 March 1987.
Pilav v. Bosnia and Herzegovina, Case No. 41939/07, 9 June 2016.
Pudarić v. Bosnia and Herzegovina, Case No. 55799/18, 8 December 2020.
Sejdić and Finci v. Bosnia and Herzegovina [Grand Chamber], Case Nos. 27996/06 and 34836/06, 22 December 2009.
Zornić v. Bosnia and Herzegovina, Case No. 3681/06, 15 July 2014.

Inter-American Court of Human Rights

Case of the Kaliña and Lokono Peoples v. Suriname, Series C No. 309, 25 November 2015.
Case of the Kichwa Indigenous People of Sarayaku v. Ecuador, Series C No. 245, 27 June 2012.
Case of the Mayagna (Sumo) Awas Tingni Community v. Nicaragua, Series C No. 7, 31 August 2001.
Case of the Moiwana Community v. Suriname, Serie C No. 124, 15 June 2005.
Case of the Saramaka People v. Suriname, Series C No. 172, 28 November 2007.

International Court of Justice

Legal Consequences of the Separation of the Chagos Archipelago from Mauritius in 1965, Advisory Opinion, (2019) ICJ Reports 95.

East Timor (Portugal v. Australia), Judgment, (1995) ICJ Reports 90.

Accordance with International Law of the Unilateral Declaration of Independence in Respect of Kosovo, Advisory Opinion, (2010) ICJ Reports 403.

Legal Consequences for States of the Continued Presence of South Africa in Namibia (South West Africa) notwithstanding Security Council Resolution 276 (1970), Advisory Opinion, (1971) ICJ Reports 16.

Legal Consequences of the Construction of a Wall in the Occupied Palestinian Territory, Advisory Opinion, (2004) ICJ Reports 136.

Western Sahara, Advisory Opinion, (1975) ICJ Reports 12.

Figures and Tables

Figures

Tables

Introduction

1 Unfolding the Subject

Societies divided along ethnic, linguistic, religious, or cultural lines give rise to practical challenges of great importance. In fact, the tensions between ethnocultural groups may result in violence (permanent discrimination, civil conflict, ethnic cleansing, genocide) or, even in the absence of violence, have a corrosive effect on the political dynamics of the state, creating a stalemate in political institutions or even a constitutional crisis. In Bosnia-Herzegovina, ethnic divisions were exploited by political actors in order to fuel nationalist claims, resulting in one of the most violent wars witnessed on European soil since the Second World War. Eventually, the Dayton Peace Agreement ended the war in 1995, introducing a set of complex power-sharing arrangements to hold the system in check. In practice, the complexity of the constitutional settlement is so great and pervasive at every level of governance that institutional crises are the norm. This means that the political system is unable to deal effectively with important issues such as high levels of emigration, economic crisis, endemic corruption, and secessionist threats. Dayton brought peace to Bosnia-Herzegovina, but not a sustainable solution in the long term.

Many other examples could be recalled, both more and less problematic than Bosnia-Herzegovina. Comparative studies on the arrangements adopted in divided societies indicate that there is no magic formula or one-size-fits-all solution, as there are lots of different factors that may influence constitutional design. Therefore, the reality of their implementation must always be taken into account in order to effectively deal with these challenges. With that in mind, this book does not purport to find a definitive answer to the many questions that arise in divided societies. Instead, the overall aim is to look at the topic from a different perspective in order to explore alternative explanations and offer valuable insights into the subject. In particular, the research attempts to sew together the scholarship on constitutional design for divided societies with that on federalism, as the two find a middle ground in the introduction of constitutional asymmetries in divided multi-tiered systems.

 | DOI:10.1163/9789004739109_002

2 Terminological Clarifications

Before diving deeper into the subject, it is worth briefly defining four essential concepts that the book will deal with, in order to facilitate understanding of the overall research.

2.1 *Constitutional Design, Constitution-Making*

Constitutional design may be defined as the imaginative process according to which government structures and fundamental rights are modelled. Albeit linked to constitution-making, the two should be considered different concepts.[1] In fact, constitutional design is the vision, the process that precedes and accompanies the drafting phase, as well as the outcome of this process, while constitution-making is the process in which the design is operationalised in the drafting of a new constitution. In the current research, the expressions "constitutional design", "constitutional engineering", and "institutional architecture", are broadly considered synonyms, even though they may emphasise different aspects of the process of constitutional design. "Constitutional engineering" stresses the adjustment of certain mechanisms in the original design at a later stage, e.g., through constitutional amendments, while "institutional architecture" highlights the institutions established on the basis of the design.

2.2 *Federal States, Federal Systems, Multi-tiered Systems*

In federal theory, federalism as a concept has not yet found a comprehensive and widely accepted definition.[2] Since this research does not seek to contribute to a re-definition of the debate on a general theory of federalism, this book takes a pragmatic approach, relying on the conception of federalism as an overall idea, founded on Elazar's principle of "self-rule and shared rule"[3] among constituent units. Moreover, it makes reference to federalism

1 See Tom Ginsburg, "Introduction," in *Comparative Constitutional Design*, ed. Tom Ginsburg (Cambridge: Cambridge University Press, 2012), 1–14.

2 See Anna Gamper, "A 'Global Theory of Federalism': The Nature and Challenges of a Federal State," *German Law Journal* 6, no. 10 (2005): 1297–1318; Francesco Palermo and Karl Kössler, *Comparative Federalism* (Oxford: Hart Publishing, 2017), 13–19; Patricia Popelier, *Dynamic Federalism: A New Theory for Cohesion and Regional Autonomy* (London and New York: Routledge, 2021), 9–45.

3 Daniel J. Elazar, *Exploring Federalism* (Tuscaloosa and London: University of Alabama Press, 1987), 5.

as a process rather than as a fixed design, as theorised by Friedrich.[4] For this reason, this research refers to the category of "multi-tiered systems" (MTS), namely those systems with multiple tiers of government in which the central level coexists with subnational entities (SNEs) that have lawmaking powers.[5] This makes it possible to include as many manifestations of federalism as possible, encompassing also those systems wishing to distance themselves from the strict definition of a "federation", such as regional or devolutionary systems. In this research, what matters is not the formal name that constitutional systems decide to adopt to describe themselves (federation, regional state, unitary state with devolution of powers), but the existence of multiple levels of government interacting with each other and possibly creating constitutional asymmetries within the system.

2.3 *Divided Societies, Multinationalism*

This book mainly refers to the concept of "divided society" as defined by Choudhry: "As a category of political and constitutional analysis, a divided society is not merely a society which is ethnically, linguistically, religiously, or culturally diverse. [...] Rather, what marks a divided society is that these differences are politically salient – that is, they are persistent markers of political identity and bases for political mobilisation. Ethnocultural diversity is translated into political fragmentation. In a divided society, political claims are refracted through the lens of ethnic identity, and political conflict is synonymous with conflict among ethno-cultural groups".[6] For methodological purposes, this research also includes those societies that are only "partially divided",[7] meaning those societies in which ethnocultural divisions may

4 See Carl J. Friedrich, *Constitutional Government and Democracy: Theory and Practice in Europe and America* (Waltham: Blaisdell Publishing Company, 1968); Carl J. Friedrich, "New Tendencies in Federal Theory and Practice," *Jahrbuch des Öffentliches Rechts* 14 (1965); Carl J. Friedrich, *Trends of Federalism in Theory and Practice* (New York: Frederick A. Praeger, 1968).

5 For more on multi-tiered systems, see Palermo and Kössler, *Comparative Federalism*, 8; Patricia Popelier and Maja Sahadžić, eds., *Constitutional Asymmetry in Multinational Federalism* (Cham, Switzerland: Palgrave Macmillan, 2019), 4; Maja Sahadžić, *Asymmetry, Multinationalism and Constitutional Law* (London and New York: Routledge, 2020), 44–45; Popelier, *Dynamic Federalism*, 50–51.

6 Sujit Choudhry, "Bridging Comparative Politics and Comparative Constitutional Law," in *Constitutional Design for Divided Societies*, ed. Sujit Choudhry (Oxford: Oxford University Press, 2008), 4–5.

7 Nicolò Paolo Alessi and Francesco Palermo, "Intergovernmental Relations and Identity Politics in Italy," in *Intergovernmental Relations in Divided Societies: A Comparative Perspective*, ed. Yonatan Fessha and Karl Kössler (Cham: Palgrave Macmillan, 2022), 185.

exist only in limited parts of the territory where the minorities are located (e.g., South Tyrol in Italy with the *Südtiroler Volkspartei*, representing the German-speaking and Ladin-speaking minority), while in the rest of the territory the same divisions are legally irrelevant.

The term "divided society" partly overlaps with Stepan's definition of the multinational state as a state that has territorially based differences rooted in linguistic, religious, cultural, and ethnic identities, and in which there are political groups that aim to build political sovereignty or an independent state (or states) around these territorially based differences.[8] However, the two may be distinguished in terms of their perspectives, justifying my choice. First of all, the category of divided society first makes reference to the societal level, while multinationalism tends to indicate the institutional and territorial manifestations of ethnocultural differences, thus referring to a multinational state (and not society). This leads to a substantial difference between the two, namely their focus on territory. If in Stepan's definition, the territory plays an essential role, as also demonstrated by Sahadžić,[9] the fact that ethnocultural differences cover the entire territory or are present in only limited parts is irrelevant to defining a divided society.

A good example of the distinction between the two terms is offered by Northern Ireland. Northern Ireland is considered a classic example of a divided society by the literature, but it cannot be classified as a multinational state. Conversely, the United Kingdom, of which Northern Ireland is an integral part, can be considered a multinational state specifically because Northern Ireland constitutes a territorial manifestation of ethnocultural differences. *Vice versa*, the United Kingdom can also be considered a divided society because it displays different identities (Scottish, Northern Irish, Welsh), which become markers for political mobilisation (e.g., regional political parties such as the Scottish National Parties, Sinn Féin, Plaid Cymru).

Moreover, the violent or non-violent conflict arising from ethnocultural groups in divided societies has led, and still leads, to processes of constitutional design in order to accommodate such differences. It could be argued that divided societies that underwent a process of constitutional design to

8 Alfred Stepan, "Towards a New Comparative Politics of Federalism, Multinationalism, and Democracy: Beyond Rikerian Federalism," in *Federalism and Democracy in Latin America*, ed. Edward L. Gibson (Baltimore, Maryland: Johns Hopkins University Press, 2004), 39.

9 Following Stepan's definition, Sahadžić identifies three sub-properties of multinationalism: *territorial* differences based on language, religion, culture, and ethnicity; the *territorial* embeddedness of these differences; the existence of claims to more important political autonomy based on these differences (see Sahadžić, *Asymmetry*, 73).

accommodate competing claims may later become multinational states. The conflict may then persist, but not necessarily lead to a new process of constitutional design. However, since the focus of this book is on constitutional design, and on the introduction of constitutional asymmetries as a distinct model of constitutional design for divided societies, the preferred term will be divided society. This also explains why multicultural states (e.g., the US, Germany, Austria), which have significant internal diversity but where such diversity does not translate into political mobilisation even in limited parts of the territory, will not be considered as either multinational states or divided societies.

Such clarifications are of crucial importance, as this distinction will constitute one of the criteria used to select the 12 case studies.[10]

2.4 *Asymmetry, Asymmetries*

A final terminological clarification concerns the core concept of this book, i.e., constitutional asymmetries. Chapter 2 will further distinguish between political and constitutional asymmetries, as well as among the manifestations of asymmetries in different legal dimensions. However, what should be clarified here is that this research will intentionally use "asymmetries" in its plural form,[11] instead of simply "asymmetry", as is more commonly used.[12] As simple as it might seem, using the plural instead of the singular is a choice coherent with the overall conceptual framework of this book, which frames constitutional asymmetries as a plural and multidimensional constitutional phenomenon. Referring to asymmetries makes the idea of a flexible model more immediate, suggesting that, more often than not, there are (and can be) different constitutional asymmetries in place in the same constitutional systems, that these can vary across systems and across dimensions, and that plural

10 For more on the selection criteria and the properties identified to detect a divided society, see Chapter 3, paragraph 2.3.

11 As already done by Francesco Palermo, Karl Kössler, and Carolin Zwilling, eds., *Asymmetries in Constitutional Law: Recent Developments in Federal and Regional Systems* (Bolzano/Bozen: Accademia Europea di Bolzano, 2009).

12 See, for instance, David Milne, "Asymmetry in Canada: Past and Present," *Asymmetry Series – IIGR, Queen's University*, 2005, 1–8; Patricia Popelier and Maja Sahadžić, eds., *Constitutional Asymmetry in Multinational Federalism* (Cham: Palgrave Macmillan, 2019); Ferran Requejo and Klaus-Jürgen Nagel, eds., *Federalism Beyond Federations: Asymmetry and Processes of Resymmetrisation in Europe* (Farnham, England: Ashgate, 2011); Sahadžić, *Asymmetry*; Ronald L. Watts, "A Comparative Perspective on Asymmetry in Federations," *Asymmetry Series – IIGR, Queen's University*, no. 4 (2005): 1–7; Charles D. Tarlton, "Symmetry and Asymmetry as Elements of Federalism: A Theoretical Speculation," *The Journal of Politics* 27, no. 4 (1965): 861–74.

identities and needs can be addressed through differential arrangements.[13] Therefore, the choice to use "asymmetries" consistently was guided by the desire to also reflect the composite nature of this constitutional model in the terminology employed in this book.

3 Theoretical Aims of the Research

The challenges arising from societies characterised by profound internal diversity present the law with the fundamental task of devising a series of instruments capable of promoting pluralism, as well as the inclusion and participation of minorities in the democratic life of the system.[14] This has stimulated a lively debate among scholars, who have proposed different constitutional models for dealing with diversity and avoiding structural inequality and discrimination. In the field of political science, McGarry, O'Leary, and Simeon have identified two main approaches in the literature on constitutional design for plural societies, namely accommodation and integration. The former refers to the group of models built on the assumption that ethnocultural diversity is meant to be enduring and that, for this reason, the state should recognise and promote the plurality of identities in the public sphere.[15] Examples of proposals belonging to this approach are the consociational model theorised by Lijphart[16] and the "incentive model" proposed by Horowitz.[17] Conversely, scholars of the integrationist approach believe that ethnocultural differences do not necessarily result in political fragmentation and that the state should promote a common public identity while allowing ethnocultural pluralism in the private sphere.[18] In the field of comparative constitutional law, the theoretical development of different models of diversity treatment has found a

13 As Chapter 2 will further explain, this does not mean that asymmetries are the solution to all problems. There are potential challenges that need to be accounted for.

14 See Jens Woelk and Francesco Palermo, "From Minority Protection to a Law of Diversity? Reflections on the Evolution of Minority Rights," *European Yearbook of Minority Issues Online* 3, no. 1 (2003): 5–13; Nicolò Paolo Alessi, *A Global Law of Diversity* (London and New York: Routledge, 2024).

15 John McGarry, Brendan O'Leary, and Richard Simeon, "Integration or Accommodation? The Enduring Debate in Conflict Regulation," in *Constitutional Design for Divided Societies*, ed. Sujit Choudhry (Oxford: Oxford University Press, 2008), 41.

16 See Arend Lijphart, "Consociational Democracy," *World Politics* 21, no. 2 (1969): 207–25.

17 See Donald Horowitz, "Democracy in Divided Societies," *Journal of Democracy* 4, no. 4 (1993): 18–38.

18 See Brian Barry, *Culture and Equality: An Egalitarian Critique of Multiculturalism* (Cambridge: Harvard University Press, 2001).

space that is still somewhat limited, but not marginal. In fact, the essential contribution of Toniatti led to the first formulation of four constitutional models,[19] later refined by Palermo and Woelk.[20] The treatment of diversity finds room in the so-called promotional model and, in fully institutionalised form, in the multinational model. In these two models, constitutional systems cope with the existence of internal diversity by adopting a set of differential instruments aimed at ensuring equality in a substantive and not just a formal sense.[21] Thus, in such systems, the solutions adopted are not only based on the principle of non-discrimination, but also include provisions for the protection of so-called special rights (e.g., religious, cultural, linguistic rights) and self-government arrangements.[22] In this context, autonomy, in its territorial and non-territorial dimensions, is particularly relevant as part of the possible solutions to promote internal pluralism and protect minorities,[23] as also shown by the scholarship advocating for a dynamic approach to federalism.[24]

This book argues that the introduction of constitutional asymmetries in divided multi-tiered systems can be framed as a dynamic constitutional model to accommodate ethnocultural diversity. In the literature on asymmetric federalism, constitutional asymmetries are considered a valuable tool for resolving ethnic and territorial conflicts.[25] Moreover, they represent a com-

---

19 Cfr. Roberto Toniatti, "Minorities and Protected Minorities: Constitutional Models Compared," in *Citizenship and Rights in Multicultural Societies*, ed. Tiziano Bonazzi and Michael Dunne (Edinburgh: Edinburgh University Press, 1996), 193–220.

20 See Francesco Palermo and Jens Woelk, *Diritto costituzionale comparato dei gruppi e delle minoranze* (Milan: Wolters Kluwer, 2021), 43–71.

21 Palermo and Woelk, *Diritto costituzionale comparato*, 53–68.

22 Palermo and Woelk, *Diritto costituzionale comparato*, 33–8.

23 See Arend Lijphart, "Consociation and Federation: Conceptual and Empirical Links," *Canadian Journal of Political Science* 12, no. 3 (1979): 499–516; John McGarry and Brendan O'Leary, "Federation as a Method of Ethnic Conflict Regulation," in *From Power Sharing to Democracy*, ed. Sid Noel (Montréal: McGill-Queen's University Press, 2005), 263–96; Donald Horowitz, "The Many Uses of Federalism," *Drake Law Review* 55 (2007): 953–66.

24 See, especially, Carl J. Friedrich, "Federal Constitutional Theory and Emergent Proposals," in *Federalism: Mature and Emergent*, ed. A. W. Macmahon (New York: Russell and Russell Inc, 1955), 513–17; Carl J. Friedrich, *Trends of Federalism in Theory and Practice* (London: Pall Mall Press, 1968). For some more recent references, see Patricia Popelier, *Dynamic Federalism* (London and New York: Routledge, 2021).

25 See Tarlton, "Symmetry and Asymmetry"; Robert Agranoff, ed., *Accommodating Diversity: Asymmetry in Federal States* (Baden-Baden: Nomos Verlagsgesellschaft, 1999); Marc Weller and Katherine Nobbs, eds., *Asymmetric Autonomy and the Settlement of Ethnic Conflict* (Philadelphia and Oxford: University of Pennsylvania Press, 2010).

mon ground among the models developed by the literature, intertwining accommodation and integration. Constitutional asymmetries also allow for flexibility, as they can be introduced to different degrees of intensity to accommodate internal diversity. This can happen not only in multinational federations (e.g., Belgium, India) but also in those systems that are "partially divided societies"[26] and do not identify themselves as federations (e.g., Italy, Spain, the United Kingdom).[27] Therefore, the introduction of constitutional asymmetries in systems characterised by deep internal diversity can be considered a dynamic instrument fully attributable to the idea of federalism as a process, capable of responding to the challenges raised by internal diversity and ethnocultural pluralism. However, legal scholarship has not yet framed constitutional asymmetries as a dynamic constitutional model (only as an instrument) to accommodate ethnocultural diversity, nor has it explored the role played by constitutional courts in reshaping the degree of constitutional asymmetries.

4 Research Questions and Methodology

Given these premises, the book aims to answer two research questions related to how the introduction of constitutional asymmetries provides a dynamic constitutional model to accommodate ethnocultural diversity in divided multi-tiered systems, and what the role of constitutional courts is in reshaping the degrees of constitutional asymmetries in these systems. Related to these research questions, this book intends to test two hypotheses. The first hypothesis is that constitutional asymmetries come in different degrees and, as such, can be a flexible constitutional model for the accommodation of ethnocultural diversity in divided multi-tiered systems, whereas the second hypothesis is that constitutional courts tend to interpret constitutional asymmetries as a threat to the integrity of multi-tiered systems and, through their decisions, generally reduce the degree of asymmetry.

To answer the research questions and test the research hypotheses, the book relies on an array of comparative constitutional law methodologies, combining functional, empirical, and case-law analyses. The comparative analysis of constitutional asymmetries is conducted through a systematic

26 Alessi and Palermo, "Intergovernmental Relations," 185 ff.

27 See Guerino D'Ignazio, ed., *Integrazione europea e asimmetrie regionali* (Milan: Giuffrè, 2007); Roberto Toniatti, "Asimmetrie regionali, identità culturale e competitività dei territori," in *Il futuro della specialità regionale alla luce della revisione costituzionale*, ed. Francesco Palermo and Sara Parolari (Napoli: ESI, 2016), 13–43.

measure of asymmetries in divided multi-tiered systems. The measure of asymmetries is achieved by relying on Popelier's indexes on subnational autonomy,[28] that conceptualise autonomy along three dimensions: status, powers, and fiscal arrangements. The use of Popelier's indexes allows for a precise measure of the autonomy of subnational entities in multi-tiered systems, from which it is possible to derive asymmetry scores for each dimension, depicting a more complete picture of how asymmetries can vary in degree across dimensions. This also allows us to conduct a systematic comparison of legal frameworks across constitutional systems, and to classify the systems according to their degree of asymmetry (high, medium, low), thus satisfying the classificatory aim of comparative legal research. The book employs a selection of Popelier's indexes to measure constitutional asymmetries in 12 divided multi-tiered systems: Belgium, Bosnia and Herzegovina, Canada, Malaysia, Myanmar, India, Indonesia, Iraq, Italy, Pakistan, Spain, and the United Kingdom. The cases have been selected along three selection criteria: they qualify as divided societies; they are multi-tiered systems; and they are constitutionally asymmetrical.

Moreover, the book relies on the same conceptualisation of asymmetries along the three dimensions to analyse the case law of constitutional courts. The study first reviewed the federalism-related jurisprudence of the apex courts of the 12 case studies and then selected those courts that addressed asymmetries in their decisions. The courts resulting from this selection are the Indian Supreme Court, the Constitutional Court and the Supreme Court of Indonesia, the Italian Constitutional Court, and the Spanish Constitutional Tribunal. The book analyses the general attitude of each court on asymmetries and the specific dimensions of asymmetries involved in the court's decisions over time, allowing for an assessment of resymmetrisation or asymmetrisation trends.

Finally, the book adopts a decolonial comparative approach, relying on an emerging strand of interdisciplinary research dedicated to imprinting a decolonial perspective on comparative law[29] and comparative constitutional

28 See Popelier, *Dynamic Federalism*, 84–85.

29 See Daniel Bonilla Maldonado, *Legal Barbarians: Identity, Modern Comparative Law, and the Global South* (Cambridge: Cambridge University Press, 2021); Roger Merino, "Decolonial Theory and Comparative Law," in *The Cambridge Handbook of Comparative Law*, ed. Mathias Siems and Po Jen Yap (Cambridge: Cambridge University Press, 2024), 408–25; Lena Salaymeh and Ralf Michaels, "Decolonial Comparative Law: A Conceptual Beginning," *Rabels Zeitschrift Für Ausländisches Und Internationales Privatrecht* 86, no. 1 (2022): 166–88.

studies.[30] Indeed, the book is interested in consistently integrating constitutional systems in the Global South into the analysis, and in questioning the implied superiority of the Global North in traditional federal scholarship.

5 Structure of the Book

The overall structure of the book takes the form of two parts, consisting of a total of five chapters, excluding the introduction and the comparative conclusion. The two parts of the book (i.e., Part 1 on the impact of constitutional design and Part 2 on the role of courts) address two interrelated aspects that derive from the interest in assessing asymmetries on the books (i.e., constitutional design) and in action (i.e., the interpretation of asymmetrical provisions given by courts). Although few courts have addressed asymmetries in their case law, this is still a relevant aspect that adds to the current federal and constitutional scholarship that has widely explored the role of courts in federal systems, especially related to de/centralisation trends, but not in the dynamics involving asymmetries.

The first chapter opens Part 1 of the book, dedicated to constitutional design, and is broadly divided into three sections, providing the theoretical foundations of the book. The first section is dedicated to constitutional design as a research field and then focuses on the scholarship on constitutional design for divided societies, discussing the recurring themes in the debate. Specifically, the chapter integrates political and legal perspectives on the constitutional models for the treatment of diversity, combining the four models identified by comparative constitutional scholarship (i.e., repressive, liberal, promotional, multinational) with the two approaches developed by political scientists (i.e., accommodationist and integrationist). Then, the second paragraph addresses the theoretical and empirical links between federalism and constitutional design, linking together these two strands of literature and emphasising their respective relevance in the debate of diversity governance. Finally, the chapter puts constitutional asymmetries at the core of the research. To do so,

30 See Philipp Dann, Michael Riegner, and Maxim Bönnemann, eds., *The Global South and Comparative Constitutional Law* (Oxford: Oxford University Press, 2020); Philipp Dann, "Southern Turn, Northern Implications: Rethinking the Meaning of Colonial Legacies for Comparative Constitutional Studies," *Comparative Constitutional Studies* 1, no. 2 (2023): 174–96; Daniel Bonilla Maldonado, *Constitutionalism of the Global South: The Activist Tribunals of India, South Africa, and Colombia* (Cambridge: Cambridge University Press, 2013).

the paragraph addresses the dynamic conception of federalism as a process, rather than a static institutional structure, outlining the relative debate in federal theory and briefly reviewing the implementation of such a conception in processes of conflict resolution. The synthesis of this theoretical chapter results in the conceptualisation of constitutional asymmetries as a dynamic instrument to address internal diversity in flexible terms, capable of adapting to different systems while preserving territorial and political integrity.

Then, Chapter 2 is entirely dedicated to the definition of asymmetries, relying on the scholars who have progressively refined the theory on asymmetrical federalism. The chapter tackles some fundamental theoretical distinctions, such as the one between political and constitutional asymmetries, and clarifies the fact that the book chose to focus only on constitutional asymmetries to allow a more rigorous comparative analysis. Then, the chapter critically discusses the different proposals advanced by the literature to measure constitutional asymmetries, outlining the innovative aspects as well as the pitfalls of these previous attempts. The chapter also explains Popelier's indexes on subnational autonomy, i.e., the indexes employed in the book to measure asymmetries. The use of Popelier's indexes allows for a rigorous comparative analysis, not only across case studies but also across dimensions of asymmetries, as shown in the following comparative chapter. Moreover, through the use of standardised indexes, it is possible to classify asymmetries according to different degrees of intensity (i.e., low, medium, and high), in order to convey a more complete picture of asymmetries. Finally, the remaining part of the second chapter deals with the legal and extra-legal factors that contribute to explaining the different manifestations of constitutional asymmetries in the case studies. The main legal factors identified in the book are the territorial distribution of asymmetries, the legal procedure to introduce asymmetries, the homogenous or heterogeneous design of subnational entities, and the actors involved in the constitution-making process. Conversely, the extra-legal factors are the historical reasons and periodisation, the process of formation of the multi-tiered system, the geopolitical position of the system, and wealth.

Having defined the theoretical framework of the research, Chapter 3 delves into the comparison across case studies and concludes the first part of the book. First, the chapter tackles some necessary methodological considerations, retracing the lively debate on the comparative method, outlining the main comparative constitutional law methodologies, and explaining the case selection criteria. This first paragraph situates the book within the current methodological debate in comparative law, with a particular interest in two developing fields: empirical legal studies, and decolonial comparative law. The book relates to both insofar as it employs standardised indexes to analyse a medium-N universe of cases and aims to consistently integrate the constitutional traditions of the Global South. Then, the rest of the chapter addresses in depth the comparison of cases for each degree of asymmetry (i.e., low, medium, and high), first commenting on the autonomy scores for each constitutional system and then on the resulting asymmetry scores. The focal point of interest is to explore the different manifestations of asymmetries, assessing whether asymmetry is pervasive in all dimensions (i.e., status, powers, fiscal arrangements) or conversely only concentrated in one or a few dimensions, but not all. For each degree of asymmetry and for each case study, subnational autonomy and asymmetry are first reviewed in detail at the subnational entity level and then on average at the country level. The outcome of the comparison is a more refined assessment, analysing asymmetries not only across cases but also within cases, examining whether the degree varies across the dimensions of asymmetry. Indeed, the analysis shows that asymmetries vary significantly across cases and across dimensions, and that asymmetries do not necessarily involve every dimension of status, powers, and fiscal arrangements. Moreover, for each degree of asymmetry, the chapter also considers the asymmetries "in action", without ignoring the reality of implementation and the relative impact on the constitutional and political system.

Chapter 4 opens Part 2 of the book, exploring the role of courts. The chapter examines the relationship between courts and diversity from two different perspectives. The first perspective addresses how constitutional courts deal with the internal diversity of their constitutional systems, analysing four landmark cases decided by constitutional courts that played a meaningful role in the accommodation of diversity, namely the 1996 *First Certification Judgment* of the Constitutional Court of South Africa, the 2000 *Constituent Peoples'* case of the Constitutional Court of Bosnia-Herzegovina, the 1998 *Reference Re Secession of Québec* of the Supreme Court of Canada, and the 1985 *Shah Bano* case of the Supreme Court of India. The same section addresses how supranational courts have addressed issues related to internal diversity and minority rights, i.e., the International Court of Justice and the issue of self-determination, the European Court of Human Rights and power-sharing arrangements, and the Inter-American Court of Human Rights and the rights of indigenous peoples. Moreover, the section reviews the contribution of two quasi-judicial bodies in addressing ethnocultural diversity, i.e., the Badinter Commission and the African Commission on Human and Peoples' Rights. Then, the second perspective analysed in the fourth chapter explores how diversity can also be reflected within courts, addressing two peculiar compositions of courts, i.e., the so-called "power-sharing courts", and the "hybrid constitutional courts", comparing courts such as the BiH Constitutional Court, the Constitutional Court of Belgium, and the Constitutional Court of Kosovo. Finally, the chapter concludes with a reflection on the use of foreign law by (domestic and supranational) courts to address internal diversity, which often finds inspiration in other judicial decisions related to the protection of the fundamental rights of minorities.

The fifth and final chapter focuses on the role of constitutional courts in multi-tiered systems, reviewing the models of constitutional adjudication adopted in the case studies and exploring whether courts display a centralist or federalist behaviour. The comparative analysis of the constitutional and supreme courts that have developed a rich federalism-related jurisprudence shows that, generally, courts tend to adopt a centralist attitude, strengthening the centre and expanding the powers of the central level of government. Then, the chapter focuses on those courts that have addressed asymmetries in their case law, i.e., India, Indonesia, Italy, and Spain. In these four systems, constitutional or supreme courts have developed a rich federalism-related jurisprudence and played a crucial role in reshaping the degree of asymmetries in their systems, often during critical times for political stability and territorial integrity. Overall, the comparative analysis of constitutional case law shows that courts tend to reduce asymmetries, thus following a resymmetrisation trend. This is the case for the Spanish Constitutional Tribunal, the Italian Constitutional Court, and the Indian Supreme Court. Conversely, the Indonesian case appears to be an outlier since the decisions of the Constitutional Court and the Supreme Court confirmed the existing degree of (low) asymmetry. From the comparative analysis, it emerges that apex courts tend to reduce asymmetry when its degree is medium (i.e., India, Italy, Spain) while confirming it when it is low (i.e., Indonesia), and that apex courts have shown a changing behaviour not only over time but also among dimensions. Overall, the chapter confirms that courts have a significant impact on the degree of asymmetries and should be consistently integrated into the study of asymmetries.

Finally, the last section of the book takes up the research questions and draws conclusions from the previous chapters. Specifically, this concluding section relies on a comparative analysis to outline the core findings of the book, namely the dynamic nature of constitutional asymmetries and the significant role played by constitutional and supreme courts in (re)shaping the degree of asymmetries. Moreover, the Conclusion acknowledges the limitations of the study and sets out possible further developments.

Bibliography

Agranoff, Robert, ed. *Accommodating Diversity: Asymmetry in Federal States*. Baden-Baden: Nomos Verlagsgesellschaft, 1999.

Choudhry, Sujit, ed. *Constitutional Design for Divided Societies: Integration or Accommodation?* Oxford: Oxford University Press, 2008.

Dann, Philipp. "Southern Turn, Northern Implications: Rethinking the Meaning of Colonial Legacies for Comparative Constitutional Studies." *Comparative Constitutional Studies* 1, no. 2 (2023): 174–96.

Elazar, Daniel J. *Exploring Federalism*. Tuscaloosa and London: University of Alabama Press, 1987.

Friedrich, Carl J. *Trends of Federalism in Theory and Practice*. London: Pall Mall Press, 1968.

Gagnon, Alain-G., and Arjun Tremblay. *Advanced Introduction to Federalism*. Cheltenham, UK and Northampton, MA: Edward Elgar, 2024.

Horowitz, Donald L. "Democracy in Divided Societies." *Journal of Democracy* 4, no. 4 (1993): 18–38.

Lijphart, Arend. "Constitutional Design for Divided Societies." *Journal of Democracy* 15, no. 2 (2004): 96–109.

Palermo, Francesco, and Karl Kössler. *Comparative Federalism: Constitutional Arrangements and Case Law*. London: Hart Publishing, 2017.

Palermo, Francesco, and Jens Woelk. *Diritto costituzionale comparato dei gruppi e delle minoranze*. Milano: Wolters Kluwer, 2021.

Popelier, Patricia. *Dynamic Federalism: A New Theory for Cohesion and Regional Autonomy*. London and New York: Routledge, 2021.

Popelier, Patricia, and Maja Sahadžić, eds. *Constitutional Asymmetry in Multinational Federalism*. Cham: Palgrave Macmillan, 2019.

Requejo, Ferran, and Klaus-Jürgen Nagel, eds. *Federalism beyond Federations: Asymmetry and Processes of Resymmetrisation in Europe*. Farnham, England: Ashgate, 2011.

Sahadžić, Maja. *Asymmetry, Multinationalism and Constitutional Law: Managing Legitimacy and Stability in Federalist States*. London and New York: Routledge, 2020.

Salaymeh, Lena, and Ralf Michaels. "Decolonial Comparative Law: A Conceptual Beginning." *Rabels Zeitschrift Für Ausländisches Und Internationales Privatrecht* 86, no. 1 (2022): 166–88.

Stepan, Alfred. "Towards a New Comparative Politics of Federalism, Multinationalism, and Democracy: Beyond Rikerian Federalism." In *Federalism and Democracy in Latin America*, edited by Edward L. Gibson, 29–84. Baltimore, Maryland: Johns Hopkins University Press, 2004.

Tarlton, Charles D. "Symmetry and Asymmetry as Elements of Federalism: A Theoretical Speculation." *The Journal of Politics* 27, no. 4 (1965): 861–74.

Toniatti, Roberto. "Minorities and Protected Minorities: Constitutional Models Compared." In *Citizenship and Rights in Multicultural Societies*, edited by Tiziano Bonazzi and Michael Dunne, 193–220. Edinburgh: Edinburgh University Press, 1996.

Watts, Ronald L. "A Comparative Perspective On Asymmetry In Federations." *Asymmetry Series – IIGR, Queen's University*, no. 4 (2005): 1–7.

Woelk, Jens, and Francesco Palermo. "From Minority Protection to a Law of Diversity? Reflections on the Evolution of Minority Rights." *European Yearbook of Minority Issues Online* 3, no. 1 (2003): 5–13.

PART 1

The Role of Constitutional Design

CHAPTER 1

Constitutional Design, Federalism, and Asymmetries

1 Introduction

As anticipated in the Introduction, this first chapter lays down the theoretical framework on which the research is built, i.e., the constitutional models available to accommodate ethnocultural diversity. The brief review of these models is developed to frame constitutional asymmetries as a distinct model of constitutional design for divided societies and to explore the first research question, related to how the introduction of constitutional asymmetries can provide a dynamic constitutional model to accommodate ethnocultural diversity. First, the chapter deals with the concept of constitutional design, defined as the imaginative process according to which government structures and fundamental rights are modelled, and then focuses on the debate on divided societies. Without purporting to be exhaustive, the chapter reviews the classic literature on these topics as well as the constitutional models for the management of diversity identified in the legal and political scholarship, outlining the roots of the debate as well as the recurring problems that make the topic still relevant today. Then, the third paragraph addresses the theoretical and empirical links between federalism and constitutional design, linking together these two strands of literature and emphasising their respective relevance in the debate on diversity governance. Finally, the chapter puts constitutional asymmetries at the core of the research. To do so, the paragraph addresses the dynamic conception of federalism as a process, rather than a static institutional structure, outlining the debate in federal theory and briefly reviewing the implementation of that conception in processes of conflict resolution. In light of the theoretical review provided by this chapter, it will be possible to frame constitutional asymmetries as a dynamic constitutional model to manage diversity. Given its greater flexibility than other models, this chapter suggests that the introduction of constitutional asymmetries is also more appropriate than the federal institutional structure, as will be shown by reference to the case studies analysed in this book.

 | DOI:10.1163/9789004739109_003

2 Constitutional Design for Divided Societies

2.1 *Literature Background on Constitutional Design*

Constitution making is more art than science.[1]

Though not strictly a scientific expression, constitutional design may first be defined as a human effort to impact the future.[2] In fact, constitution drafters attempt to regulate human behaviour on the basis of tentative speculations as to how the institutions they are designing will work in reality. They make an effort to imagine the best possible solution for the constitutional system they intend to regulate, to guarantee its functioning. By doing so, they make predictions on what the outcome of their design might be, considering the inevitable compromises typical of every process of constitution-making. However, as predicting the future goes far beyond any human capability, constitution makers found their design on probabilistic guesses.[3]

In more technical terms, constitutional design is the process according to which governmental structures are modelled, as well as fundamental rights and principles.[4] The term "design" has often been contested and is not the only term used to indicate the same concept.[5] The basis for such contestation is that the term could imply a technocratic paradigm that does not fit the reality in which constitutions are drafted, often subject to political conflicts or even violence. For this reason, Horowitz observed that the term "constitutional process" would be more appropriate, as it is closer to the reality of constitution-making.[6] It is also worth clarifying that constitution-making and constitutional design are strictly linked, but they are not the same. In fact, constitution-making is the process in which a new constitution is drafted

1 Tom Ginsburg, "Introduction," in *Comparative Constitutional Design*, ed. Tom Ginsburg (Cambridge: Cambridge University Press, 2012), 2.

2 Richard Simeon, "Constitutional Design and Change in Federal Systems: Issues and Questions," *Publius: The Journal of Federalism* 39, no. 2 (2009): 242.

3 Ginsburg, "Introduction," 1.

4 Simeon, "Constitutional Design," 243.

5 For example, Giovanni Sartori preferred to use the expression "constitutional engineering" in Giovanni Sartori, *Comparative Constitutional Engineering* (New York: New York University Press, 1997). "Institutional design" is often used as well.

6 Donald Horowitz, "Constitutional Design: Proposals versus Processes," in *The Architecture of Democracy*, ed. Andrew Reynolds (Oxford: Oxford University Press, 2012), 15–36.

and later adopted,[7] while constitutional design can be considered a mindset, an imaginative process which precedes and accompanies the drafting phase, and which is guided by the belief that "desirable social and political outcomes may be accomplished through optimal institutional planning and implementation".[8] However, as Ginsburg observes, "as long there is constitution-making, there will be attempts at constitutional design".[9]

Whatever the expression used, two interlinked characteristics of constitutional design should be emphasised to get to its essence: constitutional design tends to be inherently normative, and most importantly, it is comparative in its nature.[10] In fact, in order to design how institutions should work, constitution drafters should look at and learn from prior experiences, as polities may face recurrent problems and challenges.[11] The normative goal of constitutional design may be enhancing the democratic credentials of a political system,

---

7 Jennifer Widner identified five stages of constitution-making to guide practitioners: drafting, consultation, deliberation, adoption, and ratification. See Jennifer Widner, "Proceedings," *Workshop on Constitution Building Process* (Princeton University, 17–20 May 2007). For other references on constitution-making, see David Landau and Hanna Lerner, eds., *Comparative Constitution Making* (Cheltenham and Northampton: Edward Elgar Publishing, 2019); Sujit Choudhry and Tom Ginsburg, eds., *Constitution Making* (Cheltenham and Northampton: Edward Elgar Publishing, 2016); Giuseppe de Vergottini, *Diritto costituzionale comparato* (Milano: Wolters Kluwer, 2019): 232–62; Julia Raue and Patrick Sutter, eds., *Facets and Practices of State-Building* (Leiden: Nijhoff, 2009); Edward McWhinney, *Constitution-Making: Principles, Process, Practice* (Toronto: University of Toronto Press, 1981); Claude Klein and András Sajó, "Constitution-Making: Process and Substance", in *The Oxford Handbook of Comparative Constitutional Law*, ed. Michel Rosenfeld and András Sajó (Oxford: Oxford University Press, 2012), 419–41.

8 Ran Hirschl, "The 'Design Sciences' and Constitutional 'Success'," *Texas Law Review* 87 (2009): 1339.

9 Ginsburg, "Introduction," 2.

10 Such a statement can be further justified by recalling the well-known concept of "migration of constitutional ideas" or "circulation of constitutional models" that can be found in the literature on comparative constitutionalism. See, for example, Giuseppe de Vergottini, "Constitutional Law and the Comparative Method," in *Encyclopedia of Contemporary Constitutionalism*, ed. Javier Cremades and Cristina Hermida (Cham: Springer International Publishing, 2020), 3–4; Gábor Halmai, "Constitutional Transplants," in *The Cambridge Companion of Comparative Constitutional Law*, eds. Roger Masterman and Robert Schütze (Cambridge: Cambridge University Press, 2019), 580–603; Vlad Perju, "Constitutional Transplants, Borrowing, and Migrations," in *The Oxford Handbook of Comparative Constitutional Law*, ed. Michel Rosenfeld and András Sajó (Oxford: Oxford University Press, 2012), 1304–27; Sujit Choudhry, ed., *The Migration of Constitutional Ideas* (Cambridge: Cambridge University Press, 2006). This aspect will be further explored in Chapter 3, when dealing with the comparative method in comparative constitutional law.

11 Ginsburg, "Introduction," 2.

increasing accountability and transparency, and balancing the principle of majority rule with political pluralism. At the same time, constitutional design also acts at a more practical level, aiming to improve the quality and effectiveness of public policy making, and to support political, cultural, and economic development.[12] In doing so, adopting a comparative approach is fundamental to navigating the domain of constitutional design, balancing between borrowing models and tailoring to the local polity, and between conventional choices and creative innovations.[13] Moreover, comparative studies offer new perspectives on different aspects of the process of constitution-making, facilitating a better understanding of choices faced and decisions made by drafters while crafting a new constitution.[14]

The roots of constitutional design lie far back in history. Aristotle, in *Politics* (VII–VIII), produced a systematic evaluation of the constitutions of the Greek city-states. Even though constitutions were analysed by adopting normative and universalistic terms, the Greek philosopher discovered variations among different experiences and concluded his analysis by emphasising that mixed constitutions would be the best solution for an ideal polity, thus rejecting the ideal types. The advent of the modern age brought forward a new set of analyses by political theorists such as Machiavelli, Montesquieu, and John Stuart Mill. Once again, their comparative analyses of constitutions aimed to inform normative design for new constitutions. Then, in the seventeenth century, constitutional design made its first appearance as an instrument to resolve possible constitutional problems. In fact, state-builders in the Netherlands engaged in an extensive comparative analysis of ancient and contemporary constitutional models in order to address the problems of the nascent Dutch republic. A century later, the comparative approach to the study of constitutions was adopted by lesser-known scholars such as Gottfried Achenwall and Johann Heinrich Gottlieb von Justi, who undertook comparative studies of political forms.[15]

However, constitutional design in its contemporary sense is strictly associated with the spread of the written constitutional form, and thus with

---

12 Hirschl, "The 'Design Sciences'," 1339.

13 Ginsburg, "Introduction," 2.

14 Justin Blount, Zachary Elkins, and Tom Ginsburg, "Does the Process of Constitution Making Matters?," in *Comparative Constitutional Design*, ed. Tom Ginsburg (Cambridge: Cambridge University Press, 2012), 33–4.

15 Miguel Gonzáles Marcos, "Comparative Law at the Service of Democracy: A Reading of Arosemena's Constitutional Studies of the Latin American Governments," *Boston University Law Review* 21 (2003): 313.

constitution-making.[16] In fact, conceiving of the constitution as an integrated text is the starting point of the process of constitutional design, as it is precisely the moment at which institutions have to be designed following a purposive project. This mindset led Enlightenment political thinkers to interpret constitutions as "devices to channel self-interest into larger public ends".[17] By doing so, they engaged in comparative studies of what were the desirable features for the newly designed political institutions, prompting a debate on what would be the most appropriate model. Therefore, comparative inquiries with rationalist ends of optimal design are at the heart of modern constitutions.[18] In the eighteenth century, the next wave of constitution-making came in Latin America, and liberal models were channelled through the 1812 Cádiz Constitution, influencing many others.[19] In each process of constitution-making, the drafters sought to borrow the best from other models while adapting them to the local context and introducing original innovations. In the meantime, in Western Europe as well as in Japan, state-builders adopted the new technology of the written constitutional form, and, as in the previous century, they engaged in practical comparisons about which institutions were optimal, using a mixed method of positive and normative analysis.

As we can see, early scholarship on constitutional design was deeply case-driven and responsive to constitutional events, such as the revolutions of the eighteenth century, the constitutional wave of the nineteenth century, and the World Wars in the first half of the twentieth century. Much of the analysis was merely descriptive[20] and focused, in particular, on execu-

---

16 Ginsburg, "Introduction," 2.

17 Ginsburg, "Introduction," 3.

18 Ibidem.

19 In particular, the 1821 Constitution of Gran Colombia, the 1823 and 1828 Constitutions of Peru, the 1826 Constitution of Argentina, the 1828 Constitution of Chile, the 1830 Constitution of New Granada, the 1830 Constitution of Venezuela, and the 1830 Constitution of Uruguay.

20 Ginsburg recalls some exceptions. Kantorowicz examined the Weimar Constitution to ascertain the political goals of the designers and how they met them (see Hermann Kantorowicz, "The New German Constitution in Theory and Practice," *Economica* 19 (1927): 37–62). Chapman undertook a similar operation with the Cuban Constitution (see Charles E. Chapman, "The Cuban Constitution and Congress," *California Law Review* 14, no. 1 (1925): 947–54). Finally, Arangio-Ruiz addressed the evolution of constituent power in Italy from 1848 onwards (see Gaetano Arangio-Ruiz, "The Amendments to the Italian Constitution," *Annals of the American Academy of Political and Social Science* 6 (1895): 1824–1872).

tive-legislative relations,[21] as well as on forms of territorial organisation of power, such as regionalism or federalism. The second half of the last century brought about two developments that provided ground for the growth of scholarship on comparative constitutional design. The first development was academic, with the revival of institutionalism[22] in the social sciences. This meant a renewed emphasis on individual agency embedded in broader institutional structures and on the influence that structures had on determining outcomes.[23] The second was a historical development, namely the so-called third wave of democratisation,[24] bringing about major turning points such as the Portuguese revolution in 1974, the fall of the Soviet Union and Yugoslavia, and the overall end of the Cold War in the 1990s. The dissolution of the USSR and the Yugoslav federation marked the emergence of new states and new constitution-making processes, which prompted a new round of debates about which model of constitutional design was the most appropriate. As will be further explained in the next paragraph, in this phase, constitutional design became central to addressing the challenges that arise in ethnically divided societies, with a renewed interest in federalism.

Today, constitutional design is more relevant than ever. The conflicts in the Middle East (e.g., Iraq, Afghanistan, Syria, Yemen) will need some form of resolution and constitutional reconstruction. Constitution designers will be called upon to help the drafters in imagining which institutions would improve governance and guarantee the functioning of the constitutional system. Recalling Ginsburg's words ("Today, there is much demand for wisdom and knowledge, largely driven by real-world constitutional designers")[25], this research was developed expressly considering the importance of remembering reality while examining different constitutional design models. However,

21 See Charles Albert, S. M. Lindsay, and Leo S. Rowe, "Supplement: Constitution of the Kingdom of Italy," *Annals of the American Academy of Political and Social Science* 5 (1894): 1–44.

22 See, for example, James G. March and Johan P. Olsen, *Rediscovering Institutions* (New York: Free Press, 1989); Walter Powell and Paul DiMaggio, *The New Institutionalism in Organizational Analysis* (Chicago: University of Chicago Press, 1991).

23 Ginsburg, "Introduction," 4.

24 The expression "wave of democratization" was coined by Samuel P. Huntington in 1991, identifying three waves (see Samuel P. Huntington, "Democracy's Third Wave," *Journal of Democracy* 2, no. 2 (Spring 1991): 12–34), while Jon Elster makes reference to seven "waves of constitution-making" (see Jon Elster, "Forces and Mechanisms in the Constitution-Making Process," *Duke Law Journal* 45 (1995): 368–73).

25 Ginsburg, "Introduction," 4.

the search for "best practice" does not encounter many areas in which a clear consensus has been reached. In fact, the eternal dispute on the optimal form of government, split between presidentialism and parliamentarism,[26] is far from being resolved, as it is strongly influenced by ideological choices, identity and nationalism,[27] and power relations. In other domains, such as electoral systems and the mechanisms of judicial appointments, it has been possible to identify slightly more consensus among scholars.

Over the last decade, scholars have extensively debated constitutional design[28] and its overall sense. On the one hand, part of the literature intends constitutional design as a useful instrument to guide constitution drafters,[29] adopting a "pragmatic vision of constitution-making as a response to concrete problems and challenges".[30] Some scholars have even attempted to define a number of "general principles".[31] In particular, Lutz, by stressing the link between constitutional design (and constitutionalism) and Western political philosophy,[32] identified eight general principles of constitutional

26 Markus Böckenförde, "The Design of the Executive Branch," in *A Practical Guide to Constitution Building*, ed. Böckenförde Markus, Hedling Nora, and Wahiu Winluck (Stockholm: International IDEA, 2011), 147–83.

27 See, for example, Sujit Choudhry, "Managing Linguistic Nationalism through Constitutional Design: Lessons from South Asia," *International Journal of Constitutional Law* 7, no. 4 (2009): 577–618; Sujit Choudhry, "Citizenship and Federations: Some Preliminary Reflections," in *The Federal Vision: Legitimacy and Levels of Governance in the US and the EU*, ed. Kalypso Nicolaidis and Robert Howse (Oxford: Oxford University Press, 2001), 377–402.

28 The main references on constitutional design have been Tom Ginsburg, ed., *Comparative Constitutional Design* (Cambridge: Cambridge University Press, 2012); Adrian Vermule, *Mechanisms of Democracy* (Oxford: Oxford University Press, 2009); Walter F. Murphy, *Constitutional Democracy* (Baltimore: Johns Hopkins University Press, 2007); Edward V. Schneier, *Crafting Constitutional Democracies* (Lanham: Rowman & Littlefield, 2006); Donald S. Lutz, *Principles of Constitutional Design* (Cambridge: Cambridge University Press, 2006); Ian Shapiro and Stephen Macedo, eds., *Designing Democratic Institutions* (New York and London: New York University Press, 2000).

29 For example, Hydén and Venter constructed a common framework and evaluated constitutional design processes in terms of the representativeness of the process, the mechanisms used to create the document and aggregate interests, and, finally, the extent of popular participation. See Göran Hydén and Denis Venter, eds., *Constitution-Making and Democratisation in Africa* (Pretoria: Africa Institute of South Africa, 2001).

30 Hirschl, "The 'Design Sciences'," 1340.

31 Lutz, *Principles of Constitutional Design*, 209–20.

32 In Lutz's view, constitutional designers, as well as political philosophers, assess the reasons *why* it would be appropriate to adopt one model rather than another. Another common element between the two is the stretch between the ideal and the actual, as both fields must face the "limits imposed by the world of politics". In fact, Lutz clarifies

design.[33] Of course, Lutz is aware of the fact that the term "principle" is problematic, as it might imply "something that sounds like a science",[34] which is far from being the case in the study of politics and constitutions, which necessarily involves normative, analytic, and empirical considerations. For the purposes of the current review, the precise content of Lutz's principles is not relevant, but they are useful in identifying an understanding of constitutional design as a domain that, even if not a precise science, can be an instrument to achieve a goal: crafting a new constitution following an integrated and coherent project, while having to deal with reality.

On the other hand, another part of the literature is sceptical of the actual relevance of constitutional design. For example, Hirschl[35] is quite critical of the ability of constitutional design to address global challenges, which go beyond constitutions alone. In fact, Hirschl emphasises the gap between planning and implementation, coming to a series of possibilities[36] about how to define the "success" of constitutional design. One of the most debated is the ability to actually implement prefixed constitutional aspirations. In particular, scholars disagree on the respective weight that constitutional design should have compared to a developed rights-supportive environment. Indeed, some argue that, in maintaining democratic political institutions, constitutional arrangements (and a bill of rights) are less important than the existence of favourable sociocultural conditions.[37] This would imply that, in order for a de-

---

that "constitutional design is always condition by some vision of the ideal, but institutions rest on real people in the actual world", and he warns about the possible dangers of aiming for a perfect and ideal result, as institutions are inevitably imperfect (see Lutz, *Principles of Constitutional Design*, 209–212).

33 The eight principles are: 1. Match the government to the people. 2. Seek the best possible political system under the circumstances, not the ideal. 3. Political power is an unavoidable danger that must be understood and faced. 4. The idea of a constitution is to marry justice with power. 5. Distribution of power. 6. Collective decision-making as a complete system of interlocking institutions. 7. Systems of institutions should be grounded in a coherent theory apparent from the behavioural implications. 8. A constitution does not rely only on history and the present but also on probable future developments (see Lutz, *Principles of Constitutional Design*, 218–20).

34 Lutz, *Principles of Constitutional Design*, 216.

35 Hirschl, "The 'Design Sciences'," 1339–74.

36 These are: endurance; actual implementation of constitutional aspirations; contribution in accomplishing substantive goals such as democracy, prosperity, and human development; (in)ability of constitutions to address some of the world's biggest challenges; and the real success rate of constitutions in mitigating existential tensions in conflict or post-conflict settings.

37 See Robert A. Dahl, "Thinking about Democratic Constitutions: Conclusions from Democratic Experience," in *Political Order*, ed. Ian Shapiro and Russell Hardin (New York:

mocracy to endure in a given polity, a vibrant civil society and a rights-supportive culture is more important than a correctly structured institutional setting.[38] Conversely, others believe that constitutional design is essential in structuring political institutions and in limiting power,[39] which are the very foundations of a polity. In this respect, the present research is situated between the two extremes, as constitutional design is considered something necessary but not sufficient.[40] Without a support structure fostering democratic culture and political pluralism in civil societies, constitutional design is to be considered incomplete, as it ends up being ineffective in supporting a full democracy. As will become evident in the next paragraph, this is especially true when it comes to divided societies.[41]

2.2 *The Debate on Constitutional Design for Divided Societies*

The most vivid scientific debate on constitutional design is provided by discussions on divided societies. The first necessary remark concerns the striking difference between the considerable scientific production in the field of comparative politics,[42] and the rather modest one in the domain of comparative

New York University Press, 1998), 175–8; Robert D. Putnam, Robert Leonardi, and Raffaella Nanetti, *Making Democracy Work* (Princeton: Princeton University Press, 1993), 91–99.

38 Hirschl, "The 'Design Sciences'," 1356.

39 Sartori argues that constitutions are, first of all, procedures designed to ensure a controlled exercise of power, and that contemporary constitution-makers have forgotten the incentive-monitored and incentive-sustained character of constitutions. See Sartori, *Comparative Constitutional Engineering*, 195–201.

40 Hirschl, "The 'Design Sciences'," 1355.

41 Along these lines, Epp believes that having a bill of rights matters to the extent that a support structure for legal mobilisation (rights-advocacy organisations, rights-supportive lawyers, law schools, governmental rights-enforced agencies, legal-aid schemes) is well developed. See Charles R. Epp, *The Rights Revolution* (Chicago: University of Chicago Press, 1998), 14.

42 Among many others, see Adrian Guelke, *Democracy and Ethnic Conflict: Advancing Peace in Deeply Divided Societies* (Basingstoke and New York: Palgrave Macmillan, 2004); Donald Horowitz, *Ethnic Groups in Conflict* (Berkeley: University of California Press, 2001); Hanna Lerner, *Making Constitutions in Deeply Divided Societies* (Cambridge: Cambridge University Press, 2011); Arend Lijphart, "Constitutional Design for Divided Societies," *Journal of Democracy* 15, no. 2 (2004): 96–109; Arend Lijphart, *Patterns of Democracy* (New Haven and London: Yale University Press, 2012); Joanne McEvoy and Brendan O'Leary, eds., *Power Sharing in Deeply Divided Societies* (Philadelphia: University of Pennsylvania Press, 2013); Shamshad Pasarlay, "Dialogic Incrementalism in Deeply Divided Societies," *International Journal of Constitutional Law* (2024): 1–36; Andrew Reynolds, ed., *The Architecture of Democracy* (Oxford: Oxford University Press, 2002); Joseph

constitutional law.[43] Both Issacharoff[44] and Choudhry[45] observe that, unfortunately, comparative constitutional law has been a side discipline in this vibrant debate. Yet despite this, it should occupy centre stage, as constitutions play a crucial role in dealing with the challenges that arise in divided societies. Precisely for this reason, the ultimate goal of this research is to "bridge comparative politics and comparative constitutional law through a genuinely interdisciplinary conversation",[46] from a theoretical as well as a methodological point of view. In fact, the following pages will attempt to look at constitutional design for divided societies, as well as asymmetric federalism, from a constitutional law perspective, by drawing on the foundations of the debate in comparative politics.

Belmont, Mainwaring, and Reynold, when introducing one of the most important works on the topic,[47] offer a threefold motivation for focusing on institutional design as a way to manage conflict in divided societies. First, they maintain that "in the short term, structural, cultural, and international factors that affect the prospects for building a stable democracy cannot be changed profoundly",[48] while political institutions can be shaped in order to increase the probability of a democratic management of ethnocultural conflicts. Second, they support the idea that democracy can be sustained even in countries that face daunting structural and cultural obstacles, showing a good dose of optimism. Third, the three scholars believe that it is precisely in divided societies that constitutional design may have the greatest impact and that it can make a difference to democratic conflict resolution. Their motivations in want-

---

Siegle, "Constitutional Design: Vital but Insufficient for Conflict Management," *Ethnopolitics* 15, no. 5 (2016): 533–7.

43 The main references in the field of comparative constitutional law are Sujit Choudhry, ed., *Constitutional Design for Divided Societies: Integration or Accommodation?* (Oxford: Oxford University Press, 2008); Yash Ghai, ed., *Autonomy and Ethnicity: Negotiating Competing Claims in Multi-Ethnic States* (Cambridge: Cambridge University Press, 2000); Colin Harvey and Alex Schwartz, *Rights in Divided Societies* (Oxford and Portland: Hart Publishing, 2012); Stephen Tierney, *Constitutional Law and National Pluralism* (Oxford: Oxford University Press, 2004).

44 Samuel Issacharoff, "Constitutionalizing Democracy in Fractured Societies," *Texas Law Review* 82 (2004): 1870.

45 Choudhry, "Bridging," 7.

46 Choudhry, "Bridging," 13.

47 Andrew Reynolds, ed., *The Architecture of Democracy* (Oxford: Oxford University Press, 2002).

48 Katharine Belmont, Scott Mainwaring, and Andrew Reynolds, "Introduction," in *The Architecture of Democracy*, ed. Andrew Reynolds (Oxford: Oxford University Press, 2002), 2.

ing to address these issues are quite explicative of the centrality of constitutions in the overall process of constitutional design. Another interesting note is their pragmatism: they do not intend to predict the future or to proselytise, as it is impossible to prescribe a univocal set of institutional arrangements to be applied in all divided societies.[49] This pragmatic approach is crucial when diving into the domain of constitutional design for divided societies, as there is no magic formula capable of fitting all polities. Rather, it is an attempt to define a broad frame which has to be adapted to the specific divided society.

Coming more specifically to the scientific debate, this was first led by two main scholars, Lijphart and Horowitz, who both assumed as their paradigm the majoritarian democracy modelled on the Westminster system. They both agreed on the fact that a purely procedural conception of democracy was inadequate for divided societies because, even if the procedure was correctly executed, minorities may be permanently excluded from the decision-making process. Starting from this assumption, the two scholars sharply disagreed on the possible solutions, proposing two radically different models. These will be further analysed in the next section. For the current introduction, it is sufficient to mention that Lijphart promotes consociational (or power-sharing) democracy, while Horowitz advocates a centripetal democracy. Their competing proposals were reflected in real-time, contemporary events, as they wrote against the backdrop of the third wave of democratisation.[50] For the last three decades, the debate has been polarised between these two sets of proposals. More recently, McGarry, O'Leary, and Simeon reframed the debate, distinguishing two more general approaches: accommodation and integration. The key distinction between the two is their attitude towards the durability of ethnocultural differences: accommodationists believe that ethnocultural divisions are resilient and durable; integrationists reject the idea that ethnic differences should necessarily translate into political differences, and they argue for the possibility of a common public identity.[51]

2.3 *Constitutional Models for Diversity Governance*

In the field of political science, McGarry, O'Leary, and Simeon have identified two main approaches in the literature to constitutional design for plural soci-

49 Belmont, Mainwaring, and Reynolds, "Introduction," 3.

50 Choudhry, "Bridging," 22–3.

51 John McGarry, Brendan O'Leary, and Richard Simeon, "Integration or Accommodation? The Enduring Debate in Conflict Regulation," in *Constitutional Design for Divided Societies: Integration or Accommodation?*, ed. Sujit Choudhry (Oxford: Oxford University Press, 2008), 41.

eties, namely accommodation and integration. The former refers to the group of models built on the assumption that ethnocultural diversity is meant to be enduring and that, for this reason, the state should recognise and promote a plurality of identities in the public sphere.[52] Examples of proposals belonging to this approach are the consociational model theorised by Lijphart[53] and the "incentive model" proposed by Horowitz.[54] In contrast, scholars of the integrationist approach believe that ethnocultural differences do not necessarily result in political fragmentation and that the state should promote a common public identity while allowing ethnocultural pluralism in the private sphere.[55]

In the field of comparative constitutional law, attention to different models of diversity treatment has found a space that is still somewhat limited but not marginal. In fact, Italian legal doctrine boasts the essential contribution of Toniatti in the first formulation of four constitutional models,[56] later taken up and deepened by Palermo and Woelk.[57] These models are the repressive model, the liberal model, the promotional model, and the multinational model. The following sections will address each model, integrating the two conceptual frameworks.

2.3.1 The Repressive or Assimilationist Model

A first "counter-intuitive" constitutional model identified by Toniatti is the so-called "repressive nationalist state."[58] It may appear as a paradoxical model

52 McGarry, O'Leary, and Simeon, "Integration or Accommodation," 41.

53 See Arend Lijphart, "Consociational Democracy," *World Politics* 21, no. 2 (1969): 207–25; Arend Lijphart, *Democracy in Plural Societies: A Comparative Exploration* (New Haven and London: Yale University Press, 1977); Arend Lijphart, "The Wave of Power-Sharing Democracy," in *The Architecture of Democracy*, ed. Andrew Reynolds (Oxford: Oxford University Press, 2002), 37–54.

54 Cfr. Donald Horowitz, "Constitutional Design: Proposals v. Processes," in *The Architecture of Democracy*, edited by Andrew Reynolds (Oxford: Oxford University Press, 2002), 15–36; Donald Horowitz, *Ethnic Groups in Conflict* (Berkeley: University of California Press, 2001); Donald Horowitz, "Democracy in Divided Societies," *Journal of Democracy* 4, no. 4 (1993): 18–38.

55 See, for example, Brian Barry, *Culture and Equality: An Egalitarian Critique of Multiculturalism* (Cambridge: Harvard University Press, 2001).

56 Cfr. Roberto Toniatti, "Minorities and Protected Minorities: Constitutional Models Compared," in *Citizenship and Rights in Multicultural Societies,* ed. Tiziano Bonazzi and Michael Dunne (Edinburgh: Edinburgh University Press, 1996), 273–307.

57 See Francesco Palermo and Jens Woelk, *Diritto costituzionale comparato dei gruppi e delle minoranze* (Milan: Wolters Kluwer, 2021), 43–71.

58 For more on the repressive model, see Toniatti, "Minorities and Protected Minorities," 206; Palermo and Woelk, *Diritto costituzionale comparato*, 44–7.

insofar as this is a model that does not protect diversity but, conversely, seeks to achieve uniformity and impose a national identity on others through the enactment of repressive policies and legislation. In other words, the repressive model promotes assimilation, seeking the erasure of private and public differences between and among citizens, as well as the creation of a common public identity. This can happen through fusion, meaning the mixture of two or more communities into something new (A + B = C), or acculturation, namely the adoption and absorption of the dominant culture by a community (A + B = A). For instance, the repressive state might ban the use of minority languages in schools or public offices, as well as impose the translation of names, surnames, and placenames. This is, for instance, what happened during the Japanese colonisation of Korea, with the imposition of the Japanese language and the translation of Korean names to Japanese names to erase Korean language and culture.[59] Similarly, the same happened to ethnocultural minorities during Nazi-fascism in Europe, when linguistic minorities in South Tyrol were faced with the "option" to either renounce their language and culture to preserve their land or abandon their lands to retain their identity.[60] It should be noted that repressive policies towards minorities may be adopted even by so-called liberal democracies, as in the case of the Baltic countries such as Estonia and Latvia, where, for a long time, national legislation prevented Russian-speaking minorities from acquiring citizenship.[61] Even though these policies have been progressively dismantled, including through the ratification of the Framework Convention on National Minorities (FCNM) of the Council of Europe, in Latvia, the imposition of two reservations on the application of the FCNM led to enduring discrimination against the Russian minority, repeatedly legitimised by the Latvian Constitutional Court.[62]

59 See Wonmo Dong, *Japanese Colonial Policy and Practice in Korea, 1905–1945: A Study in Assimilation* (Ann Arbor, Michigan: Georgetown University, 1965). Yoko Motani, "Towards a More Just Educational Policy for Minorities in Japan: The Case of Korean Ethnic Schools," *Comparative Education* 38, no. 2 (2002): 225–37; Soon-Yong Pak and Keumjoong Hwang, "Assimilation and Segregation of Imperial Subjects: 'Educating' the Colonised during the 1910–1945 Japanese Colonial Rule of Korea," *Paedagogica Historica* 47, no. 3 (2011): 377–97.

60 See Keith Lowe, "European Fascism and its Aftermath," in *Routledge International Handbook of Diversity Studies*, ed. Steven Vertovec (London and New York: Routledge, 2014), 159–65; Palermo and Woelk, *Diritto costituzionale comparato*, 45.

61 Palermo and Woelk, *Diritto costituzionale comparato*, 46.

62 This is due to the fact that the Constitutional Court deemed the Russian-speaking community not a minority but descendants from previous Russian occupants (see Palermo and Woelk, *Diritto costituzionale comparato*, 47; Ryo Nakai, "The Influence of Party

What is important to stress is that sometimes the integrationist model of diversity governance is misinterpreted as assimilation, since some integrationist scholars are not against voluntary assimilation as an ultimate goal, or they see it as a positive by-product of integration. Nonetheless, neither integration nor accommodation requires cultural conformity across the public or private dimensions of life.[63] On the one hand, if it is true that integrationists support the development of a common public identity, it is also true that they promote the maintenance of ethnocultural differences in the private sphere, or at least they show indifference towards such differences. On the other hand, accommodationists support the maintenance of those divisions both in the private and in the public sphere. Whatever the attitude towards ethnocultural identities, both models firmly reject any form of coercive assimilation, condemning ethnocide, linguicide, and theocide.[64]

2.3.2 The Integrationist or Liberal Model

Following the previous definition of integration, the integrationist model of constitutional design "aims at equal citizenship", turning "a blind eye to difference for public purpose".[65] The integrationist approach corresponds to what Toniatti defines as the "agnostic liberal national states".[66] These are indifferent to the maintenance of ethnocultural identities and are exclusively concerned with the protection of individual rights and formal equality of citizens before the nation, as enshrined (although differently) in the US and French constitutions.[67] As written by Barry, one of the most prominent scholars in the integrationist field, integration can be defined as the privatisation of national, ethnic, and cultural differences,[68] capturing the liberal philosophy behind integration. In fact, advocates of integrationist arrangements for divided socie-

---

Competition on Minority Politics: A Comparison of Latvia and Estonia," *Journal of Ethnopolitics and Minority Issues in Europe* 13, no. 1 (2014): 57–85).

63 McGarry, O'Leary, and Simeon, "Integration or Accommodation," 42–3.

64 Forced assimilation can assume many forms, from the stigmatisation of local dialects to the erasure of minority history from school curricula to the illegalisation of minority ethno-cultural parties.

65 McGarry, O'Leary, and Simeon, "Integration or Accommodation," 45.

66 See Toniatti, "Minorities and Protected Minorities," 206; Palermo and Woelk, *Diritto costituzionale comparato*, 47–53.

67 For the characterisation of the US and French models, see Palermo and Woelk, *Diritto costituzionale comparato*, 48–50.

68 Brian Barry, *Culture and Equality: An Egalitarian Critique of Multiculturalism* (Cambridge: Harvard University Press, 2001), 19–62; Brian Barry, "Political Accommodation and Consociational Democracy," *British Journal of Political Science* 5, no. 4 (1975): 477–505.

ties believe that political instability and conflict are the result of group-based partisanship in the public sphere, namely within political institutions. To avoid such conflict, integrationists advise against ethnocultural political parties,[69] and favour cross-cutting parties. In the same spirit, the integrationist model backs electoral systems that require winners to achieve broad-based support and promotes executives that favour candidates who rise above ethnocultural factions. Besides, they discourage the delegation of some public policy functions to minority groups, and they oppose any form of territorial or non-territorial autonomy based on groups. Integration is the dominant goal, and it embodies the received wisdom regarding conflict regulation and conflict resolution in the longer-established democracies. International political actors such as the European Union, the United Nations, the World Bank, the International Monetary Fund, and the OSCE's High Commissioner on National Minorities (HCNM)[70] generally advocate for integration. Among state actors, the supporters of integration may vary, as they may be large majorities, small minorities, middlemen minorities, or indigenous people. Conversely, large minorities, especially when territorially concentrated and nationally mobilised, are firmly opposed to integration.[71] McGarry, O'Leary, and Simeon identify three main groups within the integrationist field, briefly analysed below.

This first group of integrationists is the so-called "republican integrationists" and are supporters of the civic "nation-state". They derive inspiration from those political thinkers who considered the conditions under which city-states or agrarian republics would flourish, such as Niccolò Machiavelli, James Harrington, Jean-Jacques Rousseau, Thomas Jefferson, and Immanuel Kant. They all believed that "citizens needed sufficient property and sufficient

---

69 On the ban of ethnonationalist parties, see Palermo and Woelk, *Diritto costituzionale comparato*, 50–3; Matthias Basedau et al., "Ethnic Party Bans in Africa: A Research Agenda," *German Law Journal* 8, no. 6 (2007): 617–34; Matthias Basedau and Anika Moroff, "Parties in Chains: Do Ethnic Party Bans in Africa Promote Peace?" *Party Politics* 17, no. 2 (2011): 205–22; Matthijs Bogaards, Matthias Basedau, and Christof Hartmann, eds., *Ethnic Party Bans in Africa* (London and New York: Routledge, 2013).

70 See, for example, The Ljubljana Guidelines on Integration of Diverse Societies, published by the HCNM in 2012, available at https://www.osce.org/files/f/documents/0/9/96883.pdf (last accessed 19 January 2023). Another meaningful document is the Thematic Commentary No. 4 on the Scope of Application of the Framework Convention for the Protection of National Minorities, adopted by the Council of Europe in 2016, available at https://bit.ly/34gi1kG (last accessed 19 January 2023).

71 See Will Kymlicka, "The Internationalization of Minority Rights," in *Constitutional Design for Divided Societies: Integration or Accommodation?*, ed. Sujit Choudhry (Oxford: Oxford University Press, 2008), 138–9.

equality to be sturdy and independent of the state and oppressive social organisations".[72] Republicans veer towards integral nationalism, in an assimilationist direction. Overall, they support civic virtue among citizens, shared citizenship, education, language, religion, and military service, and most of all, they are the strongest advocates of a nation of individuals, opposing any form of group-based advantage. The clearest examples of republicanism are French Jacobinism and Turkish Kemalism.

Unlike republican integrationists, liberals have a less expansive view of what should be publicly homogenised. In general terms, liberals are champions of the nation-state and of international liberal institutions, promoting the construction of a cosmopolitan political order. The ancestors of liberal integrationism are to be found in utilitarianism and rights-based defences of the value of liberty. If republicans promote a community of individuals, liberals' key premise is the individual *per se*. In fact, liberals support those conditions that enable strong individuals; they value political competition, and they promote liberal values such as choice, freedom, and equality. They disagree with accommodationist coercive solidarity and oppose differences in treatment on the grounds of culture, though they allow it based on morality or ability. Liberal integrationism is particularly popular in the United States, following the tradition of Charles-Louis de Secondat, Montesquieu, and John Locke.[73]

The concept of the nation-state divides the socialist integrationist field: some believe it constitutes a barrier to the creation of a global socialist civilisation, while others see it as a bastion against capitalism. After the focus of republicans on the community and liberals on the individual, the key component for socialists is the social class. They regard distributive justice as the public priority of the state, and social democrats regard substantive social citizenship as the best means to realise it.[74] From their perspective, ethnocultural politics inhibit the "correct" working-class politics. In fact, the capitalist order profits from ethnocultural divisions and the fact that such divisions obscure the similar interests of members of different communities. Socialists advocate for a strong welfare state, with redistribution and public investment in deprived areas to deal with the presumed "material bias" of ethnic or other collective identity, at the cost of temporarily supporting positive action poli-

72 McGarry, O'Leary, and Simeon, "Integration or Accommodation," 46.

73 McGarry, O'Leary, and Simeon, "Integration or Accommodation," 46–8.

74 See Thomas Humphrey Marshall and Tom Bottomore, eds., *Citizenship and Social Class* (London: Pluto Press, 1992).

cies to achieve equality.[75] Social integrationism is popular with the European left and Marxists around the world, including the South African Communist Party.

2.3.3 The Promotional Model

Placed in an intermediate position between the integrationist/liberal model and the accommodationist/multinational model, the promotional model is adopted by those constitutional systems characterised by the presence of a dominant majority group and one or several minority groups. In promotional systems, the recognition, protection, and promotion of diversity and minorities are founding elements of the constitutional system. As argued by Palermo and Woelk, "if the classic liberal model guarantees the right to be equal, the promotional model recognises the right to be different."[76] In other words, these systems aim to ensure equality in a substantive and not just a formal sense. Therefore, the solutions adopted are not only based on the principle of non-discrimination but also on the provision of a series of "special rights," such as differential rules for political participation and electoral rights, linguistic and religious rights, and forms of self-government. Although the specific promotional arrangements can vary significantly among constitutional systems, Palermo and Woelk argue that they all represent a combination of individual and collective rights that, in some parts of the territory, may recall the fully institutionalised multinational model (analysed in the following section).[77]

Generally speaking, five main promotional sets of arrangements can be identified. A first solution is the explicit recognition of minorities as constitutive elements of the constitutional system, entrenching their protection in the form of the state. This is the case with the 2012 Hungarian Constitution, which recognises in the Preamble that "the nationalities living with us form part of the Hungarian political community and are constituent parts of the State" and proclaims its commitment to "promoting and safeguarding [...] the languages and cultures of nationalities living in Hungary".[78] Similarly, in Art. XXIX, the Hungarian Constitution reiterates the recognition of minorities as constitutive elements of the state and provides for linguistic and

75 McGarry, O'Leary, and Simeon, "Integration or Accommodation," 50.

76 Palermo and Woelk, *Diritto costituzionale comparato*, 54 [English translation by the author.]

77 Ibidem.

78 Constitution of Hungary – Preamble.

cultural rights (Art. XXIX(1)),[79] as well as self-government (Art. XXIX(2) and (3)).[80] Then, a second set of arrangements includes differentiated treatments in the constitutional or national legal framework of specific parts of the territory. This is perfectly exemplified by the special status of the Åland Islands within the Finnish constitutional system.[81] The differentiated status of the Åland Islands is provided for in Art. 120 of the Finnish Constitution, which recognises essential guarantees. These include the right to self-government, with a directly elected subnational parliament enjoying wide legislative autonomy, the introduction of a sort of "regional citizenship" (the so-called right of domicile)[82] and the limitation of central legislative and executive competences in specific matters, especially the mandatory use of Finnish. A third promotional solution concerns the possibility to access special rights if determined (often numerical) conditions are met, without a previous territorial entrenchment. For instance, the 2001 Ohrid Agreement, signed in North Macedonia to end the hostilities between the governmental forces and the Albanian military groups, provides that minority languages can be recognised as official languages at the municipal level wherever they are spoken by more than 20% of the population of that municipality.[83] A fourth strategy that promotional states can implement is the right of a mi-

---

79 Constitution of Hungary – Art. XXIX(1): "Nationalities living in Hungary shall be constituent parts of the State. Every Hungarian citizen belonging to any nationality shall have the right to freely express and preserve his or her identity. Nationalities living in Hungary shall have the right to use their native languages and to the individual and collective use of names in their own languages, to promote their own cultures, and to be educated in their native languages."

80 Constitution of Hungary – Art. XXIX: "(2) Nationalities living in Hungary shall have the right to establish local and national self-governments. (3) The detailed rules relating to the rights of nationalities living in Hungary, the nationalities, the requirements for recognition as a nationality, and the rules for the election of the self-governments of nationalities at local and national level shall be laid down in a cardinal Act. A cardinal Act may provide that recognition as a nationality shall be subject to a certain length of time of presence and to the initiative of a certain number of persons declaring to be members of the nationality concerned."

81 See Pertti Joenniemi, "The Åland Islands Issue," in *The Nordic Peace*, ed. Clive Archer and Pertti Joenniemi (London and New York: Routledge, 2017), 88–104; Lauri Hannikainen and Frank Horn, eds., *Autonomy and Demilitarisation in International Law: The Åland Islands in Changing European Context* (Leiden: Martinus Nijhoff Publishers, 1997).

82 See Heidi Öst, "The Concept of the Åland Islands' Regional Citizenship and Its Impact on the Inclusion of Migrants," *European Yearbook of Minority Issues Online* 13, no. 1 (2016): 220–32.

83 See Armend Reka, "The Ohrid Agreement: The Travails of Inter-Ethnic Relations in Macedonia," *Human Rights Review* 9, no. 1 (2008): 55–69.

nority to political participation, through the adoption of promotional policies and legislation on political representation, the establishment of consultative bodies and the presence of liaison offices between minority groups and central institutions. An example of this strategy is the presence of ombudsmen for minorities in Sweden and Finland, that in specific circumstances are also able to submit petitions to the Constitutional Courts.[84] Finally, a rather controversial technique to promote the recognition of minority and group rights is the so-called *Millet* or "pillar" system, that has been adopted in some parts of the world and, but for its partial (and not full) institutionalisation, closely resembles the multinational model. This technique entails the provision of separate and self-governed systems for minority groups to manage certain matters, such as education or family and personal laws. The *Millet* system was anciently used in the Ottoman empire[85] to manage the coexistence of different religious groups and is partly still in place in some Middle Eastern countries, such as Lebanon, Egypt, Israel, Jordan, and Syria, or in India with the personal law system that will be discussed when addressing the *Shah Bano* case in Chapter 4. The "European variation" of this system is the traditional Dutch *verzuiling* ("pillar") system aimed at reaching "tolerance through separation."[86] According to such system, each religious group, i.e., the Protestant majority and the Catholic minority, enjoy legal recognition of the right to self-government in religious, cultural, and educational activities. Unsurprisingly, this institutional system of separation and its risk of creating internal segregation has attracted many criticisms and has been put under pressure by the increasing pluralism of contemporary societies.[87]

---

84 See Linda C. Reif, *The Ombudsman, Good Governance, and the International Human Rights System* (Leiden: Martinus Nijhoff Publishers, 2004).

85 See Jan Erk, "Non-Territorial Millets and Autonomy in the Ottoman Empire," in *Minority Accommodation through Territorial and Non-Territorial Autonomy*, ed. Tove Malloy and Francesco Palermo (Oxford: Oxford University Press, 2015), 119–32; Karen Barkey and George Gavrilis, "The Ottoman *Millet* System: Non-Territorial Autonomy and its Contemporary Legacy," in *Non-Territorial Autonomy in Divided Societies*, ed. John Coakley (London and New York: Routledge, 2018), 24–42.

86 Palermo and Woelk, *Diritto costituzionale comparato*, 58.

87 Matthijs Bogaards, "Consociationalism in the Netherlands: Polder Politics and Pillar Talk," in *Power-Sharing in Europe: Past Practice, Present Cases, and Future Directions*, ed. Soeren Keil and Allison McCulloch (Cham: Springer, 2021), 19–42.

2.3.4 The Accommodationist or Multinational Model

According to McGarry, O'Leary, and Simeon, accommodation[88] can take different forms. Despite the differences, they all have an essential common feature: they all require the "recognition of more than one ethnic, linguistic, national, or religious community in the state".[89] Such institutionalisation of diversity broadly corresponds to the multinational model identified by Toniatti, who defines the multinational state as a constitutional system "framed in terms of both the territorial organisation of its institutional system and substantive legislation in order to incorporate and reflect the multinationality of its permanent social pattern on a paritarian basis".[90] In general terms, the accommodationist or multinational model aims to secure the coexistence of different identities within the same state, allowing secession only if successful implementation of any form of accommodation proves impossible.[91] McGarry, O'Leary, and Simeon identify three main accommodationist approaches (i.e., consociationalism, centripetalism, and multiculturalism), briefly analysed below.

2.3.4.1 *Consociational Democracy*

The main theorist of consociationalism is Arend Lijphart, who dedicated a substantial part of his work[92] to power sharing.[93] Lijphart's definition of consociational democracy started as a contrast to the majoritarian interpretation of democracy, modelled on the Westminster system. In fact, Lijphart believes that the inherently competitive character of majoritarianism is not appropri-

88 More on accommodationist models can be found in Toniatti, "Minorities and Protected Minorities," 195–220.

89 McGarry, O'Leary, and Simeon, "Integration or Accommodation," 52.

90 Toniatti, "Minorities and Protected Minorities," 207; Palermo and Woelk, *Diritto costituzionale comparato*, 58–68.

91 For more on secession see the references listed in note 156.

92 Lijphart's major essays on power-sharing are collected in Arend Lijphart, *Thinking about Democracy* (London and New York: Routledge, 2008).

93 For further references on power sharing, see Allison McCulloch, "Consociational Settlements in Deeply Divided Societies: The Liberal-Corporate Distinction," *Democratization* 21, no. 3 (2014): 501–18; Feargal Cochrane, Neophytos Loizides, and Thibaud Bodson, *Mediating Power-Sharing: Devolution and Consociationalism in Deeply Divided Societies* (London and New York: Routledge, 2018); Soeren Keil and Allison McCulloch, eds., *Power-Sharing in Europe: Past Practice, Present Cases, and Future Directions* (Cham: Palgrave Macmillan, 2021); Joanne McEvoy and Brendan O'Leary, eds., *Power Sharing in Deeply Divided Places* (Philadelphia, Pennsylvania: University of Pennsylvania Press, 2013); Marc Weller, Barbara Metzger, and Niall Johnson, eds., *Settling Self-Determination Disputes: Complex Power-Sharing in Theory and Practice* (The Hague: Martinus Nijhoff, 2008).

ate for divided or plural societies, as it would create conflict between the majority and the opposition. If, in the Westminster model majority and opposition generally alternate in government, in plural societies it is impossible that the competition will actually lead to a governmental alternation between the majority and the minorities. On the contrary, in divided societies, majority rule would create a condition of perpetual exclusion of minorities from political power, as well as discrimination and loss of allegiance to the regime. Therefore, Lijphart argues that divided societies require a consociational model of democracy (also called "power-sharing democracy").[94]

Lijphart observes that scholars on divided societies have reached a certain amount of agreement on some essential points.[95] Firstly, they agree on the fact that divided societies pose a serious problem for democracy, and the challenges that those societies give rise to make it more difficult to establish and maintain a democracy than in a homogeneous society. Secondly, experts agree that these challenges are greater in not-yet-democratic or not-fully-democratic regimes than in well-established democracies. The third point that Lijphart mentions is not exactly a point of universal agreement, as it is precisely the issue over which the dispute with Horowitz originated. This is that "the two ingredients for successful democracy in divided societies are the sharing of executive power and group autonomy".[96] These two elements are what Lijphart defines as the "primary characteristics" of consociational democracy.[97] With power sharing, Lijphart means the equal participation of representatives of the significant ethnocultural groups in the executive, while autonomy may be translated in territorial or non-territorial terms.[98] In the first case, autonomy assumes the characteristics of federalism and decentralisation, while in the second it means the groups' authority to manage their

94 Lijphart, *Patterns of Democracy*, 30–3.

95 Lijphart, "The Wave," 38.

96 Lijphart, "The Wave," 38–9.

97 Arend Lijphart, "Multiethnic Democracy," in *The Encyclopedia of Democracy*, ed. Seymour Lipset, vol. III (London and New York: Routledge, 1995), 859.

98 For more recent works on territorial and non-territorial autonomy, see Marc Weller and Katherine Nobbs, eds., *Asymmetric Autonomy and the Settlement of Ethnic Conflicts* (Philadelphia: University of Pennsylvania Press, 2010); Michael Keating and Alain-G. Gagnon, eds., *Political Autonomy and Divided Societies: Imagining Democratic Alternatives in Complex Settings* (London: Palgrave Macmillan, 2012); Tove Malloy and Francesco Palermo, eds., *Minority Accommodation through Territorial and Non-Territorial Autonomy* (Oxford: Oxford University Press, 2015); Dawn Walsh, *Territorial Self-Government as a Conflict Management Tool* (Cham, Switzerland: Springer International Publishing, 2018); Felix Schulte, *Peace through Self-Determination: Success and Failure of Territorial Autonomy* (Cham: Springer International Publishing, 2020).

own internal affairs, especially in the educational and cultural sectors. As we will analyse in the subsequent section and have in part already mentioned, Horowitz has a completely different stance on this issue. To these two primary characteristics, Lijphart adds two "secondary characteristics",[99] namely proportionality and mutual veto. By proportionality, Lijphart refers to the proportional electoral system, preferable to the first-past-the-post system typical of majority rule. In fact, Proportional Representation (PR) is considered a more appropriate system as it allows for broader representation of minorities, which would otherwise be excluded.[100] Finally, in consociational democracies, groups should have the option to exercise veto power on vital interest issues that may affect the rights and autonomy of minorities.[101]

Power-sharing democracy has attracted many criticisms, which Lijphart summarises[102] in six main categories: (1) It is not sufficiently democratic; (2) it cannot work in practice; (3) a key explanation for its failure is that it does not contain incentives for moderate behaviour; (4) regional autonomy may lead to secession and territorial partitions; (5) it strengthens rather than weakens the cohesion and distinctiveness of ethnic groups, and thus increases conflict between them; and (6) both primary as well as secondary characteristics are based on European or Western experience, and thus they are unsuitable for multiethnic societies in other parts of the world. Lijphart responds to each criticism.[103] To the first argument, he simply observes that the mere alternation between majority and opposition governments is modelled on the majoritarian model of democracy, and it does not exhaust the full range of democratic possibilities. Concerning the critics' argument that it is impossible to make a decision when power is shared, Lijphart replies that there are successful examples that demonstrate it is indeed possible to have functioning democratic institutions in consociational democracies. Lijphart also adds that even if power sharing fails, as it did in Cyprus in 1963 and in Lebanon in 1975, it should be repaired rather than replaced, as it constitutes the best chance of successful conflict resolution. The criticism concerning incentives is the one put forward by Horowitz, to which Lijphart responds by stating that if it is true that coalescence and compromise are analytically different, as to coalesce does not necessarily mean to compromise, it is also true that parties have the general inclination to want to be included in the cabinet, and that

99 Lijphart, "The Wave," 39.
100 Lijphart, "Constitutional Design," 99–101.
101 Lijphart, "Constitutional Design," 107.
102 Lijphart, "The Wave," 40.
103 Lijphart, "The Wave," 41–5.

especially in divided societies this represents a sufficient incentive to compromise. To the arguments concerning territorial autonomy, Lijphart observes that there is no empirical evidence that confirms the link between autonomy and secession. On the contrary, granting group autonomy may be an effective means of regional conflict resolution.[104] The same logic applies to the risk of ethnic conflict, as the existence of strong and autonomous groups may not necessarily lead to political confrontation among them. On the contrary, if correctly designed, they may have a constructive role in conflict resolution. Concerning the last criticism, Lijphart opposes many examples of power-sharing democracies in the non-Western world, along with many non-Western scholars who emphasise that majority rule goes against their native traditions of trying to reach a consensus, recalling the essential basis of power sharing. Even though Lijphart strongly defends his theory, there is an "especially valid and serious criticism",[105] namely that the key concepts of power sharing have been particularly hard to define and measure with a confident amount of precision. Lijphart admits the impossibility of coming to a satisfying answer and thus concludes that "this is an insoluble problem and that we shall simply have to live with concepts that have very important theoretical and policy significance but cannot be measured precisely".[106]

2.3.4.2 *Centripetal Democracy*

The most prominent critic of consociational theory can be considered Donald Horowitz, who proposes instead the so-called "incentive approach" (or "centripetalism"[107] as defined by McGarry, O'Leary, and Simeon). Before moving to the analysis of Horowitz's approach, it is useful to first consider his criticisms of Lijphart's theory. As previously mentioned, Horowitz questions the motivations that lead ethnocultural groups to share power in a consociation, considering them inadequate and unconvincing. The desire to be included in the cabinet is not enough of an incentive to share power, especially in cases of large groups which could alone gain the majority of votes in the electoral

---

104 See also Will Kymlicka, "The Internationalization of Minority Rights," in *Constitutional Design for Divided Societies*, ed. Sujit Choudhry (Oxford: Oxford University Press, 2008), 111–40.

105 Lijphart, "The Wave," 46.

106 Ibidem.

107 The incentive approach supporters emphasise moderation and compromise, thus an overall convergence of political actors, while consociation is deemed to generate centrifugal politics (see McGarry, O'Leary, and Simeon, "Integration or Accommodation," 53–6).

competition.[108] The same applies to political élites and their degree of tolerance towards other ethnocultural groups: statesmanship alone is not enough. Another criticism concerns cultural autonomy. As cultural matters are habitually divisive issues, they go straight to the heart of the conflict, and to accord equal recognition to all cultures, religions, and languages has three different effects. First, it means to concede equal ownership, contrary to what groups are normally willing to concede. Second, it means to concede the issue of group superiority, which can be contested by reference to disputes over cultural superiority and primacy. Lastly, it means to concede the issue of the identity of who will dominate, which would otherwise be regulated by limitations on languages and educational streams associated with competitors.[109] A final criticism moved by Horowitz against Lijphart's consociational theory is the failure to distinguish between pre-electoral and post-electoral coalitions. In fact, the coalitions recommended in a consociation are post-electoral coalitions, which do not typically compromise on inter-ethnic issues but rather on the division of portfolios in the shared cabinet. By contrast, pre-electoral coalitions would foster compromise on ethnic issues.[110] Moving away from these criticisms, Horowitz proposes a theory based on incentives promoting moderation among ethno-cultural groups. Following this logic, Horowitz recommends the use of the Alternative Vote (AV) as the electoral system, as the multipolar fluidity of vote pooling would facilitate inter-ethnic accommodation. Conversely, PR and Single Transferable Vote (STV)[111] would favour ethnic parties, not fostering moderation.[112] Vote pooling would require at least the winning candidates to pool votes from among different ethnic voters in order to gain the majority. This logic is also reflected in the choice of the form of government: a single presidency rising above ethnic politics.[113] Even though Horowitz recognises that the incentive approach is difficult to adopt, he believes that once adopted it has a great advantage: it can prevent the crystallisation of identities and the emergence of more severe conflict.[114]

---

108 Horowitz, "Constitutional Design," 20.
109 Horowitz, "Constitutional Design," 22.
110 Ibidem.
111 Some accommodationists prefer the STV version of proportional representation, as it has a higher effective threshold than most forms of list-based proportional representation, and it may facilitate transfers in favour of candidates and parties prepared to maintain power-sharing.
112 McGarry, O'Leary, and Simeon, "Integration or Accommodation," 53.
113 Choudhry, "Bridging," 22.
114 Horowitz, "Constitutional Design," 25.

2.3.4.3 *Multiculturalism*

The accommodationist version of multiculturalism is something different from what we generally associate with the concept. In fact, in accommodationist terms, multiculturalism should entail some respect for a group's self-governance in matters defined as important, as well as some broad appreciation of the principle of proportional representation of all groups in key public institutions (although not necessarily by quotas). Then, it should offer a share of public political power through consociational arrangements,[115] and it should provide for territorially based communities to share power through a pluralist federation or a pluralist union state respecting historic nationalities, languages, or religions.[116] Moreover, multiculturalism should promote public schools for national minorities, as well as other forms of cultural autonomy. By contrast, Western multiculturalism has avoided such policies and is limited to tolerance of such differences in the private domain while promoting integration in the public sphere.[117]

3 Federalism and Constitutional Design: Theoretical and Empirical Links

From the review of the constitutional models to accommodate ethnocultural diversity, autonomy, in its territorial and non-territorial dimensions, appears to emerge as a particularly relevant feature in the possible solutions to promote internal pluralism and protect minorities. This paragraph briefly reviews the theoretical and empirical links between federalism and constitutional design.

3.1 *The Scholarship on Constitutional Design and the Relevance of Federalism*

In the literature on constitutional design, federalism often makes an appearance. As already recalled in the previous pages, the territorial organisation of power as regionalism or federalism provided one of the main factors on which

---

115 For this reason, multiculturalism has also been defined as a semi-consociation, as it presents some of the distinctive elements of a typical consociation but not others (see Christopher McCrudden and Brendan O'Leary, *Courts and Consociations. Human Rights versus Power Sharing* (Oxford: Oxford University Press, 2013), 9–10).

116 McGarry, O'Leary, and Simeon, "Integration or Accommodation," 57–8.

117 McGarry, O'Leary, and Simeon, "Integration or Accommodation," 56–7.

the original case-driven analyses focused.[118] Besides, Lutz includes federalism in his "general principles of constitutional design" when discussing the issue of the distribution of power.[119] Moreover, Simeon provided a checklist of the main issues and questions on constitutional design and amendments in federal systems.[120] Interestingly, Simeon observed that views on the fundamental goals of federalism influence the process of constitutional design, as federalism could be intended as an integral element of liberal democracies, founded on the separation of powers and on checks and balances (i.e., the United States), or as a device for the development and delivery of public services (i.e., Germany and Australia), or again as a device for managing conflicts in territorially divided societies (i.e., Canada, Belgium, Spain).[121] Each process entails a set of "institutions and rules that would provide incentives for leaders to promote and sustain certain values, and limit behaviour that undermines them".[122] Therefore, the two domains of constitutional design and federalism are deeply intertwined. This becomes even more evident once we shift to the literature on constitutional design for divided societies.[123] In fact, this consol-

---

118 Ginsburg, "Introduction," 3–4.

119 Lutz, *Principles of Constitutional Design*, 219–20: "A critical problem in constitutional design is the distribution of power: Why should we distribute power, and how should we do it? Consider separation of powers, *federalism*, institutional complexity, and accountability. Evaluate basic constitutional models: the parliamentary model (constraint by tradition) versus the separation of powers model (constraint by institutional complexity); the mixed regime model (balance) versus the presidential model (legitimate force); the framework model (process over content) versus the code model (content over process); and the covenant model (communitarian civic relationships) versus the manifesto model (communitarian transformational relationships)."

120 Simeon identified a series of issues, such as the number and character of the constituent units, the division of powers, fiscal arrangements, intergovernmental relations, representation at the centre, and judicial review, some of which will be discussed in Chapter 2 while explaining the legal factors conducive to constitutional asymmetry (see Simeon, "Constitutional Design," 241–61).

121 Simeon, "Constitutional Design," 243.

122 Ibidem.

123 See for references: Liam Anderson, *Federal Solutions to Ethnic Problems: Accommodating Diversity* (London and New York: Routledge, 2013); Sujit Choudhry and Nathan Hume, "Federalism, Secession and Devolution: From Classical to Post-Conflict Federalism," in *Comparative Constitutional Law*, ed. Tom Ginsburg and Rosalind Dixon (Cheltenham: Edward Elgar, 2011); Jan Erk and Lawrence M. Anderson, *The Paradox of Federalism: Does Self-Rule Accommodate or Exacerbate Ethnic Divisions?* (London and New York: Routledge, 2013); Yash Ghai, *Autonomy and Ethnicity: Negotiating Competing Claims in Multi-Ethnic States* (Cambridge: Cambridge University Press, 2000); Michael Keating and Alain-G. Gagnon, eds., *Political Autonomy and Divided Societies: Imagining Democratic Alternatives in Complex Settings* (London: Palgrave Macmillan, 2012); Neophytos Loi-

idates the suggestion that federalism is one of the possible arrangements to address internal divisions along ethnocultural lines,[124] as both the integrationist and accommodationist sides include federalism in their models.

On the one hand, on the integrationist side, federalism is not supported by all groups. If republicans are generally the champions of a centralised and unitary state, following a monistic concept of sovereignty,[125] liberal integrationists are strong supporters of the federal model over the unitary state, through the creation of national federations, as they believe that liberty is better protected through the division and separation of powers. Nevertheless, liberals oppose ethno-federations, since these may encourage secession and separatism.[126]

On the other hand, among the accommodationists, Horowitz believes that federalism or regional autonomy can have positive effects on divided societies, preserving multipolar fluidity, acting in aid of the electoral system, fostering intra-group competition in homogeneous federal units, or providing political socialisation among different groups in heterogeneous units.[127] The main supporter of centripetalism also believes that federalism has "conciliatory potential",[128] as it may allow stateside minorities to become regional majorities, as well as potentially facilitating asymmetrical autonomy arrangements for regions with distinctive identities and issues. Moreover, federations disperse power from the centre, generally inhibiting authoritarianism, and provide a training ground for local politicians and party leaders to engage in ethnic bargaining at the local level.[129] On the accommodationist

---

zides, Iosif Kovras, and Kathleen Ireton, "Introduction: Federalism, Reconciliation, and Power-Sharing in Post-Conflict Societies," *Federal Governance* 8, no. 2 (2011): 1–14; Dawn Walsh, *Territorial Self-Government as a Conflict Management Tool* (Cham, Switzerland: Springer International Publishing, 2018).

124 Hirschl, "The 'Design Sciences'," 1366–7; Palermo and Kössler, *Comparative Federalism*, 97–111; Elazar, *Exploring Federalism*, 248–51. For more on federalism and conflict resolution, see, for example, Soeren Keil, "Federalism as a Tool of Conflict Resolution," in *A Research Agenda for Federalism Studies*, ed. John Kincaid (Cheltenham: Edward Elgar Publishing, 2019), 151–61; Soeren Keil and Elisabeth Alber, "Introduction: Federalism as a Tool of Conflict Resolution," *Ethnopolitics* 19, no. 4 (2020): 329–41; Elisabeth Alber and Michael G. Breen, "Federalism and Ethnic Relations," in *Encyclopedia of Contemporary Constitutionalism*, ed. Javier Cremades and Cristina Hermida (Cham: Springer International Publishing, 2022), 1–26.

125 McGarry, O'Leary, and Simeon, "Integration or Accommodation," 48.

126 McGarry, O'Leary, and Simeon, "Integration or Accommodation," 49.

127 Horowitz, "Constitutional Design," 25.

128 Donald Horowitz, *A Democratic South Africa? Constitutional Engineering in a Divided Society* (Berkeley: University of California Press, 1992), 214.

129 Horowitz, "The Many Uses of Federalism," 958–62.

side, McGarry, O'Leary, and Simeon also identify a model called "territorial pluralism", which is especially prevalent in pluralist or ethno-federations,[130] namely those federations with internal boundaries that respect ethnocultural divisions.[131]

For his part, Lijphart dedicated part of his work to the link between consociations and federations,[132] considering them both as models of non-majoritarian democracy[133] viable to address the problems of plural societies, and identifying the conditions under which a consociation is also a federation, and those under which a federation is also a consociation. From the comparison of the core elements of consociational and federal theories, Lijphart starts by observing that one of the primary characteristics of power sharing, i.e., segmental autonomy, can take territorial and non-territorial forms,[134] and most of the time, territorial segmental autonomy is translated into federal arrangements.[135] Therefore, a consociation is also a federation when: the segments of plural societies are geographically concentrated;[136] the boundaries between the federal units follow segmental boundaries; and the other federal

130 However, territorial pluralism as a model of accommodating diversity can also be found in formally unitary states (e.g., United Kingdom, Spain, Denmark), as long as they recognise historic nationalities and their boundaries.

131 McGarry, O'Leary, and Simeon, "Integration or Accommodation," 53, 63–7. See also Palermo and Kössler, *Comparative Federalism*, 98–101; Alain-G. Gagnon and Arjun Tremblay, "Federalism and Diversity: A New Research Agenda," in *A Research Agenda for Federalism Studies*, John Kincaid, ed. (Cheltenham: Edward Elgar Publishing, 2019), 129–139.

132 See Arend Lijphart, "Consociation and Federation: Conceptual and Empirical Links," *Canadian Journal of Political Science / Revue Canadienne de Science Politique* 12, no. 3 (1979): 499–515; Arend Lijphart, "Federal, Confederal, and Consociational Options for the South African Plural Society," in *Conflict and Compromise in South Africa*, ed. Robert I. Rotberg and John Barrett (Lexington, Massachusetts: Lexington Books, 1980), 51–75; Arend Lijphart, "Non-Majoritarian Democracy: A Comparison of Federal and Consociational Theories," *Publius: The Journal of Federalism* 15 (1985): 3–15.

133 Lijphart, "Non-Majoritarian Democracy," 4.

134 Lijphart observes that federalism offers an excellent opportunity for group autonomy when groups are geographically concentrated, thus opting for a territorial form of autonomy. By contrast, when the groups are geographically dispersed, autonomy can be instituted on a non-territorial basis in fields such as education and culture (see Lijphart, "The Wave," 51–2).

135 Lijphart, "Consociation and Federation," 505.

136 As also suggested by Livingston in his definition of "federal societies", meaning a federation that is needed when the constitutional system has diverse, geographically concentrated, and politically mobilised communities (see William S. Livingston, *Federalism and Constitutional Change* (Oxford: Oxford University Press, 1956)).

principles are applied as well.[137] Lijphart also highlighted the consociational elements in federal theory, arguing that the latter embodies all the basic principles of consociational theory. In fact, federal units enjoy a high degree of autonomy in organising their internal affairs (autonomy); all units participate in the decision-making process at the central level of government in the federal chamber (power sharing in grand coalitions); the federal chamber is often composed according to the idea of proportionality as a minimum and minority representation (proportionality); and the amendment procedure of the federal constitution generally requires the consent of the federal units (veto power).

However, Lijphart specified that not every consociation is a federation, nor is every federation necessarily a consociation.[138] First of all, a federal structure does not entail democracy,[139] thus a federation can only be a consociation if it has a democratic regime. Second, a consociation operates in the context of a divided society, while a federation may also occur in homogeneous societies (e.g., Australia, Germany, Austria, the United States); therefore, "only federations in plural societies can be consociations".[140] Moreover, a federation is a consociation only if all four basic principles of a power-sharing democracy are present, whereas federal systems where the scope of autonomy of the subnational units is extensive can be considered consociations.[141] Perhaps the most

---

137 Lijphart makes specific reference to the necessary requirements of a central-regional division of power, internal constitutional autonomy and decentralised government, bicameralism, minority representation in the federal chamber, and a written constitution specifying the division of powers.

138 Lijphart, "Consociation and Federation," 509–12.

139 Lijphart offers a few examples: Soviet Union, Czechoslovakia, Argentina, Brazil. However, if Lijphart assumes that consociation and consociational democracy are synonymous, many critics have questioned the compatibility of power-sharing with democracy (see, for example, Christine Bell, "Power-Sharing and Human Rights Law," *The International Journal of Human Rights* 17, no. 2 (2013): 204–37). Daniel J. Elazar, in 1987, defined this specific assumption of consociations as inherently democratic as "problematic", arguing that there is no guarantee that democracy will actually prevail within the different segments (see Daniel J. Elazar, *Exploring Federalism* (Tuscaloosa and London: University of Alabama Press, 1987), 24–5).

140 Lijphart, "Consociation and Federation," 509.

141 Such passage in Lijphart's work appears to be somewhat enigmatic, as he states that "only *decentralized* federations can be consociations". However, the term "decentralized federations" seems to be redundant, as the principle of self-rule and shared rule necessarily implies a form of decentralization. Perhaps, what Lijphart is referring to is the extensiveness of the scope in which subnational units (i.e., the "segments") may exercise their autonomy (i.e., self-rule) (see Lijphart, "Consociation and Federation," 509–10). Moreover, in a later work, Lijphart observes that "most federal systems are decentralized

interesting point raised by Lijphart, especially for the purpose of this research, is the one concerning symmetry and asymmetry in federal systems.[142] Recalling Charles D. Tarlton's definition, Lijphart identified asymmetric federations as the only ones that can also be considered consociations, since asymmetric federal systems are "composed of political units corresponding to differences of interest, character, and makeup that exist within the whole society".[143] On a related note, a final condition is that a federation should consist of as many units as there are segments in a divided society in order to be defined as a consociation as well.

3.2 *Federal Theory and the Relevance of Constitutional Design for Divided Societies*

Moving to the federal scholarship's perspective, it is interesting to recall two authors who have examined the link between federalism and consociationalism, both starting from Lijphart's work. The first was Ivo D. Duchacek,[144] who argued that "the inevitably consociational origin of federalism neither requires nor promises a continuation of consociationalism in the future management of the federal system".[145] The "consociational cradle" Duchacek was referring to in his article concerns the initial compact among political actors, requiring their initial consensus to give birth to a "future federal nation".[146] However, the author is convinced that such a consociational birth does not entail the rejection of majoritarianism, since "from inter-elite summit there emerges a commitment to a majoritarian decision mode".[147] Instead, Duchacek closely associates consociations and confederal systems, as consociational principles (e.g., consensus, veto rights) prevail in the cases of loose confederations where there is no interest or commitment to building a common sovereign identity.[148]

– in fact, there are no cases in the pure "federal and centralized" category at all – and most unitary systems are centralized." (see Lijphart, *Patterns of Democracy*, 179).

142 It is interesting to note that, in a later work, Lijphart used the expression "congruent/incongruent" instead of "symmetry/asymmetry", since, in his opinion, the latter is most often used to describe the different degree of distribution of powers and thus tends to be confusing (see Lijphart, *Patterns of Democracy*, 184).

143 Tarlton, "Symmetry and Asymmetry," 869.

144 Ivo D. Duchacek, "Consociational Cradle of Federalism," *Publius: The Journal of Federalism* 15 (1985): 35–48.

145 Duchacek, "Consociational Cradle," 47.

146 Duchacek, "Consociational Cradle," 35.

147 Duchacek, "Consociational Cradle," 47.

148 Duchacek, "Consociational Cradle," 46–7.

The second author was Daniel J. Elazar,[149] who observed that "in the latter half of the 1970s, students of both [federalism and consociationalism] began to explore the other's theories in an attempt to determine points of convergence and difference".[150] On the one hand, federal scholars referred to consociational arrangements as "non-territorial federalism"; on the other, consociationalists discovered consociational dimensions in federal polities. Aside from Lijphart's contribution to identifying the links between the two, Elazar argued that one main difference between federalism and consociationalism is that the former involves structures as well as processes of government, while the latter involves processes only, which can be embodied by law but not necessarily in the same way as in federal systems. Nonetheless, Elazar defines both concepts as political and social phenomena, although consociationalism could be considered even more of a social phenomenon than federalism.[151] Indeed, federalism is essentially understood in terms of relations among governments, while consociationalism emphasises the relations among different ethnocultural groups. Therefore, Elazar's conclusion concerns the different focus of federalism and power sharing towards the polity: federalism focuses on the form, whereas consociationalism focuses on the regime.[152] When federalism purports to go beyond the mere form towards the character of the regime as well, then federalism and consociationalism "relate to each other on a more symmetrical basis".[153]

Perhaps the most evident link between the two scholarships is the debate on the viability of multinational federalism in a context of ethnocultural diversity.[154] Once again, such debate originated in the 1990s, after the breakup of

---

149 Elazar, *Exploring Federalism*, 18–26.

150 Elazar, *Exploring Federalism*, 19.

151 Elazar, *Exploring Federalism*, 21.

152 Elazar, *Exploring Federalism*, 22.

153 Elazar, *Exploring Federalism*, 26.

154 For some references on multinational federalism as a model of constitutional design to compose and manage internal diversity, see Michael Burgess and John Pinder, eds., *Multinational Federations* (London and New York: Routledge, 2011); Ernest Gellner, *Nations and Nationalism* (Hoboken, New Jersey: Blackwell Publishers, 1983); Alain-G. Gagnon and James Tully, eds., *Multinational Democracies* (Cambridge and New York: Cambridge University Press, 2001); Anna Mastromarino, *Il federalismo disaggregativo. Un percorso costituzionale negli Stati multinazionali* (Milano: Giuffrè, 2010); Wayne J. Norman, *Negotiating Nationalism: Nation-Building, Federalism, and Secession in the Multinational State* (Oxford and New York: Oxford University Press, 2006); Ferran Requejo and Klaus-Jürgen Nagel, eds., *Federalism beyond Federations: Asymmetry and Processes of Resymmetrisation in Europe* (Farnham, England: Ashgate, 2011); Michel Seymour and Alain-G. Gagnon, eds., *Multinational Federalism: Problems and Prospects* (London:

three multinational federations: the USSR, Yugoslavia, and Czechoslovakia. For some scholars, the disintegration of these federations served as a demonstration of the nonviability of multinational federalism in diverse societies, as it did not prevent the collapse of the political system. However, it can be argued that the three former ethno-federations did not collapse because the model was unfit to accommodate diversity, but because federalism was not introduced in properly democratic regimes, and it was not followed by political pluralism and guarantees of fundamental rights protection.[155] Critics of multinational federations, as integrationists, also argue that this model would encourage secession, since it would provide nationality-based subnational units with incentives and political resources that may eventually lead to secession.[156] Proponents of multinational federalism respond to this critique

---

Palgrave Macmillan UK, 2012); Stepan, "Towards a New Comparative Politics of Federalism," 29–84.

155 John McGarry and Brendan O'Leary, "Federation as a Method of Ethnic Conflict Regulation," in *From Power Sharing to Democracy*, ed. Sid Noel (Montréal: McGill-Queen's University Press, 2005), 274–81; Michael Burgess and Franz Gress, "Symmetry and Asymmetry Revisited," in *Accommodating Diversity: Asymmetry in Federal States*, ed. Robert Agranoff (Baden-Baden: Nomos, 1999), 54–5.

156 For further references on secession and self-determination, see Antoni Abat i Ninet, *Constitutional Law and Politics of Secession* (London and New York: Routledge, 2023); Rainer Bauböck, "Why Stay Together? A Pluralist Approach to Secession and Federalism," in *Citizenship in Diverse Society*, ed. Will Kymlicka and Wayne Norman (Oxford: Oxford University Press, 2000), 366–94; Rainer Bauböck, "A Multilevel Theory of Democratic Secession," *Ethnopolitics* 18, no. 3 (2019): 227–46; Harry Beran, "A Liberal Theory of Secession," *Political Studies* 32, no. 1 (1984): 21–31; Pau Bossacoma Busquets, *Morality and Legality of Secession* (Cham, Switzerland: Palgrave Macmillan, 2020); Allen Buchanan, "Theories of Secession," *Philosophy & Public Affairs* 26, no. 1 (1997): 31–61; Carlos Closa, Costanza Margiotta, and Giuseppe Martinico, eds., *Between Democracy and Law: The Amorality of Secession* (New York: Routledge, 2019); Donald L. Horowitz, "The Cracked Foundations of the Right to Secede," *Journal of Democracy* 14, no. 2 (2003): 5–17; Michael Keating, "Is a Theory of Self-Determination Possible?," *Ethnopolitics* 18, no. 3 (2019): 315–23; Will Kymlicka, "Federalism and Secession: At Home and Abroad," *Canadian Journal of Law & Jurisprudence* 13, no. 2 (2000): 207–24; Percy B. Lehning, ed., *Theories of Secession* (London and New York: Routledge, 2005); Susanna Mancini, *Minoranze autoctone e Stato. Tra composizione dei conflitti e secessione* (Milano: Giuffrè, 1996); Susanna Mancini, "Rethinking the Boundaries of Democratic Secession: Liberalism, Nationalism, and the Right of Minorities to Self-Determination," *International Journal of Constitutional Law* 6, no. 3–4 (2008): 553–84; Susanna Mancini, "Secession and Self-Determination," in *The Oxford Handbook of Comparative Constitutional Law, ed. Michel Rosenfeld and András Sajó* (Oxford: Oxford University Press, 2012), 481–500; Susanna Mancini, "Costituzionalismo, federalismo e secessione," *Istituzioni del Federalismo* 35, no. 4 (2014): 779–805; Avishai Margalit and Joseph Raz, "National Self-Determination," *Journal of Philosophy* 87, no. 9 (1990): 439–61; Costanza Margiotta, *L'ultimo diritto. Profili*

not by denying the risk of secession,[157] but by claiming that sufficient autonomy is a valuable solution to address internal political and ethnocultural divisions, avoiding the risk of secession and therefore the disintegration of the state.[158]

For the purpose of this research, it is interesting to recall the four different positions identified by McGarry and O'Leary on the value of federalism as a method of accommodating ethnocultural diversity. First, the so-called "Jacobin position" supports unitarism rather than federalism, as the latter would contribute to the rise of ethnocentrism. The "federalism as nation building position" is essentially the solution advocated by liberal integrationists; as previously recalled, they support the creation of national federations rather than multinational federations. Drawing from the Marxist tradition, the "Cosmopolitan position" recognises the value of federalism as a means to accommodate diversity, but only if accepted in the framework of the realisation of global communism. Finally, supporters of multinational federalism believe that federalism can be valuable both in order to accommodate national and ethnic differences, as well as to ensure the preservation of liberal democratic rights. What is even more relevant for the purpose of this book is that McGarry and O'Leary also argue that multinational federalists advocate for the institutionalisation of asymmetric federalism,[159] a nexus that was also highlighted by Alfred Stepan, who claimed that "all of the long-standing multinational federal democracies are constitutionally asymmetrical".[160] As observed by Palermo and Kössler, a sound verification of the viability of multi-

---

storici e teorici della secessione (Bologna: Il Mulino, 2005); Giuseppe Martinico and Giacomo Delledonne, eds., *The Canadian Contribution to a Comparative Law of Secession* (Cham, Switzerland: Palgrave Macmillan, 2019); Margaret Moore, *National Self-Determination and Secession* (Oxford: Oxford University Press, 1998); Wayne Norman, *Negotiating Nationalism: Nation-Building, Federalism, and Secession in the Multinational State* (Oxford: Oxford University Press, 2006); Nikos Skoutaris, "Mind the Gap Between Federalism and Secession: The Relationship Between Two (In)compatible Concepts," *Perspectives on Federalism* 16, no. 1 (2024): 211–36; Venice Commission, "Report on Self-Determination and Secession," CDL-INF(2000)2, 1999; Daniel Weinstock, "Constitutionalizing the Right to Secede," *Journal of Political Philosophy* 9, no. 2 (2001): 182–203; Christopher Heath Wellman, *A Theory of Secession*, 1st ed. (Cambridge: Cambridge University Press, 2005).

157 See, for example, Kymlicka, "Federalism and Secession: At Home and Abroad."

158 Palermo and Kössler, *Comparative Federalism*, 98.

159 McGarry and O'Leary, "Federation," 266–73.

160 See Alfred Stepan, "Federalism and Democracy: Beyond the U.S. Model," *Journal of Democracy* 10, no. 4 (1999): 29–30; Alfred Stepan, "Towards a New Comparative Politics of Federalism," 40.

national federalism is impossible, because constitutional design models are too influenced by methodological bias, as well as highly susceptible to variations and extra-legal factors (e.g., socio-economic, cultural, or political factors), to identify "an unambiguous causal link between multinational federalism and secession".[161]

Finally, it should be recalled that, in federal theory, there are several authors who link the principles of federalism to the idea of a changing society. In the 1950s, for example, Livingston coined the expression "federal society," specifically denoting those federal systems delineated according to social diversity and internal pluralism.[162] Similarly, Friedrich, drawing on the thought of Althusius,[163] introduced a new approach, the so-called "dynamic federalism," which conceives of federalism not as a rigid institutional scheme but as a process capable of adapting to social developments.[164] More recently, Kincaid and Tarr,[165] Burgess,[166] Popelier[167] and Tierney,[168] and have again focused on the evolutions of federal systems in response to political and social changes, highlighting their dynamic capacity. Thus, federalism seems to prove to be a complex of principles and tools capable of adapting to the challenges raised by divided societies.

4 Constitutional Asymmetries as a Dynamic Constitutional Model

In the analysis of the link between constitutional design for divided societies and federalism, asymmetric federalism was recalled more than once: Lijphart believes that only asymmetric federal systems can be considered consociations; Horowitz argues that asymmetrical autonomy in federal systems may have conciliatory potential; McGarry and O'Leary recall the institutionalisa-

161 Palermo and Kössler, *Comparative Federalism,* 100.

162 See William S. Friedrich, Livingston, "A Note on the Nature of Federalism," *Political Science Quarterly* 67, no. 1 (1952): 81–95.

163 See, especially, Friedrich, "Federal Constitutional Theory and Emergent Proposals."

164 See Friedrich, *Trends of Federalism in Theory and Practice.*

165 See John Kincaid and Alan Tarr, eds., *Constitutional Origins, Structure, and Change in Federal Countries* (Montréal: McGill-Queen's University Press, 2005).

166 Michael Burgess, *In Search of the Federal Spirit* (Oxford: Oxford University Press, 2013).

167 Popelier, *Dynamic Federalism*; Patricia Popelier, "Federal Dynamics and Stability," in *The Making and Ending of Federalism*, ed. Peter Bußjäger, Mathias Eller, and Julia Oberdanner (Leiden and Boston: Brill | Nijhoff, 2024), 92–116.

168 See Stephen Tierney, *The Federal Contract: A Constitutional Theory of Federalism* (Oxford: Oxford University Press, 2022).

tion of asymmetric federalism in multinational federations; and Stepan claims that all multinational federal democracies are constitutionally asymmetrical. Moreover, constitutional asymmetries also appear in the bulk of federal literature that has been dedicating increasing attention to federalism as a tool for conflict resolution, comparatively exploring the adoption of the federal structure by several ethnically divided states such as Belgium, Canada, and India.[169] An effective explanation for the reason why federalism is regarded as an instrument to manage diversity is offered by India. In fact, for Indian constitution-makers, federalism was seen as a constitutional device that could engage with its extraordinary heterogeneity, displaying multiple cross-cutting identities based on language, religion, caste, tribe, and region.[170] According to Nesiah, federalism "embodied and institutionalised those values that represented their own hopes and aspirations for independent India: democratic, pluralistic, and politically stable."[171] In this respect, the federal model was designed in cooperative terms to grant multiple and heterogeneous communities "an institutional mechanism for engaging with the nation,"[172] while preserving the unity of the nation. However, some federal scholars have argued that:

> Effective decentralisation […] requires revisiting the traditional federal theory on constitutional asymmetry. Asymmetry can no longer be considered as the exception, as a driver for disunity that carries the risk of

---

169 See Giancarlo Rolla, "Federalismo e regionalismo in tempi di transizione," *Federalismi.it*, Special Issue no. 2 (2018): 2–22; McGarry and O'Leary, "Federation as a Method of Ethnic Conflict Regulation;" John McGarry and Brendan O'Leary, "Territorial Approaches to Ethnic Conflict Settlement," in *The Routledge Handbook of Ethnic Conflict*, ed. Karl Cordell and Stefan Wolff (London ; New York: Routledge, 2016), 240–56; Matteo Nicolini, Francesco Palermo, and Enrico Milano, eds., *Law, Territory and Conflict Resolution: Law as a Problem and Law as a Solution* (Leiden and Boston: Brill Nijhoff, 2016); Alex Danilovich and Francis Owtram, "Federalism as a Tool to Manage Conflicts and Associated Risks," in *Iraqi Federalism and the Kurds*, ed. Alex Danilovich (London and New York: Routledge, 2016), 13–48; Guerino D'Ignazio and Anna Margherita Russo, eds., "Asimmetria e conflitti territoriali nel quadro dell'integrazione europea," *Istituzioni del Federalismo*, no. 2 (2018); Soeren Keil and Elisabeth Alber, eds., *Federalism as a Tool of Conflict Resolution* (London and New York: Routledge, 2021); Soeren Keil, "Federalism and Conflict Resolution: Mixed Success?" in *Teaching Federalism*, ed. John Kincaid and J. Leckrone (Cheltenham and Northampton: Edward Elgar Publishing, 2023), 154–64.

170 Vasuji Nesiah, "Federalism and Diversity in India," in *Autonomy and Ethnicity: Negotiating Competing Claims in Multi-Ethnic States*, ed. Yash Ghai (Cambridge: Cambridge University Press, 2000), 53.

171 Ibidem

172 Nesiah, "Federalism and Diversity in India," 53–4.

> secession. If the complexity of a conflict needs to be matched by the complexity of solutions to the respective conflict, as earlier argued, then the implementation of asymmetry in conflict resolution has to be on top of the agenda, for all parties involved, and structural fears as to its use must be overcome by procedural guarantees that contribute to capacity- and trust-building across levels of government and beyond volatile politics.[173]

On these premises, it can be easily argued that constitutional asymmetries are a valuable arrangement to accommodate diversity[174] and to address ethnic and territorial conflicts.[175]

However, the theoretical stand of this book aims to go even further, claiming that the introduction of constitutional asymmetries in divided multi-tiered systems can be framed as a dynamic constitutional model to accommodate ethnocultural diversity,[176] insofar as they provide a middle ground between previous constitutional models.[177] In fact, constitutional asymmetries allow for more flexibility,[178] an element often missing in consociations or national federations. As will be explored in the rest of the book, different degrees of constitutional asymmetries were introduced to deal with diversity not only in multinational federations (e.g., Belgium, India) but also in formally unitary states that are "partially divided societies" (e.g., United Kingdom, Spain, Italy) with regional or devolutionary arrangements.[179] Precisely

---

173 Keil and Alber, "Introduction," 335.

174 Weller, "Introduction," 1.

175 See Tarlton, "Symmetry and Asymmetry;" Robert Agranoff, ed., *Accommodating Diversity: Asymmetry in Federal States* (Baden-Baden: Nomos Verlagsgesellschaft, 1999); Weller and Nobbs, *Asymmetric Autonomy.*

176 Patricia Popelier and Maja Sahadžić, "Linking Constitutional Asymmetry with Multinationalism," in *Constitutional Asymmetry in Multinational Federalism*, ed. Patricia Popelier and Maja Sahadžić (Cham: Palgrave Macmillan, 2019), 2.

177 See also Choudhry, "Bridging," 32–35.

178 Stefan Wolff, "Cases of Asymmetrical Territorial Autonomy," in *Asymmetric Autonomy and the Settlement of Ethnic Conflicts*, ed. Marc Weller and Katherine Nobbs (Philadelphia: University of Pennsylvania Press, 2010), 24.

179 See Guerino D'Ignazio, ed., *Integrazione europea e asimmetrie regionali* (Milano: Giuffrè, 2007); Anna Mastromarino, "Il diritto comparato alle prese con il multiculturalismo: una sfida aperta. Il federalismo disaggregativo nella teoria dei tipi di Stato," *Diritto Pubblico Comparato ed Europeo*, no. 3 (2010): 964–99; Matteo Monti, *Federalismo disaggregativo. Secessione e asimmetria in Italia e Spagna* (Torino: Giappichelli Editore, 2021); Marco Olivetti, "Il federalismo asimmetrico belga e le sue recenti evoluzioni," in *Integrazione europea e asimmetrie regionali*, ed. Guerino D'Ignazio (Milano: Giuffrè, 2007), 63–90; Giancarlo Rolla, "Federalismo e regionalismo in Europa. Alcune riflessioni sulle dina-

for this reason, this research explores constitutional asymmetries in divided multi-tiered systems (MTS) as an encompassing term for all those systems with multiple tiers of government in which the central level coexists with subnational entities (SNEs) having lawmaking powers.[180] This exemplifies the fact that constitutional asymmetries can be more easily acceptable than the federal model altogether,[181] as a traditional federation can be perceived as a threat to the territorial integrity of the state, encouraging secession or separatism. However, this did not exclude the introduction of constitutional asymmetries in order to accommodate specific national minorities.[182] Moreover, we recalled that liberal integrationists oppose multiethnic federalism and support instead national federations (such as the US or Germany), but these federations tend to be symmetrical, meaning that all subnational units have an equal relationship with each other and with the centre. The benefits of the federal idea of self-rule and shared rule cannot be denied, but a purely symmetrical solution would reduce those benefits in divided or partially divided societies, since it would not recognise the specific needs of some subnational entities. Conversely, the introduction of constitutional asymmetries in divided multi-tiered systems might preserve the integrity of the state and represent a more efficient application of the principle of self-rule and shared

miche in atto," *Diritto Pubblico Comparato ed Europeo* no. Speciale (2019): 657–84; Anna Margherita Russo, *Pluralismo territoriale e integrazione europea: asimmetria e relazionalità nello Stato autonomico spagnolo. Profili comparati (Belgio e Italia)* (Napoli: Editoriale scientifica, 2010); Francesco Palermo, Karl Kössler, and Carolin Zwilling, eds., *Asymmetries in Constitutional Law. Recent Developments in Federal and Regional Systems* (Bolzano/Bozen: Accademia Europea di Bolzano, 2009); Requejo and Nagel, eds., *Federalism beyond Federations*; Maja Sahadžić and Patricia Popelier, "Constitutional Asymmetry through an Empirical Lens: A Federal Device for Diverse Systems," in *Comparative Federalism*, ed. Félix Mathieu, Dave Guénette, and Alain-G. Gagnon (Cham: Springer Nature Switzerland, 2024), 45–65; Raffaele Bifulco, "Differenziazioni e asimmetrie nella teoria federale contemporanea," *Diritti Regionali*, no. 1 (2020): 139–72.

180 For more on multi-tiered systems, see paragraph 2.2 of the Introduction and Popelier and Sahadžić, "Linking Constitutional Asymmetry with Multinationalism," 4; Sahadžić, *Asymmetry*, 44–5; Popelier, *Dynamic Federalism*, 50–1.

181 Wolff, "Cases of Asymmetrical Territorial Autonomy," 24.

182 This was the case for Northern Ireland and Scotland in the United Kingdom, for Catalonia and the Basque Country in Spain, and for South-Tyrol in Italy (see Robert Agranoff, "Power Shifts, Diversity and Asymmetry," in *Accommodating Diversity: Asymmetry in Federal States*, ed. Robert Agranoff (Baden-Baden: Nomos Verlagsgesellschaft, 1999), 12–13).

rule among the subnational units and with the centre.[183] Finally, as will clearly emerge in the next chapter, constitutional asymmetries are also more widely acceptable because they are not a fixed institutional structure but rather can be introduced to different degrees of intensity.[184] In other words, constitutional asymmetries appear to be capable of responding to the challenges raised by internal diversity and ethnocultural pluralism and are flexible enough to adapt to different systems while preserving territorial and political integrity.

For all these reasons, the introduction of constitutional asymmetries in divided multi-tiered systems can be framed as a dynamic instrument fully attributable to the idea of federalism as a process, as "federal asymmetries result from the challenge of diversity within federal societies."[185]

5 Concluding Remarks

This introductory chapter had two main objectives. The first was to retrace the origins of the debate on constitutional design for divided societies, tackling the recurrent problems and emphasising the reasons why it is a topic still relevant today. This was achieved by reviewing the literature on constitutional design in general and on divided societies in particular, so that the peculiarities of the latter could emerge more clearly.

The second objective was to explain why this research frames constitutional asymmetries as the middle ground between the scholarship on constitutional design and that on federalism, as well as between the accommodationist and integrationist models of constitutional design. Federalism and asymmetries are recurrent elements in the theoretical debate on both approaches (i.e., integration and accommodation), and the chapter shows how and why constitutional asymmetries seem to be the most acceptable solution to accommodate internal diversity in a divided, multi-tiered system. Indeed, they allow for more flexibility than the consociational or the "fully-fledged" federal model, and they were introduced in federations as well as in regional or devolved states, which do not accept the use of federal terminology to describe themselves.

183 Michael Burgess, "The Paradox of Diversity – Asymmetrical Federalism in Comparative Perspective," in *Asymmetries in Constitutional Law*, ed. Francesco Palermo, Carolin Zwilling, and Karl Kössler (Bolzano/Bozen: Accademia Europea di Bolzano, 2009), 25–6.

184 Burgess, "The Paradox of Diversity," 24.

185 Agranoff, "Power Shifts," 11.

The next chapter builds on this preliminary analysis to dive deep into the theoretical and operational definitions of constitutional asymmetries in divided multi-tiered systems, reviewing different methods to properly measure asymmetries and identifying the legal and extra-legal factors that are conducive to constitutional asymmetries.

Bibliography

Abat i Ninet, Antoni. *Constitutional Law and Politics of Secession*. London and New York: Routledge, 2023.

Aboultaif, Eduardo Wassim, Soeren Keil, and Allison McCulloch, eds. *Power-Sharing in the Global South: Patterns, Practices and Potentials*. Cham, Switzerland: Palgrave Macmillan, 2024.

Addante, Luca. "Tra Sartori e Lijphart: una tipologia delle forme di governo democratiche." *Rivista Italiana Di Scienza Politica*, no. 2 (2003): 225–56.

Aggestam, Karin, and Annika Björkdahl, eds. *Rethinking Peace Building: The Quest for Peace in the Middle East and the Western Balkans*. London and New York: Routledge, 2014.

Alber, Elisabeth, and Michael G. Breen. "Federalism and Ethnic Relations." In *Encyclopedia of Contemporary Constitutionalism*, edited by Javier Cremades and Cristina Hermida, 1–26. Cham: Springer International Publishing, 2022.

Albert, Richard, and Yaniv Roznai, eds. *Constitutionalism Under Extreme Conditions*. Cham, Switzerland: Springer, 2020.

Alessi, Nicolò Paolo. *A Global Law of Diversity: Evolving Models and Concepts*. London and New York: Routledge, 2024.

Anderson, George, and Sujit Choudhry. "Devolution and Federalism in Collapsed States: Constitutional Process and Design." *Forum of Federations*, 2020, p. 31.

Anderson, Liam. *Federal Solutions to Ethnic Problems: Accommodating Diversity*. 1st ed. London and New York: Routledge, 2013.

Aroney, Nicholas, Erin F Delaney, and Stephen Tierney. "Federal Exceptionalism and Constituent Power: Afterword to the Foreword by Sergio Verdugo." *International Journal of Constitutional Law* 21, no. 4 (2023): 1182–88.

Awengo Dalberto, Séverine. "Hidden Debates over the Status of the Casamance during the Decolonization Process in Senegal: Regionalism, Territorialism, and Federalism at a Crossroads, 1946–62." *The Journal of African History* 61, no. 1 (2020): 67–88.

Baldin, Serena, Lucio Pegoraro, and Angelo Rinella. *Tre lezioni sul federalismo*. Trieste: Edizioni Università di Trieste, 1999.

Barnsley, Ingrid, and Roland Bleiker. "Self-Determination: From Decolonization to Deterritorialization." *Global Change, Peace & Security* 20, no. 2 (2008): 121–37.

Barry, Brian. *Culture and Equality: An Egalitarian Critique of Multiculturalism*. Cambridge: Harvard University Press, 2001.

Bauböck, Rainer. "A Multilevel Theory of Democratic Secession." *Ethnopolitics* 18, no. 3 (2019): 227–46.

Bauböck, Rainer. "Multinational Federalism: Territorial or Cultural Autonomy?" *Iwe Working Paper Series*, no. 15 (2001): 71.

Bauböck, Rainer. "Why Stay Together? A Pluralist Approach to Secession and Federalism." In *Citizenship in Diverse Society*, edited by Will Kymlicka and Wayne Norman, 366–94. Oxford: Oxford University Press, 2000.

Bell, Christine. "Constitutionalising Conflict: Beyond Constituent Power – Afterword to the Foreword by Sergio Verdugo." *International Journal of Constitutional Law* 21, no. 4 (2023): 1189–97.

Bell, Christine. "Power-Sharing and Human Rights Law." *The International Journal of Human Rights* 17, no. 2 (2013): 204–37.

Belser, Eva Maria, Thea Bächler, Sandra Egli, and Lawrence Zünd, eds. *The Principle of Equality in Diverse States: Reconciling Autonomy with Equal Rights and Opportunities*. Leiden and Boston: Brill | Nijhoff, 2021.

Beran, Harry. "A Liberal Theory of Secession." *Political Studies* 32, no. 1 (1984): 21–31.

Berg, Eiki. "Examining Power-Sharing in Persistent Conflicts: De Facto Pseudo-Statehood versus de Jure Quasi-Federalism." *Global Society* 21, no. 2 (2007): 199–217.

Böckenförde, Markus, Nora Hedling, and Winluck Wahiu. *A Practical Guide to Constitution Building*. Stockholm: International IDEA, 2011.

Bogaards, Matthijs, Ludger Helms, and Arend Lijphart. "The Importance of Consociationalism for Twenty-First Century Politics and Political Science." *Swiss Political Science Review* 25, no. 4 (2019): 314–56.

Bormann, Nils-Christian, Lars-Erik Cederman, Scott Gates, Benjamin A. T. Graham, Simon Hug, Kaare W. Strøm, and Julian Wucherpfennig. "Power Sharing: Institutions, Behavior, and Peace." *American Journal of Political Science* 63, no. 1 (2019): 84–100.

Bossacoma Busquets, Pau. *Morality and Legality of Secession*. Cham, Switzerland: Palgrave Macmillan, 2020.

Boulden, Jane, and Will Kymlicka. *International Approaches to Governing Ethnic Diversity*. Oxford: Oxford University Press, 2015.

Breen, Michael G. "The Origins of Holding-Together Federalism: Nepal, Myanmar, and Sri Lanka." *Publius: The Journal of Federalism* 48, no. 1 (2018): 26–50.

Buchanan, Allen. "Theories of Secession." *Philosophy & Public Affairs* 26, no. 1 (1997): 31–61.

Burgess, Michael. *Comparative Federalism: Theory and Practice*. London and New York: Routledge, 2006.

Burgess, Michael. *In Search of the Federal Spirit*. Oxford: Oxford University Press, 2013.

Burgess, Michael, and John Pinder, eds. *Multinational Federations*. London and New York: Routledge, 2011.

Cassese, Antonio. *Self-Determination of Peoples: A Legal Reappraisal*. Cambridge: Cambridge University Press, 1995.

Choudhry, Sujit. "Citizenship and Federations: Some Preliminary Reflections." In *The Federal Vision: Legitimacy and Levels of Governance in the US and the EU*, edited by Kalypso Nicolaidis and Robert Howse, 377–402. Oxford: Oxford University Press, 2001.

Choudhry, Sujit, ed. *Constitutional Design for Divided Societies: Integration or Accommodation?* Oxford: Oxford University Press, 2008.

Choudhry, Sujit. "Managing Linguistic Nationalism through Constitutional Design: Lessons from South Asia." *International Journal of Constitutional Law* 7, no. 4 (2009): 577–618.

Choudhry, Sujit. "Semi-Presidentialism as Power Sharing." Stockholm, Sweden: International IDEA, 2014.

Choudhry, Sujit, ed. *The Migration of Constitutional Ideas*. Cambridge: Cambridge University Press, 2006.

Choudhry, Sujit, and Tom Ginsburg, eds. *Constitution Making*. Cheltenham: Edward Elgar Publishing, 2016.

Choudhry, Sujit, and Nathan Hume. "Federalism, Secession and Devolution: From Classical to Post-Conflict Federalism." In *Comparative Constitutional Law*, edited by Tom Ginsburg and Rosalind Dixon, 356–84. Cheltenham: Edward Elgar, 2011.

Cochrane, Feargal, Neophytos Loizides, and Thibaud Bodson. *Mediating Power-Sharing: Devolution and Consociationalism in Deeply Divided Societies*. London and New York: Routledge, 2018.

Contiades, Xenophon, and Alkmene Fotiadou, eds. *Routledge Handbook of Comparative Constitutional Change*. London and New York: Routledge, 2020.

Cordell, Edited Karl, and Stefan Wolff, eds. *The Routledge Handbook of Ethnic Conflict*. London and New York: Routledge, 2016.

Delaney, Erin F., and Ruth Mason. "Solidarity Federalism." *Notre Dame Law Review* 98, no. 2 (2022): 617–70.

Delledonne, Giacomo, Giuseppe Martinico, and Patricia Popelier. "Re-Exploring Subnational Constitutionalism." *Perspective on Federalism* 6, no. 2 (2014).

Dersso, Solomon A. *Taking Ethno-Cultural Diversity Seriously in Constitutional Design: A Theory of Minority Rights for Addressing Africa's Multiethnic Challenge*. Leiden and Boston: Brill | Nijhoff, 2012.

Dirri, Adriano. *Federalismi africani: pluralismo e centralismo in Sudafrica, Nigeria ed Etiopia*. Torino: Giappichelli Editore, 2024.

Duchacek, Ivo. *Comparative Federalism: The Territorial Dimension of Politics*. Ann Arbor: University of Michigan Press, 1970.

Duchacek, Ivo D. "Consociational Cradle of Federalism." *Publius: The Journal of Federalism* 15, no. 2 (1985): 35–48.

Dumont, Hugues, and Mathias El Berhoumi. "La reconnaissance constitutionnelle du droit de demander la sécession dans les états plurinationaux." In *Constitutionnalisme, droits et diversité : mélanges en l'honneur de José Woehrling*, edited by Alain-G Gagnon and Pierre Noreau, 467–503. Montréal: Éditions Thémis, 2017.

Dumont, Hugues, and Mathias El Berhoumi. "L'état Fédéral Plurinational : Tentative De Définition Juridique." *Libejeune*, 2017, 28.

Elazar, Daniel J. *Exploring Federalism*. Tuscaloosa and London: University of Alabama Press, 1987.

Elster, Jon. "Forces and Mechanisms in the Constitution-Making Process." *Duke Law Journal* 45, no. 2 (1995): 364–96.

Erk, Jan, and Lawrence M. Anderson, eds. *The Paradox of Federalism: Does Self-Rule Accommodate or Exacerbate Ethnic Divisions?* London and New York: Routledge, 2010.

Federico, Veronica, and Hugh Corder. *The Quest for Constitutionalism*. London and New York: Routledge, 2014.

Fejzula, Merve. "The Cosmopolitan Historiography of Twentieth-Century Federalism." *The Historical Journal* 64, no. 2 (2021): 477–500.

Fessha, Yonatan T., Karl Kössler, and Francesco Palermo, eds. *Intergovernmental Relations in Divided Societies*. Cham: Palgrave Macmillan, 2022.

Fessha, Yonatan Tesfaye. *Ethnic Diversity and Federalism: Constitution Making in South Africa and Ethiopia*. Burlington, VT: Ashgate, 2010.

Fombad, Charles M., and Nico Steytler. *Decentralisation and Constitutionalism in Africa*. Oxford: Oxford University Press, 2019.

Fong, Brian C. H., and Atsuko Ichijo, eds. *The Routledge Handbook of Comparative Territorial Autonomies*. London and New York: Routledge, 2022.

Francioni, Francesco, and Martin Scheinin, eds. *Cultural Human Rights*. Leiden and Boston: Brill | Nijhoff, 2008.

Friedrich, Carl J. *Constitutional Government and Democracy: Theory and Practice in Europe and America*. Waltham: Blaisdell Publishing Company, 1968.

Friedrich, Carl J. "Federal Constitutional Theory and Emergent Proposals." In *Federalism: Mature and Emergent*, edited by Arthur W. Macmahon, 512–18. New York: Russell and Russell Inc., 1955.

Friedrich, Carl J. "New Tendencies in Federal Theory and Practice." *Ahrbuch Des Öffentliches Rechts* 13 (1965).

Friedrich, Carl J. *Trends of Federalism in Theory and Practice*. London: Pall Mall Press, 1968.

Gagnon, Alain, and James Tully, eds. *Multinational Democracies*. Cambridge and New York: Cambridge University Press, 2001.

Gagnon, Alain-G., and Arjun Tremblay, eds. *Federalism and National Diversity in the 21st Century*. Cham: Springer International Publishing, 2020.

Gamper, Anna. "A 'Global Theory of Federalism': The Nature and Challenges of a Federal State." *German Law Journal* 6, no. 10 (2005): 1297–318.

Gebeye, Berihun Adugna. *A Theory of African Constitutionalism*. Oxford: Oxford University Press, 2021.

Ginsburg, Tom, ed. *Comparative Constitutional Design*. New York: Cambridge University Press, 2012.

Ginsburg, Tom, Zachary Elkins, and Justin Blount. "Does the Process of Constitution-Making Matter?" *Annual Review of Law and Social Science* 5 (2009): 201–23.

Guelke, Adrian, ed. *Democracy and Ethnic Conflict: Advancing Peace in Deeply Divided Societies*. Basingstoke and New York: Palgrave Macmillan, 2004.

Hilpold, Peter. "UN Standard-Setting in the Field of Minority Rights." *International Journal on Minority and Group Rights* 14, no. 2–3 (2007): 181–205.

Hirschl, Ran. "The 'Design Sciences' and Constitutional 'Success.'" *Texas Law Review* 87 (2009): 1339–74.

Horowitz, Donald. *A Democratic South Africa? Constitutional Engineering in a Divided Society*. Berkeley: University of California Press, 1992.

Horowitz, Donald. "Constitutional Design: Proposals Versus Processes." In *The Architecture of Democracy*, edited by Andrew Reynolds, 15–36. Oxford: Oxford University Press, 2002.

Horowitz, Donald. *Ethnic Groups in Conflict*. Berkeley: University of California Press, 2001.

Horowitz, Donald. "The Many Uses of Federalism." *Drake Law Review* 55 (2007): 953–66.

Horowitz, Donald. "Democracy in Divided Societies." *Journal of Democracy* 4, no. 4 (1993): 18–38.

Horowitz, Donald. "The Cracked Foundations of the Right to Secede." *Journal of Democracy* 14, no. 2 (2003): 5–17.

Issacharoff, Samuel. "Constitutionalizing Democracy in Fractured Societies." *Texas Law Review* 82 (2004): 1861–93.

Issacharoff, Samuel. "Democracy and Collective Decision Making." *International Journal of Constitutional Law* 6, no. 2 (2008): 231–66.

Keating, Michael. "Is a Theory of Self-Determination Possible?" *Ethnopolitics* 18, no. 3 (2019): 315–23.

Keating, Michael, and Alain-G Gagnon, eds. *Political Autonomy and Divided Societies: Imagining Democratic Alternatives in Complex Settings*. Cham: Palgrave Macmillan, 2012.

Keil, Soeren. "Federalism as a Tool of Conflict-Resolution: The Case of Bosnia and Herzegovina." *L'Europe En Formation* 363, no. 1 (2012): 205–18.

Keil, Soeren, and Elisabeth Alber. "Introduction: Federalism as a Tool of Conflict Resolution." *Ethnopolitics* 19, no. 4 (2020): 329–41.

Keil, Soeren, and Allison McCulloch, eds. *Power-Sharing in Europe: Past Practice, Present Cases, and Future Directions*. Cham: Palgrave Macmillan, 2021.

Kincaid, John, and Alan Tarr, eds. *Constitutional Origins, Structure, and Change in Federal Countries*. Montréal: McGill-Queen's University Press, 2005.

Kymlicka, Will. "Federalism and Secession: At Home and Abroad." *Canadian Journal of Law & Jurisprudence* 13, no. 2 (2000): 207–24.

Kymlicka, Will. "Minority Rights." In *The Oxford Handbook of International Political Theory*, edited by Chris Brown and Robyn Eckersley. Oxford University Press, 2018.

Kymlicka, Will. *Multicultural Odysseys: Navigating the New International Politics of Diversity*. Oxford: Oxford University Press, 2007.

Kymlicka, Will. "Multiculturalism and Minority Rights: West and East." *Journal on Ethnopolitics and Minority Issues in Europe* (*JEMIE*) 14, no. 4 (2016): 1–26.

Kymlicka, Will. "The Internationalization of Minority Rights." In *Constitutional Design for Divided Societies: Integration or Accommodation?*, edited by Sujit Choudhry, 111–40. Oxford: Oxford University Press, 2008.

Kymlicka, Will. *The Rights of Minority Cultures*. Oxford: Oxford University Press, 1995.

Kymlicka, Will, and W. J. Norman, eds. *Citizenship in Diverse Societies*. Oxford ; New York: Oxford University Press, 2000.

La Pergola, Antonio. *Residui contrattualistici e struttura federale nell'ordinamento degli Stati Uniti*. Milan: Giuffrè, 1969.

Landau, David. "Constitution-Making Gone Wrong." *Alabama Law Review* 64 (2013).

Law, David S., ed. *Constitutionalism in Context*. Cambridge: Cambridge University Press, 2022.

Lee, Feng-yu, and Tse-min Lin. "Institutions, Contexts, and Ethnic Violence in Comparative Perspective." *International Political Science Review* 42, no. 3 (2020): 400–415.

Lehning, Percy B., ed. *Theories of Secession*. London and New York: Routledge, 2005.

Lennox, Corinne, and Damien Short. *Handbook of Indigenous Peoples' Rights*. London and New York: Routledge, 2016.

Lerner, Hanna. *Making Constitutions in Deeply Divided Societies*. Cambridge: Cambridge University Press, 2011.

Lijphart, Arend. "Consociation and Federation: Conceptual and Empirical Links." *Canadian Journal of Political Science* 12, no. 3 (1979): 499–516.

Lijphart, Arend. “Consociational Democracy.” *World Politics* 21, no. 2 (1969): 207–25.

Lijphart, Arend. “Constitutional Design for Divided Societies.” *Journal of Democracy* 15, no. 2 (2004): 96–109.

Lijphart, Arend. *Democracy in Plural Societies: A Comparative Exploration*. New Haven and London: Yale University Press, 1977.

Lijphart, Arend. “Multiethnic Democracy.” In *The Encyclopedia of Democracy*, edited by Seymour Lipset, 853–65. London and New York: Routledge, 1995.

Lijphart, Arend. “Non-Majoritarian Democracy: A Comparison of Federal and Consociational Theories.” *Publius: The Journal of Federalism* 15 (1985): 3–15.

Lijphart, Arend. *Thinking about Democracy: Power Sharing and Majority Rule in Theory and Practice*. London and New York: Routledge, 2008.

Livingston, William S. “A Note on the Nature of Federalism.” *Political Science Quarterly* 67, no. 1 (1952): 81–95.

Livingston, William S. *Federalism and Constitutional Change*. Oxford: Oxford University Press, 1956.

Loizides, Neophytos, Iosif Kovras, and Kathleen Ireton. “Introduction Federalism, Reconciliation, And Power-Sharing In Post-Conflict Societies.” *Federal Governance* 8, no. 2 (2011): 1–14.

Loughlin, John, John, Kincaid, and Wilfried Swenden, eds. *Routledge Handbook of Regionalism and Federalism*. London and New York: Routledge, 2013.

Lustick, Ian S. “Lijphart, Lakatos, and Consociationalism.” *World Politics* 50, no. 1 (1997): 88–117.

Lutz, Donald S. *Principles of Constitutional Design*. Cambridge: Cambridge University Press, 2006.

Macklem, Patrick. “Minority Rights in International Law.” *International Journal of Constitutional Law* 6, no. 3–4 (2008): 531–52.

Malloy, Tove. “Towards a New Paradigm of Minority Law-Making: A Rejoinder to Palermo and Woelk’s Law of Diversity.” *European Yearbook of Minority Issues Online* 4, no. 1 (2004): 1–28.

Malloy, Tove, and Francesco Palermo, eds. *Minority Accommodation through Territorial and Non-Territorial Autonomy*. Oxford: Oxford University Press, 2015.

Mancini, Susanna. *Minoranze autoctone e Stato: tra composizione dei conflitti e secessione*. Milano: Giuffrè, 1996.

Mancini, Susanna. “Rethinking the Boundaries of Democratic Secession: Liberalism, Nationalism, and the Right of Minorities to Self-Determination.” *International Journal of Constitutional Law* 6, no. 3–4 (2008): 553–84.

Mancini, Susanna. “Secession and Self-Determination.” In *The Oxford Handbook of Comparative Constitutional Law*, edited by Michel Rosenfeld and András Sajó, 481–500. Oxford: Oxford University Press, 2012.

Marko, Joseph. "Equality and Difference: Political and Legal Aspects of Ethnic Group Relations." In *Vienna International Encounter on Some Current Issues Regarding the Situation of National Minorities*, edited by Franz Matscher, 67–97. Kehl: N. P. Engel Verlag, 1997.

Marko, Joseph. "What Is Wrong with the Concept of Multinational Federalism? Some Thoughts about the Interrelationship between the Concepts of (Multi-)Nationalism, Federalism, Power Sharing, and Conflict Resolution." *Ethnopolitics* 19, no. 4 (2020): 416–32.

Marko, Joseph, and Sergiu Constantin, eds. *Human and Minority Rights Protection by Multiple Diversity Governance: History, Law, Ideology and Politics in European Perspective*. London and New York: Routledge, 2019.

Martinico, Giuseppe, and Giacomo Delledonne, eds. *The Canadian Contribution to a Comparative Law of Secession*. Cham, Switzerland: Palgrave Macmillan, 2019.

Mastromarino, Anna. *Il federalismo disaggregativo. Un percorso costituzionale negli Stati multinazionali*. Milano: Giuffrè, 2010.

Mathieu, Félix, Dave Guénette, and Alain-G. Gagnon, eds. *Comparative Federalism: A Pluralist Exploration*. Cham: Springer Nature Switzerland, 2024.

McCrossan, Michael, and Kiera L. Ladner. "Eliminating Indigenous Jurisdictions: Federalism, the Supreme Court of Canada, and Territorial Rationalities of Power." *Canadian Journal of Political Science* 49, no. 3 (2016): 411–31.

McCrudden, Christopher, and Brendan O'Leary. *Courts and Consociations: Human Rights versus Power Sharing*. Oxford: Oxford University Press, 2013.

McCulloch, Allison. "Consociational Settlements in Deeply Divided Societies: The Liberal-Corporate Distinction." *Democratisation* 21, no. 3 (2014): 501–18.

McCulloch, Allison, and Eduardo Wassim Aboultaif. "Territorial and Institutional Settlement in the Global South and Beyond." In *Oxford Research Encyclopedia of International Studies*, 2023.

McCulloch, Allison, and John McGarry, eds. *Power-Sharing: Empirical and Normative Challenges*. London and New York: Routledge, 2017.

McEvoy, Joanne, and Brendan O'Leary, eds. *Power Sharing in Deeply Divided Places*. Philadelphia, Pennsylvania: University of Pennsylvania Press, 2013.

Moore, Margaret. *National Self-Determination and Secession*. Oxford: Oxford University Press, 1998.

Nicolini, Matteo. *Legal Geography: Comparative Law and the Production of Space*. Cham: Springer International Publishing, 2022.

Nicolini, Matteo. "'Writing the Earth and Representing the World': The Cartographical Ambitions of Comparative Law." *The Journal of Comparative Law* 19, no. 1 (2024): 79–101.

Nicolini, Matteo, Francesco Palermo, and Enrico Milano, eds. *Law, Territory and Conflict Resolution: Law as a Problem and Law as a Solution*. Leiden and Boston: Brill | Nijhoff, 2016.

Noel, Sid, ed. *From Power Sharing to Democracy: Post-Conflict Institutions in Ethnically Divided Societies.* Montréal: McGill-Queen's University Press, 2005.

Norman, Wayne. *Negotiating Nationalism: Nation-Building, Federalism, and Secession in the Multinational State.* Oxford: Oxford University Press, 2006.

Norris, Pippa. *Driving Democracy: Do Power-Sharing Institutions Work?* Cambridge: Cambridge University Press, 2008.

Oberschall, Anthony. *Conflict and Peace Building in Divided Societies.* London and New York: Routledge, 2007.

Palermo, Francesco, and Karl Kössler. *Comparative Federalism: Constitutional Arrangements and Case Law.* London: Hart Publishing, 2017.

Palermo, Francesco, and Jens Woelk. *Diritto costituzionale comparato dei gruppi e delle minoranze.* Milano: Wolters Kluwer, 2021.

Papillon, Martin. "Indigenous Peoples and Federalism: In or Out?" In *Teaching Federalism*, edited by John Kincaid and J. Leckrone, 210–20. Cheltenham: Edward Elgar Publishing, 2023.

Pasarlay, Shamshad. "Dialogic Incrementalism in Deeply Divided Societies." *International Journal of Constitutional Law* 22, no. 2 (2024): 318–53.

Pejic, Jelena. "Minority Rights in International Law." *Human Rights Quarterly* 19, no. 3 (1997): 666–85.

Perju, Vlad. "Constitutional Transplants, Borrowing, and Migrations." In *The Oxford Handbook of Comparative Constitutional Law*, edited by Michel Rosenfeld and András Sajó, 1304–27. Oxford: Oxford University Press, 2012.

Popelier, Patricia. *Dynamic Federalism: A New Theory for Cohesion and Regional Autonomy.* London and New York: Routledge, 2021.

Popelier, Patricia. "Federal Dynamics and Stability." In *The Making and Ending of Federalism*, edited by Peter Bußjäger, Mathias Eller, and Julia Oberdanner, 92–116. Leiden and Boston: Brill | Nijhoff, 2024.

Raue, Julia, and Patrick Sutter, eds. *Facets and Practices of State-Building.* Leiden: Nijhoff, 2009.

Requejo, Ferran, and Klaus-Jürgen Nagel, eds. *Federalism Beyond Federations: Asymmetry and Processes of Resymmetrisation in Europe.* Farnham, England: Ashgate, 2011.

Requejo, Ferran, and Marc Sanjaume-Calvet, eds. *Defensive Federalism: Protecting Territorial Minorities from the "Tyranny of the Majority."* London and New York: Routledge, 2022.

Reynolds, Andrew. *The Architecture of Democracy: Constitutional Design, Conflict Management, and Democracy.* Oxford: Oxford University Press, 2002.

Robert, Schütze. "Political Philosophy of Federalism." In *Max Planck Encyclopedia of Comparative Constitutional Law.* Oxford University Press, 2023.

Sartori, Giovanni. *Comparative Constitutional Engineering*. New York: New York University Press, 1997.

Schneier, Edward V. *Crafting Constitutional Democracies*. Lanham: Rowman & Littlefield, 2006.

Schulte, Felix. *Peace through Self-Determination: Success and Failure of Territorial Autonomy*. Cham: Springer International Publishing, 2020.

Senehi, Jessica, Imani Michelle Scott, Sean Byrne, and Thomas G. Matyók, eds. *Routledge Handbook of Peacebuilding and Ethnic Conflict*. 1st ed. London and New York: Routledge, 2022.

Shapiro, Ian, and Stephen Macedo, eds. *Designing Democratic Institutions*. New York and London: New York University Press, 2000.

Siegle, Joseph. "Constitutional Design: Vital but Insufficient for Conflict Management." *Ethnopolitics* 15, no. 5 (2016): 533–37.

Simeon, Richard. "Constitutional Design and Change in Federal Systems: Issues and Questions." *Publius: The Journal of Federalism* 39, no. 2 (2009): 241–61.

Tarr, Alan, Robert F. Williams, and Joseph Marko, eds. *Federalism, Subnational Constitutions, and Minority Rights*. Westport: Praefer, 2004.

Teitel, Ruti. "Transitional Jurisprudence: The Role of Law in Political Transformation." *The Yale Law Journal* 106 (1997): 2009–80.

Tierney, Stephen. *Constitutional Law and National Pluralism*. Oxford: Oxford University Press, 2004.

Tierney, Stephen. *The Federal Contract: A Constitutional Theory of Federalism*. 1st ed. Oxford: Oxford University Press, 2022.

Toniatti, Roberto. "Minorities and Protected Minorities: Constitutional Models Compared." In *Citizenship and Rights in Multicultural Societies*, edited by Tiziano Bonazzi and Michael Dunne, 193–220. Edinburgh: Edinburgh University Press, 1996.

Tremblay, Arjun, and Alain-G. Gagnon. "Multinational, Multicultural, Intercultural, and Plurinational Federalism." In *Teaching Federalism*, edited by John Kincaid and J. Leckrone, 141–53. Cheltenham: Edward Elgar Publishing, 2023.

Venice Commission. "A General Legal Framework to Facilitate the Settlement of Ethno-Political Conflicts in Europe," 2000.

Venice Commission. "Report on Self-Determination and Secession," 1999.

Verdugo, Sergio. "Is It Time to Abandon the Theory of Constituent Power?" *International Journal of Constitutional Law* 21, no. 1 (2023): 14–79.

Verdugo, Sergio. "Is It Time to Abandon the Theory of Constituent Power? A Rejoinder." *International Journal of Constitutional Law* 21, no. 4 (2023): 1213–24.

Vermule, Adrian. *Mechanisms of Democracy*. Oxford: Oxford University Press, 2009.

Watts, Ronald L. *Comparing Federal Systems*. Montréal and Kingston: McGill-Queen's University Press, 2008.

Watts, Ronald L. "Models of Federal Power Sharing." *International Social Science Journal* 53, no. 167 (2002): 23–32.

Watts, Ronald L. "Multinational Federations in Comparative Perspective." In *Multinational Federations*, edited by Michael Burgess and John Pinder, 225–47. Abingdon: Routledge, 2007.

Watts, Ronald L. "Typologies of Federalism." In *Routledge Handbook of Regionalism & Federalism*, edited by John Loughlin, John Kincaid, and Wilfried Swenden. London and New York: Routledge, 2013.

Weller, Marc, Barbara Metzger, and Niall Johnson, eds. *Settling Self-Determination Disputes: Complex Power-Sharing in Theory and Practice*. The Hague: Martinus Nijhoff, 2008.

Weller, Marc, and Stefan Wolff, eds. *Autonomy, Self Governance and Conflict Resolution: Innovative Approaches to Institutional Design in Divided Societies*. London and New York: Routledge, 2005.

Woelk, Jens, and Francesco Palermo. "From Minority Protection to a Law of Diversity? Reflections on the Evolution of Minority Rights." *European Yearbook of Minority Issues Online* 3, no. 1 (2003): 5–13.

Wolff, Stefan. "Complex Power-Sharing and the Centrality of Territorial Self-Governance in Contemporary Conflict Settlements." *Ethnopolitics* 8, no. 1 (2009): 27–45.

CHAPTER 2

Defining Asymmetries in Multi-tiered Systems

1 Introduction

Having reviewed the background on constitutional design for divided societies and identified constitutional asymmetries as an intermediate model of constitutional design, this chapter is dedicated to the definition of constitutional asymmetries in multi-tiered systems. The first paragraph defines asymmetries – reviewing the main literature on the topic, from the origins of the concept to its more recent developments, distinguishing between *de jure* (constitutional) and *de facto* (political) asymmetries, and the related challenges that may arise in asymmetrical divided multi-tiered systems.

Then, the following paragraph provides for a framework to "measure" constitutional asymmetries, reviewing previous attempts that have emerged in the scholarship and explaining the method adopted in this book. The employed method is based on the conceptualisation of autonomy and asymmetry along the three dimensions of status, powers, and fiscal arrangements, as tested by Popelier and Sahadžić in their works.[1]

Then, the last part of the chapter is dedicated to the factors conducive to constitutional asymmetries, distinguishing between legal and extra-legal factors. Specifically, this research identified four main legal factors: the territorial distribution of constitutional asymmetries; the procedures to introduce constitutional asymmetries; the design of the subnational entities; and the constitution-making process. Conversely, the extra-legal factors that come into play in asymmetrical divided multi-tiered systems relate to their geopolitical, socio-economic, and historical nature, such as the historical period in which asymmetries were introduced, the geopolitical position of the constitutional system (i.e., Global South or Global North), and the distribution of socio-economic resources within the system.

1 See Popelier, *Dynamic Federalism*; Sahadžić, *Asymmetry*; Popelier and Sahadžić, eds., *Constitutional Asymmetry*.

 | DOI:10.1163/9789004739109_004

2 Between Theory and Practice

2.1 *Introducing the Concept*

The origins of the concept of symmetry and asymmetry in federal theory can be traced back to the aforementioned article by Charles D. Tarlton, who in 1965 first introduced the notion of symmetry as "the extent to which component states share in the conditions and thereby the concerns more or less common to the federal system as a whole", while asymmetry "expresses the extent to which component states do not share in these common features".[2] According to Tarlton, whether the relationship is symmetrical or asymmetrical depends on the participation of federal units in the "pattern of social, cultural, economic, and political characteristics of the federal system",[3] thus first highlighting a political nature of asymmetry. As Lijphart did in his work, Tarlton also recalled Livingston's socio-cultural theory of federalism,[4] linking such theory to asymmetric federalism. Indeed, in his opinion, an asymmetric federal government is the one that best corresponds to the real "federal society" beneath political institutions.[5]

While recalling Livingston, Tarlton also makes reference to the constitutional nature of asymmetry, namely to the "varying degrees of autonomy and power".[6] Up until Tarlton's essay, the idea of asymmetries in federal systems had only been implicitly mentioned,[7] and symmetry was assumed to be the norm within federations.[8] This was due to the fact that, traditionally, federal states were created as centripetal (or "coming-together") federations, by pooling together sovereignty. Establishing a symmetric relationship between member states was therefore the priority in order to guarantee federal equality. By the same logic, symmetry was also adopted within specific dimensions,

2 Tarlton, "Symmetry and Asymmetry," 861.

3 Ibidem.

4 Livingston criticised the over-emphasis on legalistic concerns in classic federal theory, pointing out that the institutional design does not necessarily express the social, cultural, and political reality of the society under study.

5 Tarlton, "Symmetry and Asymmetry," 869.

6 Tarlton, "Symmetry and Asymmetry," 869: "The asymmetrical federal system would be one in which, as Livingston says of federal systems generally, the diversities in the larger society find political expression through local governments possessed of varying degrees of autonomy and power."

7 See for example Livingston, "A Note on the Nature of Federalism."

8 Watts, "A Comparative Perspective on Asymmetry in Federations," 1.

i.e., the division of legislative power.[9] With the shift towards "holding-together" or centrifugal federations, the focus was necessarily on the constitutional provisions granting differentiated rights to the subnational units in order to preserve the unity of the state, thus enshrining federal asymmetries in their constitutions. Therefore, it is now considered legally wrong to count asymmetries as the exception, as "asymmetry is not less essential to federalism than symmetry".[10]

Since its first publication, Tarlton's essay has been revisited by federal scholars. In 1999, Burgess and Gress discussed some of Tarlton's assumptions,[11] identifying four main objections. First, they argue that the claim made by Tarlton concerning the impossibility of "discern[ing] interests that could be clearly considered mutual or national in scope"[12] is an exaggeration, as the quality of asymmetry does not depend on this "wide-ranging criterion".[13] Moreover, accepting this kind of assumption would enable a dangerous misconception that looms over asymmetry, i.e., the stigma of disloyalty to the national interest,[14] when on the contrary asymmetric federations actually witness a "constant shifting pattern of overlapping interests and concerns"[15], ensuring overall legitimacy and political stability. The second objection concerns Tarlton's assertion about the relationship between conflict and asymmetry, and conversely the one between harmony and symmetry. Tarlton states that "the degree of harmony or conflict within a federal system can be thought as a function of the symmetrical or asymmetrical pattern prevailing within the system", even though most federal systems are in an intermediate position between the "complete harmony symmetrical model and the complete conflict asymmetrical model".[16] However, Burgess and Gress believe that this is not helpful, as the nature of such conflict is not further explored, and the centre-subnational unit relations that may cause conflict are also dependent on the specific power relations and overall political sta-

9 Francesco Palermo, "Asymmetries in Constitutional Law – An Introduction," in *Asymmetries in Constitutional Law*, ed. Francesco Palermo, Carolin Zwilling, and Karl Kössler (Bolzano/Bozen: Accademia Europea di Bolzano, 2009), 12–13.

10 Palermo, "Asymmetries in Constitutional law," 11.

11 Burgess, and Gress, "Symmetry and Asymmetry Revisited," 44–47. See also Michael Burgess, *Comparative Federalism: Theory and Practice* (London and New York: Routledge, 2006), 211–215.

12 Tarlton, "Symmetry and Asymmetry," 869.

13 Burgess, and Gress, "Symmetry and Asymmetry Revisited," 46.

14 Burgess, *Comparative Federalism*, 213.

15 Burgess, and Gress, "Symmetry and Asymmetry Revisited," 46.

16 Tarlton, "Symmetry and Asymmetry," 871.

bility of the federal system.[17] Then, Burgess and Gress question Tarlton's assumption that a condition of predominant diversity should be a unitary and centralised system, instead of a federal system, in order to control centrifugal forces and the "secession-potential".[18] As they observe, though it is not clear what Tarlton actually meant, his suggestion of centralisation instead of federalism would be "a quite remarkable preference in the 1990s".[19] Finally, the last objection concerns Tarlton's rejection of the politics of recognition, once again advocating for "increased coordination and coercion",[20] being overall sceptical about the feasibility of federalism while dealing with diversity. As Burgess and Gress highlight, Tarlton "was very much an American author writing from a particular perspective", and with an overriding concern for the "secession-potential inherent in federations".[21]

The concept of asymmetry was later refined in the literature[22] with the adoption of a series of distinctions, widening the theoretical framework on federal asymmetries. First of all, Watts[23] introduced the distinction between

---

17 Burgess, and Gress, "Symmetry and Asymmetry Revisited," 46.

18 Tarlton, "Symmetry and Asymmetry," 871–873.

19 Burgess, and Gress, "Symmetry and Asymmetry Revisited," 47.

20 Tarlton, "Symmetry and Asymmetry," 874.

21 Burgess, and Gress, "Symmetry and Asymmetry Revisited," 47.

22 Starting from the recalled essay by Tarlton, the main literature on asymmetric federalism has been founded on (in chronological order): Ivo Duchacek, *Comparative Federalism: The Territorial Dimension of Politics* (Ann Arbor: University of Michigan Press, 1970), 276–309; Daniel J. Elazar, *Exploring Federalism* (Tuscaloosa and London: University of Alabama Press, 1987); Robert Agranoff, ed., *Accommodating Diversity: Asymmetry in Federal States* (Baden Baden: Nomos Verlagsgesellschaft, 1999); Rainer Bauböck, "United in Misunderstanding? Asymmetry in Multinational Federations," *ICE Working Paper Series*, no. 26 (2002): 1–52; Ronald L. Watts, "A Comparative Perspective on Asymmetry in Federations," *Asymmetry Series – IIGR, Queen's University* 4 (2005): 1–7; Michael Burgess, *Comparative Federalism: Theory and Practice* (London and New York: Routledge, 2006), 209–225; John McGarry, "Asymmetry in Federations, Federacies and Unitary States," *Ethnopolitics* 6, no. 1 (2007): 105-116; Francesco Palermo, Carolin Zwilling, and Karl Kössler, eds., *Asymmetries in Constitutional Law. Recent Development in Federal and Regional Systems* (Bolzano/Bozen: Accademia Europea di Bolzano, 2009); Marc Weller and Katherine Nobbs, eds., *Asymmetric Autonomy and the Settlement of Ethnic Conflicts* (Philadelphia: University of Pennsylvania Press, 2010); Ferran Requejo and Kalus-Jürgen Nagel, eds., *Federalism Beyond Federations. Asymmetry and Processes of Resymmetrisation in Europe* (Farnham, England: Ashgate, 2011); Patricia Popelier and Maja Sahadžić, eds., *Constitutional Asymmetry in Multinational Federalism* (London: Palgrave Macmillan, 2019); Maja Sahadžić, *Asymmetry, Multinationalism and Constitutional Law* (London and New York: Routledge, 2020).

23 See Ronald L. Watts, "The Theoretical and Practical Implications of Asymmetrical Federalism," in *Accommodating Diversity: Asymmetry in Federal States*, ed. Robert Agranoff

two types of asymmetries: *de jure* (or constitutional) and *de facto* (or political), further analysed in the next section. Briefly, the former indicates the asymmetries entrenched in the constitutional and legal framework; the latter refers to the actual asymmetries deriving from social, cultural, and economic differences in a federal system. Next, Burgess distinguished between preconditions leading to asymmetries and the outcomes.[24] The former defines asymmetries as the social reality, and therefore they are "what really exists". Burgess further distinguished between two categories of preconditions: socio-economic (the regional demographic and socio-economic disparities, and territorial differences); and cultural-ideological (religious, linguistic, territorial, cultural, and ethno-national patterns). Following the same conceptual shift from federalism to federation, the asymmetrical outcomes derive from the preconditions of asymmetries. Another distinction drawn by Agranoff is the one between vertical asymmetry, referring to the relationship of one level to the others (e.g., national or second-tier government), and horizontal asymmetry, meaning the differentiation of status and rights among component units.[25] However, it could be argued that horizontal asymmetry can always be reframed in terms of vertical asymmetries, as the difference between component units depends on the relationship that they have with the central level. Another interesting aspect to consider is that symmetry and asymmetry must be framed in relational terms: "a change toward asymmetry affects overall symmetry",[26] and "federal systems seek a sort of balance between asymmetry and symmetry".[27] Finally, as already mentioned, asymmetries can also vary both in kind and in their degree of intensity.

2.2 De Facto *and* De Jure *Asymmetries*

Since the core of this research involves constitutional asymmetries, it is worth further exploring the distinction between *de facto* and *de jure* asymmetries.[28] As previously mentioned, the former refers to "the actual practices or relation-

---

(Baden-Baden: Nomos, 1999), 24–42; Ronald L. Watts, "A Comparative Perspective on Asymmetry in Federations," *Asymmetry Series - IIGR, Queen's University*, no. 4 (2005): 1–7; Ronald L. Watts, *Comparing Federal Systems* (Montréal: McGill-Queen's University Press, 2008), 125–130.

24 See Burgess, *Comparative Federalism*, 215–217; Burgess, "The Paradox of Diversity," 24; Burgess, and Gress, "Symmetry and Asymmetry Revisited," 48–56.

25 Agranoff, "Power Shifts," 17.

26 Agranoff, "Power Shifts," 20.

27 Agranoff, "Power Shifts," 21.

28 For a recent overview on *de facto* and *de jure* asymmetries, see Sahadžić, *Asymmetry*, 16–42.

ships arising from the impact of cultural, social and economic differences among constituent units within a federation",[29] while the latter to the asymmetries "embedded in constitutional and legal processes, where constituent units are treated differently under the law".[30] Multi-tiered systems may present different kinds and degrees of both *de jure* and *de facto* asymmetries, and it has been observed that constitutional asymmetries often result from the incorporation of political asymmetries in the constitution.[31]

2.2.1 Political Asymmetries

Within multi-tiered systems, political asymmetries may take different forms. There may be variations in the size of the territory and of the population, as well as in the wealth of constituent units, within one or more dominant member states, or the "relative powerlessness of particularly small member states".[32] Differences in wealth can be explained by variations in labour mobility, resources and infrastructures. There may also be variations in the relative power exercised by each unit, identity, and political landscape. Differences in the exercise of power relate to the variety of political cultures within different constituent units, the variations in identity refer to the ethnic, cultural, linguistic, and religious differences.[33]

2.2.2 Constitutional Asymmetries

Some multi-tiered systems have translated their political asymmetries into constitutional asymmetries, by entrenching them in their constitutional frameworks. Constitutional asymmetries may manifest in different ways. In a broad sense, they may emerge insofar as central level constitutions try to moderate political asymmetries by adjusting the number, size and boundaries of the component units, and the representation in the second chamber, even though asymmetry continues to be significant.[34] In a narrow sense, they may emerge as a different distribution of power and competences among the constituent units.[35] In fact, constitutions may do so to recognise significant variations in geographical size and population or their social and cultural compo-

---

29 Watts, "A Comparative Perspective," 2.

30 Ibidem.

31 Agranoff, "Power Shifts," 16; Popelier and Sahadžić, *Constitutional Asymmetries*, 489–492.

32 Watts, "The Theoretical and Practical Implications," 30.

33 Popelier and Sahadžić, "Linking Constitutional Asymmetry with Multinationalism," 5.

34 Watts, "The Theoretical and Practical Implications," 36.

35 Francesco Palermo, "«Divided We Stand»: l'asimmetria negli ordinamenti composti," in *Processi di devolution e transizioni costituzionali negli Stati unitari (dal Regno Unito all'Europa)*, ed. Alessandro Torre (Torino: Giappichelli, 2007), 159-160.

sition and economic situation. Generally, the literature identifies three domains in which constitutional asymmetries may be identified: status of the constituent units; distribution of powers and competences; fiscal autonomy.[36]

Starting from the first element (i.e., status), constitutional design may introduce asymmetrical arrangements following asymmetrical territorial features and may delineate subnational entities within a diverse institutional framework. However, Sahadžić observed that the literature has neglected the issue of institutional autonomy in subnational entities, given that they may organise their own legislative and executive bodies.[37] Moreover, representation in central institutions may be subject to constitutional asymmetry, concerning the composition of the central level legislature and voting.[38] Indeed, in chambers where the distribution of seats is weighted by the population of the member states, larger states would have more influence in policy-making and legislation than smaller states. This effect may be moderated by a particular regional basis for coalitions within governing parties or by an equal representation of constituent units in the federal chamber. Following the same logic, other forms of asymmetry may involve the bodies responsible for the conduct of intergovernmental relations among the different levels of government.[39]

Moving to the second domain (i.e., powers), Watts identifies three main constitutional approaches to establishing *de jure* asymmetry in the distribution of powers: by increasing the federal authority; by increasing the jurisdiction of particular member states; by allowing for asymmetry in a formally symmetrical distribution of powers among component units.[40]

Then, fiscal autonomy is strictly interconnected with the status and distribution of powers, as "the level of fiscal power may indicate the capacity of subnational entities to define their distinct status".[41] A higher level of fiscal autonomy would determine the relative autonomy and power of subnational entities, and vice versa.[42] Specifically, fiscal autonomy (and thus constitutional asymmetry) may be displayed in their taxing powers, power to raise revenues, spending capacity, reliance on transfers, and budgetary control.[43] Moreover, multi-tiered systems have often adopted asymmetrical transfers

36 Palermo, "Asymmetries in Constitutional Law," 12.
37 Sahadžić, *Asymmetry*, 32–33.
38 Sahadžić, *Asymmetry*, 34–36; Palermo, "«Divided We Stand»," 161–164.
39 Watts, "The Theoretical and Practical Implications," 33–40.
40 Watts, "The Theoretical and Practical Implications," 37.
41 Sahadžić, *Asymmetry*, 41.
42 Ibidem.
43 Ibidem.

and schemes of redistribution and equalisation in order to make the fiscal capacities of the member states more symmetrical.[44]

The reason why this research chose to focus on constitutional asymmetries rather than on political asymmetries can be found in Weller's words: *de jure* asymmetries offer "greater clarity" and "the existence or extent of asymmetry can be immediately identified through a study of the formal constitutional and legislative instruments establishing the state".[45] Moreover, as already argued, by entrenching political asymmetries in the constitutional and legal processes, *de jure* asymmetries may constitute a way of accommodating ethnocultural diversity in the attempt to preserve the integrity and cohesion of the state. Therefore, constitutional asymmetries allow for a more precise analysis, functional to the objective of this research, without losing "sight on the reality of their implementation".[46]

2.3 *Asymmetries, Mixed Legal Systems, and the Legacy of Colonialism*

A less-explored legal expression of asymmetry is linked to the conservation of legal specificities in one or more subnational unit. For example, Palermo recalls the maintenance of civil law in otherwise common law legal systems, e.g., Québec, Scotland, Puerto Rico, or the presence of peculiar legal institutions, e.g., the *derecho foral* in the Basque Country and in Navarre, or the *geschlossener Hof* in South-Tyrol.[47] Another example of this kind of constitutional asymmetry is provided by Indonesia, where the Law 11/2006 on the Governing of Aceh authorises the province to implement Islamic law.[48] This provision later allowed the enactment of the Islamic Criminal Code in 2014, thus making Aceh the only Indonesian province where Islamic law is directly applied to both Muslim and non-Muslim citizens, and raising concerns over human rights protection.[49] Similarly, since the early 2000s, several northern states in Nigeria have adopted Islamic criminal codes, raising concerns over the pro-

44 Watts, "The Theoretical and Practical Implications," 38.

45 Marc Weller, "Introduction," in *Asymmetric Autonomy and the Settlement of Ethnic Conflicts*, ed. Marc Weller and Katherine Nobbs (Philadelphia: University of Pennsylvania Press, 2010), 8.

46 Ibidem.

47 Palermo, "«Divided We Stand»," 163.

48 Law no. 11 of 2006 "On the Governing of Aceh," Art. 125–127.

49 Simon Butt, "Provincial Asymmetry in Indonesia: What Is so 'Special' About It? A Country Study of Constitutional Asymmetry in Indonesia," in *Constitutional Asymmetry in Multinational Federalism*, ed. Patricia Popelier and Maja Sahadžić (Cham: Palgrave Macmillan, 2019), 247–248.

tection of the human rights of minorities and vulnerable groups.[50] The asymmetrical outcomes of mixed legal systems can vary substantially among constitutional systems.[51] For instance, the presence of more legal traditions can lead to constitutional asymmetries in the organisation of the judiciary, as in Canada with the appointment of three judges from Québec in the Supreme Court or in the United Kingdom, where Scotland retained its own legal and judicial system based on Scots law. In other contexts, the adoption of Islamic criminal codes in specific parts of a territory has had a substantial impact on fundamental rights protection and at times called into question the integrity of the legal system. Moreover, if in the case of Canada and the United Kingdom the constitutional recognition of the civil law tradition resulted in further integration of the legal system and the accommodation of legal pluralism, in contexts that experienced colonial domination such as Nigeria and Indonesia, the territorial implementation of Islamic criminal law appeared to compress legal and religious pluralism. This was as these countries not only imposed Islamic *shari'a* over common/civil law and customary law but also applied it to non-Muslim citizens.

Although the study of the intersections between constitutional asymmetries and mixed legal systems has attracted only limited attention in the literature,[52] it provides a fascinating perspective not only on the study of constitutional asymmetry, but also on the legacies of colonialism in public law and federal studies.[53] In fact, colonialism was central to the formation of mixed

---

50 See Mohammed H. A. Bolaji, "Shari'ah in Northern Nigeria in the Light of Asymmetrical Federalism," *Publius: The Journal of Federalism* 40, no. 1 (2010): 114–35.

51 A more detailed analysis can be found in Lidia Bonifati, "Constitutional Asymmetries and Mixed Legal Systems. New Itineraries of Legal Comparison," *Rivista di Diritti Comparati*, no. 3 (2024): 156–180.

52 See Giuseppe Martinico, "L'origine 'mista' dell'asimmetria canadese," in *Il costituzionalismo canadese a 150 anni dalla Confederazione. Riflessioni comparatistiche*, ed. Giacomo Delledonne, Giuseppe Martinico, and Leonardo Pierdominici (Pisa: Pisa University Press, 2017), 15–30.

53 See Séverine Awenengo Dalberto, "Hidden Debates over the Status of the Casamance During the Decolonization Process in Senegal: Regionalism, Territorialism, and Federalism at a Crossroads, 1946–62," *The Journal of African History* 61, no. 1 (2020): 67–88; Michael Burgess, *The British Tradition of Federalism* (London: Leicester University Press, 1995); Cheikh Anta Babou, "Decolonization or National Liberation: Debating the End of British Colonial Rule in Africa," *The Annals of the American Academy of Political and Social Science* 632, no. 1 (2010): 41–54; John Kendle, *Federal Britain* (London: Routledge, 1997); Shahal Khoso, "Postcolonial Federalism: A Conceptual Analysis for Tracing State-Formation in the Global South," *Nationalism and Ethnic Politics* 30, no. 4 (2024); Steven L. Solnick, "Federalism and State-Building: Post-Communist and Post-Colonial Perspectives," in *The Architecture of Democracy*, ed. Andrew Reynolds

legal systems as the affirmation of colonial power passed through the imposition of the colonisers' legal systems and often of the federal structure.[54] This was the case with British common law over French civil law in Québec, Scots law in Scotland, Islamic *shari'a* and customary laws in Nigeria and India,[55] and Dutch civil law over Islamic *shari'a* and customary laws in Indonesia.[56] Particularly in the Global South, the imposition of the colonisers' legal systems was firmly linked to a political intent to pursue civilisation and exploitation of the colonies, radically transforming the previous legal landscape.[57] Specifically, Lawan observed that, in Nigeria, "the [British] conquerors claimed that Islamic *shari'a* was inadequate to cope with the commercial activities of the new colony. They believed that English law was the best system to serve their interests. Therefore, they designed an endless and self-perpetuating process of legal domination."[58] Similarly, the Dutch colonial experience in Indonesia consolidated a legal structure based on race and ethnicity that endured even after independence.[59] Moreover, the Dutch colonial presence led to a departure from the previous co-existence between customary law and Islamic legal institutions, creating a sharp demarcation between the two by supporting the former and restricting the latter.[60] Salim argued that the evolution of the post-independence Indonesian legal system led to a shift from the colonial system of discrimination based on race to a revised system where discrimination was based on religion.[61] This seems to suggest that the asymmetries generated by the implementation of Islamic criminal law in the Indonesian prov-

---

(Oxford: Oxford University Press, 2002), 171–205; Alain-G Gagnon and Arjun Tremblay, *Advanced Introduction to Federalism* (Cheltenham, UK and Northampton, MA: Edward Elgar, 2024), 131–143.

54 See especially Michael Collins, "Decolonisation and the 'Federal Moment,'" *Diplomacy & Statecraft* 24, no. 1 (2013): 21–40.

55 See Christian R. Burset, *An Empire of Laws: Legal Pluralism in British Colonial Policy* (New Haven and London: Yale University Press, 2023).

56 See Arskal Salim, *Contemporary Islamic Law in Indonesia: Sharia and Legal Pluralism*, Exploring Muslim Contexts (Edinburgh: Edinburgh Univ. Press, 2015).

57 See Khaled Abou El Fadl, "The Islamic Legal Tradition," in *The Cambridge Companion to Comparative Law*, ed. Mauro Bussani and Ugo Mattei (Cambridge: Cambridge University Press, 2012), 310–311; Rodolfo Sacco, "The Sub-Saharan Legal Tradition," in *The Cambridge Companion to Comparative Law*, ed. Mauro Bussani and Ugo Mattei (Cambridge: Cambridge University Press, 2012). 321–326; Mamman Lawan, "Islamic Law and Legal Hybridity in Nigeria," *Journal of African Law* 58, no. 2 (2014): 305.

58 Lawan, "Islamic Law and Legal Hybridity in Nigeria," 305.

59 Salim, *Contemporary Islamic Law in Indonesia*, 30.

60 Salim, *Contemporary Islamic Law in Indonesia*, 31.

61 Salim, *Contemporary Islamic Law in Indonesia*, 30.

ince of Aceh and the northern states of Nigeria were a reaction against previous colonial policies that restricted the jurisdiction of Islamic *shari'a*.

The issue of constitutional asymmetries in mixed legal systems also recalls the link between federalism and legal pluralism, that has been increasingly explored by legal scholarship[62] (although not yet from an asymmetrical perspective). Specifically, Topidi observes that federalism and legal pluralism "can [...] be joined from a pragmatic perspective as their manifestations and operationalization matter in order to reflect on ways to manage and reconcile difference within plural societies".[63] Indeed, the federal dimension of legal pluralism can emerge in both territorial and non-territorial manifestations.[64] Recalling the previous examples, constitutional systems can design a territorial implementation of the different legal traditions in specific subnational entities, as with Québec in Canada or Aceh in Indonesia. However, the federal dimension of legal pluralism also presents non-territorial manifestations. Once again, some instances are provided by the application of Islamic *shari'a* in personal and civil law matters in Nigeria, India, and Indonesia, both in colonial and post-colonial times, or the presence of alternative religious jurisdictions, especially *shari'a* courts, in countries such as the UK, Israel or Greece.[65] Interestingly, Gagnon and Tremblay argue that while Canadian fed-

62 See Paul Schiff Berman, "Federalism and International Law through the Lens of Legal Pluralism," *Missouri Law Review* 73, no. 4 (2008): 1149–84; Erin Ryan, "Federalism as Legal Pluralism," in *The Oxford Handbook of Global Legal Pluralism*, ed. Paul Schiff Berman (Oxford: Oxford University Press, 2020), 491–531; Kiriaki Topidi, "Federalism, Legal Pluralism and the Law of Diversity," in *Federalism and the Law of Diversity*, ed. Nicolò Paolo Alessi, and Martina Trettel (Leiden and Boston: Brill, 2025), 181–204.

63 Topidi, "Federalism, Legal Pluralism and the Law of Diversity," 189.

64 Ibidem.

65 On the introduction of alternative religious jurisdictions in liberal constitutional systems, and the related challenges, see Asher Maoz, "Enforcement of Religious Courts' Judgments Under Israeli Law," *Journal of Church and State* 33, no. 3 (1991): 473–94; Martin Edelman, *Courts, Politics, and Culture in Israel* (Charlottesville: University of Virginia Press, 1994); Daphna Hacker, "Religious Tribunals in Democratic States: Lessons from the Israeli Rabbinical Courts," *Journal of Law and Religion* 27, no. 1 (2012): 59–81; Gila Stopler, "The Challenge of Strong Religion in the Liberal State," *Boston University International Law Journal* 32, no. 2 (2014): 411–48; Angelo Rinella, "Pluralismo giuridico e giurisdizioni religiose alternative," *DPCE online*, no. 4 (2018): 1005–13; Angelo Rinella, *La Shari'a in Occidente. Giurisdizioni e diritto islamico: Regno Unito, Canada e Stati Uniti d'America* (Bologna: Il Mulino, 2021); Angelo Rinella and Maria Francesca Cavalcanti, "I Tribunali islamici in Occidente: Gran Bretagna e Grecia, profili di diritto comparato," *Diritto Pubblico Comparato ed Europeo*, no. 1 (2017): 69–118; Maria Francesca Cavalcanti, *Giurisdizioni alternative e* legal pluralism*: le minoranze islamiche negli ordinamenti costituzionali occidentali* (Napoli: Editoriale scientifica, 2023).

eralism allowed a limited legal pluralism by recognising the distinct legal system of Québec, it failed to do the same in respect of the legal orders of Indigenous peoples, that "have yet to receive the same degree of recognition and protection".[66] Also relevant to this issue, scholars like McCrossan and Ladner,[67] and similarly McKerracher,[68] have argued that the "Aboriginal Rights and Treaty Rights" under section 35 of the 1982 Constitution Act are not a sufficient instrument to create a strong legal pluralism since they eliminated the Indigenous laws pertaining to territorial jurisdiction. Though far from the focus of this research, further research could explore how asymmetrical arrangements could provide flexible solutions to accommodate the plurality of legal traditions.

2.4 *The Challenges Deriving from Constitutional Asymmetries*

To conclude this first theoretical section on constitutional asymmetries, it is important to not only acknowledge the potential of constitutional asymmetry as a distinct constitutional model to manage diversity, but also to be aware that "asymmetry is not a panacea for the resolution of territorial self-determination disputes" and it is thus a "double-edged sword whose application requires careful consideration of potential consequences".[69] Even though the potential risks deriving from asymmetries have been acknowledged and discussed by some federal scholars,[70] these have not been consistently addressed in the federal literature in order to find a definite answer to the challenges that constitutional asymmetries can give rise to.

Above all, the balance between constitutional asymmetries and the principle of equality appears to be one of the most pressing and recurrent issues in the debate.[71] Indeed, some scholars tend to draw a parallel between symmetry

66 Alain-G Gagnon and Arjun Tremblay, *Advanced Introduction to Federalism* (Cheltenham, UK and Northampton, MA: Edward Elgar, 2024), 136.

67 In particular, the authors critically addressed the Supreme Court of Canada's decision in *Tsilhqot'in Nation v. British Columbia* [2014 SCC 44] that for the first time recognised Aboriginal title under section 35(1), and they substantially reduced the wide-reaching nature of this decision in terms of actual protection of Indigenous rights (see McCrossan, Michael, and Kiera L. Ladner. "Eliminating Indigenous Jurisdictions: Federalism, the Supreme Court of Canada, and Territorial Rationalities of Power," *Canadian Journal of Political Science* 49, no. 3 (2016): 411–31).

68 See Kelty McKerracher, "Relational Legal Pluralism and Indigenous Legal Orders in Canada," *Global Constitutionalism* 12, no. 1 (2023): 133–53.

69 Wolff, "Cases of Asymmetrical Territorial Autonomy," 25.

70 See for example Bauböck, "United in Misunderstanding."

71 See David Milne, "Equality or Asymmetry: Why Choose?," in *Options for a New Canada*, ed. Ronald L. Watts and Douglas M. Brown (Toronto: University of Toronto Press, 1991),

and equality, and consequently between asymmetry and inequality. For instance, on the asymmetrical distribution of powers, Bauböck argued that "unequal powers of constituent units translate into unequal representation of citizens in federal government and thus can been seen to violate a commitment to equal federal citizenship".[72] This was the case, for instance, of the proposals for increased asymmetries in Canada to accommodate Québec nationalism, that were questioned by other provinces "on the ground that asymmetry would conflict with the principle of provincial equality and, in the eyes of some critics, would imply a privileged position for Quebec".[73] However, in his assessment of the relationship between asymmetry and equality in the Canadian federation, Milne found "the logic of uniformity might be flawed in thinking that, if provincial constitutions are no uniform, they are then by definition unequal".[74] In fact, Milne observed that, despite the presence of constitutional asymmetries, all provinces share a "fundamental equality" in respect of the basic distribution of powers under the Canadian Constitution, and such "juridical equality" is emphasised by the formal equality of all provinces in exercising their opting-out rights.[75] As such, the constitutional asymmetry entrenched in the Canadian Constitution does not appear to undermine the fundamental equality of provinces. This view is also share by Kymlicka, who held that equality among individuals does not necessarily need to be translated into equality of power across the federal units.[76] Particularly relative to asymmetrical federal systems, Kymlicka further argued that:

> On the contrary, special status for nationality-based units can be seen as promoting this underlying moral equality, since it ensures that the na-

285–307; Bauböck, "United in Misunderstanding," 19–22; Sahadžić, *Asymmetry*, 180–196; Maja Sahadžić, "Constitutional Asymmetry and Equality in Multinational Systems with Federal Arrangements," in *The Principle of Equality in Diverse States: Reconciling Autonomy with Equal Rights and Opportunities* ed. Eva Maria Belser, et al. (Leiden: Brill, 2021), 36–61; Monti, *Federalismo disintegrativo*, 77–90.

72 Bauböck, "United in Misunderstanding," 19–20.

73 Ronald L. Watts, "Federalism and Diversity in Canada," in *Autonomy and Ethnicity. Negotiating Competing Claims in Multi-Ethnic States*, ed. Yash Ghai (Cambridge: Cambridge University Press, 2000), 35.

74 Milne, "Equality or Asymmetry," 292.

75 Ibidem.

76 See Will Kymlicka, *Finding Our Way. Rethinking Ethnocultural Relations in Canada* (Oxford: Oxford University Press, 1998); Will Kymlicka, "Is Federalism a Viable Alternative to Secession?," in *Theories of Secession*, ed. Percy B Lehning (London and New York: Routledge, 2005), 109–47.

> tional identity of minorities receives the same concern and respect as that of the majority nation.[77]

When it comes to divided societies, the complexity enshrined in the concept of equality finds its utmost expression in the tension between the individual and collective dimensions, as "equality becomes plural when it needs to provide support for the accommodation of differences".[78] In a recent study, Sahadžić assessed the impact of constitutional asymmetry on equality, and argued for example that "a bicameral legislature leaves spaces for discussion about equality, especially with regards to the second chamber".[79] However, she further observed that the principle of equality is not violated by a weighted representation of subnational entities in the second chamber, as long as the first chamber respects the principle of equal representation. Another aspect linked to representation and inequality concerns the right of a representative to vote on matters that do not concern that entity, or possibly convincing other representatives not to vote on matters that concern only their entity.[80] Then, differences in the application of powers of self-organisation can be regarded as a threat to equality,[81] but in this case a different application does not entail different powers, as subnational entities would be given the same powers of self-organisation. Thus, the issue concerns differences in the procedures, and not asymmetries in powers. Finally, another potential threat to equality is provided by an uneven distribution of fiscal resources.[82] Indeed, resource-rich and resource-poor subnational entities are likely to be oriented towards different expectations, the former advocating for the return of revenues to the entity that generated them, the latter for proportional revenue sharing. It has been noted that, despite some systems adopting asymmetrical fiscal policies to address differences in wealth, the outcome has sometimes been that the richest subnational entities appear to suffer under such an asymmetrical design.[83] The impact of constitutional asymmetries on equality still needs to be further explored, but the exploratory research con-

77 Kymlicka, "Is Federalism a Viable Alternative to Secession," 127.

78 Sahadžić, *Asymmetry*, 181; Ferran Requejo, "Federalism and the Quality of Democracy in Multinational Contexts: Present Shortcomings and Possible Improvements," in *Federalism and Territorial Cleavages*, ed. Ugo M. Amoretti and Nancy G. Bermeo (Baltimore: Johns Hopkins University Press, 2004), 263.

79 Sahadžić, "Constitutional Asymmetry and Equality," 53.

80 Ibidem.

81 Sahadžić, "Constitutional Asymmetry and Equality," 54.

82 Ibidem.

83 Sahadžić, "Constitutional Asymmetry and Equality," 54–55.

ducted by Sahadžić provides an essential starting point for further developments in the literature.

Overall, the debate over the relationship between asymmetry and equality appears to recall the fundamental distinction between formal and substantive equality not only as a pillar of constitutionalism[84] but also of minority rights.[85] In this respect, Toniatti argued that the development of asymmetries should be combined with "the reasonableness of the principle of equality between territories, under which common discipline is required for equal situations and reasonably differentiated discipline is required in reasonably different situations".[86] As observed by Watts even in the early 2000s,

> Much of the intensive constitutional debate in Canada has turned around the issue of the degree of which the current asymmetry might be increased to accommodate Quebec's concerns and the degree to which might undermine equality among the provinces. This Canadian experience suggests that constitutional asymmetry may be an essential element in accommodating distinct groups within a federation but also that there may be limits beyond which asymmetry itself may contribute to divisiveness.[87]

Strictly interconnected to equality, two other ideas are also invoked when dealing with the challenges posed by constitutional asymmetries, namely those of legitimacy and stability.[88] Indeed, these are substantiated by the con-

---

84 See for instance Norman Dorsen et al., eds., *Comparative Constitutionalism. Cases and Materials* (Eagan, Minnesota: West Academic, 2016), 839-1000; Susan Baer, "Equality," in *The Oxford Handbook of Comparative Constitutional Law*, ed. Michel Rosenfeld, and András Sajó (Oxford: Oxford University Press, 2012), 982-1001; Kate O'Regan and Nick Friedman, "Equality," in *Comparative Constitutional Law*, ed. Tom Ginsburg and Rosalind Dixon (Cheltenham, UK and Northampton, MA: Edward Elgar, 2011), 473–503; Brun-Otto Bryde and Michael Ashley Stein, "General Provisions Dealing with Equality," in *Routledge Handbook of Constitutional Law*, ed. Mark Tushnet, Thomas Fleiner, and Cheryl Saunders (London and New York: Routledge, 2013), 287–300.

85 See especially Kristin Henrard, "Equality Considerations and their Relations to Minority Protections, State Constitution Law, and Federalism," in *Federalism, Subnational Constitutions, and Minority Rights*, ed. G. Alan Tarr, Robert F. Williams, and Josef Marko (Westport: Praeger, 2004), 25–40; Palermo and Woelk, *Diritto costituzionale comparato*, 32–35.

86 Toniatti, "Asimmetrie regionali," 40 [English translation by the author].

87 Watts, "Federalism and Diversity in Canada," 43.

88 See Sahadžić, *Asymmetry*, 179–253.

cepts of equality, transparency, and cohesion,[89] as they are considered to be safeguards to both legitimacy and stability.[90] Specifically, Sahadžić suggested that constitutional asymmetries tend to undermine stability and legitimacy in multinational asymmetrical federal systems,[91] detecting pitfalls in all three concepts (i.e., equality, transparency, cohesion) and in all three dimensions of autonomy and asymmetry, namely status, powers and competences, and fiscal autonomy.[92] To counter such pitfalls and find a sustainable balance, Sahadžić proposes a series of constitutional safeguards, specifically structural-institutional, political, economic, and public safeguards.[93]

A related recurring objection to constitutional asymmetries is that, when taken to its extreme, the undermining of stability and legitimacy can lead to secession.[94] However, more often than not, what appears to increase the chances of secession is the denial of asymmetries, not their existence.[95] In his comparative study of asymmetry and secessionist trends in Italy and Spain, Monti noted that the negotiation of asymmetries to manage the specificities of some subnational entities has actually prompted an "anti-secessionist function of asymmetry",[96] stabilising the constitutional system. Conversely, Monti showed how their denial ignited and legitimised secessionist claims, amplifying the political consensus of independentist movements.[97] A similar conclusion was reached also by Saxena, who observed that the asymmetrical provisions in the Indian federation "have reduced the secessionist potential of an extremely diverse society by accommodating diverse groups and providing them with a share in governance of the country".[98] In this respect, it is possible to identify a similarity also with Ghai's argument in respect of political claims based on ethnicity:

89 See also Bauböck, "United in Misunderstanding," 15–22.

90 Sahadžić, "Constitutional Asymmetry and Equality," 39.

91 Sahadžić, *Asymmetry*, 239.

92 Sahadžić, *Asymmetry*, 240.

93 Sahadžić, *Asymmetry*, 241–243.

94 On this debate, see Chapter 1, paragraph 3.2.

95 On the debate over the constitutionalisation of secession in asymmetrical states, see in particular Susanna Mancini, "Costituzionalismo, federalismo e secessione," *Istituzioni del Federalismo* 35, no. 4 (2014): 780.

96 Monti, *Federalismo disintegrativo*, 393.

97 Monti, *Federalismo disintegrativo*, 394.

98 Rekha Saxena, "Asymmetrical Federalism in India: Promoting Secession or Accommodating Diversity?," in *Revisiting Unity and Diversity in Federal Countries*, ed. Alain-G. Gagnon and Michael Burgess (Leiden and Boston: Brill | Nijhoff, 2018), 373.

> Sometimes (especially when the claims are denied) there is progression from modest to the more substantial demands, including a fundamental re-design of the state or even secession (arguing that only through this radical reform can legitimate demands be met).[99]

Nevertheless, the anti-secessionist potential of asymmetries to accommodate ethnocultural diversity should always be reconciled with the principle of equality, to make asymmetries sustainable for the entire constitutional system. The concept of the "sustainability" of constitutional asymmetries has been previously explored by Martinico, who framed the concept as the exercise of federal asymmetries according to procedural and substantive guarantees to safeguard the constitutional core of the constitutional system.[100] Therefore, if sustainable, asymmetries are a valuable instrument of integration, and not disintegration, of diverse federal systems.[101]

Although further research is still needed to find a more comprehensive answer to the challenges of constitutional asymmetries, it is helpful to frame these potential risks in terms of federal dynamics, providing dynamic answers to potential inequalities arising from constitutional asymmetries. In this respect, the concept of sustainable asymmetry appears to be closely linked to the idea of a constant search for a balance between autonomy and cohesion, between self-rule and shared rule, and between integration and disintegration. As written by Martinico:

> [...] asymmetry is a game between centripetal and centrifugal forces, and here again one can find interesting clues from comparative studies: indeed, the debate on the possible negative implications of asymmetry leads to the identification of the existence of a constitutional core of principles and values whose respect makes asymmetry sustainable [...].[102]

99 Yash Ghai, "Ethnicity and Competing Notions of Rights," in *Rights in Divided Societies*, ed. Colin Harvey and Alex Schwartz (Oxford and Portland: Hart Publishing, 2012), 55.

100 Specifically, Martinico relied on Patrick Glenn's definition of sustainability as "the provenability to hold together, to sustain, mutually inconsistent sub-traditions, [and to] achieve complexity" (see Martinico, "L'origine 'mista' dell'asimmetria canadese," 30; Patrick Glenn, *Legal Traditions of the World: Sustainable Diversity in Law* (Oxford: Oxford University Press, 2014), 368).

101 Giuseppe Martinico, "Quanto è sostenibile l'integrazione (asimmetrica) sovranazionale. Note di diritto comparato," *Istituzioni del Federalismo* 2 (2018): 299.

102 Giuseppe Martinico, "Asymmetry as an Instrument of Differentiated Integration: The Case of the European Union," *European Journal of Law Reform* 18, no. 2 (2016): 143.

However, the (re)negotiation of what constitutes the core principles and values that would make asymmetries sustainable should be anchored to the development and nurturing of the culture of autonomy.[103] In fact, as already observed by Palermo:

> The rules of the law of diversity are inevitably subject to constant revision with respect to their proportionality, efficiency, and sustainability. These rules are directly linked to the changes of the societal reality that they regulate. Accordingly, the task of finding workable legal solutions to the treatment of diversity is constantly in progress and, given the nature of the issues involved, never completely finished.[104]

3 Measuring Constitutional Asymmetries

Having theoretically defined constitutional asymmetries, we can now shift towards a more "operational" definition. It may have been established that constitutional asymmetries can emerge to different degrees, yet in the literature there are no systematic comparative analyses on how to systematically explore these differences in intensity. In the field of comparative politics, some interesting attempts to classify the degrees of federalism and decentralisation have been conducted by Lijphart and Requejo, who both develop their own set of indicators. On the one hand, Lijphart mixed the dichotomies of federal/unitary states and decentralised/centralised states, showing the close link between the two sets, as most federal systems are decentralised, and most unitary systems are centralised.[105] Moreover, Lijphart identified a few indicators to measure the degree of federalism: the cameral structure,[106] the flexibility of the constitution and the existence of judicial review,[107] the independence of the central bank.[108] On the other hand, Requejo conceptualised federalism along four axes: uninational/plurinational; unitarianism/federal-

103 On the culture of autonomy, see Roberto Toniatti, *La cultura dell'autonomia: le condizioni pre-giuridiche per un'efficace autonomia regionale* (Trento: Università degli Studi di Trento, 2018).

104 Francesco Palermo, "Accommodating Differences: The Present and Future of the Law of Diversity," *Vermont Law Review* 30 (2006): 432.

105 The only exceptions of unitary and decentralised states are Japan and the Nordic countries (see Lijphart, *Patters of Democracy*, 177–179).

106 Lijphart, *Patterns of Democracy*, 201–203.

107 Lijphart, *Patterns of Democracy*, 218–219.

108 Lijphart, *Patterns of Democracy*, 236–238.

ism; centralisation/decentralisation; symmetry/asymmetry.[109] For each axis, Requejo developed a set of indicators. Regarding the symmetry/asymmetry axis, the author did not draw any distinction between the degrees of asymmetry, but simply between states which clearly display a number of asymmetries and those which do not,[110] thus reinforcing the claim that a systematic study on the degree of asymmetry is yet to be undertaken. However, it is interesting to recall Requejo's conclusion regarding the link between plurinational federal systems and asymmetries, that "plurinational federations/regional states are more asymmetrical in constitutional terms than uninational federations".[111]

Moving more specifically to the measurement of constitutional asymmetries, a range of previous research can be reviewed.

3.1 *Palermo: The Application of Game Theory*

A fascinating perspective on how to determine the extent of asymmetry in multi-tiered systems is offered by Palermo, who applied game theory to asymmetries in federal systems and identified three different scenarios: zero sum games (cooperative theories); positive/negative sum games (prisoner paradox), and equilibrated outcomes (Nash equilibrium).[112] In the first case, as the overall level of asymmetry in the constitutional system is constant, then the increase of the degree of asymmetry in one constituent unit leads to the decrease of the degree in another unit, as it is a zero-sum game. In other words, the asymmetry granted to one unit is translated into the loss of asymmetry by another unit, since it is considered a limited resource. Palermo recalls the example of the Italian regional system, where the failed constitutional reform of 2016 would have reduced the autonomy of ordinary regions to increase that of the special regions.[113] The second scenario provides that the final sum of asymmetry may be positive (overall gain for the system) or negative (overall loss for the system). In a complex system such as the European Union, the territorial competition for resources, in the absence of cooperation, may lead to a great advantage for some at the expense of others, as in the prisoner paradox.[114] Finally, the third scenario leads to a more equilibrated

---

109 Ferran Requejo, "Federalism and Democracy," in *Federal Democracies*, ed. Michael Burgess and Alain G. Gagnon (London and New York: Routledge, 2010), 284–291.

110 Requejo, "Federalism and Democracy," 286.

111 Requejo, "Federalism and Democracy," 289.

112 Francesco Palermo, "Asimmetria come forma e formante dei sistemi composti," *Istituzioni del Federalismo*, vol. 2 (2018), 268–271.

113 Palermo, "Asimmetria come forma e formante," 270.

114 Palermo, "Asimmetria come forma e formante," 271.

and efficient outcome for all units, in which asymmetry is at the minimum level.

Even though this approach does not systematise or quantify the degrees of constitutional asymmetry in a multi-tiered system, it does provide an example of a theoretical framework that applies a quantitative discipline (i.e., mathematics) to the legal field.

3.2 *Sahadžić: A First Measure of Constitutional Asymmetry*

A more refined measure of constitutional asymmetry can be found in Sahadžić's research. In her comparative study, she confirmed that constitutional asymmetries are more likely to occur in multinational multi-tiered systems than in non-multinational frameworks,[115] as previously argued by Requejo[116] and Stepan.[117] To explore this link, Sahadžić measured the degree of constitutional asymmetry (mild, moderate, strong)[118] on the basis of three indicators (status, powers and competences, fiscal autonomy), each having several sub-indicators.[119] To assign scores to each indicator and sub-indicator, Sahadžić relied on qualifying respondents' questionnaires designed following a Likert scale and distributed to a number of national experts. In respect of the distinct status of a subnational entity, namely "the power of the subnational entity to define its specific position at the central level",[120] Sahadžić explored whether the status of a specific subnational entity is recognised in constitutional or legal acts at the central level; whether the subnational entity has institutional autonomy; whether a subnational entity enjoys the guarantees of representation in central level institutions that put them in a different position; whether a subnational entity is favoured through a specific scheme of involvement in constitutional reform procedures and decision-making in the central institutions; whether a subnational entity benefits from veto powers in central level institutions; whether there are specific locks to ensure the protection of autonomy at the central level; and whether the central government has the power to supervise the content of decisions made by a subnational entity.[121] Concerning the distribution of powers and competences, Sahadžić intended to track "the extent, type, and nature of assigned powers and allocated com-

115 Sahadžić, *Asymmetry*, 83.
116 Requejo, "Federalism and Democracy," 289.
117 Stepan, "Federalism and Democracy," 29–30.
118 Sahadžić, *Asymmetry*, 80–84.
119 Sahadžić, *Asymmetry*, 76–79.
120 Sahadžić, *Asymmetry*, 76.
121 Sahadžić, *Asymmetry*, 77.

petences".[122] She examined whether a specific subnational entity enjoys a broader or narrower set of competences; whether difference exists in the techniques of allocation of powers for a specific subnational entity; whether there is a distinction between different sets of competences for specific subnational entities; whether a subnational entity is allowed to opt-in or opt-out with regard to specific competences; whether a subnational entity has an opportunity to exercise autonomy at a different speed; and whether a subnational entity has the power to formulate measures enforced in the subnational entity.[123] Finally, with regard to fiscal autonomy, Sahadžić analysed whether "tax-raising and expenditure autonomy of the subnational entity is restricted, substantial, or the same compared with the other subnational entities".[124] To do so, she explored whether a subnational entity has the power to raise its own taxes; whether a subnational entity has the discretion to set bases and rates for major taxing powers; whether a subnational entity has the power to raise revenues; whether a subnational entity is responsible for spending capacity when budgetary power is delegated to the entity; whether a subnational entity relies on transfers; and whether a subnational entity is subject to budgetary control over borrowing.[125]

Sahadžić's work is extremely helpful because she set a baseline against which constitutional asymmetry can be measured, albeit the choice of a Likert scale allows for a degree of subjectivity, hindering the potential for cross-country comparability of results. Nonetheless, thanks to her comparative analysis, Sahadžić provided for a descriptive analysis of strong and weak asymmetries,[126] as summarised in the following table.

3.3 *Popelier: The Autonomy and Cohesion Index*

Starting from Friedrich's approach to federalism as a process rather than as a fixed design,[127] Popelier developed a theory based on the balance between

122 Ibidem.

123 Sahadžić, *Asymmetry*, 77–78.

124 Sahadžić, *Asymmetry*, 78.

125 Ibidem.

126 Sahadžić, *Asymmetry*, 84–88.

127 See Carl J Friedrich, *Constitutional Government and Democracy: Theory and Practice in Europe and America* (Waltham: Blaisdell Publishing Company, 1968); Carl J Friedrich, "New Tendencies in Federal Theory and Practice," *Jahrbuch des Öffentliches Rechts* 14 (1965); Carl J Friedrich, *Trends of Federalism in Theory and Practice* (New York: Frederick A. Praeger, 1968).

TABLE 2.1 Strong v. weak constitutional asymmetries for status, powers, and fiscal arrangements

Intensity	Status of constituent units	Qualitative indicators	
		Distribution of powers	**Fiscal powers**
Weak	– Representation/involvement in decision-making varies but not to the extent that under-empowered subnational entities cannot weigh in on central decision-making; – Central oversight is in place with some detailed differentiation.	Subnational entities have different sets of powers, but only in detail.	All subnational entities have more or less the same fiscal powers, even if variations are noticeable as to conditions or forms.
Strong	– The privileged status results in a quasi-veto power; – Central oversight is absent with regard to privileged entities, but preponderant towards others.	Some subnational entities have substantially more (or less) power than others.	Some subnational entities have substantial fiscal autonomy, whereas others have (almost) none.

Source: Sahadžić, *Asymmetry*, 84-88

both autonomy and cohesion,[128] as well as on the notion of flexibility as "essential to respond to the exigencies of the moment".[129] To do so, the author developed a series of standardised indexes to measure subnational autonomy and cohesion, to be employed in cross-case comparative analysis. Indeed, this framework allows for measurement of the autonomy of component units ac-

128 See Patricia Popelier, *Dynamic Federalism. A New Theory for Cohesion and Regional Autonomy* (London and New York: Routledge, 2021).

129 Popelier, *Dynamic Federalism*, 56.

cording to the same three dimensions used by Sahadžić (status, powers, fiscal arrangements), assigning a score for each indicator to each subnational unit. According to Popelier, "status" refers to the identification of the subnational entities; "powers" concern the allocation of legislative, executive, administrative and judicial powers to the central and subnational entities; and "fiscal arrangements" refer to the financial relationships between the central and the subnational levels of authority.[130] The scores are then all converted to a value between 0 and 1, and the systems are then qualified as low (0 to 0.33), medium (0.34 to 0.66), and high (0.67 to 1) in respect of their degree of autonomy. This allows for the evaluation of autonomy for each indicator, as well as on an overall basis (obtained as a mean of the three values). Although Popelier's indexes have not been widely tested yet apart from their detailed application to the Belgian context and are not primarily interested in the study of constitutional asymmetry, the author acknowledged that asymmetry can be measured through the use of her indexes.[131]

3.4 *Measuring Asymmetries Combining Quantitative and Qualitative Methods*

As the objective of this research is not only to describe, but also to measure constitutional asymmetry to depict a more nuanced picture and produce comparable cross-country results, Popelier's model for measuring the autonomy of subnational entities is taken as reference and tested on 12 case studies. Despite the fact that Popelier's primary interest was not asymmetry but the balance between autonomy and cohesion, measurement of subnational autonomy is the essential first step towards measuring constitutional asymmetry. Indeed, the value of constitutional asymmetry is derived by the subtraction of the values of autonomy previously calculated, in terms of every dimension or in the overall spread.

Before moving to the explanation of the functioning of the indexes in measuring asymmetry, it should be added that another reason that led to the adoption of Popelier's autonomy indexes relate to her attempt to build a new theory of dynamic federalism. In such a theory, the idea of constitutional asymmetries as a flexible solution to accommodate diversity in divided societies fits quite easily. Moreover, Popelier justified the legal-institutional approach of her theory by arguing that "institutional instruments and procedures can be subjected to constitutional engineering",[132] namely one of the

---

130 Popelier, *Dynamic Federalism*, 54.
131 Popelier, *Dynamic Federalism*, 84.
132 Popelier, *Dynamic Federalism*, 57.

theoretical pillars of this book. Although Popelier adopted a maximalist approach, her indexes can be reduced "to a more practical toolbox"[133] thus taking a minimalist approach. Indeed, her subnational autonomy indexes are widely comprehensive, and a selection had to be made to conduct a feasible measurement of autonomy (and then asymmetry). The indexes were selected on the basis of the objective of this research, i.e., those aspects that were more likely to highlight asymmetry, as briefly summarised in the following table.

For "status", the selected categories were constitutional self-definition, subnational constitutional autonomy, legislative level, executive level, and organisation of courts. More precisely, Popelier constructed the category of constitutional self-definition along two sets of indicators. The first examines "whether the tier is recognised as a constituent unit of the entire system",[134] while the second measures the power to secede. Similarly, to measure subnational constitutional autonomy, the index focused on the strength of the power to adopt subnational constitutions through the adoption of two indicators. The first measured the scope of constitutional autonomy, namely to what extent subnational entities can decide how to organise themselves, while the second assessed the extent to which subnational entities (SNEs) can take these decisions autonomously.[135] Moreover, Popelier identified four categories of constitutional matters: identity clauses, representative structures and the organisation of public authority, fundamental rights, and policy principles.[136] Then, concerning the legislative level, autonomy was represented by two indicators: one for shared rule, namely the representation of SNEs in the central lawmaking body, and another for self-rule, namely the presence of a subnational lawmaking body. A similar approach was taken at the executive level as well, taking into account the representation of SNEs in the central executive body and at the subnational level.[137] Finally, the index on the organisation of courts examined whether subnational entities can organise their own courts, with additional scores if the SNE is represented in central supreme courts.[138]

Moving to the "powers" indicator, the selected subcategories were the scope of powers, the allocation techniques, the political federalism dispute resolution, and the judicial dispute resolution. To measure the scope of

133 Popelier, *Dynamic Federalism*, 69.
134 Popelier, *Dynamic Federalism*, 92-93.
135 Popelier, *Dynamic Federalism*, 105.
136 Ibidem.
137 Popelier, *Dynamic Federalism*, 116.
138 Popelier, *Dynamic Federalism*, 134–135.

TABLE 2.2 Selected indexes for the measure of autonomy

Indicator	Categories
Status	Self-definition Subnational constitutional autonomy Legislative level Executive level Organisation of courts
Powers	Scope of powers Allocation techniques Political federalism dispute resolution Judicial federalism dispute resolution
Fiscal arrangements	Subnational taxes

Source: Popelier, *Dynamic Federalism*, 54 ff

powers, Popelier identified five categories: economic purposes, political control, multinational conflict management, territorial management, or the residual category.[139] The allocation techniques refer to whether SNEs enjoy administrative or implementation powers, concurrent powers, and exclusive powers.[140] Concerning political federalism dispute resolution, from an autonomy perspective, the issue revolves around the extent to which the subnational entity has control over the management of political conflict,[141] while the index on judicial federalism dispute resolution examines the representation of the particular subnational entity in the appointment procedure of judges.[142]

Finally, for the "fiscal arrangements" dimension, the selected category was subnational taxes, namely whether SNEs have tax autonomy.[143] It should be clarified that Popelier's indexes on fiscal arrangements are much more comprehensive, including the assessment of borrowing powers, shared tax revenues, conditional grants, and fiscal discipline rules. Despite offering a complete picture of subnational autonomy in the fiscal domain, with an eye to feasibility the present research decided to focus on only one of these indexes.

139 Popelier, *Dynamic Federalism*, 140–141.
140 Popelier, *Dynamic Federalism*, 148–151.
141 Popelier, *Dynamic Federalism*, 165–166.
142 Popelier, *Dynamic Federalism*, 169–170.
143 Popelier, *Dynamic Federalism*, 182–183.

The choice to select the index on subnational taxes has to do with the fact that having taxation powers makes subnational entities "less dependent on decisions adopted by the central government",[144] irrespective of their actual use of such powers, and thus is used as a proxy of subnational autonomy and asymmetries in fiscal relations. Therefore, the index on subnational taxes measures whether subnational entities have taxation powers, and if so whether they can set the base and/or rate of only minor taxes or also of major taxes, such as personal income, value-added, or corporate taxes. Another aspect that is assessed is whether subnational entities can raise taxes with or without substantial limitations from the central authority. Moreover, the index measures whether subnational entities can introduce new taxes and provide relief. As already mentioned, asymmetries in the subnational taxing powers are used as a proxy for asymmetries in the fiscal domain. However, for a complete picture on the asymmetries in fiscal arrangements it would be necessary to assess subnational autonomy in all indexes of the fiscal dimension, as this would offer greater clarity on the asymmetries actually in place.

Coming to more operational terms, the measurement of constitutional asymmetry was conducted in the following three stages. First, for each case study two subnational entities had to be selected, and it is appropriate to explain the reasoning behind such selection.[145] As a general principle, the selection of subnational entities followed a "most different cases" logic,[146] to grasp the wider divide in terms of autonomy and thus asymmetry. Such difference was mainly displayed in terms of size and population density, comparing the biggest/smallest and most/least populous subnational units. Additionally, where different types of subnational units were present, the most and least autonomous type were taken as units of analysis. For example, for Italy the two selected SNEs were Aosta Valley, since it is the smallest and least populous unit, and it is a special region, and Lombardy, since it is the most populous ordinary region, and one of the biggest in terms of territorial size. Then, once the two subnational entities were selected, the second step involved calculating the degree of autonomy for each SNE, following Popelier's selected autonomy index. Specifically, the measure of autonomy relied on three indicators

144 Popelier, *Dynamic Federalism*, 182.

145 More details on the selection of the subnational entities for each case study can be found in Chapter 3.

146 Hirschl, "The Question of Case Selection," 139–142.

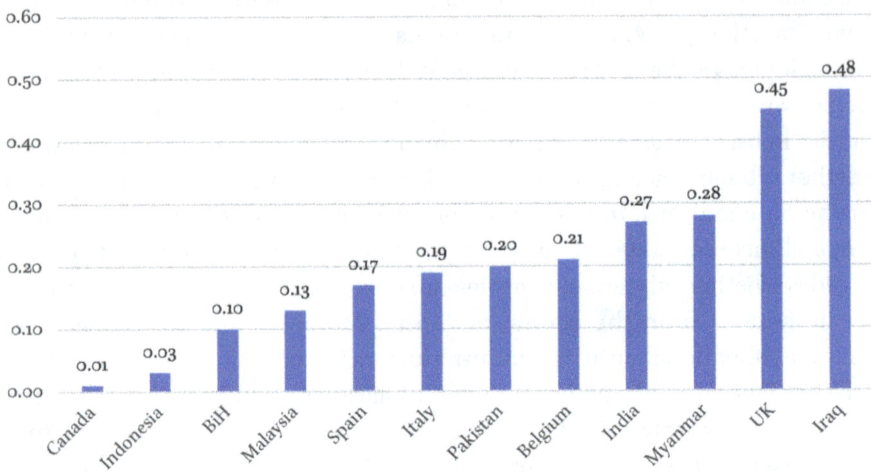

FIGURE 2.1 Constitutional asymmetry scores for the 12 case studies (average value)
SOURCE: AUTHOR'S ANALYSIS ON PRIMARY DATA

(status, powers, fiscal arrangements) and on the relative sub-categories. Finally, the scores for constitutional asymmetry were derived by subtracting the autonomy scores of the two selected SNEs.[147]

Figure 2.1 shows the scores of constitutional asymmetry at the country level for each case study, whereas Figure 2.2 shows the scores of constitutional asymmetry for each dimension in each case study.

Once all the constitutional asymmetry scores for the case studies were calculated (for each dimension and overall), these were converted through min-max normalisation[148] so that it was possible to compare the values across dimensions and overall.[149] Following Popelier's strategy, the conversion allowed us to rely on the percentiles to qualify the degrees of constitutional asymmetry as low (0–0.33), medium (0.34–066), and high (0.67–1).[150] The next chapter provides the comparative analysis on the autonomy and asymmetry scores, analysing the 12 case studies for each degree of low, medium, and high constitutional asymmetry.

147 See the Appendices for the details of the subnational autonomy scores and asymmetry scores for each case study.
148 Min-max normalisation performs a linear transformation on the original data while preserving the relationship among the original data values (see Jiawei Han, Jian Pei Micheline Kamber, *Data Mining: Concepts and Techniques* (Amsterdam: Morgan Kaufmann, 2012), 113–114).
149 See Appendix 1 for the resulting converted values of constitutional asymmetry.
150 Popelier, *Dynamic Federalism*, 84.

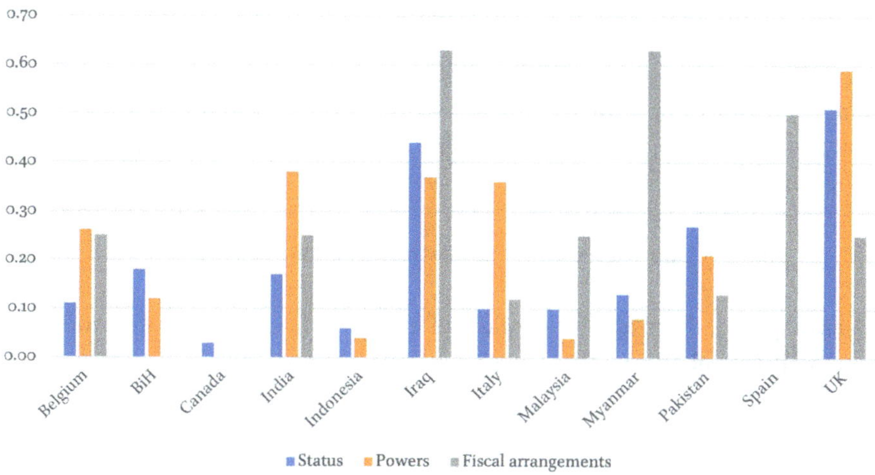

FIGURE 2.2 Constitutional asymmetry scores for each dimension of asymmetry in the 12 case studies.
SOURCE: AUTHOR'S ANALYSIS ON PRIMARY DATA

Before concluding this section, it is necessary to make one final clarification that serves as a general disclaimer for the rest of the book. The method and analytical strategy proposed in this research are far from aiming to provide absolute truths on the complex constitutional phenomenon of constitutional asymmetries. Some degree of subjectivity is inevitable, insofar as much depends on the choices that are made by the researcher while employing the method, especially concerning the subnational entities that are selected for the study. However, the aim of this book was not to transform comparative constitutional law in a research field that is not, i.e., a hard science, but rather to rely on some methodological instruments that have the potential to enhance the scope of comparative legal research. What mattered was not finding out the incontrovertible truth about constitutional asymmetries in divided multi-tiered systems but building a research design that allows for rigorous comparison across cases and, most of all, for the replication of such strategy by other researchers.[151] This would further enrich the study of constitutional

151 As noted by Hancké: "Social science is a debate, which revolves around solving puzzles, and which is based on the idea that theories and facts are caught in a three-cornered fight. Relevant data both falsify an existing theory and allow for the development of a new theory. Research design is the practical manifestation of these philosophical insights in the way we conduct social science: it provides logical links between question, debate, working hypothesis, and data so that you can turn plausible ideas into convincing arguments" (Bob Hancké, *Intelligent Research Design* (Oxford and New York: Oxford University Press, 2009), 33).

asymmetries, by employing the same method in other case studies, or selecting different subnational entities, or even assigning different scores for the same categories. After all, as Popelier wrote in the Introduction to her book, "it takes an entire research community to develop a theory".[152]

4 Factors Conducive to Constitutional Asymmetries

As anticipated, there are both legal and extra-legal factors that are conducive to constitutional asymmetries, each briefly outlined below.

4.1 *Legal Factors*

With the expression "legal factor", this research refers to those factors of constitutional design that are embedded in the law. Specifically, since constitutional asymmetries are considered a distinct model of constitutional design, this paragraph reviews the legal factors that are likely to explain the introduction of different degrees of constitutional asymmetry. The following sections aims to explore four legal factors that unpack four main dynamics: how many SNEs enjoy differentiated autonomy (i.e., the territorial distribution of asymmetry); how differentiated autonomy can be granted to SNEs (i.e., the legal procedures); how SNEs are designed (i.e., the internal distribution of ethnonational groups); and how international and subnational actors influence the degree of asymmetry (i.e., the constitution-making process). Certainly, the number of legal factors identified in this paragraph is not imagined to be exhaustive, and follow-up research may discover other factors that would further enrich the analysis and sharpen the understanding of constitutional asymmetries.[153]

4.1.1 Territorial Distribution

A first legal factor concerns how constitutional asymmetries are distributed within the territory, as they may involve one or more of the subnational entities that make up the federal system, or only some peripheral political enti-

152 Popelier, *Dynamic Federalism*, 5.

153 Other legal factors might include the presence of judicial review and the design of constitutional courts, the representation of subnational entities in the central level legislature, the mechanisms for intergovernmental relations, the presence of eternity clauses in the constitution, the degree of flexibility in the constitution (see also Simeon, "Constitutional Design," 246–248).

ties.[154] Comparative federal studies show that differentiated autonomy can be granted to almost all component units but one (e.g., England in the UK); to more than one unit, but not all units (e.g., the special regions in Italy); to only one unit (e.g., the Kurdistan Region in Iraq). This categorisation shifts the focus from the type of territorial settlement to the number of subnational entities involved in the negotiation for more autonomy. Indeed, the literature tends to classify asymmetrical settlements by making reference to the unitary/federal dichotomy,[155] a distinction that is superfluous once we refer to multi-tiered systems, i.e., those systems which present forms of decentralisation in even one subnational unit within the territory.[156] Moreover, Simeon has already suggested that the number and character of the constituent units is especially relevant for divided societies, since a small number of units could lead to instability, possibly resulting in secession, while a large number may be conducive to the opposite condition, i.e., subnational governments subordinate to the central level.[157]

Looking comparatively at the 12 case studies in this book, it is possible to appreciate the wide variations among federal arrangements, which can be grouped into three categories. The first category is composed of the majority of constitutional systems, that opt to provide differentiated autonomy to more than one subnational entity (but not all) to address territorial specificities. This is the case in Italy, where the five special regions (Aosta Valley, Trentino/South Tyrol, Friuli Venezia-Giulia, Sicily, and Sardinia) enjoy differentiated forms of autonomy compared to the other 15 ordinary regions. Italian special regions were the first to be established at the outset of Italian regionalism in 1948, with ordinary regions becoming effective only in the early 1970s. The Italian case is also helpful in exploring how asymmetrical settlements can vary substantially within the same context, as in Italy each special region has a different system of powers that has been negotiated bilaterally with the central authority and is guaranteed by a "special statute" approved with constitutional procedures. Moreover, after the 2001 reform of Title V of the Constitu-

154 Watts, "The Theoretical and Practical Implications," 28.

155 Generally, the literature identifies four main types of asymmetrical settlements: a unitary state may grant autonomy status to just one unit (the so-called "federacy"); a unitary state may grant different degrees of autonomy to more than one unit; a multi-tiered system may grant a differentiated status to one or more of its constituent units; a multi-tiered system may institutionalise asymmetry among its constituent units (see See John McGarry, "Asymmetry in Federations, Federacies, and Unitary States," *Ethnopolitics* 6, no. 1 (2007): 105–116; Weller, "Introduction," 8–9).

156 For terminology references, see Introduction (n 5).

157 Simeon, "Constitutional Design," 246.

tion, perspectives on asymmetry became multidimensional, opening a path for ordinary regions to negotiate for more autonomy from the central level (or at least consider this). Another formally unitary state, i.e., Indonesia, has granted more autonomy to five entities, i.e., the regions of Aceh, Papua, and West Papua, and the two cities of Jakarta and Yogyakarta. With specific reference to Aceh and Papua, the asymmetrical provisions introduced in the Indonesian constitutional framework derive from the decades of civil war in Aceh and Papua between the separatist movements and the national armed forces. Both regions claimed specific religious (in the case of Aceh) and cultural differences (in the case of Papua) than the rest of Indonesia. In three federal states, i.e., India, Malaysia, and Myanmar, asymmetrical provisions were introduced in the set-up of the federations to address the presence of multiple ethnic, religious, cultural, and linguistic identities. This took the form of differentiated forms of autonomy for Sabah and Sarawak in Malaysia, and for the North-East states (and the state of Jammu and Kashmir until 2019) in India. For its part, Myanmar represents a rather peculiar case insofar as the 2008 Constitution established two types of subnational entities and relative space for asymmetries. On the one hand, the ethnic states and the Bamar regions[158] are designed as symmetrical entities enjoying equal status and powers, despite having different names. On the other hand, the 2008 Constitution introduced the Self-Administered Areas, that can take the form of Self-Administered Divisions or Self-Administered Zones. Finally, the Belgian federal system provides for different types of entities, i.e., the communities and the regions, and created space for differentiation. For instance, the Constitution entitles the Flemish and French Speaking Communities to overlap with the respective regions (as opted for by the Flemings), whereas the German Speaking Community can only establish agreements with the Walloon Region to exercise some of the regional competences.

Then, a second category of case study includes those constitutional systems that show a differentiated treatment of only one subnational entity, that enjoys significantly more or less autonomy. The most evident case is Iraq, where the 2005 Constitution provides for the establishment of only the Kurdistan region, enjoying a degree of autonomy that is almost incomparable to the autonomy of governorates, that still are recognised as an autonomous tier of government. At the other end of the spectrum, in Pakistan and in the UK, the multi-tiered systems have only one subnational entity enjoying less autonomy than the others. In Pakistan, the autonomous region of Gilgit-Baltistan has less

158 The Bamar people is the majority ethnic group in Myanmar.

autonomy than the other provinces, and in the UK, England is the only British nation that has not benefited from the devolution process.

Finally, a third category is constituted of those countries that established differential autonomy provisions in limited parts of the territory but only in determined dimensions. For instance, in Canada constitutional asymmetry is detectable only in the status dimension, whereas there is symmetry in the other two dimensions of powers and fiscal arrangements. In Bosnia-Herzegovina the two entities and the autonomous district of Brčko differ in the fiscal domain, as it enjoys less autonomy than the entities. Similarly, in Spain, the initial constitutional asymmetry has been progressively reduced and the only dimension where it is prominent is fiscal autonomy.

Before moving to the following factor, it is necessary to make some clarifications regarding Myanmar and the United Kingdom, that will also serve the comparative analysis conducted in Chapter 3. First, it could be argued that Myanmar does not qualify as an asymmetrical federal system, given the pervasive presence of military groups controlling parts of the territory and the fact that the system has long been under military rule. However, the inclusion of Myanmar among the case studies was functional to display the discrepancy between asymmetry on the books and asymmetry in action. If the constitutional asymmetries entrenched by the 2008 Constitution are rather limited and emerge mainly in the fiscal domain, Myanmar *de facto* is deeply asymmetrical (i.e., economic, ethnic, religious divides across the territory) and was highly asymmetrical *de jure* in the previous 1947 Constitution. As explained by Breen, the 1947 Constitution provided for a substantial differentiation between types of subnational entities, that did not depend on the military control of the territory, but rather the constitutional provisions regulating political representation in central institutions, powers, and fiscal arrangements.[159] Moreover, Breen observed that "asymmetry between ethnic nationalities and the Bamar, and among ethnic nationalities, was a source of tension".[160] This suggests that at the outset of the federal system, asymmetry among nationalities and the dominant group was not designed to be reconciled with the principle of equality, to the point that it became one of the factors that eventually led to conflict among groups and the suspension of subnational autonomy. Then, in reference to the 2008 Constitution, the author argues that "a largely

159 Micheal Breen, "Asymmetry or Equality? Ethnic Nationalities in a Bamar-Dominated State. A Country Study of Constitutional Asymmetry in Myanmar," in *Constitutional Asymmetry in Multinational Federalism*, ed. Patricia Popelier and Maja Sahadžić (Cham: Palgrave Macmillan, 2019), 341–368.

160 Breen, "Asymmetry or Equality," 362.

symmetrical constitution does not mean ethnic neutrality"[161] and does not necessarily entail equality, suggesting that even constitutional symmetry did not erase the existing asymmetry and unequal treatment of ethnocultural groups. Therefore, Myanmar is an extremely interesting case to consider when looking at how asymmetry shaped the constitutional and political history of the system, and its relative impact on current dynamics.

A second clarification concerns the United Kingdom and the methodological choice to frame England as a subnational entity enjoying almost zero autonomy, since England did not benefit from the asymmetrical devolution process as Scotland, Wales, and Northern Ireland. Indeed, the "English Question" emerges regularly in legal scholarship, and it has been recently addressed after Brexit[162] and following the constitutional debate on devolution reforms in the UK.[163] The resulting asymmetry also emerges in the representation in Westminster, as "an obvious anomaly is that MPs at Westminster representing Scottish constituencies can vote on English legislation while MPs representing English constituencies no longer vote on devolved matters".[164] As will emerge more clearly in Chapter 3, the degree of asymmetry in the UK is not to be taken in absolute terms, but rather depends on the methodological choices I made and justified to grasp the widest divide among subnational entities and thus the widest asymmetry. However, as anticipated in the previous pages, constitutional asymmetry is a relational and dynamic concept, that depends on the object of analysis.

4.1.2 Legal Procedures

The second legal factor is strictly related to the number of subnational entities enjoying differentiated autonomy and concerns the procedures to introduce asymmetries in the legal framework. Constitutional asymmetries may be predetermined and codified in the constitution or may be permitted by providing for a general procedure,[165] leaving the opportunity open to the constituent units to self-determine themselves and negotiate more autonomy.[166] From a

161 Breen, "Asymmetry or Equality," 363.

162 Stephen Tierney, "Brexit and the English Question," in *The Law and Politics of Brexit*, ed. Federico Fabbrini (Oxford: Oxford University Press, 2017), 95–114.

163 Peter Leyland, "Navigating the Constitutional Path to English Devolution: How Not to Crack an Old Chestnut in a Disunited Kingdom?," *Istituzioni Del Federalismo* 3 (2023): 567–98.

164 Leyland, "Navigating the Constitutional Path to English Devolution," 568.

165 Palermo, "«Divided We Stand»," 164–165.

166 Such logic recalls the concepts of pre-determination and self-determination of groups entitled to share power in a consociation made by Lijphart. In the first case, entitled

comparative overview of the case studies, the former procedure is the one followed by Belgium,[167] Bosnia-Herzegovina,[168] India,[169] Iraq,[170] and Malaysia,[171] whereas the latter can be detected in Spain.[172] Interestingly, the Italian Constitution displays a mixture of both procedures, entrenching the special status of the five specific regions (Art. 116(1)), while providing a general procedure to ordinary regions that might want more autonomy in specific sectors (Art. 116(3)).[173] Palermo observed that the second procedure allows further development of the flexible and functional characteristics of the asymmetrical process, and this approach relies on a strong culture of cooperation, founded on asymmetrical cooperation between the centre and the peripheries.[174]

Moreover, constitutional asymmetries are often introduced by bilateral acts,[175] as in the case of South Tyrol with the De Gasperi-Gruber Agreement in 1946, later to be integrated into the Constitution. This was also the case with Russia during the period of "wild federalism" between 1985 and 1993. In this period, several bilateral agreements were negotiated between some subnational entities and the central government, creating a substantial asymmetry among entities (later erased by the central government).[176] Another example

---

groups are specified in the constitutional text (e.g., the so-called "constituent peoples" in the BiH constitutional preamble); in the other case, entitled groups may manifest themselves in a later stage, after the adoption of the constitution, thus resulting in a more flexible and inclusive arrangement (see Lijphart, "The Wave," 50–51; Lijphart, *Thinking about Democracy*, 66–74).

167 Constitution of Belgium – Title I.

168 Constitution of Bosnia-Herzegovina – Art. I(3), Art. III, Art. VI(4).

169 Constitution of India – Art. 370–371, Schedule 5 and 6, Art. 239AA.

170 Constitution of Iraq – Art. 117(1).

171 Constitution of Malaysia – Art. 161E.

172 Art. 143 and 144 of the Spanish Constitution provides for a procedure to establish Autonomous Communities without identifying them in advance.

173 Constitution of Italy – Art. 116(3): "Additional special forms and conditions of autonomy, related to the areas specified in art. 117, paragraph three and paragraph two, letter l)- limited to the organisational requirements of the Justice of the Peace -and letters n) and s), may be attributed to other Regions by State Law, upon the initiative of the Region concerned, after consultation with the local authorities, in compliance with the principles set forth in art. 119. Said Law is approved by both Houses of Parliament with the absolute majority of their members, on the basis of an agreement between the State and the Region concerned."

174 Palermo, "Divided We Stand," 165.

175 Palermo, "Divided We Stand," 167–169.

176 See Elena A. Kremyanskaya, "Constitutional Asymmetry in Russia: Issues and Developments. A Country Study of Constitutional Asymmetry in the Russian Federation," in *Constitutional Asymmetry in Multinational Federalism*, ed. Patricia Popelier and Maja Sahadžić (Cham: Palgrave Macmillan, 2019), 403–405.

is provided by Myanmar, where asymmetry was also negotiated through bilateral agreements and ceasefires, before the adoption of the 1974 and 2008 Constitutions. On this point, Popelier argues that bilateral agreements have the potential to give SNEs the opportunity to negotiate for more autonomy, thus leading to higher asymmetry.[177]

Finally, in other contexts, constitutional asymmetry was introduced through national legislation, as in the case of Canada with the enactment of the Supreme Court Act 1985 providing the appointment for three judges from Québec, and in the case of the United Kingdom with the acts of Westminster Parliament regulating devolution in Scotland, Wales, and Northern Ireland. Similarly, the different status of Gilgit-Baltistan in Pakistan was recognised by the Gilgit-Baltistan Empowerment and Self-Governance Order in 2009, whereas in Indonesia the special autonomy of Aceh and Papua is regulated by Law 11/2006 on Aceh Special Autonomy and Law 21/2001 on Special Autonomy for Papua Province.

Another related aspect that is interesting to note is that constitutional asymmetries were introduced both by states with a written constitution (e.g., Belgium, Italy, Spain), as well as through ordinary legislation by states that do not have a single homogeneous constitutional text (e.g., United Kingdom). This element was also analysed by Lijphart concerning the degree of federalism depending on the rigidity or flexibility of the constitution. According to Lijphart, the more rigid the constitution (i.e., the more difficult it is to amend), the higher the degree of federalism and decentralisation.[178]

4.1.3 Homogeneous or Heterogeneous Design of the Subnational Entities

The third legal factor concerns the internal distribution of ethnocultural groups in the subnational entities, namely whether the SNEs were designed as homogeneous or heterogeneous.[179] As also confirmed by the literature on constitutional design, this is a relevant aspect. Horowitz suggested that homogeneous units may foster intra-group competition at the expense of an exclusive inter-group competition, while the groups in heterogeneous units have more experience in political socialisation, as politicians from different groups become used to dealing with each other at the lower level before they need to

177 Popelier, *Dynamic Federalism*, 223–224.

178 Lijphart, *Patterns of Democracy*, 204–225.

179 See also Matteo Nicolini, *Legal Geography: Comparative Law and the Production of Space* (Cham: Springer International Publishing, 2022).

do so at the centre.[180] For his part, Lijphart observed that territorial autonomy (and thus federalism) is desirable where there is a homogeneous distribution of groups, while non-territorial autonomy in sectors such as education and culture is more appropriate where the distribution of groups is heterogeneous.[181] Moreover, Simeon observed that the "drawing of borders is a much-neglected issue in comparative federalism; but it is a critical issue in the design of new federations",[182] since once they are drawn, borders can be difficult to change as "interests and identities coalesce around them".[183]

The divided multi-tiered systems analysed in this book display a variety of designs when it comes to the internal composition of subnational entities. Some systems have established homogeneous units where ethnocultural groups are territorially concentrated (as Belgium, and Iraq), others heterogeneous (as India and Pakistan), and some others a mixture of both. This latter configuration is present in the majority of constitutional systems, where ethnocultural groups are concentrated only in some parts of the territory, whereas the rest of the subnational entities are homogeneous. Of course, even in this case there are some variations in the balance between the number of homogeneous entities vis-à-vis heterogeneous entities. In Canada, Italy, Spain, and the UK, the number of homogeneous subnational entities is higher than heterogeneous ones, whereas in Indonesia, Malaysia and Myanmar the opposite is true, with a predominance of heterogeneous entities. Finally, in some other cases, such as Bosnia-Herzegovina, we find a more balanced situation, as the 1995 Dayton Peace Agreement confirmed the establishment of two entities: a heterogeneous Bosniac-Croat entity and a homogeneous Serb entity.

4.1.4 Constitution-Making Process

Finally, another interesting legal factor revolves around the constitution-making process,[184] and in particular around the actors involved in such processes and their impact on constitutional asymmetry.[185] As previously argued

180 Horowitz, "Constitutional Design," 25.
181 Lijphart, "The Wave," 51.
182 Simeon, "Constitutional Design," 246.
183 Ibidem.
184 For more on this issue, see also Simeon's discussion on the role played by citizens, politicians, experts, international actors, and courts (Simeon, "Constitutional Design," 252–254).
185 Cfr. Angustias Hombrado, "Learning to Catch the Wave? Regional Demands for Constitutional Change in Contexts of Asymmetrical Arrangements," *Regional & Federal Studies* 21, no. 4–5 (2011): 479–501.

by Lollini and Palermo, contemporary constitutions are "no longer a mere and single act of political will, but a more complex series of constitutional facts and acts, including political, judicial and international conditionality, and in the end it becomes a legally-driven process and procedure".[186] In this context, the role of comparative constitutional law is pivotal, as "there is no modern constitution-building nor constitution-making without a massive use of comparative (and international) law".[187] Generally, this research makes reference to four main constitution-making processes,[188] depending on the actors involved: written constitutions "imposed" by international actors on another state (i.e., external process);[189] constitutions written by national actors with the direct involvement of external or international actors (i.e., internationally assisted process);[190] constitutions written by national actors involving subna-

186 Andrea Lollini and Francesco Palermo, "Comparative Law and the Proceduralization of Constitution-Building Processes," in *Facets and Practices of State-Building*, ed. Julia Raue and Patrick Sutter (Leiden and Boston: Brill | Nijhoff, 2009), 302. On this argument, see also Francesco Biagi, *Constitution-Building After the Arab Spring A Comparative Perspective* (Cambridge: Cambridge University Press, 2025), 59 ff.

187 Lollini and Palermo, "Comparative Law and the Proceduralization of Constitution-Building Processes," 302.

188 For more on constitution-making models, see de Vergottini, *Diritto costituzionale comparato*, 215–247; Andrew Arato, "Forms of Constitution Making and Theories of Democracy," *Cardozo Law Review* 17, no. 2 (1995): 191–231; David Landau and Hanna Lerner, eds., *Comparative Constitution Making* (Cheltenham: Edward Elgar Publishing, 2019); Sujit Choudhry and Tom Ginsburg, eds., *Constitution Making* (Cheltenham: Edward Elgar Publishing, 2016); Tom Ginsburg, Zachary Elkins, and Justin Blount, "Does the Process of Constitution-Making Matter?," *Annual Review of Law and Social Science* 5 (2009): 201–23. For a focused analysis on divided societies, see Hanna Lerner, *Making Constitutions in Deeply Divided Societies* (Cambridge: Cambridge University Press, 2011); Clark B. Lombardi and Shamshad Pasarlay, "Constitution-Making for Divided Societies: Afghanistan," in *Constitutionalism in Context*, ed. David S. Law, 1st ed. (Cambridge: Cambridge University Press, 2022), 89–112.

189 Comparatively speaking, this is the case of Japan after WWII and of former colonies, see Richard Albert, Xenophon Contiades, and Alkmene Fotiadou, *The Law and Legitimacy of Imposed Constitutions* (London and New York: Routledge, 2020); Yasuo Hasabe, "Imposed Constitutions (Constitutions Octroyées)," in *Max Plank Encyclopedia of Comparative Constitutional Law*, ed. Rainer Grote, Frauke Lachenmann, and Rüdiger Wolfrum (Oxford: Oxford University Press, 2016).

190 As in the case of Bosnia and Herzegovina, previously recalled, or Iraq, see for example Philipp Dann, "International Influence of Post-Conflict Constitution-Making," in *Order from Transfer*, ed. Günter Frankenberg (Cheltenham and Northampton: Elgar Publishing, 2013), 243–260; Philipp Dann and Zaid Al-Ali, "The Internationalized *Pouvoir Constituant* – Constitution-Making Under External Influence in Iraq, Sudan and East Timor," *Max Planck Yearbook of United Nations Law* 10 (2006): 423–63; Cheryl Saunders, "International Involvement in Constitution Making," in *Comparative Constitution Mak-*

tional actors (i.e., participatory process);[191] constitutions written only by national actors within a constituent assembly (i.e., internal process).[192]

Considering the different actors involved in the process in the 12 case studies, the involvement of international actors, rather than national or even subnational actors in the process might substantially influence the model of constitutional design adopted in the system, since the international community might endorse one model rather than another.[193] In fact, the role of international actors in the processes of constitution making in divided societies was particularly meaningful in cases such as Bosnia-Herzegovina, Iraq, and (at a local level) Northern Ireland, where power-sharing arrangements and asymmetrical solutions were strongly supported by the United States and the rest of the international community. In four other systems, former colonial power played an important role in the process of constitution making. This was the

---

ing, ed. David Landau and Hanna Lerner (Cheltenham, UK ; Northampton, MA: Edward Elgar Publishing, 2019), 69–89; Nicolas Maziau, "Le costituzioni internazionalizzate. Aspetti teorici e tentativi di classificazione," *Diritto Pubblico Comparato ed Europeo* 4 (2002): 1397–1420; Antoni Abat i Ninet, *Constitutional Crowdsourcing Democratising Original and Derived Constituent Power in the Network Society* (Cheltenham, UK: Edward Elgar Publishing, 2021).

191 See for example Francesco Palermo, "Participation, Federalism and Pluralism: Challenges to Decision-Making and Responses by Constitutionalism," in *Citizen Participation in Multilevel Democracies*, ed. Cristina Fraenkl-Haeberle (Leiden and Boston: Brill Publishing, 2015), 31–47; Palermo and Kössler, *Comparative Federalism*, 111–122; Jonathan Wheatley and Fernando Mendez, eds., *Patterns of Constitutional Design: The Role of Citizens and Elites in Constitution-Making* (Farnham, England: Ashgate, 2013).

192 On the theory of constituent power, see Costantino Mortati, *La teoria del potere costituente* (Macerata: Quodlibet Ius, 2020); Gaetano Silvestri, "Il potere costituente come problema teorico-giuridico," in *Scritti in onore di Leopoldo Elia. Vol. II* (Milano: Giuffrè, 1999): 1615–1634; Pietro Giuseppe Grasso, "Potere costituente," *Enciclopedia del Diritto*, XXXIV (1985), 657 ss; Alessandro Pace, *Potere costituente, rigidità costituzionale, autovincoli legislativi* (Padova: CEDAM, 2002); Marina Calamo Specchia, "La costituzione tra potere costituente e mutamenti costituzionali," *Rivista AIC*, no. 1 (2020): 266–95; Matilda Arvidsson, Leila Brännström, and Panu Minkkinen, eds., *Constituent Power: Law, Popular Rule, and Politics* (Edinburgh: Edinburgh University Press, 2020); Sergio Verdugo, "Is It Time to Abandon the Theory of Constituent Power?," *International Journal of Constitutional Law* 21, no. 1 (2023): 14–79; Nicholas Aroney, Erin F Delaney, and Stephen Tierney, "Federal Exceptionalism and Constituent Power: Afterword to the Foreword by Sergio Verdugo," *International Journal of Constitutional Law* 21, no. 4 (2023): 1182–88; Sergio Verdugo, "Is It Time to Abandon the Theory of Constituent Power? A Rejoinder," *International Journal of Constitutional Law* 21, no. 4 (2023): 1213–24; Héctor López Bofill, *Law, Violence and Constituent Power. The Law, Politics and History of Constitution Making* (London and New York: Routledge, 2023).

193 See Kymlicka, "The Internationalization of Minority Rights"; Simeon, "Constitutional Design," 254.

case in Canada, India, Malaysia, and Myanmar, which all experienced British colonialism and relative processes of constitution making during decolonisation. Finally, it should also be acknowledged that in the majority of cases subnational actors were involved in the constitution making process and thus were able to negotiate more autonomy. Particularly emblematic cases are Belgium, where the linguistic groups played (and still play) a determining role in the re-design of the system, Indonesia and Malaysia, where the subnational entities that then enjoyed more autonomy (i.e., Aceh and Papua, and Sabah and Sarawak) were directly involved in the constitution-making process that eventually introduced constitutional asymmetry to accommodate their claims.

4.2 *Extra-legal Factors*

Given the predominant legal focus of this book, the extra-legal factors conducive to asymmetries are only briefly reviewed below, to highlight the global dynamics in which the 12 case studies are placed.[194]

4.2.1 Historical Reasons and Periodisation

A first extra-legal factor that should be considered is the role played by history in the introduction of asymmetrical arrangements. Indeed, having different perspectives in mind, both Huntington and Elster coined two similar and inter-related expressions, respectively "waves of democratisation"[195] and "waves of constitution-making",[196] to look at global political and constitutional history. On the one hand, in Huntington's periodisation, the focus is on democratisation, identifying three waves of democratisation and corresponding counter-waves of authoritarian backsliding. In Huntington's theorisation,[197] the first wave started in 1828 and lasted until 1922, followed by a counter-wave characterised by the rise of Nazism and Fascism (between

194 This paragraph reflects mainly on the role played by history, geopolitics and wealth, but other significant extra-legal factors might be the power ratio, autocracy, and separatism, as observed by Sahadžić (see Sahadžić, *Asymmetry*, 89–95; Nicholas Aroney, and John Kincaid, "Introduction: Courts in Federal Systems," in *Courts in Federal Countries: Federalists or Unitarists?* ed. Nicholas Aroney, and John Kincaid (Toronto: University of Toronto Press, 2017), 18–22).

195 Samuel P. Huntington, "Democracy's Third Wave," *Journal of Democracy* 2, no. 2 (1991): 12–34.

196 Jon Elster, "Forces and Mechanisms in the Constitution-Making Process," *Duke Law Journal* 45, no. 2 (1995): 368–373.

197 For a critical perspective, see Renske Doorenspleet, "Reassessing the Three Waves of Democratization," *World Politics* 52, no. 3 (2000): 384–406.

1922 and 1942). The second wave occurred between 1943 and 1962, followed by a second counter-wave dominated by the rise of authoritarian regimes in Latin America, Asia, Africa, and South-Eastern Europe (between 1958 and 1975). Finally, the third wave began in 1974 with the fall of Salazar in Portugal and lasted until the mid-1990s, with the dissolution of the USSR and Yugoslavia. As already mentioned in the previous chapter, the third wave of democratisation marked a turning point in the renewed interest in constitutional design, especially in cases of deeply divided societies.[198]

On the other hand, the focus of Elster's seven waves is on the process of constitution making, understood as the drafting and adoption of new constitutions. According to such periodisation, the first wave occurred in late eighteenth century, with the written constitutions of the US, Poland, and France. The second broke out after the 1848 revolutions in Europe, where many countries adopted new constitutions. Then, the next two waves occurred in the aftermath of the World Wars, with the adoption of the Weimar constitution, the new constitution of Poland and of Czechoslovakia after the First World War, and the new constitutions in Italy, Germany, and Japan which were adopted under the influence of the Allied Powers after the Second World War. The fifth wave followed the process of decolonisation between the 1940s and 1960s, with the break-up of the British and French colonial empires, beginning with the new constitutions of India and Pakistan and of many African countries, closely modelled on those of the previous colonial powers.[199] Then, a sixth wave of constitution making occurred in the mid-1970s with the fall of dictatorships in Portugal, Spain, and Greece. Finally, the last wave of constitution making was linked to the fall of communist regimes in Eastern Europe in the aftermath of the fall of the Berlin Wall and the break-up of the Soviet Union, Yugoslavia, and Czechoslovakia. In also worth noticing that Elster believed that some of these waves were spurious or accidental, such as the temporal proximity of the new constitutions drafted in the first or sixth waves, while others are nonspurious, being triggered by the same event (e.g., the end of the two World Wars, the process of decolonisation) or by a chain reaction (e.g., the fall of communist regimes after 1989).[200]

It is interesting to recall such "waves" because, in the case of constitutional asymmetries, Weller observes that "asymmetrical state-building is a feature of the ongoing second wave of post-Cold War settlements to secessionist con-

198 See Chapter 1, paragraph 2.1.

199 See also Simeon, "Constitutional Design," 249.

200 Elster, "Forces and Mechanisms," 371.

flicts".[201] Indeed, the end of the Cold War and the dissolution of the ethno-federation brought about a dramatic change in the international arena, with the formation of new states in Central and Eastern Europe, and it can be observed that some "waves" (i.e., the third/seventh wave, depending on the author's periodisation) brought more asymmetries than others. Furthermore, Sahadžić confirmed that historical reasons seem to contribute significantly to constitutional asymmetries in multinational multi-tiered systems, in all three dimensions of *de jure* asymmetries (status, powers and competences, fiscal autonomy).[202] Therefore, history should be an element which is taken into account when analysing the introduction of constitutional asymmetries, since it could be a significant explanatory factor.

4.2.2 Process of Formation

Strictly linked to history is the formation process of the multi-tiered system. Indeed, according to federal scholarship, until roughly World War I federal systems were formed following a "coming-together" process, by uniting previously sovereign entities.[203] After the 1920s, due to the reconfiguration of the geopolitical landscape, most federal settlements were "holding-together" systems, resulting from a transfer of power from a unitary state.[204] Regarding the latter process of formation, Stepan argued that political systems with strong unitary features might decide that the best way to preserve democracy in a country would be to "devolve power constitutionally", turning the polities into a federal settlement.[205] This is especially true for systems where centrifugal forces threatened the integrity of the state, often on the basis of ethnocultural identity markers.[206]

As already mentioned in the previous chapter, Stepan established a link between the features of coming-together/holding-together and symmetry/asymmetry, holding that coming-together federal systems tend to be symmetrical, while holding-together federal systems tend to be multinational and

---

201 Weller, "Introduction," 7.

202 In particular, she recalls examples such as Bosnia and Herzegovina with the signing of the post-conflict Dayton Agreement; Northern Ireland with the signing of the Good Friday Agreement; Iraq with the drafting of a new constitution under international influence and supervision; Pakistan with its reshuffling of the British colonial rule (see Sahadžić, *Asymmetry*, 89-95).

203 Palermo and Kössler, *Comparative Federalism*, 42–43.

204 Palermo and Kössler, *Comparative Federalism*, 43.

205 Stepan, "Federalism and Democracy," 22.

206 See, for example, the cases of India, Belgium, and Spain also recalled by Stepan.

asymmetrical.[207] Therefore, as Palermo and Kössler conclude, "historical origins are indeed very relevant in shaping the constitutional features of federal states. [...] It is important to identify historical cycles that have determined the ways of forming federations."[208] Thus, the process and dynamics leading to the formation of a multi-tiered system should be taken into account when analysing the system, in order to better frame and explain the introduction of asymmetries.

4.2.3 Global North v. Global South

Related to the previous aspects is also the geopolitical position of the country in which constitutional asymmetries were introduced. In fact, in the literature on constitutional design, the bias of the divide between "the West" and "the rest" remains noticeable. Issacharoff argued this point while comparing Bosnia-Herzegovina and South Africa.[209] In both cases the adoption of a consociational model (transitional or permanent) was strongly influenced by the Western orientation or influence, even though neither country is properly in the Global North. As previously mentioned, Lijphart's critics have argued that the consociational model would only work in Western countries, while he responds with consociational experiences of non-Western countries such as Lebanon, Malaysia, Colombia, and South Africa.[210] Another interesting perspective is the one offered by Horowitz, who talks about "bias and distortions",[211] and the relative attractiveness of alternative constitutional models across states and the interpretation of constitutional experiences within states. More specifically, the colonial impact of France and the United Kingdom had a deep impact on post-colonial conditions, that can and indeed do change, but powerful networks, habits, and pressures can stunt this. Horowitz also suggested that divided societies have to look to other divided societies in other regions of the world, rather than less divided societies.[212] Inter-regional boundaries also constitute powerful impediments to constitutional borrow-

---

207 Stepan, "Federalism and Democracy," 29–30.

208 Palermo and Kössler, *Comparative Federalism*, 44.

209 Issacharoff, "Constitutionalizing Democracy," 1881–1883.

210 Lijphart, "The Wave," 45.

211 Horowitz, "Constitutional Design," 31.

212 For example, Lijphart suggested that Nigeria should have looked at the experience of Switzerland rather than the US, since the author considers the former a divided society. However, it is hard to define Switzerland as a "divided society", as even if there are diverse identities these do not give rise to political conflict or autonomy claims. Aside from this debatable issue, it should be noted that Lijphart equally suggested that a non-Western country should have looked at the experience of a Western country.

ings, again in a logic of Global North v. Global South, and Horowitz concluded that there is not yet completely free trade in constitutional innovations.

Therefore, the geopolitical position of the multi-tiered system could be taken into account in the analysis as a control factor, assessing the impact of whether it belongs to the so-called "Global South" or "Global North".

4.2.4 Wealth

The last and perhaps most obvious extra-legal factor to take into account is the wealth of subnational entities within a multi-tiered system. Sahadžić observed that wealth emerges as a decisive factor in the intensity of constitutional asymmetry, since particularly wealthy subnational entities might use it to push for more autonomy, thus resulting in more asymmetry in the system. This is reflected in asymmetries in status, powers and competences, and fiscal autonomy,[213] and several examples might be recalled, such as Catalonia and the Basque Country in Spain, Flanders in Belgium, Scotland in the United Kingdom, the Kurdistan Region in Iraq. Moreover, Burgess also identified socio-economic factors as one of the preconditions of asymmetry, as "large regional economic disparities that lead inevitably to differential demands and expectations within federations".[214]

In conclusion, wealth should be considered a crucial control factor for the introduction of constitutional asymmetries in a multi-tiered system, especially in relation to asymmetries in fiscal arrangements.

5 Concluding Remarks

This chapter sought to dive deeper into the analysis of asymmetries in multi-tiered systems to provide a sound theoretical and operational framework for the comparative analysis and the following examination of the role played by courts in Part II. More specifically, it recalled the distinction between *de facto* and *de jure* asymmetries and explored the different dimensions of constitutional asymmetries (status, powers, fiscal arrangements) that will be taken into account in the comparative analysis of the 12 case studies in the next chapters. As mentioned earlier in the chapter, this research focuses on constitutional (rather than political) asymmetries as they offer greater analytical clarity and can be measured more effectively.

---

213 Sahadžić, *Asymmetry*, 89–95.

214 Burgess, *Comparative Federalism*, 216.

Moreover, by reviewing the scholarship on asymmetries in federal theory, a second task of this chapter was to highlight the gaps still present in the literature, namely the lack of systematic analysis of the degrees of constitutional asymmetries in divided multi-tiered systems, as well as consideration of the explanations of such differences in intensity. Similarly, relying on previous research, the chapter proposed a method to measure constitutional asymmetries to conduct rigorous cross-case comparison, relying on Popelier's autonomy indexes. Finally, the chapter reviewed the legal and extra-legal factors that are distinctive elements of constitutional design and conducive to the introduction of constitutional asymmetries, to offer a broader context for asymmetries in divided multi-tiered systems.

Bibliography

Agranoff, Robert, ed. *Accommodating Diversity: Asymmetry in Federal States*. Baden-Baden: Nomos Verlagsgesellschaft, 1999.

Alessi, Nicolò Paolo, and Martina Trettel, eds. *Federalism and the Law of Diversity*. Leiden and Boston: Brill | Nijhoff, 2025.

Arato, Andrew. "Forms of Constitution Making and Theories of Democracy." *Cardozo Law Review* 17, no. 2 (1995): 191–231.

Bauböck, Rainer. "United in Misunderstanding? Asymmetry in Multinational Federations." *Ice Working Paper Series*, no. 26 (2002): 1–52.

Bennett, T W. "Comparative Law and African Customary Law." In *The Oxford Handbook of Comparative Law*, edited by Mathias Reimann and Reinhard Zimmermann, 2nd ed., 652–80. Oxford: Oxford University Press, 2019.

Berman, Paul Schiff. "Federalism and International Law through the Lens of Legal Pluralism." *Missouri Law Review* 73, no. 4 (2008): 1149–84.

Berman, Paul Schiff. "The New Legal Pluralism." *Annual Review of Law and Social Science* 5, no. 1 (2009): 225–42.

Berman, Paul Schiff, ed. *The Oxford Handbook of Global Legal Pluralism*. Oxford: Oxford University Press, 2020.

Bifulco, Raffaele. "Differenziazioni e asimmetrie nella teoria federale contemporanea." *Diritti Regionali*, no. 1 (2020): 139–72.

Bolaji, Mohammed H. A. "Shari'ah in Northern Nigeria in the Light of Asymmetrical Federalism." *Publius: The Journal of Federalism* 40, no. 1 (2010): 114–35.

Bonifati, Lidia. "Asymmetries and Mixed Legal Systems: New Itineraries of Legal Comparisons." *Rivista di Diritti Comparati*, no. 3 (2024): 156–180.

Burgess, Michael. *Comparative Federalism: Theory and Practice*. London and New York: Routledge, 2006.

Burset, Christian R. *An Empire of Laws: Legal Pluralism in British Colonial Policy*. New Haven and London: Yale University Press, 2023.

Butt, Simon. "Religious Conservatism, Islamic Criminal Law and the Judiciary in Indonesia: A Tale of Three Courts." *The Journal of Legal Pluralism and Unofficial Law* 50, no. 3 (2018): 402–34.

Cassidy, Julie. "The Legacy of Colonialism." *The American Journal of Comparative Law* 51, no. 2 (2003): 409–56.

Cavalcanti, Maria Francesca. *Giurisdizioni alternative e* legal pluralism*: le minoranze islamiche negli ordinamenti costituzionali occidentali.* Napoli: Editoriale scientifica, 2023.

Cortese, Fulvio, and Jens Woelk. *Autonomie speciali e regionalismo italiano. Un Bilancio.* Milano: Franco Angeli, 2023.

Dann, Philipp, and Zaid Al-Ali. "The Internationalized Pouvoir Constituant – Constitution-Making Under External Influence in Iraq, Sudan and East Timor." *Max Planck Yearbook of United Nations Law* 10 (2006): 423–63.

D'Atena, Antonio. "Passato, presente … e futuro delle autonomie regionali speciali." *Rivista AIC*, no. 4 (2014): 1–15.

D'Ignazio, Guerino, ed. *Integrazione europea e asimmetrie regionali.* Milano: Giuffrè, 2007.

D'Ignazio, Guerino, and Anna Margherita Russo, eds. "Asimmetria e conflitti territoriali nel quadro dell'integrazione europea." *Istituzioni Del Federalismo* 2 (2018).

Dirri, Adriano. "Asimmetria costituzionale e pluralismo identitario negli Stati federali multinazionali: le (diverse) asimmetrie di Etiopia, Iraq, India." *Rivista Gruppo Di Pisa* 3, no. 2 (2020): 365–85.

Fejzula, Merve. "The Cosmopolitan Historiography of Twentieth-Century Federalism." *The Historical Journal* 64, no. 2 (March 2021): 477–500.

Gagnon, Alain-G, and Michael Burgess, eds. *Revisiting Unity and Diversity in Federal Countries*. Leiden and Boston: Brill | Nijhoff, 2018.

Ghai, Yash. "Constitutional Asymmetries: Communal Representation, Federalism, and Cultural Autonomy." In *The Architecture of Democracy: Constitutional Design, Conflict Management, and Democracy*, edited by Andrew Reynolds, 141–70. Oxford: Oxford University Press, 2002.

Glenn, Patrick. *Legal Traditions of the World: Sustainable Diversity in Law*. Oxford: Oxford University Press, 2014.

Hallaq, Wael B. *Restating Orientalism: A Critique of Modern Knowledge*. New York: Columbia University Press, 2018.

Henrard, Kristin. "Equality Considerations and Their Relations to Minority Protections, State Constitution Law, and Federalism." In *Federalism, Subnational Constitutions, and Minority Rights*, edited by Alan Tarr, Robert F. Williams, and Joseph Marko, 25–40. Westport: Praefer, 2004.

Hooker, M.B. *Legal Pluralism: An Introduction to Colonial and New-Colonial Laws.* Oxford: Oxford University Press, 1975.

Lawan, Mamman. "Islamic Law and Legal Hybridity in Nigeria." *Journal of African Law* 58, no. 2 (October 2014): 303–27.

Lev, Daniel S. *Legal Evolution and Political Authority in Indonesia.* Leiden: Brill, 2000.

Lindsey, Tim, and Simon Butt. *Indonesian Law.* Oxford: Oxford University Press, 2018.

Mallat, Chibli. "Comparative Law and the Islamic (Middle Eastern) Legal Culture." In *The Oxford Handbook of Comparative Law*, edited by Mathias Reimann and Reinhard Zimmermann, 2nd ed., 624–51. Oxford: Oxford University Press, 2019.

Mancini, Susanna. "Costituzionalismo, federalismo e secessione." *Istituzioni del Federalismo* 35, no. 4 (2014): 779–805.

Mancuso, Salvatore. *African Law(s) : Comparative Insights on the African Lawscape.* Leiden and Boston: Brill, 2024.

Martinico, Giuseppe. "Asymmetry as an Instrument of Differentiated Integration: The Case of the European Union." *European Journal of Law Reform* 18, no. 2 (2016): 139–58.

Martinico, Giuseppe. "L'origine 'mista' dell'asimmetria canadese." In *Il costituzionalismo canadese a 150 anni dalla Confederazione. Riflessioni comparatistiche*, edited by Giacomo Delledonne, Giuseppe Martinico, and Leonardo Pierdominici, 15–30. Pisa: Pisa University Press, 2017.

Martinico, Giuseppe. "Quanto è sostenibile l'integrazione (asimmetrica) sovranazionale. Note di diritto comparato." *Istituzioni del Federalismo* 2 (2018): 287–300.

Martinico, Giuseppe, and Matteo Monti, eds. "New Trends in Comparative Federalism." *Perspectives on Federalism* 16, no. 1 (2024): 1–291.

Mawani, Renisa. "Law and Colonialism: Legacies and Lineages." In *The Handbook of Law and Society*, edited by Austin Sarat and Patricia Ewick, 1st ed., 417–32. Wiley, 2015.

McCrossan, Michael, and Kiera L. Ladner. "Eliminating Indigenous Jurisdictions: Federalism, the Supreme Court of Canada, and Territorial Rationalities of Power." *Canadian Journal of Political Science* 49, no. 3 (2016): 411–31.

McGarry, John. "Asymmetric Autonomy in the United Kingdom." In *Asymmetric Autonomy and the Settlement of Ethnic Conflicts*, edited by Marc Weller and Katherine Nobbs, 148–79. Philadelphia: University of Pennsylvania Press, 2012.

McGarry, John. "Asymmetry in Federations, Federacies and Unitary States." *Ethnopolitics* 6, no. 1 (2007): 105–16.

McKerracher, Kelty. "Relational Legal Pluralism and Indigenous Legal Orders in Canada." *Global Constitutionalism* 12, no. 1 (2023): 133–53.

Michaels, Ralf. "Global Legal Pluralism." *Annual Review of Law and Social Science* 5, no. 1 (2009): 243–62.

Milne, David. "Asymmetry in Canada: Past and Present." *Asymmetry Series – IIGR, Queen's University*, 2005, 1–8.

Milne, David. "Equality or Asymmetry: Why Choose?" In *Options for a New Canada*, edited by Ronald L Watts and Douglas M. Brown, 285–307. Toronto: University of Toronto Press, 1991.

Monti, Matteo. *Federalismo disintegrativo. Secessione e asimmetria in Italia e Spagna*. Torino: Giappichelli Editore, 2021.

Motta, Riccardo. "Approccio classico e approccio critico al pluralismo giuridico." *Materiali per una storia della cultura giuridica*, no. 2 (2004): 345–62.

Olivetti, Marco. "Il federalismo asimmetrico belga e le sue recenti evoluzioni." In *Integrazione europea e asimmetrie regionali*, edited by Guerino D'Ignazio, 63–90. Milan: Giuffrè, 2007.

Olivetti, Marco. "Il regionalismo differenziato alla prova dell'esame parlamentare." *Federalismi.it* 6 (2019): 2–40.

Örücü, Esin. "What Is a Mixed Legal System: Exclusion or Expansion?" *Journal of Comparative Law* 3, no. 1 (2008): 34–52.

Otto, Jan Michiel, ed. *Sharia Incorporated: A Comparative Overview of the Legal Systems of Twelve Muslim Countries in Past and Present*. Leiden: Leiden University Press, 2010.

Palermo, Francesco. "Asimmetria come forma e formante dei sistemi composti." *Istituzioni del Federalismo* 2 (2018): 255–71.

Palermo, Francesco. "«Divided We Stand». L'asimmetria negli ordinamenti composti." In *Processi di devolution e transizioni costituzionali negli Stati unitari (dal Regno Unito all'Europa)*, edited by Alessandro Torre, 149–69. Torino: Giappichelli Editore, 2007.

Palermo, Francesco. "Federalismo asimmetrico e riforma della Costituzione italiana." *Le Regioni*, no. 2/3 (1997): 291–310.

Palermo, Francesco. "La coincidenza degli opposti: l'ordinamento tedesco e il federalismo asimmetrico." *Federalismi.it*, no. 3 (2017): 18.

Palermo, Francesco, Karl Kössler, and Carolin Zwilling, eds. *Asymmetries in Constitutional Law. Recent Developments in Federal and Regional Systems*. Bolzano/Bozen: Accademia Europea di Bolzano, 2009.

Palmer, Valentine Vernon. "Mixed Legal Systems." In *The Cambridge Companion to Comparative Law*, edited by Mauro Bussani and Ugo Mattei, 368–83. Cambridge: Cambridge University Press, 2012.

Palmer, Valentine Vernon. "Mixed Legal Systems ... and the Myth of Pure Laws." *Louisiana Law Review* 67, no. 4 (2007): 1205–18.

Palmer, Valentine Vernon. "Two Rival Theories of Mixed Legal Systems." *Journal of Comparative Law* 3, no. 1 (2008): 7–33.

Palmer, Valentine Vernon, Mohamed Y. Mattar, and Anna Koppel, eds. *Mixed Legal Systems, East and West.* Wey Court East, Union Farm, Farnham, Surrey, England ; Burlington, VT: Ashgate, 2015.

Plessis, Jacques du. "Comparative Law and the Study of Mixed Legal Systems." In *The Oxford Handbook of Comparative Law*, edited by Mathias Reimann and Reinhard Zimmermann, 2nd ed., 474–501. Oxford: Oxford University Press, 2019.

Popelier, Patricia, and Maja Sahadžić, eds. *Constitutional Asymmetry in Multinational Federalism.* Cham: Palgrave Macmillan, 2019.

Requejo, Ferran, and Klaus-Jürgen Nagel, eds. *Federalism Beyond Federations. Asymmetry and Processes of Resymmetrisation in Europe.* Farnham, England: Ashgate, 2011.

Rinella, Angelo. *La Shari'a in Occidente. Giurisdizioni e diritto islamico: Regno Unito, Canada e Stati Uniti d'America.* Bologna: Il Mulino, 2021.

Rinella, Angelo. "Pluralismo giuridico e giurisdizioni religiose alternative." *DPCE online*, no. 4 (2018): 1005–13.

Rinella, Angelo, and Maria Francesca Cavalcanti. "I Tribunali islamici in Occidente: Gran Bretagna e Grecia, profili di diritto comparato." *Diritto Pubblico Comparato ed Europeo*, no. 1 (2017): 69–118.

Rolla, Giancarlo. "Alcune considerazioni in merito al fondamento costituzionale del regionalismo speciale. L'apporto del diritto comparato." *Federalismi.it*, no. 13 (2015): 2–22.

Rolla, Giancarlo. "Federalismo e regionalismo in Europa. Alcune riflessioni sulle dinamiche in atto." *Diritto Pubblico Comparato ed Europeo*, no. Speciale (2019): 657–84.

Rolla, Giancarlo. "Federalismo e regionalismo in tempi di transizione." *Federalismi.it* 2/2018 (2018): 2–22.

Ruskola, Teemu. "Legal Orientalism." *Michigan Law Review* 101, no. 1 (2002): 179–234.

Russo, Anna Margherita. *Pluralismo territoriale e integrazione europea: asimmetria e relazionalità nello Stato autonomico spagnolo. Profili comparati (Belgio e Italia).* Napoli: Editoriale scientifica, 2010.

Ryan, Erin. "Federalism as Legal Pluralism." In *The Oxford Handbook of Global Legal Pluralism*, edited by Paul Schiff Berman, 491–531. Oxford: Oxford University Press, 2020.

Sahadžić, Maja. *Asymmetry, Multinationalism and Constitutional Law: Managing Legitimacy and Stability in Federalist States.* London; New York: Routledge, 2020.

Sahadžić, Maja. "Constitutional Asymmetry and Equality in Multinational Systems with Federal Arrangements." In *The Principle of Equality in Diverse States: Reconciling Autonomy with Equal Rights and Opportunities*, edited by Eva Maria Belser, et al., 36–61. Leiden: Brill, 2021.

Sahadžić, Maja, and Patricia Popelier. "Constitutional Asymmetry Through an Empirical Lens: A Federal Device for Diverse Systems." In *Comparative Federalism*, edited by Félix Mathieu, Dave Guénette, and Alain-G. Gagnon, 45–65. Cham: Springer Nature Switzerland, 2024.

Saïd, Edward W. *Orientalism*. New York: Pantheon Books, 1978.

Salim, Arskal. *Contemporary Islamic Law in Indonesia: Sharia and Legal Pluralism*. Exploring Muslim Contexts. Edinburgh: Edinburgh Univ. Press, 2015.

Saunders, Cheryl. "International Involvement in Constitution Making." In *Comparative Constitution Making*, edited by David Landau and Hanna Lerner, 69–89. Cheltenham, UK and Northampton, MA: Edward Elgar Publishing, 2019.

Saxena, Rekha. "Asymmetrical Federalism in India: Promoting Secession or Accommodating Diversity?" In *Revisiting Unity and Diversity in Federal Countries*, edited by Alain-G. Gagnon and Michael Burgess, 362–76. Leiden and Boston: Brill | Nijhoff, 2018.

Suberu, Rotimi T. "Religion and Institutions: Federalism and the Management of Conflicts over Sharia in Nigeria." *Journal of International Development* 21, no. 4 (2009): 547–60.

Tarlton, Charles D. "Symmetry and Asymmetry as Elements of Federalism: A Theoretical Speculation." *The Journal of Politics* 27, no. 4 (1965): 861–74.

Toniatti, Roberto, and Davide Strazzari, eds. *Legal Pluralism in Europe and the Ordre Public Exception: Normative and Judicial Perspectives*. Trento: The Pluralist Papers Ebooks, 2016.

Watts, Ronald. *Comparing Federal Systems*. 3rd ed. Montréal and Kingston: McGill-Queen's University Press, 2008.

Watts, Ronald L. "A Comparative Perspective On Asymmetry In Federations." *Asymmetry Series – IIGR, Queen's University*, no. 4 (2005): 1–7.

Weller, Marc, and Katherine Nobbs, eds. *Asymmetric Autonomy and the Settlement of Ethnic Conflicts*. Philadelphia: University of Pennsylvania Press, 2010.

Yadudu, Auwalu H. "Colonialism and the Transformation of Islamic Law in Northern States of Nigeria." *Journal of Legal Pluralism and Unofficial Law*, no. 32 (1992): 103–40.

CHAPTER 3

Constitutional Asymmetries from a Comparative Perspective

1 Introduction

This chapter delves into the comparison across case studies and concludes the first part of the book dedicated to constitutional design. First, the chapter tackles some necessary methodological considerations related to the comparative method, retracing the debate on the comparative method, outlining the main comparative constitutional law methodologies, and explaining the case selection criteria. This first paragraph situates the book within the current methodological debate in comparative law, with a particular interest in two developing fields: empirical legal studies, and decolonial legal studies. The book relates to both insofar as it employs standardised indexes to analyse a medium-N universe of cases to conduct the comparative analysis and aims to consistently include the constitutional traditions of the Global South.

Then, the rest of the chapter addresses in detail the comparison of cases for each degree of asymmetry (i.e., low, medium, and high), first commenting on the subnational autonomy scores and then on the resulting asymmetry scores. The focal point of interest is to explore the different manifestations of asymmetries, assessing whether asymmetry is pervasive across all dimensions (i.e., status, powers, fiscal arrangements) or conversely only concentrated in one or a few dimensions, but not all. For each case study, subnational autonomy and asymmetry are first reviewed in detail at the subnational entity level and then overall at the country level.[1]

Moreover, for each degree of asymmetry, the chapter also considers the asymmetries "in action", as it aims at not ignoring the reality of implementation and the relative impact on the constitutional and political system. Indeed, the book focuses on asymmetries as entrenched in the constitutional and legal framework, but this does not necessarily mean that they are translated into (or reflect) reality.

1 See the Appendices for subnational autonomy scores for each dimension and at the country level, and the original and converted values of constitutional asymmetry for each dimension and at the country level.

 | DOI:10.1163/9789004739109_005

Before delving into the comparative analysis, it should be briefly remembered that to measure constitutional asymmetry in each constitutional system, first the subnational autonomy scores were measured for two selected subnational entities, according to a "most different" selection logic,[2] and then these scores were subtracted to derive the constitutional asymmetry scores. Subnational autonomy and thus constitutional asymmetry were conceptualised along three dimensions: status, powers, and fiscal arrangements.[3]

Along Popelier's analytical strategy for measuring subnational autonomy and cohesion, the resulting constitutional asymmetry scores, for each dimension and at the country level, are converted to values between 0 and 1 to enable a coherent comparison.[4] Moreover, percentiles are used to qualify the degrees of asymmetry and of subnational autonomy as low (0.00–0.33), medium (0.34–0.66), and high (0.67–1.00).

Table 3.1 summarises the degrees of asymmetry, both for each dimension and at the country level. From Table 3.1, it emerges that some systems display symmetry in some dimensions of subnational autonomy, despite being asymmetrical overall and in other dimensions. For instance, in Bosnia and Herzegovina, asymmetry overall is low, and more specifically is medium in status and low in powers, but absent in fiscal arrangements. Similarly, in Canada, the only asymmetrical dimension is status, whereas the other two dimensions are completely symmetrical. Moreover, it emerges that asymmetry does not maintain the same degree across dimensions, as neither case displays the same degree of asymmetry consistently in every dimension. Even in the cases with a high degree of asymmetry, there is one dimension with a lower degree than the others. This the case in the UK and Iraq, which display a high degree of asymmetry overall and in two dimensions out of three, but a medium degree of asymmetry in the remaining one. As explained in Chapter 2, this outcome confirms that the proposed method to measure asymmetry enables a more refined analysis, combining the use of quantitative and qualitative methods.

According to the degrees of constitutional asymmetry at the country level (i.e., "overall degree" column) shown in Table 3.1, among the 12 case studies there are four cases with a low degree of constitutional asymmetry (Canada, Indonesia, Bosnia and Herzegovina, Malaysia), six cases with a medium degree of constitutional asymmetry (Spain, Italy, Pakistan, Belgium, India,

2 See Hirschl, "The Question of Case Selection," 139–142.

3 See Chapter 2, paragraph 3, for more details on the measure of subnational autonomy and constitutional asymmetry.

4 Popelier, *Dynamic Federalism*, 84.

TABLE 3.1 Degrees of asymmetry in the 12 case studies (for each dimension and overall)

Country	Dimension of asymmetry			Overall degree
	Status	Powers	Fiscal arrangements	
Belgium	Low	Medium	Medium	Medium
Bosnia and Herzegovina	Medium	Low	Symmetrical	Low
Canada	Low	Symmetrical	Symmetrical	Low
India	Low	Medium	Medium	Medium
Indonesia	Low	Low	Symmetrical	Low
Iraq	High	Medium	High	High
Italy	Low	Medium	Low	Medium
Malaysia	Low	Low	Medium	Low
Myanmar	Low	Low	High	Medium
Pakistan	Medium	Medium	Low	Medium
Spain	Symmetrical	Symmetrical	High	Medium
UK	High	High	Medium	High

Myanmar), and two cases of high constitutional asymmetry (Iraq and the United Kingdom).

2 Methodological Considerations

2.1 *The Debate over the Comparative Method*

The field of comparative law has long discussed the challenges arising from the use of the comparative method. These criticisms have traditionally been related to the (im)possibility of "legal transplants"[5] and the relative Watson-

5 See William Ewald, "Comparative Jurisprudence (II): The Logic of Legal Transplants," *American Journal of Comparative Law* 43, no. 4 (1995): 489–510; Michele Graziadei, "Legal Transplants and the Frontiers of Legal Knowledge," *Theoretical Inquiries in Law* 10, no. 2 (2009): 723–743; Morton J. Horwitz, "Constitutional Transplants," *Theoretical Inquiries in Law* 10, no. 2 (2009): 535–560; Vlad Perju, "Constitutional Transplants, Borrowing, and Migrations," in *The Oxford Handbook of Comparative Constitutional Law*, ed. Michel Rosenfeld and András Sajó (Oxford: Oxford University Press, 2012), 1304–27.

Legrand debate based on modern-doctrinalist frameworks[6] or conversely on critical and postmodern theories.[7] As regards constitutional law, the comparative method raised a number of challenges.[8] Jackson links these to the goals and functions of comparison, such as to develop a better understanding of constitutional systems; to enhance capacity for self-reflection and to develop a better understanding of one's own system; to develop an understanding of normatively preferable "best practice"; and to answer questions asked by domestic constitutional doctrine.[9] These goals entail a series of obstacles, such as the time needed to develop expertise, language barriers, the difficulties in establishing normative concepts, and the risk of "cherry-picking". Jackson concludes that a good way to face these challenges could be a comparative analysis combining functionalism and contextualism (i.e., contextualised functionalism), in order to reconcile the strengths and weaknesses of both approaches.

However, the overarching challenge that comparative constitutional law faces is the lack of a solid framework for the methodological aspects of comparative analyses (e.g., its research design, case selection criteria, and data analysis), as extensively pointed out in the literature.[10] In this respect, while

6 See Alan Watson, *Legal Transplants: An Approach to Comparative Law*, London, 1993; Alan Watson, "From Legal Transplants to Legal Formants," *American Journal of Comparative Law* 43, no 3 (1995): 469–476.

7 See Pierre Legrand, "The Impossibility of 'Legal Transplants'," *Maastricht Journal of European and Comparative Law* 4, no. 2 (1997): 111–124; Pierre Legrand, "What «Legal Transplants»?," in *Adapting Legal Cultures*, ed. David Nelken and Johannes Feest (Oxford: Oxford University Press, 2001), 55–69.

8 On the challenges of comparative constitutional law, especially in constitutional adjudication, see also Cheryl Saunders, "The Use and Misuse of Comparative Constitutional Law," *Indiana Journal of Global Legal Studies* 13, no. 1 (2006): 37–76.

9 Vicki Jackson, "Comparative Constitutional Law: Methodologies," in *The Oxford Handbook of Comparative Constitutional Law*, ed. Michel Rosenfeld and András Sajó (Oxford: Oxford University Press, 2012), 69–70.

10 See for example Ran Hirschl, "Comparative Methodologies," in *The Cambridge Companion of Comparative Constitutional Law*, ed. by Roger Masterman, and Robert Schütze (Cambridge: Cambridge University Press, 2019), 11–39; Ran Hirschl, "The Question of Case Selection in Comparative Constitutional Law," *The American Journal of Comparative Law*, no. 11 (2003): 125–155; Ran Hirschl, *Comparative Matters: The Renaissance of Comparative Constitutional Law* (Oxford: Oxford University Press, 2014); Mathias Reimann, "The Progress and Failure of Comparative Law in the Second Half of the Twentieth Century," *The American Journal of Comparative Law* 50, no. 4 (2002): 671–700; Cheryl Saunders, "The Use and Misuse of Comparative Constitutional Law," *Indiana Journal of Global Legal Studies* 13, no. 1 (2006): 37–76; Bönnemann Maxim and Jung Laura, "Critical Legal Studies and Comparative Constitutional Law," in *Max Planck Encyclopedia of Comparative Constitutional Law*, ed. Rainer Grote, Frauke Lachenmann, and Rüdiger Wolfrum (Oxford: Oxford University Press, 2017). For some attempts at systematising

acknowledging the value of the classical approaches to comparative inquiry, Hirschl[11] argues that comparative constitutional law should be directed towards the "next level" of comparative analysis, namely "causal inference through controlled comparison",[12] allowing the researcher to make causal claims and better grasp the causes and the consequences of constitutional phenomena.[13] This approach thus aspires to build a theory through causal inference, as also suggested by King, Keohane, and Verba, and is based on the notion that a solid theory requires not only the clarification and description of concepts but also the development of causal explanations for that phenomenon.[14] A fascinating criticism of Hirschl's approach has been advanced by von Bogdandy, based on a Hegelian understanding of the law as an expression of "objective spirit". According to this understanding, legal scholarship is concerned with phenomena characterised by intersubjectivity and normativity.[15] Therefore, the main elements at the core of legal research are the understanding of normative validity, and the construction and maintenance of nor-

---

the comparative method, see Giuseppe de Vergottini, "Constitutional Law and the Comparative Method," in *Encyclopaedia of Contemporary Constitutionalism*, ed. Javier Cremades and Cristina Hermida (Cham: Springer International Publishing, 2020), 1–42; Stephen Gardbaum, "How Do and Should We Compare Constitutional Law?," in *Comparing Comparative Law*, ed. Samantha Besson, Lukas Heckendorn, and Samuel Jube (Lausanne: Swiss Institute of Comparative Law, 2017), 109–26; Christopher McCrudden, "What Does It Mean to Compare, and What Should It Mean?," in *Comparing Comparative Law*, ed. Samantha Besson, Lukas Heckendorn, and Samuel Jube (Lausanne: Swiss Institute of Comparative Law, 2017), 61–84; John C. Reitz, "How to Do Comparative Law," *The American Journal of Comparative Law* 46, no. 4 (1998): 617–636; Rodolfo Sacco, "Legal Formants: A Dynamic Approach to Comparative Law (Instalments I & II)," *The American Journal of Comparative Law* 39, no. 1 & (1991): 1–34; 343–401.

11 In particular, Hirschl refers to three main types of comparative inquiry: freestanding, single-country studies; comparative reference aimed at self-reflection through analogy, distinction and contrast; comparative research aimed at concept generation and thinking tools through multi-faceted descriptions. Applied to constitutional law, Hirschl proposed eight types of constitutional comparison: research on a foreign legal order; genealogical or taxonomical classification; comparison to find the best solution to a given problem (functional comparative law); comparative law to serve as a reflection on one's legal order; comparative law to illustrate theoretical assumptions; small-N analyses in a social-scientific style to find causal relationships; large-N analyses which find correlations based on statistical analysis (see Hirschl, "Comparative Methodologies," 18–19).

12 Hirschl, "The Question of Case Selection," 126.

13 Hirschl, "Comparative Methodologies," 18.

14 See Gary King, Robert O. Keohane, and Sidney Verba, *Designing Social Inquiry: Scientific Inference in Qualitative Research* (Princeton, N.J: Princeton University Press, 1994).

15 Armin von Bogdandy, "Comparative Constitutional Law as a Social Science? A Hegelian Reaction to Ran Hirschl's Comparative Matters," *MPIL Research Paper Series* 09 (2016), 2.

mative meaning, whereas Hirschl argues that a social-scientific explanation should occupy centre stage in the analysis. Conversely, von Bogdandy raises doubts about the effective contribution of causal inference and causal explanations since these are perceived as playing only a limited role in the understanding, interpretation, and application of the law.[16] Moreover, another element of disagreement between the two scholars concerns the leadership role attributed by Hirschl to comparative politics, at the expense of comparative constitutional law, as Hirschl argues that only political science methods formulate theoretical models and reach concrete and generalisable findings. For his part, von Bogdandy observes that this constitutes a limited perspective of the discipline and raises questions about the applicability of the methods proposed by Hirschl to the domain of comparative constitutional law.[17] However, the most fundamental point of divergence concerns the very aim of the comparative approach in constitutional law. If according to Hirschl the aim should be to explain, von Bogdandy claims that this would mean denying other forms of knowledge that go beyond mere description and classification and sit alongside causal explanations, namely the "hermeneutical understanding of intersubjective phenomena".[18] Therefore, he supports a hermeneutical procedure of comparative law, which aims to reach an understanding arising "from a synthesis of a multiplicity of elements in their manifold relationships".[19] What is interesting to note is that such an approach is not viewed in opposition to causal inference, but it warns against the perils of making causality the "supreme aim of research".[20]

Finally, the work of Meuwese and Versteeg is worth mentioning, as they advanced some proposals on the use of quantitative methods in comparative constitutional law.[21] In particular, the authors argue that comparative constitutional scholars might benefit from the methodological toolkit proper of comparative politics and comparative political economy. This would allow

16 von Bogdandy, "Comparative Constitutional Law as a Social Science," 5.

17 von Bogdandy, "Comparative Constitutional Law as a Social Science," 8–9.

18 von Bogdandy, "Comparative Constitutional Law as a Social Science," 10.

19 Ibidem.

20 Ibidem.

21 See Anne Meuwese, and Mila Versteeg, "Quantitative Methods for Comparative Constitutional Law", in *Practice and Theory of Comparative Law*, ed. by Maurice Adams, and Jacco Bomhoff (Cambridge: Cambridge University Press, 2012), 230–257. On the use of quantitative methods in comparative law, see also Pier Giorgio Monateri and Mauro Balestrieri, *Quantitative Methods in Comparative Law* (Cheltenham, UK and Northampton, MA: Elgar Publishing, 2023); Mathias Siems, *Comparative Law* (Cambridge: Cambridge University Press, 2022), 207–254.

researchers to "describe the law, engage in systematic comparisons of legal systems, and, if used properly, make causal claims".[22] Although they are aware that the use of quantitative methods in constitutional scholarship might be controversial, they advance three reasons to support their proposal. First, the use of such methods has the potential to test empirically the validity of causal claims that already permeate constitutional scholarship.[23] Second, quantitative methods might be able to manage the global dimension of the (global) challenges addressed by constitutional law. According to the authors, traditional methods, such as detailed case studies, are unable to "fully capture the globalising nature of constitutional systems around the world".[24] Once again, they recall the example of constitutional design in the post-Cold War era, arguing that a systematic empirical study[25] on the impact of constitutions on government behaviour is still needed, and could be realised through a large-N study using quantitative methods. Third, Meuwese and Versteeg observe that large quantitative legal datasets are increasingly available, and they would allow researchers to approach legal systems they are not completely familiar with.[26]

Within this methodological debate, this book is placed in an intermediate position, aiming to mix qualitative and quantitative methods to enhance legal understanding and explore constitutional dynamics, as also suggested by Meuwese and Versteeg,[27] and Siems.[28] Most importantly, this research is aware of the fact that comparative analysis cannot stop at the review of mere numbers, but rather should interpret the numbers to complement and refine understandings of complex realities.

---

22 Meuwese, and Versteeg, "Quantitative Methods," 233.

23 Meuwese, and Versteeg, "Quantitative Methods," 233–234.

24 Meuwese, and Versteeg, "Quantitative Methods," 234.

25 On the field of empirical legal studies, see for example Peter Cane and Herbert M. Kritzer, eds., *The Oxford Handbook of Empirical Legal Research* (Oxford and New York: Oxford University Press, 2010); Holger Spamann, "Empirical Comparative Law," *Annual Review of Law and Social Science* 11 (2015): 131–153; Kees van den Bos, *Empirical Legal Research* (Cheltenham, UK: Edward Elgar Publishing, 2020); Mathias Siems, "Empirical Methods," in *The Cambridge Handbook of Comparative Law*, ed. Mathias Siems and Po Jen Yap (Cambridge: Cambridge University Press, 2024), 157–76.

26 Meuwese and Versteeg, "Quantitative Methods," 235–236.

27 Meuwese and Versteeg, "Quantitative Methods," 256–257.

28 Siems, "Empirical Methods," 173–175.

2.2 *Comparative Constitutional Law Methodologies*

Traditionally, the issue of methodology (or, more correctly, methodologies) in comparative constitutional law has been explained through the argument that "methods vary in what they *aim* to do and in *who* is engaged in comparisons".[29] In fact, different actors have different goals and reasons to compare: scholars, adjudicators, and legislators are set in distinctive roles and contexts, which influence their respective methodological orientations while engaging in comparisons.[30] For instance, legal scholars may be interested in advancing research by drafting a "systematic taxonomical account of all forms and manifestations of a given constitutional phenomenon",[31] judges may look at other jurisdictions to address a case, while constitutional drafters may engage in comparison to explore relevant alternatives when seeking effective solutions to a problematic context.

To such distinctions based on the subjects and aims involved in comparison, Hirschl adds another basic distinction regarding the comparative aspects of three interrelated branches of constitutional scholarship, namely constitutional law, constitutional theory, and constitutional studies, and their respective comparative elements. Considering them separately, Hirschl defines the first as the study of constitutional texts, provisions, and principles; the second as the exploration of the "foundational principles and normative considerations that ought to guide the constitutional domain and its various stakeholders";[32] while the third is a domain which "complements legal and normative approaches to the study of constitutions, by deploying more social-scientific approaches and method to the study of constitutions and constitutional developments".[33] In relation to the current research, this last expanding body of literature in constitutional scholarship appears to be the one that better fits the purpose and method of this book, since "the constitutional domain is perceived as extending beyond constitutional texts, constitutional principles or constitutional jurisprudence, to encompass historical trends, political interests, economic incentives, strategic choices and power struggles that affect and are shaped by constitutional institutions".[34]

---

29 Jackson, "Comparative Constitutional Law: Methodologies," 54.

30 See also Giuseppe de Vergottini, "Constitutional Law and the Comparative Method," in *Encyclopedia of Contemporary Constitutionalism*, ed. Javier Cremades and Cristina Hermida (Cham: Springer International Publishing, 2020), 1–42.

31 Hirschl, "Comparative Methodologies," 17.

32 Hirschl, "Comparative Methodologies," 14.

33 Ibidem.

34 Hirschl, "Comparative Methodologies," 15.

On this note, it should be emphasised that Hirschl makes specific reference to the study of constitutional design, namely the core of this research, as a significant thread within this body of scholarship, since it combines "social-scientific empirical research with an explicit normative outlook".[35] As will be further explained in the next section, Hirschl recommends that social-science research methods are employed when attempting to better grasp constitutional phenomena in their broader context. Aside from these wider considerations, Hirschl suggests that the addition of the "comparative element" to these three branches of scholarship has created a broader catch-all category of comparative constitutional law, defined as "the study of constitutional systems or their various components across time and place, with an aim of generating some kind of analytical yield by the act of comparison".[36]

With this in mind, the following sections review the (sometimes overlapping) methodological approaches in comparative constitutional law scholarship.

2.2.1 Classificatory Approach

The first and most classic approach is the one concerned with the classification of different legal systems into the so-called "families" of law, exploring for instance the divide between civil and common law legal systems, or between centralised and decentralised constitutional review.[37] A distinct contribution to the process of classification is provided by "area studies", where a key issue is "whether there are distinctive features of constitutional development in a region",[38] due to prior occupation or colonisation, shared ethno-cultural heritage, or other geopolitical reasons. Legal scholars are not the only ones interested in legal comparison for classificatory purposes. In fact, political scientists also conduct classificatory studies focusing on particular elements of constitutional systems, e.g., electoral systems, parliamentary and presidential systems, federal and consociational forms of state organisation, which bring about new categories of constitutional systems or phenomena.[39] Moreover, in addition to works on "structural" issues, an emerging body of classificatory studies explore the trends in doctrinal and interpretative methodology, com-

35 Ibidem.
36 Hirschl, "Comparative Methodologies," 16.
37 Jackson, "Comparative Constitutional Law: Methodologies," 55.
38 Jackson, "Comparative Constitutional Law: Methodologies," 56.
39 Jackson, "Comparative Constitutional Law: Methodologies," 57.

paring the methodological approach of proportionality or balancing and formalism or originalism.[40]

As observed by Jackson, classificatory scholarship can be "backward-looking" in historical or intellectual ways, being concerned mainly with defining a framework for classification and analysis, or "forward-looking", being interested in identifying and analysing new constitutional phenomena.[41]

2.2.2 Historical Approach

Closely related to classificatory studies, the primary focus of the historical approach is to understand the development of constitutional law or constitutional systems over time, engaging in so-called "diachronic comparisons".[42] Jackson distinguishes between "genetic" and "genealogical" forms of connections among systems. The former is based on the influence that one system has on the development of another, while in the latter one or more constitutional systems grew out of another, typical of countries with a colonial past.[43] Scholars may examine how two or more systems originated from a common legal system, developing in similar or different ways over time. Moreover, they may also explore how legal concepts that exist in one legal system influence or migrate to another, focusing on the path of ideas as well as on how they are transmitted and received.[44]

The framework built by historical analyses seeks both to understand the development and functioning of a particular system (or set of systems) internally, and to make it accessible to readers from other systems.[45] In this respect, a comparison may be implicit or explicit, since the analysis can be drawn either from the description of other legal systems or by implicit normative or functional conclusions.[46]

2.2.3 Normative Approach

The third class of methodological approach has a distinct normative aspiration. According to Kommers, "the study of comparative constitutional law can be the search for principles of justice and political obligation that transcend

40 Ibidem.
41 Jackson, "Comparative Constitutional Law: Methodologies," 58.
42 See de Vergottini, "Constitutional Law and the Comparative Method," 19–21.
43 Jackson, "Comparative Constitutional Law: Methodologies," 58.
44 This last kind of historical work refers to Choudhry's concept of "migration of constitutional ideas" (see Sujit Choudhry, ed., *The Migration of Constitutional Ideas* (Cambridge: Cambridge University Press, 2009)).
45 Jackson, "Comparative Constitutional Law: Methodologies," 59.
46 Ibidem.

the culture-bound opinions and conventions of a particular political community",[47] leading to a universalist and normative approach to comparative constitutional law. Such a normative category may overlap with the other categories, since classificatory, historical, or functional approaches may be motivated by the search for transcendent constitutional principles. Having such an aspiration in mind, scholars examine foreign legal sources which aim at constructing a general theory, employing these sources to refine, support, or clarify their analysis. Recalling Hirschl's previous distinction, the normative approach falls within the domain of constitutional theory, whereas comparative analysis may be used to answer crucial jurisprudential or philosophical questions, such as the concept of the rule of law in different legal traditions, or the nature of constitutionalism.[48] Moreover, it should be added that being mainly concerned with fundamental rights, universalist scholarship tends to bring together constitutional law and international law, especially international human rights and humanitarian law.

2.2.4 Functional Approach

The functional approach is perhaps the dominant method in comparative analysis.[49] According to functionalism,[50] the focus of the comparison is (and should be) the function(s) of a particular institution or set of institutions in different constitutional systems. As observed by Jackson, functional work can be positive, not being concerned with normative questions but with "how different institutions may perform roughly equivalent roles, or how differences in institutional design may correspond with broader differences in political societies or behaviour".[51] Sometimes, it can be normative, when scholars aim at identifying what model of constitutional design or doctrine is the most suitable for producing normatively valuable consequences. However, the difference between the functional and the normative approach is in the technique of comparison, since functionalism is mainly focused on the functions of institutions or constitutional principles, and the questions of causation, rather than the purely moral and philosophical questions of the normative approach.

---

47 Donald P. Kommers, "The Value of Comparative Constitutional Law," *John Marshall Journal of Practice and Procedure*, vol. 9 (1976): 692.

48 Jackson, "Comparative Constitutional Law: Methodologies," 61.

49 Jackson, "Comparative Constitutional Law: Methodologies," 62.

50 See Ralf Michaels, "The Functional Method of Comparative Law," in *The Oxford Handbook of Comparative Law*, ed. Mathias Reimann and Reinhard Zimmermann (Oxford: Oxford University Press, 2019), 345–388.

51 Jackson, "Comparative Constitutional Law: Methodologies," 62.

The techniques through which it is possible to carry out functional comparisons may vary considerably. Jackson identifies three main techniques: conceptual functionalism, detailed case studies, and large-N studies.[52]

Conceptual functionalism partly overlaps with the classificatory approach, since scholars advance hypotheses about the reasons and ways constitutional institutions or doctrines function as they do, and about what categories or analytic criteria better explain these functions, referring to a limited number of systems to further conceptualise their hypotheses. These studies may also include economic or behavioural models of constitutional design, models that can be entirely theoretical or capable of being tested in reality against comparative examples. This further explains why this book described the field of constitutional design as "comparative in its nature".[53] For instance, legal scholars and constitutional drafters may engage in comparison to explore the relationship between different constitutional design models and the protection of fundamental rights, such as minority rights, by looking at different constitutional systems.

The second technique of functionalism is detailed case studies, an in-depth analysis of how constitutional institutions or doctrines actually work in practice, by analysing one or more systems. Case studies' analyses (should) involve a reasoned case selection process, as also suggested by Hirschl. More specifically, Hirschl suggested five forms of "logic" for selecting cases in comparative analysis.[54] The first is the "most similar cases" logic, initially proposed by Mill and later defined by the social sciences. According to this logic, "researchers should compare cases that have similar characteristics, [...] but vary in the values on the key independent and dependent variables",[55] thus isolating the significance of the key variable. This is especially suited to diachronic, cross-time comparisons within the same system. The other side of the coin is the "most different logic", which takes the opposite perspective: researchers should select cases that vary in all variables that are not central to the study, but have matching key variables, thus "emphasising the significance of consistency of the key independent variable in explaining the similar reading on the dependent variable".[56] Then, the "prototypical cases logic" provides that scholars should compare cases that serve as a "rep-

52 Jackson, "Comparative Constitutional Law: Methodologies," 63.
53 See Chapter 1, paragraph 2.1
54 See Hirschl, "The Question of Case Selection."
55 Hirschl, "The Question of Case Selection," 134.
56 Hirschl, "The Question of Case Selection," 139.

resentative exemplar of other cases exhibiting similar pertinent characteristics".[57] This logic is supposed to strongly support the arguments advanced by scholars since the cases that meet the criteria to be considered as a selected prototypical case are more likely to apply widely to others.[58] Moving to the "most difficult cases" principle, this is based on an overall idea that in formal logic would be considered as *ad absurdum*. In this way, "the confidence in the validity of a given claim is enhanced once it has proved to hold true in a case that is the most challenging or least favourable to it".[59] Finally, the "outlier cases" principle is designed to offer a new explanation for a phenomenon through the negation of valuable alternative explanations for that phenomenon.[60] Overall, a benefit of a detailed case study is the capacity to explore the ways in which different features of the system may interact with and affect the other institutions or doctrines, as well as appreciate these features in action.[61]

Finally, the third and increasingly popular technique involves large-N studies[62] designed to examine causal or collective patterns between constitutional features and other socio-political phenomena.[63] These kinds of studies rarely focus on doctrine or reasoning and are mainly conducted by political scientists, even though examples of large-N studies also exist in legal scholarship.[64] This technique is still under-developed, and draws from both qualitative and quantitative social-science methods.

It should be noted that although functionalism represents one of the dominant approaches in comparative constitutional law, it has attracted a number of critiques. For instance, Frankenberg suggested that it appears "all too easy", however the researcher tends to be unable to grasp the conceptual or socio-political foundations of legal orders other than the ones the researcher is fa-

---

57 Hirschl, "The Question of Case Selection," 142.
58 Ibidem.
59 Hirschl, "The Question of Case Selection," 145.
60 Hirschl, "The Question of Case Selection," 147.
61 Jackson, "Comparative Constitutional Law: Methodologies," 64.
62 See also Hirschl, "Comparative Methodologies," 30–34.
63 Jackson, "Comparative Constitutional Law: Methodologies," 65.
64 See for example the large-N study on constitutional longevity, by Zachary Elkins, Tom Ginsburg, and James Melton, *The Endurance of National Constitutions* (Cambridge: Cambridge University Press, 2009); Josephine De Jaegere, *Judicial Review and Strategical Behavior* (Cambridge: Intersentia, 2019); Patricia Popelier and Samantha Bielen, "How Courts Decide Federalism Disputes," *Publius: The Journal of Federalism* 49, no. 4 (2019): 587–616.

miliar with.[65] Similarly, Bomhoff warns against the perils of pure formalism, since doctrines with similar names and seemingly similar functions may actually mean different things in the reality of particular contexts.[66]

2.2.5 Contextual Approach

The core of the contextual approach to comparative inquiry is driven by the critiques moved against functionalism. Since the path adopted by public law has been described as particularly dependent on initial institutional choices, this requires close attention to specific systems operating in their own context.[67] Therefore, contextualism aims to uncover more about the context of a particular constitutional system, being concerned not only with the functions of constitutional features but also with its "socio-legal self-understanding or self-reflection".[68] Thus, contextual scholarship tries to problematise the sense of "false necessity" that may emerge from functional or universalist-normative approaches, seeking to elicit a more intense understanding of how particular paradigmatic social or political phenomena shape or are reflected in constitutional law.[69]

2.2.6 Post-/Decolonial Approach

The Eurocentric nature of modern comparative law has been a target of many criticisms, especially by the strand of literature known as postcolonial comparative law.[70] Postcolonial comparative scholars base their critiques on post-

---

65 See Günter Frankenberg, "Critical Comparisons: Re-Thinking Comparative Law," *Harvard International Law Journal* 26, no. 1 (1985): 411–456.

66 See Jacco Bomhoff, "Balancing the Global and the Local: Judicial Balancing as a Problematic Topic in Comparative (Constitutional) Law," *Hastings International and Comparative Law Review* 31, no. 2 (2008): 555–588.

67 See John Bell, "Comparing Public Law," in *Comparative Law in the 21st Century*, ed. Andrew Harding and Esin Örücü (London and New York: Kluwer Academic, 2002), 235–248.

68 Jackson, "Comparative Constitutional Law: Methodologies," 67.

69 See David S. Law, ed., *Constitutionalism in Context* (Cambridge: Cambridge University Press, 2022).

70 See Teemu Ruskola, "Legal Orientalism," *Michigan Law Review* 101, no. 1 (2002): 179–234; Daniel Bonilla Maldonado, *Legal Barbarians. Identity, Modern Comparative Law and the Global South* (Cambridge: Cambridge University Press, 2021); Judith Schacherreiter, "Postcolonial Theory and Comparative Law: On the Methodological and Epistemological Benefits to Comparative Law Through Postcolonial Theory," *Verfassung und Recht in Übersee* 49, no. 3 (2016): 291–312; Brenda Cossman, "Turning the Gaze Back on Itself: Comparative Law, Feminist Legal Studies, and the Postcolonial Project," *Utah Law Review* 2 (1997): 525–544; Sherally Munshi, "Comparative Law and Decolonizing Critique," *The American Journal of Comparative Law* 65, suppl. 1 (2017): 205–235.

colonial theories[71] and seek to overcome the role of colonialism[72] in comparative law.[73] Specifically, they have placed legal transplants within colonial expansion[74] and criticise the traditional classifications of legal families for their ethnocentric essence.[75] Accordingly, these scholars argue that Eurocentric comparative scholarship has not dedicated the necessary and adequate consideration to local culture and that the dominant position of the Global North and its legal traditions should be redressed.[76]

Despite the many attractive aspects of postcolonial comparative law, Salaymeh and Micheals have identified some limitations that risk reducing and distorting the innovative scope of postcoloniality. In particular, Salaymeh and Micheals criticise the view of postcoloniality as "importing insights from and about the Global South into a European liberal paradigm and thereby leaving Global South epistemologies behind".[77] Similarly, the two authors

71 See Peter Childs and Patrick Williams, *An Introduction to Post-Colonial Theory* (London and New York: Routledge, 1997).

72 On the different types of colonialism (i.e., *mestizo* colonialism, settler colonialism, and trade colonialism), see Ronald J. Horvath, "A Definition of Colonialism," *Current Anthropology* 13, no. 1 (1972): 45–57; Jürgen Osterhammel, and Shelley Laura Frisch, *Colonialism: A Theoretical Overview* (Princeton, NJ: Markus Wiener Publishers, 2005); Lorenzo Veracini, "Understanding Colonialism and Settler Colonialism as Distinct Formations," *Interventions* 16, no. 5 (2014): 615–633; Margaret Kohn, and Kavita Reddy, "Colonialism", in *The Stanford Encyclopedia of Philosophy*, ed. Edward N. Zalta & Uri Nodelman (Summer 2024 Edition).

73 On colonialism and comparative law, see Julie Cassidy, "The Legacy of Colonialism," *The American Journal of Comparative Law* 51, no. 2 (2003): 409–56; Shane Chalmers, "Colonialism and Law," in *Elgar Encyclopedia of Comparative Law*, ed. Jan M. Smits et al. (Cheltenham, UK and Northampton, MA: Edward Elgar Publishing, 2023), 282–91; Helge Dedek, "The Tradition of Comparative Law: Comparison and Its Colonial Legacies," in *The Cambridge Handbook of Comparative Law*, ed. Mathias Siems and Po Jen Yap (Cambridge: Cambridge University Press, 2024), 387–407.

74 Matteo Solinas, "The Nature of Legal Transplants – Inspirations from Postcolonial Scholarship," *New Zealand Association for Comparative Law Yearbook* 22 (2016): 179–216.

75 On taxonomies of legal families, see Ugo Mattei, "Three Patterns of Law: Taxonomy and Change in the World's Legal Systems," *The American Journal of Comparative Law* 45 (1997): 5–44; H. Patrick Glenn, "Comparative Legal Families and Comparative Legal Traditions," in *The Oxford Handbook of Comparative Law* (2019): 423–441; Mathias Siems, "Varieties of Legal Systems: Towards a New Global Taxonomy," *Journal of Institutional Economics* 12, no. 3 (2016): 579–602.

76 On the "provincialisation" of the Global North, see Dipesh Chakrabarty, *Provincializing Europe: Postcolonial Thought and Historical Difference* (Princeton: Princeton University Press, 2009).

77 Lena Salaymeh and Ralf Michaels, "Decolonial Comparative Law: A Conceptual Beginning," *Rabels Zeitschrift Für Ausländisches Und Internationales Privatrecht* 86, no. 1 (2022): 176.

are sceptical about the "provincialisation" of Europe and comparative law, insofar as "the application of postcolonial theory in the discipline has frequently resulted in merely inserting Global South vocabulary into Global North sentences about comparative law".[78] Therefore, according to Salaymeh and Micheals, postcolonial comparative law has not overcome the hierarchies of power relations between the Global North and the Global South, but rather has ended up reversing them.

Alongside these criticisms of postcolonial comparative law, some scholars have recently paid increasing attention to the application of decolonial theory to legal studies, and especially to comparative law.[79] Although decolonial and postcolonial theory partly overlap in that they both aim to address the role of colonialism and the supremacy of the Global North in legal production and legal scholarship, a number of distinctive elements of decolonial theory compared to postcoloniality can be identified. First, decolonial studies argue that the end of colonialism did not end "coloniality", framed as a way of thinking about power relations and legitimising colonialism and neo-colonialism while embracing universalism.[80] Second, decolonial theory "views coloniality as producing a myth of modernity",[81] as well as a narrative of colonialism as the driver of positive changes in the political, economic, scientific, and social domains. However, this narrative overshadows the enduring oppression of colonised peoples, and decolonial theory aims to acknowledge the fact the "freedom and progress of colonial societies cannot be disentangled from the

78 Ibidem.

79 See especially the work by Ralf Michaels, "Decolonial Comparative Law: FAQ," in *A Research Agenda for Comparative Law*, ed. Jaakko Husa (Cheltenham, UK: Edward Elgar, 2024), 61–86; Helge Dedek, "The Tradition of Comparative Law: Comparison and Its Colonial Legacies," in *The Cambridge Handbook of Comparative Law*, ed. Mathias Siems and Po Jen Yap (Cambridge: Cambridge University Press, 2024), 387–407; Roger Merino, "Decolonial Theory and Comparative Law," in *The Cambridge Handbook of Comparative Law*, ed. Mathias Siems and Po Jen Yap (Cambridge: Cambridge University Press, 2024), 408–25; Philipp Dann, "Southern Turn, Northern Implications: Rethinking the Meaning of Colonial Legacies for Comparative Constitutional Studies," *Comparative Constitutional Studies* 1, no. 2 (2023): 174–96; Lena Salaymeh and Ralf Michaels, "Decolonial Comparative Law: A Conceptual Beginning," *Rabels Zeitschrift Für Ausländisches Und Internationales Privatrecht* 86, no. 1 (2022): 166–88.

80 See Walter Mignolo and Catherine E. Walsh, *On Decoloniality: Concepts, Analytics, Praxis* (Durham: Duke University Press, 2018).

81 Salaymeh and Michaels, "Decolonial Comparative Law," 177. On the myth of modernity, see also Ulrich Beck, Wolfgang Bonss, and Christoph Lau, "The Theory of Reflexive Modernization: Problematic, Hypotheses and Research Programme," *Theory, Culture & Society* 20, no. 2 (2003): 1–33.

material and epistemic oppression of colonised (and neo-colonised) societies".[82] Third, the primary goal of the decolonial approach is to "expose the epistemic assumptions of the modernity/coloniality matrix",[83] resisting the "coloniality of scholarship".[84] Indeed, decolonial theory aims at rejecting the colonial construction of categories, such as national, racial, ethnic, religious, and gender classifications. Fourth, decoloniality addresses the power of universalism and coloniality by "delinking"[85] and decentring from Eurocentrism,[86] imagining alternatives to traditional categories such as the modern nation-state. However, decolonial scholars observe that delinking is not sufficient *per se* to overcome coloniality, and that "the reconstructive dimensions of decolonial scholarship are intensely challenging precisely because coloniality both eradicated many subaltern epistemologies and marks many epistemologies from the Global South as inadequate or antiquated".[87] Therefore, decoloniality aims to strengthen epistemologies from the Global South and develop anti-colonial epistemologies from other regions of the world. Finally, decolonial theory proposes "pluriversality"[88] as an alternative to Western universalism, "revealing options without any claim to universal truth or objectivity".[89]

Recently, decolonial theory has contributed to the emergence of the field of decolonial legal studies, more specifically in the study of international law,[90]

---

82 Salaymeh and Michaels, "Decolonial Comparative Law," 178.

83 Ibidem.

84 Ibidem.

85 On the concept of "delinking", see Walter D. Mignolo, "Delinking: The Rhetoric of Modernity, the Logic of Coloniality and the Grammar of Decoloniality," *Cultural Studies* 21, no. 2–3 (2007): 449–514.

86 Dann, "Southern Turn, Northern Implications," 177–178.

87 Salaymeh and Michaels, "Decolonial Comparative Law," 179.

88 See Bernd Reiter, ed., *Constructing the Pluriverse: The Geopolitics of Knowledge* (Durham: Duke University Press, 2018).

89 Salaymeh and Michaels, "Decolonial Comparative Law," 180.

90 See Antony Anghie, *Imperialism, Sovereignty and the Making of International Law* (Cambridge: Cambridge University Press, 2004); Arnulf Becker Lorca, "Eurocentrism in the History of International Law," in *The Oxford Handbook of the History of International Law*, ed. Bardo Fassbender and Anne Peters (Oxford: Oxford University Press, 2012), 1034–57; Matthew Craven, *The Decolonization of International Law* (Oxford: Oxford University Press, 2007); Nathaniel Berman, *Passion and Ambivalence: Colonialism, Nationalism, and International Law* (Leiden and Boston: Brill | Nijhoff, 2012); Lena Salaymeh, "Comparing Islamic and International Laws of War: Orthodoxy, 'Heresy,' and Secularization in the Category of Civilians," *The American Journal of Comparative Law* 69, no. 1 (2021): 136–67.

philosophy of law,[91] law and religion,[92] law and gender,[93] and constitutional law.[94] Specifically, decolonial approaches to constitutional studies have focused on decolonising societies and on "the constitutional recognition of plurinationality as a strategy for decolonising the modern nation-state's frequent imposition of national homogeneity".[95] This found space especially in the *neoconstitucionalismo latinoamericano*,[96] and the relative debate on the possibili-

91 See Peter Fitzpatrick, "The Revolutionary Past: Decolonizing Law and Human Rights," *Metodo: International Studies in Phenomenology and Philosophy* 2, no. 1 (2014): 117–133; Lena Salaymeh, "Decolonial Translation: Destabilizing Coloniality in Secular Translations of Islamic Law," *Journal of Islamic Ethics* 5, no. 1–2 (2021): 1–28.

92 See Lena Salaymeh, and Shai Lavi, "Religion is Secularised Tradition: Jewish and Muslim Circumcisions in Germany," *Oxford Journal of Legal Studies* 41, no. 2 (2021): 431–458; Timothy Fitzgerald, *Religion and the Secular: Historical and Colonial Formations* (London and New York: Routledge, 2014).

93 See María Lugones, "Towards a Decolonial Feminism," *Hypatia* 25 (2010): 742–759; María Lugones, "Heterosexualism and the Colonial/Modern Gender System," *Hypatia* 22 (2007): 186–209; Xhercis Mendez, "Notes Toward a Decolonial Feminist Methodology: Revisiting the Race/Gender Matrix," *Trans-scripts* 5 (2015): 41–56; Breny Mendoza, "Coloniality of Gender and Power," in *The Oxford Handbook of Feminist Theory*, ed. Lisa Disch and Mary Hawkesworth (Oxford: Oxford University Press, 2015), 100–122.

94 See Upendra Baxi, "Constitutionalism as a Site of State Formative Practices," *Cardozo Law Review* 21, no. 4 (2000): 1183–1210; Daniel Bonilla Maldonado, *Constitutionalism of the Global South: The Activist Tribunals of India, South Africa, and Colombia* (Cambridge: Cambridge University Press, 2013); Michael W. Dowdle, and Michael A. Wilkinson, "On the Limits of Constitutional Liberalism: In Search of Constitutional Reflexivity," in *Constitutionalism beyond Liberalism*, ed. Michael W. Dowdle, and Michael A. Wilkinson (Cambridge: Cambridge University Press, 2017), 17–37; Philipp Dann, Michael Riegner, and Maxim Bönnemann, eds., *The Global South and Comparative Constitutional Law* (Oxford: Oxford University Press, 2020); Emile Zitzke, "Decolonial Comparative Law: Thoughts from South Africa," *Rabels Zeitschrift Für Ausländisches Und Internationales Privatrecht* 86, no. 1 (2022): 189–225; Roger Merino, "Constitution-Making in the Andes: A Decolonial Approach to Comparative Constitutional Change," *Rabels Zeitschrift Für Ausländisches Und Internationales Privatrecht* 86, no. 1 (2022): 226–53; Sigrid Boysen, "Postcolonial Global Constitutionalism," in *Handbook on Global Constitutionalism*, ed. Anthony F. Lang and Antje Wiener (Cheltenham and Northampton: Edward Elgar Publishing, 2023), 166–84; Theunis Roux, "Grand Narratives of Transition and the Quest for Democratic Constitutionalism in India and South Africa," *Verfassung in Recht Und Übersee* 57, no. 1 (2024): 5–71; Erin F. Delaney, "Mapping Power: Constitutionalism and Its Colonial Legacy," in *Redefining Comparative Constitutional Law*, ed. Madhav Khosla and Vicki C. Jackson (Oxford: Oxford University Press, 2024), 385–98.

95 Salaymeh and Michaels, "Decolonial Comparative Law," 182–183.

96 See Jorge Benavides Ordóñez, "Neoconstitucionalismo, nuevo constitucionalismo latinoamericano y procesos constituyentes en la región andina," *Ius Humani* 5 (2016): 173–188; Roberto Gargarella, "Latin American Constitutionalism: Social Rights and the 'Engine Room' of the Constitution," *Notre Dame Journal of International & Comparative Law* 4

ties for overcoming colonial categories such as state power and territorial sovereignty, that systematically oppressed indigenous land rights.[97] Moreover, engaging with constitutional experiences in the Global South allows us to broaden the scope of constitutionalism by reflecting upon the colonial legacies of traditional Western categories such as democracy, human rights, and the rule of law.[98]

As noted by Salaymeh and Micheals, "a significant challenge for decolonial constitutional law may be imagining a decolonial constitution or demonstrating if a decolonial constitution can decolonise a state".[99] In this respect, the comparative method is key for "decolonising the study of law"[100] and systematically integrating the perspective of the Global South, both by studying the legal traditions and creating a genuine critical conversation among scholars. Indeed, Dann observes that "comparative law ultimately is also a hermeneutic exercise of understanding legal meaning. What is required is a layered narrative that takes into account constitutional text, interpretation, underlying the theoretical and ideological assumptions, as well as the multi-faceted contexts beyond the law".[101] Without any presumption as to whether it will be possible to find a definite answer to the complex nature of divided societies, the current research on constitutional asymmetries in divided multi-tiered systems aims at exploring "decolonial alternatives to meet the needs of indigenous and colonised societies",[102] promoting multiple legal options and reflecting upon

(2013–2014): 9–18; Almut Schilling-Vacaflor, and Detlef Nolte, eds., *New Constitutionalism in Latin America: Promises and Practices* (London and New York: Routledge, 2016); Felipe Curcó Cobos, "The New Latin American Constitutionalism: A Critical Review in the Context of Neo-Constitutionalism," *Canadian Journal of Latin American and Caribbean Studies / Revue Canadienne Des Études Latino-Américaines et Caraïbes* 43, no. 2 (2018): 212–30; Conrado Hübner Mendes, Roberto Gargarella, and Sebastián Guidi, eds. *The Oxford Handbook of Constitutional Law in Latin America* (Oxford: Oxford University Press, 2021).

97 María Itatí Dolhare, and Sol Rojas-Lizana, "The Indigenous Concept of *Vivir Bien* in the Bolivian Legal Field: A Decolonial Proposal," *The Australian Journal of Indigenous Education* 47, no. 1 (2018): 19–29; Roger Merino, "Reimagining the Nation-state: Indigenous Peoples and the Making of Plurinationalism in Latin America," *Leiden Journal of International Law* 31, no. 4 (2018): 773–792; Emile Zitzke, "A Decolonial Critique of Private Law and Human Rights," *South African Journal on Human Rights* 34, no. 3 (2018): 492–516.

98 See Dann, "Southern Turn, Northern Implications," 191–195; Sandra Fullerton Joireman, "Inherited Legal Systems and Effective Rule of Law: Africa and the Colonial Legacy," *The Journal of Modern African Studies* 39, no. 4 (2001): 571–596.

99 Salaymeh and Michaels, "Decolonial Comparative Law," 183–184.

100 Salaymeh and Michaels, "Decolonial Comparative Law," 186.

101 Dann, "Southern Turn, Northern Implications," 179.

102 Salaymeh and Michaels, "Decolonial Comparative Law," 184.

the consequences of the colonial imposition of national homogeneity in diverse states.[103]

2.3 *Case Selection*

To systematically select the 12 cases on which the comparative analysis is conducted, three main selection criteria were taken into account. The first criterion was that cases had to be classified as divided or partially divided societies. As anticipated in the Introduction, a divided or partially divided society is considered as such not just where it is ethnoculturally diverse but only if these differences also become markers of political mobilisation and translate into political fragmentation.[104] Therefore, societies that do not present both these features were excluded, as, for the purpose of this research, their being multicultural or diverse becomes irrelevant if it has no institutional or constitutional translation (e.g., the US). Moreover, it could be argued that most countries are now classifiable as multicultural or at least diverse to some extent, due to the effect of migration processes.[105] As Choudhry observes, "the age of the ethnoculturally homogeneous state, if there ever was one, is long over".[106] Aside from the conceptual clarifications, the main issue was how to detect a divided society. To this end, three elements were identified. The first and most obvious element is the presence of differences in language, ethnicity, culture, religion. Then, a rather evident indicator of a divided society is the presence of political parties[107] reflecting the political claims of distinct ethnocultural identities (e.g., the Bosniak-Muslim SDA in Bosnia-Herzegovina, the Irish-Catholic Sinn Féin in Northern Ireland, the Flemish N-VA in Belgium). The third element was whether the political conflict that arose from ethnocultural differences spurred a process of constitutional design. In Bosnia-Herzegovina, Belgium, and Iraq, just to name a few, processes of constitutional design or constitutional engineering were established to accommodate diverging political claims (as in Belgium) or even to re-design a post-conflict settlement (as in Bosnia-Herzegovina and Iraq). After all, this

103 See Dann, "Southern Turn, Northern Implications," 185–186.

104 See Introduction; Choudhry, "Bridging," 4–5.

105 See also Karl Kössler, "Beyond the Illusion of Ethno-Culturally Homogeneous Territory," in *Minority Accommodation through Territorial and Non-Territorial Autonomy*, ed. Tove Malloy and Francesco Palermo (Oxford: Oxford University Press, 2015), 245–272.

106 Choudhry, "Bridging," 5.

107 See Choudhry, "Bridging," 17–18; Donald Horowitz, "Ethnic Conflict Management for Policymakers," in *Conflict and Peacemaking in Multiethnic Societies*, ed. Joseph V. Montville (Lexington: Lexington Books, 1990), 116; Arend Lijphart, *Democracy in Plural Societies: A Comparative Exploration* (New Haven and London: Yale University Press, 1977), 3.

element recalls the very root of the literature of constitutional design for divided societies reviewed in the first chapter, namely the need to face the challenges posed by divided societies through a process of constitutional design. In conclusion, the three sub-properties to detect divided societies are: the presence of ethnocultural differences; the presence of (regional) political parties reflecting ethnocultural identities; and processes of constitutional design spurred by the political conflict among ethnocultural groups.

The second criterion to select cases was that they needed to be multi-tiered systems (MTS).[108] Given the flexibility of this definition, which could potentially include any constitutional system with any form of decentralisation, this research takes into account MTS granting legislative powers to their subnational entities. In this respect, a country such as Cyprus had to be excluded, since though the six districts provided for by the constitution do form a level of local government which is implicitly granted administrative autonomy, the constitution does not give any indication of the specific competences attributed to the district-level. Moreover, the two parts in which the island is divided are not constitutionally recognised. As in this book autonomy is constructed along the indicators of status, powers, and fiscal arrangements, Cyprus could not be meaningfully included in the analysis. However, the Cypriot ethnically divided society and its unresolved territorial reunification make it a perfect case study for a possible future application of the outcomes resulting from this research.

The third and most intuitive criterion was that cases had to display some degree of constitutional asymmetry, at least in one dimension. As the main focus of this book is constitutional asymmetry, some fascinating constitutional systems had to be excluded despite meeting the first two criteria. This was the case for South Africa, Ethiopia, Nigeria, and Russia that are widely asymmetrical *de facto* but not *de jure*.

In conclusion, the case studies meeting the three selection criteria are the following (in alphabetical order): Belgium, Bosnia and Herzegovina (BiH), Canada, India, Indonesia, Iraq, Italy, Malaysia, Myanmar, Pakistan, Spain, and the United Kingdom. It should be noted that the list resembles the one of Popelier and Sahadžić's research on constitutional asymmetries in multinational multi-tiered systems.[109] Given that the two studies are closely related, from both a theoretical and methodological perspective, it seemed reasonable to make reference to the same countries, not least to compare the respective

108 See Introduction (n 5).

109 See Patricia Popelier and Maja Sahadžić, eds., *Constitutional Asymmetry in Multinational Federalism* (Cham: Palgrave Macmillan, 2019).

outcomes of the analyses. However, some adjustments were necessary, leading to the exclusion of China and the European Union from the case studies. China does not qualify as a divided society as defined in this chapter, since despite internal ethnocultural differences localised in some entities, China is a one-party system, and therefore such diversity does not translate into the political system. Moreover, even though the European Union could classify as a divided system, it would have been the only supra-national system in the universe of cases; therefore, for the purpose of this exploratory study it was left out of the analysis.[110]

Based on the outcome of the selection process, three groups of countries can be identified for further specification: fully divided societies, partially divided societies, and formerly divided societies. The fully divided societies are Belgium, Bosnia and Herzegovina, Iraq, Malaysia, and Myanmar, since they display all three sub-properties across their entire territory: they encompass internal ethnocultural diversity, have regional or identity-based political parties, and experienced processes of constitutional design to address their internal diversity.

Then, the second group of case studies is composed of what this research calls "partially divided societies". Their inclusion was necessary to include more cases in the research, even though it meant adding a further level of specification to the selection process. Partially divided societies are considered those cases presenting the three sub-properties of divided societies only in limited parts of the territory and not necessarily in its entirety. This choice allowed me to include constitutional systems such as Italy, where internal diversity is concentrated in the subalpine regions (i.e., Aosta Valley, Trentino/South Tyrol, Friuli Venezia-Giulia); the United Kingdom, where distinctive identities are present especially in Northern Ireland and Scotland; and Spain, where constitutional arrangements were introduced to accommodate the Catalan and Basque nationalities. In these three cases, regional ethnocultural diversity is reflected in respective regional parties, such as the *Südtiroler Volkspartei* in South Tyrol and the *Union Valdôtaine* in Aosta Valley, the Scottish National Party in Scotland, and the Democratic Unionist Party and Sinn Féin in Northern Ireland, the *Esquerra Republicana de Catalunya* in Catalonia, and Basque Nationalist Party in the Basque Country. Another partially

110 Nonetheless, the European Union would be a perfect case study for future applications of the model emerging from this book, since it can be considered as a multi-tiered system having to deal with internal diversity (see, for instance, Giuseppe Martinico, "Asymmetry and Complex Adaptive (Legal) Systems: The Case of the European Union," *Maastricht Journal of European and Comparative Law* 21, no. 2 (2014): 281–99).

divided society is India, where the situation is slightly different because ethno-cultural diversity is widespread in the territory, but there is still a degree of specificity limited to some parts of the country. For example, the Muslim minority is concentrated in only few subnational entities, such as Jammu and Kashmir, Uttar Pradesh, and West Bengal, and there are also only a small number of regional parties, such as Shiromani Akali Dal (in Punjab), Jammu and Kashmir National Conference (in Jammu and Kashmir), and DMK (in Tamil Nadu). Then, the other two partially divided societies are Indonesia and Canada. In Indonesia, even though internal diversity is deeply entrenched in the history and demography of the country, regional political parties are only allowed in Aceh, one of the five regions enjoying special autonomy. In Canada, linguistic diversity is limited to Québec, home of the *Coalition Avenir Québec* and *Parti Québécois* which embody the autonomy and identity claims of the French-speaking province.

Finally, the third group of countries derives from the choice to consider a temporal perspective and include states that can be described as "formerly divided societies", i.e., constitutional systems that were divided societies but do not qualify as such anymore. This is the case with one specific country, i.e., Pakistan, where internal diversity still exists but no longer translates into political fragmentation as in the past. In Pakistan, such diversity was addressed through constitutional engineering and therefore it remains relevant for purpose of this research. Indeed, present-day Pakistan emerged after a civil war and the secession of East Pakistan, i.e., present-day Bangladesh.[111]

2.4 *The Potential Challenges of Heterogeneity*

One criticism that might be moved against the selection of such a variety of constitutional systems, belonging not only to different legal traditions but also to different forms of state, is that they are not actually comparable. Indeed, according to the EIU Democracy Index 2023,[112] only Canada, the United Kingdom, and Spain fall within the category of "full" democracies, whereas Italy, Belgium, Malaysia, India, Indonesia, and Bosnia-Herzegovina are labelled "flawed" democracies".[113] The three remaining cases, i.e., Pakistan, Iraq, and

111 See Shahal Khoso, "Postcolonial Federalism: A Conceptual Analysis for Tracing State-Formation in the Global South," *Nationalism and Ethnic Politics*, First view (2024), 1–24.

112 Economist Intelligence Unit (EIU), "Democracy Index 2023: Age of Conflict" (London: Economist Intelligence, 2024).

113 EIU, "Democracy Index 2023," 10–11.

Myanmar, are categorised as "authoritarian".[114] The debate over homogeneity as a strict requirement for legal comparison is nothing new in the field of comparative constitutional law. As noted by de Vergottini, "legal scholarship's emphasis on the requirement for system homogeneity for comparison, or on cautioning against simplistic comparisons, arises from the fact that the comparison is responsible for providing resources that will determine the adoption of constitutional texts or the harmonisation or unification of laws".[115] However, de Vergottini argued that this does not mean that heterogeneous comparisons, i.e., legal comparison among different forms of state, are not legitimate. Conversely, the study of heterogeneous systems is justifiable and legitimate within the field of comparison for scientific purposes, and as such it should not be dismissed. Certainly, the choice of heterogeneous systems must not be made lightly, and it should be relevant to the research goals and engage with in-depth analyses of the core elements of the respective constitutional systems.[116] Moreover, Salaymeh and Micheals, in their proposal for a decolonial comparative law, observe that a shared assumption in the methodological debate of comparative law is the "relative homogeneity within, and relative heterogeneity between, different legal systems".[117] This assumption necessarily implies framing the internal inconsistencies within legal systems as secondary elements, and not as constitutive features. In this respect, adopting a decolonial comparative approach contributes to "replacing homogeneity with plurality",[118] and acknowledging the multifaceted nature of constitutional asymmetries in divided multi-tiered systems.

Within the study of federalism, asymmetries, and courts, there are some notable instances of research exploring heterogeneous systems. Aside from the already mentioned research conducted by Popelier and Sahadžić[119] on asymmetry and multinational federalism, another recent work is the edited volume by Aroney and Kincaid on unitarist or federalist courts in federal countries.[120] The latter is a relevant example to recall because the authors explicitly acknowledged the heterogeneity of cases, noting that not all the examined federations were free democracies. However, they justified

114 EIU, "Democracy Index 2023," 12–13

115 de Vergottini, "Constitutional Law and the Comparative Method," 13.

116 Ibidem.

117 Salaymeh and Micheals, "Decolonial Comparative Law," 172.

118 Salaymeh and Micheals, "Decolonial Comparative Law," 186.

119 See Popelier and Sahadžić, eds., *Constitutional Asymmetry and Multinational Federalism*; Sahadžić, *Asymmetry*.

120 Nicholas Aroney and John Kincaid, eds., *Courts in Federal Countries: Federalists or Unitarists?* (Toronto: University of Toronto Press, 2017).

the inclusion of non-democratic systems precisely because they were interested in exploring the role played by courts in emerging democracies, assessing whether they took on a "consolidating role by ensuring horizontal accountability".[121]

Similarly, the choice of a wide variety of heterogeneous constitutional systems in the present study finds its justification in the fact that one of the main research objectives is to examine how internal diversity has been accommodated in different systems through the introduction of constitutional asymmetries and how constitutional courts have impacted the relative degree of asymmetry. Therefore, the main interest was not in how a specific form of state addressed asymmetry, but precisely in the variety of manifestations of constitutional asymmetry and relative constitutional interpretation across different systems. Indeed, the inclusion of heterogeneous systems allowed us to examine underexplored systems in the Global South and to appreciate how different forms of states introduced asymmetry into their constitutional framework as well as how courts interpreted asymmetry within the system. Moreover, the fact that democratic as well as non-democratic regimes have adopted constitutional asymmetries is also an indication that asymmetry can be regarded as a "neutral" constitutional instrument and is not inherently linked to the concept of democracy, further challenging the traditional Eurocentric assumptions about the relationship between federalism and democracy.[122]

Naturally, a series of challenges arose from such heterogeneity. Above all, the importance of avoiding a simplistic or superficial comparison entailed an in-depth exploration of complex cases, considering their relative constitutional and political history, as well as the often-mixed nature of the legal systems. To address the challenges of heterogeneity and avoid the risk of a purely formalistic comparison, this research acknowledged the tension between "law in the books" and "law in action".[123] Indeed, mere analysis of only the constitutional text would not have unveiled what Sartori called "façade constitutions",[124] leaving no implementation to the principles of constitutionalism. As will emerge in the rest of the chapter, each degree of constitutional asymmetry was first analysed as it is framed in the constitutional framework and

121 Aroney and Kincaid, "Introduction: Courts in Federal Countries," 24.

122 See Michael Burgess and Alain Gagnon, eds., *Federal Democracies* (London and New York: Routledge, 2010), especially the comparative chapters by Ferran Requejo, John Kincaid, and Ronald L. Watts.

123 See Roscoe Pound, "Law in the Books and Law in Action," *American Law Review*, no. 44 (1910): 12–36.

124 Giovanni Sartori, "Constitutionalism: A Preliminary Discussion," *American Political Science Review* 56, no. 4 (1962): 861.

then contextualised to consider its actual implementation. This allowed the complexity of constitutional asymmetries to be grasped, discussing how apparently low asymmetry can have a dramatic impact on fundamental rights (as in Indonesia) and how formally high asymmetry is entrenched in power relations and the denial of internal self-determination (as in Iraq). Moreover, the choice to engage in a Global North/Global South comparison comes with the inherent challenge of comparing radically different cases (e.g., Iraq and UK). However, the reason behind this choice is related to the need for dialogue among constitutional experiences, from the Global North and the Global South, without implying any superiority of the "Western liberal model". Although it may provide a challenge arising from the decolonial comparative method, overall it provides incredible opportunities of theoretical dialogue across constitutional experiences.

3 High Degree of Constitutional Asymmetry

3.1 *Autonomy and Asymmetry*

The two cases displaying a high degree of constitutional asymmetry, i.e., the United Kingdom, and Iraq, both reflect a similar trend in terms of subnational autonomy. Indeed, in these cases the high degree of asymmetry derives from a rather significant differential in terms of the subnational autonomy held by the two analysed subnational entities. In both cases, one subnational entity enjoys a medium degree of autonomy, while the other has an extremely low degree of autonomy.

The following subparagraphs look more closely at each case and their respective dimension of subnational autonomy (i.e., status, powers, fiscal arrangements), as well as at the resulting degree of asymmetry.

3.1.1 The United Kingdom

The case of the United Kingdom is rather peculiar because of the unique position of England in the British constitutional system, and some considerations had to be taken into account in order to measure subnational autonomy.[125]

125 On devolution and asymmetry in the United Kingdom, see John McGarry, "Asymmetric Autonomy in the United Kingdom," in *Asymmetric Autonomy and the Settlement of Ethnic Conflicts*, ed. Marc Weller and Katherine Nobbs (Philadelphia: University of Pennsylvania Press, 2012), 148–79; Sara Parolari, "Asymmetrical Devolutionary Tendencies and Policy-Making in the United Kingdom," in *Asymmetries in Constitutional Law*, ed. Francesco Palermo, Karl Kössler, and Carolin Zwilling (Bolzano/Bozen: Accademia Eu-

Currently, England has no distinct parliament and government, and the relative powers and competences are exercised by the UK Parliament and government. For the purposes of this study, the decision was taken to equate England with a subnational entity with sub-tiers of local government, but with no direct legislative powers, only administrative or implementation powers. Therefore, the UK parliament and government were not considered and analysed as the English parliament and government, since to do so would have been conceptually incoherent, with the further risk that it would assimilate England with the rest of the UK, disregarding the other devolved nations. Parliamentary discussions of further devolution to England are currently ongoing, but as the Select Committee on the Constitution stated in its 10th Report of Session, "there are no obvious governance changes to provide England with a distinctive voice that command political and public support. Establishing an English parliament would crystallise England's relative strength – in population and economic terms – vis-à-vis the existing devolved legislatures. This would destabilise the Union".[126]

Keeping these considerations in mind, apart from England, the other subnational entity analysed to assess subnational autonomy and constitutional asymmetry was Northern Ireland (NI), given its peculiar status within the constitutional system and the post-conflict arrangements introduced by the Belfast/Good Friday Agreement in 1998.

Looking at the subnational autonomy scores, the difference, at least at the formal level, between Northern Ireland and England is striking. Indeed, Northern Ireland displays a medium degree of subnational autonomy in both the status and powers dimensions, as well as overall, with only the fiscal arrangement dimensions being low. Conversely, England has an extremely low degree of subnational autonomy, because as anticipated it has only limited autonomy in terms of status and powers. Looking at the country level, the average scores for subnational autonomy indicate a generally low degree of autonomy, with the only exception being the dimensions of powers which displays a medium degree of subnational autonomy.

---

ropea di Bolzano, 2009), 63–76; Claudio Martinelli, "Territorial Asymmetries in the Comparative Landscape and the UK Devolution Process," *Gruppo Di Pisa*, no. 2 (2020): 505–24; Claudio Martinelli, "Il processo devolutivo come specchio delle specificità costituzionali del Regno Unito," *Istituzioni del Federalismo*, no. 4 (2018): 393–410; Peter Leyland, "The Multifaceted Constitutional Dynamics of U.K. Devolution," *International Journal of Constitutional Law* 9, no. 1 (2011): 251–73.

126 Select Committee on the Constitution, "Respect and Co-Operation: Building a Stronger Union for the 21st century", 10th Report of Session 2021–22 (20 January 2022) – HL Paper 142, chapter 7, para. 230.

As one might expect, the resulting constitutional asymmetry is rather significant, with asymmetry being high in status and powers (as well as overall), and medium in fiscal arrangements. This is not surprising given the very limited autonomy that England is currently enjoying at a formal level. Indeed, the only domains in the status dimension where Northern Ireland and England are broadly symmetrical concern the legislative level, since at the central level, both entities are represented in the British parliament through their electorates, even though the central government has to consult the NI Assembly in matters within its competence, something that is not reserved to England (as it has no legislative assembly of its own). Moreover, neither subnational entity is directly involved in the appointment of the central-level executive. In terms of all other categories of analysis on status, the asymmetries between the two entities are extremely evident and pervasive. Indeed, Northern Ireland was recognised as an autonomous part of the UK constitutional system by the Northern Ireland Act 1998, with the Belfast/Good Friday Agreement providing that Northern Ireland can decide on its constitutional status through a popular referendum, thus leaving some space to leave the union and move towards the reunification of the Irish island. Moreover, the Northern Irish Assembly adopted a series of legislation on constitutional issues, concerning fundamental rights, political organisation, and identity issues, that can be regarded as a subnational constitutional text. Also, as regards procedure, this constitutional legislation was adopted without interference from the central level. Moreover, Northern Ireland has its own directly elected assembly and an indirectly elected executive, which make laws and decisions without prior central oversight. Finally, in terms of the organisation of courts, Northern Ireland has its own court system, albeit the UK Supreme Court (UKSC) is organised at the central level, and by custom and practice is represented in the UKSC with one judge. Conversely, in England, subnational autonomy is limited to the representation of the English electorate in the Westminster parliament, leaving space for English voters and representatives to make their voices heard.

In terms of asymmetries in powers, once again the two subnational entities are rather different and the only category of analysis where they are similar is the appointment of the UKSC judges, as both subnational entities are involved in their appointments through regional judicial commissions, i.e., Judicial Appointments Commission for England and Wales, and the Judicial Appointments Commission in Northern Ireland. However, as mentioned, by custom and practice, in cases that affect Northern Ireland, the Court gives its decisions in a chamber with a judge that is, in terms of geography or identity markers, representative of Northern Ireland.

Finally, the dimension of fiscal arrangements is the one where asymmetries are less evident, as neither England nor Northern Ireland has autonomous taxing powers, but the latter can introduce new taxes as well as tax relief.

Once again, it should be noted that the choice of England as one of the two subnational entities to analyse in order to grasp constitutional asymmetries significantly impacts on the resulting degree of asymmetry. If Northern Ireland were to be compared to Scotland or Wales, the degree of constitutional asymmetry would be substantially lower, as the devolution process in the UK has reduced asymmetries in recent decades. However, England is the largest subnational entity in terms of size and population, and the area from which the majority of MPs in the central parliament are elected, yet despite all this still has no devolved government or legislature of its own, making laws and taking decisions at the entity level. This contradiction was the leading reason why it was deemed interesting to include England in the analysis.

3.1.2 Iraq

A similar reasoning as for the UK underpinned the decision to include Iraq in the sample of cases.[127] The Iraqi Constitution currently recognises only the Kurdistan Region as a federal region, while the other tiers of government, i.e., the governorates, enjoy only limited subnational autonomy and of a mostly administrative nature. Although the Constitution provides for the establishment of other federal regions,[128] Kurdistan still remains the only established region. This is also due to the fact that, since the enactment of the 2005

127 On asymmetries in Iraq, see Raad Alkadiri, "Federalism and Iraq's Constitutional Stalemate," *Chatham House Research Paper Middle East and North Africa Programme*, 2020, 1–23; Peter Bartu and Aidan MacEachern, "The Devil Is in the Details: Iraqi Kurdistan's Evolving Autonomy," in *Federalism and Decentralization in the Contemporary Middle East and North Africa* (Cambridge: Cambridge University Press, 2023), 183–202; Sean Kane, Joost R Hiltermann, and Raad Alkadiri, "Iraq's Federalism Quandary," *The National Interest*, no. 118 (2012): 20–30; John McGarry and Brendan O'Leary, "Iraq's Constitution of 2005: Liberal Consociation as Political Prescription," *International Journal of Constitutional Law* 5, no. 4 (2007): 670–98; Brendan O'Leary, "Thinking About Asymmetry and Symmetry in the Remaking of Iraq," in *Asymmetric Autonomy and the Settlement of Ethnic Conflicts*, ed. Marc Weller and Katherine Nobbs (Philadelphia: University of Pennsylvania Press, 2010), 183–212.

128 The Iraqi Constitution at Art. 117 provides that "This Constitution shall affirm new regions established in accordance with its provisions.", whereas at Art. 119 it provides that "One or more governorates shall have the right to organise into a region based on a request to be voted on in a referendum submitted in one of the following two methods: First. A request by one-third of the council members of each governorate intending to form a region. Second. A request by one-tenth of the voters in each of the governorates intending to form a region.". However, the legal procedures to establish a new region are

Constitution, the governorates that intended to organise as regions failed in their attempts.[129]

Therefore, in Iraq we can observe the reverse of the UK. Whereas England is the only subnational entity enjoying significantly less or even no autonomy compared to the others, in Iraq it is the opposite, with the Kurdistan Region being the only subnational entity enjoying significantly more autonomy than the others. The result in terms of subnational autonomy and constitutional asymmetry is rather similar. Indeed, the Kurdistan Region displays a medium degree of subnational autonomy across the indicators as well as overall. Conversely, the governorates enjoy a low degree of autonomy in status and powers, while they have no fiscal autonomy, given that the fiscal dimension of governorates is under the direct control of the central government. At the country level, Iraq is different from the previous case, because it displays on average a medium degree of subnational autonomy in the status and powers dimension, with only the fiscal arrangements dimension being slightly under the 0.33 threshold for medium autonomy, with a score of 0.32. Overall, the average autonomy score indicates that Iraq enjoys a medium degree of autonomy.

As expected, the resulting overall degree of constitutional asymmetry is high, with an even higher overall score (0.48) than the United Kingdom (0.45). As in the UK, in Iraq constitutional asymmetry is high across two dimensions (powers and fiscal arrangements) and medium in powers, but there is particular asymmetry in the fiscal arrangements dimension, whereas in the UK the highest asymmetry score was in the powers dimension.

Indeed, in Iraq, the most significant asymmetry in status emerges in the analytical category concerning subnational constitutional autonomy and the organisation of courts. In the former, the constitution provides that each region, and thus only the Kurdistan region, can adopt its own constitution defining the structure of powers and its authorities, and can adopt such a constitution without central interference. In this regard, it should be noted that despite being drafted, the Kurdistan Constitution was never formally

---

provided by the Law of the Executive Procedures regarding the Formations of Regions, Law No. 13 of 2008 (also known as "Law on Federalism").

129 It should be further noticed that governorates failed to establish new regions either because their requests were withdrawn at a later stage, or because these were denied despite the fact that the rules provided by the constitution and the Law on Federalism were followed. This especially affected the Sunni-majority governorates, which saw their constitutional right to hold a referendum to organise into a region denied by the central government (see Eva Maria Belser, "A Failure of State Transformation Rather than a Failure of Federalism? The Case of Iraq," *Ethnopolitics* 19, no. 4 (2020): 390).

adopted,[130] leaving this space for autonomy only "on the books". Moreover, concerning the organisation of courts, the Kurdistan region has its own court system, and is represented in the transitional Federal Supreme Court (according to Art. 92(2) of the Iraqi Constitution). In both categories, governorates have no subnational autonomy. Concerning the other categories (i.e., self-definition, legislative, and executive level), the differences are less evident, with both tiers of government enjoying roughly the same degree of autonomy, with governorates and the Kurdistan region having their own directly elected subnational assemblies and their own executive, but with a differentiated position for the Kurdistan region which has to be consulted by the federal government in matters affecting its interests or competences.

In terms of power, constitutional asymmetries emerge in the scope of powers and the allocation techniques, as the Kurdistan region has substantial powers in domains such as economic policies,[131] political control and organisation,[132] multinational conflict management,[133] and territorial management,[134] whereas governorates have very limited and non-substantial powers. Then, in terms of allocation techniques, the Kurdistan Region has mostly concurrent powers with priority given to subnational rule in case of conflict with federal legislation and with no central political oversight, whereas governorates have mostly administrative or implementation powers.

Finally, constitutional asymmetries in the fiscal arrangement dimension are at the extreme, as the Kurdistan Region has the power to set the base/rate of at least one major tax without upper or lower limitations by the central authority, and has the power to introduce new taxes, whereas governorates do not have taxing powers.

---

130 See Michael J. Kelly, "The Kurdish Regional Constitution within the Framework of the Iraqi Federal Constitution: A Struggle for Sovereignty, Oil, Ethnic Identity, and the Prospects for a Reverse Supremacy Clause," *Penn State Law Review* 114, no. 3 (2010): 707–808.

131 According to Popelier, the core competences in this category are economic expansion, import and export policy, regional aspects of credit policy, natural resources, commerce, tourism, transport, and energy (on this and the following categories, see Popelier, *Dynamic Federalism*, 140-141).

132 This category includes urban and spatial planning, traffic regulations, local police and public order, public services, establishment conditions, waste management, sports, and recreation.

133 Core competences in this category are linked to the protection of regional identity, such as culture, religion, education, and language.

134 This category can contain very diverse competences that may overlap with previous categories (such as spatial planning, transport, natural resources). The core territory-related competences not already included in the others would concern environment protection, land policy, agriculture and fisheries, local administration.

As in the United Kingdom, a high degree of constitutional asymmetry emerges because two very different types of subnational entities were included in the analysis. If other regions were to be established in the future, they would enjoy the same degree of autonomy as the Kurdistan region, leaving space for complete symmetry among regions. From a political perspective, this would mean reducing the differentiated position (and thus power) that the Kurdistan region is currently enjoying within the system, possibly reigniting internal conflict.

3.1.3 Comparative Overview

Looking comparatively at the results of subnational autonomy and constitutional asymmetry, we can observe a general trend. These two cases of high constitutional asymmetry derive from the difference between a medium and an extremely low degree of subnational autonomy displayed in the two subnational entities selected and analysed for each country. Indeed, the low degrees of subnational autonomy are comprised of 0.03 (i.e., England in the United Kingdom) and 0.14 (i.e., governorates in Iraq), thus are both rather close to 0, the lower extreme of the interval for low degree of autonomy. As one might expect, this generates a rather high spread in terms of subnational autonomy and thus of constitutional asymmetry. Moreover, we can observe that on average subnational autonomy tends to be low in all dimensions and overall. Iraq and to some extent the UK behave slightly differently, each having one or two dimensions (respectively status in the UK and status and powers in Iraq) going beyond the 0.33 threshold for medium subnational autonomy. Moreover, as mentioned, Iraq also has an overall average score of autonomy that is slightly over the 0.33 threshold, thus a medium degree of subnational autonomy at the country-level that is not as low as the UK.

Moreover, in the UK and Iraq, the two constitutional systems grant a differentiated level of subnational autonomy to only one specific part of the territory, respectively England and the Kurdistan Region. As already observed, these are the converse of each other, since the former enjoys significantly less autonomy, while the latter significantly more than the other subnational entities. Therefore, we can tentatively conclude that high constitutional asymmetry is displayed in constitutional systems that overall enjoy a relatively low degree of subnational autonomy, with limited parts of the territory enjoying significantly less autonomy than the others. Indeed, high constitutional asymmetry does not appear to derive from a differential between high subnational autonomy and medium or low subnational autonomy, but from a differential between medium subnational and low subnational autonomy, at the lower extreme of the interval.

3.2 *High Constitutional Asymmetry "in Action"*

For what concerns the asymmetries "in action" in the United Kingdom and Iraq, much has already been said in the previous section. If Iraq is unequivocally a case of high constitutional asymmetry, as designed by the 2005 Constitution, it is still interesting to note that the United Kingdom can easily be considered a case of low constitutional asymmetry when excluding England as a unit of analysis. As mentioned, if England is not counted as a subnational entity, the other three subnational entities have become pretty much symmetrical over time, despite the asymmetrical development of the devolution system in the UK. Indeed, due to different analytical and methodological choices, the current research offers another perspective on asymmetries to previous works on constitutional asymmetries, where these were considered minimal in the case of the UK.[135]

4 Medium Degree of Constitutional Asymmetry

4.1 *Autonomy and Asymmetry*

The six cases displaying a medium degree of constitutional asymmetry, i.e., India, Myanmar, Spain, Italy, Pakistan, and Belgium, do not share a path to subnational autonomy as the previous cases of high constitutional asymmetry do. However, they do share an overall medium degree of autonomy at the country level. The following sections briefly review the variations among cases.

4.1.1 India

Before commenting on India's autonomy and asymmetry scores, it should first be clarified that the analysis of subnational autonomy, which took place in 2022, had to take into account the Jammu and Kashmir Reorganisation Act enacted by the Indian Parliament in August 2019, which dramatically redesigned the status and powers of the Jammu and Kashmir union territory, significantly reducing the autonomy it was originally granted by Art. 370 of the Indian Constitution. The legislative provision was challenged before the Supreme Court, which eventually confirmed the reduction of asymmetries.[136]

---

135 See for example Sahadžić, *Asymmetry*, 83; Brice Dickson, "Work in Progress. A Country Study of Constitutional Asymmetry in the United Kingdom," in *Constitutional Asymmetry in Multinational Federalism*, ed. Patricia Popelier and Maja Sahadžić (Cham: Palgrave Macmillan, 2019), 481.

136 For further details of the case, see Chapter 5, paragraph 4.1

Therefore, since this study is a picture of the current constitutional framework, Jammu and Kashmir was not chosen as a subnational entity to analyse, since the peculiarities in terms of differentiated autonomy were scrapped by the 2019 legislation.

Having clarified the choice regarding the Jammu and Kashmir subnational entity, it should be added that the two subnational entities selected for the analysis were a state, Nagaland, which enjoys some degree of differentiated autonomy as one of the states in the northeast (ex. Art. 371A of the Indian Constitution), and Chandigarh, a union territory enjoying (as is largely also true of the other Indian union territories) only limited autonomy.[137]

From the analysis of subnational autonomy in India it emerges that, overall, the state of Nagaland enjoys a medium degree of subnational autonomy, resulting from a medium degree of autonomy in powers, while autonomy is low in the other two dimensions of status and fiscal arrangements. The union territory of Chandigarh, on the other hand, overall enjoys a low degree of subnational autonomy, lightly traceable only in the status and the powers dimensions of autonomy, while it has no fiscal autonomy, since this domain is under the direct control of the central government. If we observe the average scores of subnational autonomy, bearing in mind the picture at the country level, it is possible to notice that subnational autonomy scores are low, for each dimension and overall.

However, in terms of constitutional asymmetry at the country level, this translates to a medium degree of asymmetry, as the differential between the medium autonomy enjoyed by Nagaland and the low autonomy enjoyed by Chandigarh is significant. This is traceable in all dimensions of constitutional asymmetry, with the highest score in the powers dimension. Specifically, the degree of constitutional asymmetry is low in status, whereas it is medium in powers and fiscal arrangements.

Indeed, in the status dimension, the main sources of asymmetry are the legislative and executive level at the subnational entity-level, and the organisation of courts. While Nagaland (as other Indian states) has a directly elected

137 On asymmetric federalism in India, see Harihar Bhattacharyya, "States Reorganization and Accommodation of Ethno-Territorial Cleavages in India," in *Territory and Power in Constitutional Transitions*, ed. George Anderson and Sujit Choudhry (Oxford: Oxford University Press, 2019), 81–98; Harihar Bhattacharyya, *Asymmetric Federalism in India: Ethnicity, Development and Governance* (Cham: Springer Nature Switzerland, 2023); Kham Khan Suan Hausing, "Autonomy and the Territorial Management of Ethnic Conflicts in Northeast India," *Territory, Politics, Governance* 10, no. 1 (2022): 120–43; Kham Khan Suan Hausing, "Asymmetric Federalism and the Question of Democratic Justice in Northeast India," *India Review* 13, no. 2 (2014): 87–111.

assembly, which as a rule makes decisions without central oversight with only potential oversight *ex post*, union territories such as Chandigarh do not have a law-making assembly. Similarly, while Nagaland has a directly elected executive which makes decisions without central oversight with only potential oversight *ex post*, Chandigarh does not have an executive of its own, as it is governed by the central level. In terms of the organisation of courts, in the Indian states, courts are organised at the central level according to an integrated system, whereas in union territories courts are organised at the central level. In terms of powers, Indian states have substantial exclusive powers over many domains, whereas Chandigarh generally only has administrative powers or implementation powers, as it is mainly administered from the central level. Finally, subnational autonomy in fiscal arrangements is rather limited in both subnational entities, but if in Nagaland at least some form of autonomy is provided by the power to set the base and/or rate of minor taxes and to introduce subnational taxes, in Chandigarh even such minor degree of autonomy is not provided.

As we can observe, despite constitutional asymmetries being present in all three dimensions, with the highest score in powers, the widest differences are actually in the status dimension, where asymmetry concerns the executive, legislative, and judicial level, leaving Chandigarh as a subnational entity enjoying only a "minimal" degree of autonomy.

4.1.2 Myanmar

Concerning Myanmar, the selection of the two subnational entities for the measurement of subnational autonomy and constitutional asymmetry involved the Shan state, the largest and richest state in Myanmar, and the Wa Self-Administered Division (SAD), namely the largest SAD in the system.[138] It should be clarified that despite being geographically within the Shan state, the Wa Self-Administered Division is not subject to the jurisdiction of the Shan state, and therefore should be considered a subnational entity of its own. The Constitution of Myanmar establishes the tiers of both regions and states, but

138 For federalism and asymmetry in Myanmar, see Michael G. Breen, "Asymmetry or Equality? Ethnic Nationalities in a Bamar-Dominated State," in *Constitutional Asymmetry in Multinational Federalism*, ed. Patricia Popelier and Maja Sahadžić (Cham: Palgrave Macmillan, 2019), 341–68; Michael G. Breen, "The Origins of Holding-Together Federalism: Nepal, Myanmar, and Sri Lanka," *Publius: The Journal of Federalism* 48, no. 1 (2018): 26–50; Pau Sian Lian, *Federalism in Myanmar* (Lexington: Lexington Books, 2023); Alan Smith, "Ethnicity and Federal Prospect in Myanmar," in *Federalism in Asia*, ed. Baogang He, Brian Galligan and Takashi Inoguchi (Cheltenham: Edward Elgar, 2007), 188–212.

since these are completely symmetrical, it was of no interest for this study to compare a state and a region, whereas the Self-Administered Division and Self-Administered Zones are an additional tier of government and represent clusters of nationalities.

From the perspective of subnational autonomy, the case of Myanmar is rather similar to India. On the one hand, subnational autonomy, overall, is medium in the Shan state. Its highest score is for the fiscal arrangements dimension of autonomy, with a score of 0.63 (quite close to the threshold for high degree of autonomy fixed at 0.67). In the other two dimensions of autonomy, i.e., status and powers, the scores are significantly lower and describe a low degree of autonomy. On the other hand, subnational autonomy is rather low in the Wa Self-Administered Division, with the score for the dimension of powers slightly higher than the one for status, and with no fiscal autonomy, similar to the Indian case of the Chandigarh union territory. Looking at the country level (i.e., the average autonomy score), the degree of autonomy is low in each dimension of subnational autonomy as well as overall.

As with India, also in the case of Myanmar, the fact that one of the two subnational entities has a significantly lower degree of subnational autonomy than the other translates into constitutional asymmetry. Specifically, it is possible to observe that constitutional asymmetry is low in the dimension of status and powers, but high in the dimension of fiscal arrangements, resulting in a medium degree of constitutional asymmetry overall.

Specifically, in the status dimension, constitutional asymmetry concerns the legislative and judicial levels. Indeed, in the legislative domain, the electorate of the Shan state is represented in the central law-making bodies and can initiate laws. It also has its own assembly directly elected, whereas the electorate of the Wa Self-Administered Division is not directly represented in the central law-making bodies and Wa has an indirectly elected assembly. Regarding the organisation of courts, the Shan state has its own court system, even though the Supreme Court is organised at the central level, whereas Wa does not have a court system of its own. Then, in the powers dimension, constitutional asymmetries arise in the scope of powers and in the allocation techniques, since the Shan state enjoys substantial powers in matters concerning economic policies, political control and organisation, and territorial management, whereas Wa enjoys powers only in the latter two domains. Moreover, in terms of allocation techniques, the Shan state has mostly concurrent powers with priority given to central rule in case of dispute, whereas Wa has mostly administrative or implementation powers. Finally, the dimension where constitutional asymmetry is most evident is the one on fiscal arrangements. Indeed, the Shan state has the power to set the base and/or rate of property tax, without upper or lower limitations set by the central authority, and the levying of specific taxes is reserved to the Shan state, whereas Wa does not have powers to collect taxes.

4.1.3 Spain

For the Spanish case, the two selected subnational entities were the Basque Country and Andalusia, as the goal was to analyse two autonomous communities (ACs) that would reflect the widest divide in terms of internal diversity.[139] Indeed, the Basque Country is one of the smallest ACs (and with one of the highest GDP per capita in the country), having a distinctive identity and enjoying special arrangements in one of the dimensions of autonomy (i.e., the fiscal arrangements). Conversely, Andalusia is one of the largest subnational entities in Spain, in terms of population and territorial size, with one of the lowest GDP per capita.

The two selected subnational entities appear to be rather asymmetrical in reality, but when it comes to their degree of subnational autonomy, and thus to the degree of constitutional asymmetry, the picture is rather different. The Spanish Constitution provides for equal subnational autonomy in the status and powers dimensions of the Basque Country and Andalusia, both enjoying a low degree of autonomy in status, and a medium degree of autonomy in powers. The only dimension of subnational autonomy where there is a significant divide is the one on fiscal arrangements, with the Basque Country enjoying a high degree of autonomy and Andalusia a low degree of autonomy. Looking at the overall scores, both subnational entities enjoy a medium degree of subnational autonomy. At the country level, the average autonomy scores confirm that autonomy in status is low, while in powers and in fiscal arrangement it is medium, leading to an overall medium degree of subnational autonomy in the country.

---

139 For decentralisation and asymmetry in Spain, see Paul Anderson, "Decentralisation at a Crossroads: Spain, Catalonia and the Territorial Crisis," *Ethnopolitics* 19, no. 4 (2020): 342–55; Luis Medina Alcoz, "The Spanish Approach to Asymmetric Federalism," in *Asymmetries in Constitutional Law*, ed. Francesco Palermo, Karl Kössler, and Carolin Zwilling (Bolzano/Bozen: Accademia Europea di Bolzano, 2009), 49–62; Pau Bossacoma Busquets and Marc Sanjaume-Calvet, "Asymmetry as a Device for Equal Recognition and Reasonable Accommodation of Majority and Minority Nations," in *Constitutional Asymmetry in Multinational Federalism*, ed. Patricia Popelier and Maja Sahadžić (Cham: Palgrave Macmillan, 2019), 429–60; Anna Margherita Russo, *Pluralismo territoriale e integrazione europea: asimmetria e relazionalità nello Stato autonomico spagnolo. Profili comparati (Belgio e Italia)* (Napoli: Editoriale scientifica, 2010); Matteo Monti, *Federalismo disintegrativo. Secessione e asimmetria in Italia e Spagna* (Torino: Giappichelli Editore, 2021).

In terms of constitutional asymmetry, this is only traceable in the fiscal arrangements, where the score is rather high (0.50). Indeed, the Basque Country enjoys significant fiscal autonomy through a special regime that is only shared by the autonomous community of Navarre. The Basque statute of autonomy provides that the autonomous community has the power to set the base and/or rate of at least one major tax (personal and corporate income), without upper or lower limitations or other constraints set by the central authority. Specifically, the special regime of the Basque Country and Navarre is constitutionally entrenched in Additional Provision 1 of the Spanish Constitution, according to which "the Constitution protects and respects the historic rights of the territories with traditional charts (*fueros*)".[140] The traditional roots of this privilege can be found in the so-called *concierto* in the Basque Country, and *convenio* in Navarre, granting the two ACs the power to collect taxes and bilaterally agree with the central state the amount (the so-called *cupo*)[141] to be paid towards the central state expenses. For the Basque Country in particular, the legal basis of its fiscal autonomy is provided for by Title 3 of its Statute of Autonomy and the fiscal pact currently in force under the Spanish Statute 12/2002. Conversely, Andalusia falls within the ordinary regime of fiscal autonomy as provided by Art. 156 and 157 of the Spanish Constitution and has no power to substantially set the base and/or rate of taxes, but only to slightly change them.

However, since the other two dimensions are symmetrical, the overall score for constitutional asymmetry is not considerable (0.17), thus the relative converted score (0.34) falls within a medium degree of asymmetry. It should be

140 Constitution of Spain - Additional Provision 1. Concerning Additional Provision 1, some authors have observed that it provides an interesting case of "asymmetrical interpretation of history as a legitimate source of rights" (Bossacoma and Sanjaume, "Asymmetry as a Device for Equal Recognition," 454). Historically speaking, other territories such as Catalonia also had their own laws and jurisdictions (*fueros*), including their own fiscal system. However, the constitutional interpretation of that provision excluded those territories where the *fueros* were not maintained over time, without any discontinuity. Looking at the political and constitutional history of Spain, it can also be noticed that Navarre and the Basque Country maintained such historic privilege thanks to their support for the conservative reign of King Charles in the XIX century, when the *concierto* and *convenio* began. Some critics also suggest that such continuity was a reward for the non-opposition to the 1936 *coup* which brought Franco to power (see Bossacoma and Sanjaume, "Asymmetry as a Device for Equal Recognition," 454).

141 On the asymmetries in the Spanish taxing system, see Violeta Ruiz Almendral, "The Asymmetric Distribution of Taxation Powers in the Spanish State of Autonomies: The Common System and the *Foral* Tax Regimes," *Regional & Federal Studies* 13, no. 4 (2003): 41–66.

further noted that a converted score of 0.34 means that Spain is placed at the lower end of the interval for medium degree, only slightly over the 0.33 threshold between low and medium degree.

4.1.4 Italy

For the Italian case, the choice of the two subnational entities had to take into account that the Italian Constitution provided for two types of regions, i.e., special and ordinary, the former enjoying differentiated autonomy.[142] Therefore, the selection involved a special region, i.e., Aosta Valley, that is also the smallest in terms of size and population, and an ordinary region, i.e., Lombardy, which is also one of the biggest in terms of size and population. An additional reason to choose Lombardy is that it is among the ordinary regions that expressed their intention to negotiate for more autonomy as allowed by Art. 116(3) of the Italian Constitution.[143]

The two subnational entities enjoy different degrees of subnational autonomy across the dimensions. Indeed, Aosta Valley enjoys a medium degree of autonomy in status, but a high degree in powers and fiscal arrangements, producing an overall high degree of subnational autonomy. Conversely, Lombardy enjoys a medium degree in all three dimensions, as well as overall. At the country level, the average autonomy scores indicate that autonomy is medium in status and powers, while high in fiscal arrangements, producing an overall medium degree of subnational autonomy.

Constitutional asymmetry is present in all three dimensions, but to different degrees. Indeed, asymmetry is low in status and fiscal arrangements, given

---

142 On asymmetric regionalism in Italy, see Paolo Colasante, "Unity and Diversity in Italy (Partially) Asymmetric Regionalism in Light of Contemporary Constitutional Reform" in *Revisiting Unity and Diversity in Federal Countries*, ed. Alain-G. Gagnon, and Michael Burgess (Leiden and Boston: Brill | Nijhoff, 2018), 206–229; Monti, *Federalismo disintegrativo*, 291–310; Antonio D'Atena, "Passato, presente ... e futuro delle autonomie regionali speciali," *Rivista AIC*, no. 4 (2014): 1–15; Marco Olivetti, "Il regionalismo differenziato alla prova dell'esame parlamentare," *Federalismi.it* 6 (2019): 2–40; Giancarlo Rolla, "L'evoluzione dello Stato regionale in Italia: tra crisi del regionalismo omogeneo e aspirazioni a un'autonomia asimmetrica dei territori," *Le Regioni* 47, no. 1 (2019): 141–184; Giancarlo Rolla, "Alcune considerazioni in merito al fondamento costituzionale del regionalismo speciale. L'apporto del diritto comparato," *Federalismi.it*, no. 13 (2015): 2–22; Francesco Palermo and Alice Valdesalici, "Irreversibly Different," in *Constitutional Asymmetry in Multinational Federalism*, ed. Patricia Popelier and Maja Sahadžić (Cham: Palgrave Macmillan, 2019), 287–314; Francesco Palermo, "Federalismo asimmetrico e riforma della Costituzione italiana," *Le Regioni*, no. 2–3 (1997).

143 See Lorenza Violini, "L'autonomia delle Regioni italiane dopo i referendum e le richieste di maggiori poteri ex Art. 116, comma 3, Cost.," *Rivista AIC* 8, no. 4 (2018): 319–365.

that the relative autonomy scores of the two subnational entities are rather close, whereas asymmetry is medium in powers, deriving from a significant differential in terms of subnational autonomy between the two entities.

Looking more closely at how constitutional asymmetry is translated, the asymmetries in status concern almost all the categories of analysis, even though the differences are not striking. First, asymmetries emerge from the specific recognition of Aosta Valley as a special region (Art. 116(1) of the Italian Constitution) enjoying differentiated autonomy, whereas Lombardy is generally recognised as an autonomous part of the system (Art. 131 of the Italian Constitution). Then, in terms of subnational constitutional autonomy, per its special statute, Aosta Valley can make substantial arrangements in domains such as fundamental rights, identity clauses, representative structures and organisation of public authority, whereas ordinary regions can make substantial arrangements only in regard to the latter. Moreover, the differentiated position of Aosta Valley as a special region, and thus the resulting asymmetry, emerges at the legislative level, as it has to be consulted in matters affecting its interests or competences, and especially at the executive level, as it not only has to be consulted in matters affecting its interests or competences but also, due to the principle of specialty and of bilateral cooperation, it could be argued that as a special region it co-decides matters that affect its interests or competences. These provisions are limited to special regions, and thus Lombardy as an ordinary region does not enjoy the same level of autonomy.

However, the dimension of autonomy where asymmetry is widest regards powers. Indeed, in terms of scope of powers, the statute of Aosta Valley provides substantial powers in domains such as economic policy, political control, territorial management, and multinational conflict management, whereas ordinary regions have substantial powers only in the domains of economic policy and political control. In terms of the techniques of allocation of competences, Aosta Valley has mostly concurrent powers with priority given to central rule, but central interference is conditional on detailed subsidiarity or necessity conditions, as also stated by the constitutional court case-law,[144] whereas Lombardy has mostly concurrent powers with priority given to central rule. Then, when looking at the system of intergovernmental relations (IGR) for political conflict resolution, the principle of specialty provides for an equal and balanced relationship between the special region and the central authority, with an equal number of representatives on both sides in bilateral

144 It should be noted that Aosta Valley is granted more exclusive powers than ordinary regions, so in some matters it could be said that priority is given to subnational rule.

negotiations.[145] However, in respect of the other regions, it could also be argued that the special regions have a dominant position in the political dispute resolution mechanism, since such an equal relationship is not granted to ordinary regions, where the dominant position is the one of the central authorities. Moreover, Aosta Valley can initiate the dispute resolution mechanism if the central authorities have harmed its interests or exceeded its competences.

Finally, in the fiscal domain, the differences between special and ordinary regions were reduced over time, and the only asymmetry is the mechanisms in place in Aosta Valley to protect its subnational capacity to raise taxes. Otherwise, both special and ordinary regions appear to have rather symmetrical powers.

Overall, the low asymmetry in status and fiscal arrangements, but high asymmetry in powers, creates a score for constitutional asymmetry of 0.20 and a converted value of 0.38, which falls within the interval of medium degree of asymmetry.

4.1.5 Pakistan

Concerning Pakistan, subnational autonomy was measured for the province of Punjab and Gilgit-Baltistan.[146] In Pakistan, provinces all enjoy the same level of autonomy. The only part of the Pakistani territory that enjoys a different degree of autonomy is Gilgit-Baltistan, which the law defined as an "autonomous region" in the Gilgit-Baltistan Empowerment and Self-Governance Order in 2009. The territory of Gilgit-Baltistan has historically enjoyed a semi-autonomous status since its accession to Pakistan in 1947, but its differentiated constitutional status created political tensions and repeated requests to

---

145 On IGR in Italy and the joint bodies for dispute resolution between special regions and the central government, see Nicolò Paolo Alessi and Francesco Palermo, "Intergovernmental Relations and Identity Politics in Italy," in *Intergovernmental Relations in Divided Societies: A Comparative Perspective*, ed. Yonatan T. Fessha and Karl Kössler (Cham: Palgrave Macmillan, 2022), 183–218; Nicolò Paolo Alessi, "Joint Bodies – a Key Factor for Successful Autonomous Systems? The Cases of the Italian Special Regions and the Åland Islands," *Journal of Autonomy and Security Studies* 5, no. 1 (2021): 8–25.

146 On federalism and asymmetries in Pakistan, see Katharine Adeney and Filippo Boni, "Federalism and Regime Change: De/Centralization in Pakistan – 1956–2020," *Regional & Federal Studies* 33, no. 5 (2023): 725–53; Zubair Shahid and Melanie Gerster, "Subnational Empowerment for a Cohesive Federation. A Country Study of Constitutional Asymmetry in Pakistan," in *Constitutional Asymmetry in Multinational Federalism*, ed. Patricia Popelier and Maja Sahadžić (Cham: Palgrave Macmillan, 2019), 369–98; Katharine Adeney, "Democracy and Federalism in Pakistan," in *Federalism in Asia*, ed. Baogang He, Brian Galligan and Takashi Inoguchi (Cheltenham: Edward Elgar, 2007), 101–123.

mous part of the system not by the Constitution (as the provinces), but by ordinary legislation, and without being represented in the central level institutions, despite having a directly elected assembly. In terms of the organisation of courts, provinces such as Punjab have their own court system and they are represented in the Supreme Court (which is organised at the central level), whereas in Gilgit-Baltistan courts are organised at the central level. In terms of powers, asymmetries are also considerable. Indeed, provinces have powers in matters concerning economic policy, political control, multinational conflict management, and territorial management, whereas Gilgit-Baltistan does not have powers over multinational conflict management (but does over the other three categories). In terms of allocation techniques, if provinces have mostly exclusive powers, Gilgit-Baltistan has concurrent powers with priority given to central rule. Another aspect in which asymmetry is present concerns the role of subnational entities in the appointment of Supreme Court judges, as provinces are consulted on this, whereas Gilgit-Baltistan has no say over appointments. Finally, asymmetries in the fiscal arrangements dimension are minimal, as provinces have the power to set the base and/or rate of minor taxes, whereas Gilgit-Baltistan does not. However, all subnational entities in Pakistan can introduce new taxes and levies.

4.1.6 Belgium

Finally, as regards Belgium, the analysis of subnational autonomy draws directly on that already conducted by Popelier in *Dynamic Federalism*.[148] The two selected subnational entities are the Flemish Community (FC) and the German Speaking Community (GSC), as they are rather different not only in terms of size and population, but also because the FC took the opportunity granted by Art. 137 of the Belgian Constitution and merged the institutions of the Flemish community and the Flanders region into one single Flemish parliament and executive, exercising both sets of powers.

The subnational autonomy scores for the FC indicate a medium degree of autonomy in status, and a rather high degree in powers and fiscal arrangements, with the highest score in powers (0.96). Conversely, the GSC enjoys a medium degree of autonomy in status and fiscal arrangements, but a high degree of autonomy in powers. Overall, subnational autonomy is high in the FC and medium in the GSC, in a similar situation as in Italy. At the country-level, the average scores for autonomy indicate a medium degree of autonomy in status and fiscal arrangements, and a high degree of autonomy in powers.

148 For the details on the assigned scores, see Popelier, *Dynamic Federalism*, 258–268.

Overall, the degree of autonomy at the country level is medium, but the score is at the highest end of the medium interval (0.66) and is the highest in terms of subnational autonomy in the 12 case studies.

In terms of constitutional asymmetry, as with Italy and Pakistan, asymmetry is present in all dimensions; specifically it is low in status while high in powers and fiscal arrangements. Looking closely at how asymmetries are translated, in status, the main differences emerge from the legislative level, as the Dutch groups in the central parliament can veto a law, whereas the representatives from the German-Speaking Community cannot, and the executive level, as the Flemish Community is indirectly represented in the central executive through geographical or identitarian criteria, whereas the German-Speaking Community is not. This asymmetry linked to identity markers is also present in the organisation of courts, since, despite being organised at the central level, in the Flemish Community courts are embedded within the subnational legal space and the FC is indirectly represented in apex courts, whereas in the GSC this provision is not in place. Concerning the powers dimension, it is possible to observe the widest asymmetry between the two subnational entities, and the extremely high score of subnational autonomy enjoyed by the Flemish Community. Indeed, in terms of scope of powers, the FC has substantial powers in economic policy, political control, territorial management, and multinational conflict management, whereas the German-Speaking Community only holds these in the latter two domains. Moreover, in terms of political conflict dispute resolution, the FC has a dominant position in the dispute resolution mechanisms, and, like Aosta Valley, can initiate the mechanisms if its interests and competences have been harmed by the central authorities. Conversely, the German-Speaking Community does not have a dominant position in dispute resolution mechanisms, even though in an unbalanced dialogue there is still prominent representation of the GSC. Furthermore, the Flemish Community has an individual veto right in the appointment of (some) judges of the Constitutional Court, whereas the German-Speaking Community is involved through collective vote. Finally, in terms of fiscal arrangements, asymmetries emerge between the two subnational entities since the Flemish Community has the power to set the base and/or rate of at least one major tax (with constraints set by the central authority), whereas the German-Speaking Community has the power to set the base and/or rate only of minor taxes (without limitations set by the central authority).

Overall, the low asymmetry in status and the high asymmetry in powers and fiscal arrangements create a score for constitutional asymmetry of 0.21

and a relative converted score of 0.43, falling within a medium degree of asymmetry.

4.1.7 Comparative Overview

The comparative overview of the six cases sharing a medium degree of constitutional asymmetry further refines the comparison across cases, insofar as two subgroups appear to emerge. On the one hand, Spain, Italy, Pakistan, and Belgium all share a medium degree of subnational autonomy overall, with some variations. Indeed, all countries display a medium degree of subnational autonomy in at least two dimensions, with the exception of Pakistan where only the dimension of powers has a medium degree of subnational autonomy, whereas in the other two dimensions it is low (albeit close to the threshold). In Belgium and Italy, in two dimensions autonomy is medium, while in the third dimension it is high: in Belgium in the dimension of powers, in Italy in the fiscal arrangements. Conversely, in Spain autonomy is medium in two dimensions, whereas in the third dimension (status) autonomy is low. On the other hand, India and Myanmar have a low degree of subnational autonomy, with rather close scores (respectively 0.21 and 0.23). These two constitutional systems provide for a typology of subnational entity that enjoys distinctively less autonomy than the others, i.e., the union territories in India[149] and the Self-Administered Division and Self-Administered Zones in Myanmar. These were created to accommodate specific needs deriving from specific territorial locations or ethnonational identities; in the case of Myanmar this often happened after the conclusion of ceasefire (and thus bilateral) agreements.

Unsurprisingly, the difference between the two groups is also reflected in the degrees of constitutional asymmetry, as India and Myanmar show a higher value than the other four cases. If Spain, Italy, Pakistan, and Belgium are rather close in terms of values, spanning from Spain with a converted value of 0.34 to Belgium with 0.43, India and Myanmar are at the higher end of the percentile for medium asymmetry, with 0.55 for India and 0.57 for Myanmar. Therefore, these two cases could be further defined as medium/high in terms of constitutional asymmetry.

---

149 It should be noted that in India not all union territories are equal, as for example Delhi and Puducherry are given special democratic institutions, while the other union territories are governed by representatives of the central government. In order to grasp the widest divide in terms of subnational autonomy and thus asymmetry, these two territories were not selected for the analysis. It remains generally true that union territories do not enjoy the same autonomy of Indian states, but the nuances among territories should not be forgotten.

4.2 *Medium Constitutional Asymmetry "in Action"*

Within the group of cases sharing a medium degree of constitutional asymmetry, Spain and Italy offer some interesting insights not only on the evolution of asymmetries over time, but also on the difference between law on the books and law in action. Indeed, in both Italy and Spain, the constitutional asymmetries originally introduced by the newly adopted democratic constitutions were stronger than they are now. In the Spanish system, the initial asymmetry between the Basque Country and Catalonia on the one side (i.e., the "nationalities" as Art. 2 of the Constitution defines them), and the rest of the system on the other (i.e., the "regions"), has been reduced following a resymmetrisation trend, through the extension of powers to the rest of the autonomous communities, a standardisation of central legislation, the centralisation of practices, and a homogenisation of the case law. To counter this trend, both Catalonia and the Basque Country made formal proposals to re-establish a more marked asymmetry, but both proposals to reform their autonomy statutes failed. In conclusion, Bossacoma and Sanjaume argue that "it was a transitory and potential asymmetry more than a permanent and actual asymmetry",[150] and the strong potential for asymmetry allowed by the Constitution did not actualise in its later implementation.

The Italian case offers an even more nuanced picture on the implementation of asymmetries, as even the five special regions are rather different from one another, with Friuli-Venezia Giulia being established just a few years before the rest of the ordinary regions and much later than the other special regions, and with the two islands of Sicily and Sardinia never having developed what Palermo and Valdesalici define as "autonomist consciousness",[151] as they focused more on developing and strengthening ties with the central government than on taking advantage of their special autonomy. Thus, the only two special regions actually enjoying their asymmetric potential are the two small subalpine regions, namely Aosta Valley and Trentino-South Tyrol. Moreover, the constitutional developments of 1999 and 2001 significantly changed the panorama of Italian regionalism, reducing constitutional asymmetries between special and ordinary regions. Interestingly, Palermo and Valdesalici frame the discourse on constitutional asymmetries (and thus asymmetric federalism) in Italy as a pendulum that "oscillates wildly between (symmetric) centralisation and (asymmetric) decentralisation".[152] They further observe

150 Bossacoma and Sanjaume, "Asymmetry as a Device for Equal Recognition," 457.

151 Palermo and Valdesalici, "Irreversibly Different," 304.

152 Palermo and Valdesalici, "Irreversibly Different," 308.

that these oscillations have little to do with the constitutional framework but are rather tied to the political discourse and the case law of the Italian Constitutional Court. Indeed, proposed legislation to implement "differentiated autonomy" regularly emerges in the political discourse of some political parties, as Art. 116(3) of the Constitution holds the potential to reignite the discussion on further differentiation within the Italian regional system.[153] Moreover, as will be further analysed in Chapter 5, the Italian Constitutional Court significantly changed its degree of support for decentralisation and asymmetries before and after the 2001 constitutional reform and 2010 economic crises.

As already mentioned, the Indian constitutional system presented much stronger constitutional asymmetries in the (recent) past, with the distinct status of Jammu and Kashmir constitutionally entrenched in Art. 370 of the Indian Constitution up until the 2019 Jammu and Kashmir Reorganisation Act. Despite this dramatic reduction in subnational autonomy, the degree of asymmetry emerging in the current analysis is still significant and derives from the analytical choices that were made, i.e., to include two rather different types of subnational entities without ignoring the existence of union territories. Some scholars observe that India is a case of strong political asymmetry rather than constitutional asymmetries, since the overwhelming majority of Indian states, despite their extensive internal ethnocultural, demographic, and socio-economic diversity, all stand on an equal footing.[154] However, this view also derives from an analytical choice to focus only on states, that do indeed enjoy roughly the same degree of subnational autonomy, without taking into account the reality of union territories, that despite being considerably smaller are constitutionally recognised as an autonomous part of the territory. An additional reason advanced by scholars for defining India as a weak form of constitutional asymmetry stands in the political history of the country. Indeed, as Pandey observes, "it is a running theme of the Indian Constitution that political asymmetries need not to get reflected in the form of constitu-

153 The most recent example of this trend is the Law n. 86 of 26 June 2024 "Provisions for the implementation of the differentiated autonomy of the ordinary statute Regions pursuant to Article 116, third paragraph, of the Constitution." This Law will be later addressed in Chapter 5 (paragraph 4.2), in reference to the judgment 192/2024 of the Italian Constitutional Court which declared the unconstitutionality of some of its provisions.

154 Rajendra Kumar Pandey, "Accommodating Diversity, Consolidating Nationhood. A Country Study of Constitutional Asymmetry in India," in *Constitutional Asymmetry in Multinational Federalism*, ed. Patricia Popelier and Maja Sahadžić (Cham: Palgrave Macmillan, 2019), 222.

tional asymmetry to the maximum extent possible".[155] This is also translated in the fact that the asymmetrical elements of the Indian Constitution were designed to be temporary and transitional, to hold the system together during the formation of the Union before ultimately transforming India into a symmetrical federation.[156] In conclusion, the Indian case is a first good example of how asymmetries can be strongly associated with inequality (or even perpetuation of previous inequalities), and of the ideal of symmetry as a way to fully ensure equality among subnational entities, despite the different existing conditions and consequently different needs.

Myanmar is another case where constitutional asymmetries were significantly stronger in the past. The constitutional framework introduced by the 1947 Constitution was strongly asymmetrical, recognising some ethnic nationalities and not others, with different levels of representation, as well as different sets of rights and powers. This asymmetry between the Bamar majority and the non-Bamar ethnic nationalities created increasing tensions, culminating in a military coup in 1962 and in the suspension of the 1947 Constitution and the federal structure of the state. The following Constitutions in 1974 and then 2008 contain some federal elements, but asymmetries were reduced as much as possible to avoid entrenching political asymmetries in the constitutional framework. Indeed, states and regions are completely symmetrical, in order to formally ensure equality among ethnic communities. However, as with India, Myanmar still emerges as a case of high constitutional asymmetry given the presence of the Self-Administered Areas (Zones and Division), recognised by the Constitution as an autonomous part of the territory. Despite their considerably smaller size, these were introduced for smaller but clustered ethnic nationalities, and therefore are relevant in terms of autonomous units. Moreover, as Breen notes, "a largely symmetrical Constitution does not mean ethnic neutrality",[157] as the Bamar population is still in a privileged position, with Art. 3 of the Constitution recognising the special position of Buddhism, i.e., the majority, and Bamar religion, leading to the adoption of discriminatory legislation against non-Bamar religions, such as Islam. Therefore, the apparent symmetry does not necessarily translate into full equality among ethnic nationalities and disregards the existing formal asymmetry between states/regions and self-administered areas.

155 Pandey, "Accommodating Diversity", 223.
156 Ibidem.
157 Breen, "Asymmetry or Equality," 363.

Then, the Pakistani case is an interesting case of "temporary" constitutional asymmetry, as the only existing constitutional asymmetries derive from the differentiated position of Gilgit-Baltistan, that currently has "quasi-provincial" status and will eventually enjoy equal autonomy to the provinces. The roots of the differentiated position of Gilgit-Baltistan are to be found in history, as traditionally the region had been ruled by tribes, kingdoms, and dynasties.[158] Following the accession to Pakistan in 1947, it enjoyed a semi-autonomous status, even though such differentiated treatment created tensions and led to repeated calls to ensure full parity and equality in status with other provinces. After being governed by the federal government of Pakistan for decades, in 1999 the Supreme Court of Pakistan ruled that the treatment of the region should have been comparable with other provinces, and even though the changes have been slow, the *de facto* recognition of Gilgit-Baltistan as a "quasi-province" arrived in 2009 with the issuing of the Gilgit-Baltistan Empowerment and Self-Governance Order. Although the temporary nature of the asymmetries concerning Gilgit-Baltistan did not come about by explicit design, the ultimate goal is expected to be constitutional symmetry, in a rather highly politically asymmetric system.[159] Indeed, this is the reason why previous research framed Pakistan as a case of low constitutional asymmetry.[160] However, looking at the current constitutional framework, it can be seen that the asymmetries in status and powers are still significant.

Finally, it should be noted that the degree of constitutional asymmetry in Belgium largely depends on how the system is framed. If Belgium is framed as a dyadic federation revolving around the two major language groups, as it operates at the central level with the power-sharing system in place between the Dutch and French groups, constitutional asymmetries would be weaker and mainly concentrated in the fiscal domain, deriving from the merger of the community and regional institutions by the Flemish. However, such a dyadic nature is mitigated by the design of the federal structure, which also encompasses smaller entities such as the Brussels Region and the German-Speaking Community,[161] as well as the French Community Commission and the Joint

158 Zubair Shahid and Melanie Gerster, "Subnational Empowerment for a Cohesive Federation. A Country Study of Constitutional Asymmetry in Pakistan," in *Constitutional Asymmetry in Multinational Federalism*, ed. Patricia Popelier and Maja Sahadžić (Cham: Palgrave Macmillan, 2019), 384.

159 See Shahid and Gerster, "Subnational Empowerment," 377–383.

160 Sahadžić, *Asymmetry*, 83.

161 It should be noted that despite being smaller entities, the Brussels Region and the German-Speaking Community are mentioned in the Belgian Constitution in Articles 2 and 3 as being on the same level as the other regions and communities, the asymmetry

Community Commission. This creates stronger and more pervasive asymmetries, as communities and regions hold different sets of powers, and the merger of the institutions in the Flemish Community has created a concentration of powers in a single territorial entity.

5 Low Degree of Constitutional Asymmetry

5.1 *Autonomy and Asymmetry*

The four cases displaying a low degree of constitutional asymmetry do not share a common approach to subnational autonomy; rather, they seem to follow two separate trends. In Canada and Bosnia-Herzegovina, the overall degree of subnational autonomy is medium, whereas in Indonesia and Malaysia the overall degree of subnational autonomy is low. However, when looking at the resulting constitutional asymmetry, Canada and Indonesia appear to be similar to each other, while BiH and Malaysia share other similarities. Each case is briefly reviewed separately in the following sections.

5.1.1 Canada

In Canada, the two subnational entities selected to analyse were Québec, the only province where the overwhelming majority of the population is French-speaking, as well as being one of the largest and richest provinces, and Nova Scotia, one of the smallest, less rich, and least populated provinces in Canada.[162]

Looking at the subnational autonomy scores, we can observe that the two subnational entities enjoy a medium degree of autonomy in status and

---

between these and the rest of the entities thus results from the merger of the institutions in the Flemish Community.

162 On federalism and asymmetries in Canada, see Cristina Fasone, "Canada as an 'Importer' and as an 'Exporter' of Federal Arrangements: A View from Europe," *DPCE Online* 38, no. 1 (2019): 643–71; Alain-G Gagnon and Jean-Denis Garon, "Constitutional and Non-Constitutional Asymmetries in the Canada Federation," in *Constitutional Asymmetry in Multinational Federalism*, ed. Patricia Popelier and Maja Sahadžić (Cham: Palgrave Macmillan, 2019), 77–104; Alain-G. Gagnon and Guy Laforest, "The Future of Federalism: Lessons from Canada and Quebec," *International Journal* 48, no. 3 (1993): 470–91; Alain-G Gagnon and Jean-Denis Garon, "Constitutional and Non-Constitutional Asymmetries in the Canada Federation," in *Constitutional Asymmetry in Multinational Federalism*, ed. Patricia Popelier and Maja Sahadžić (Cham: Palgrave Macmillan, 2019), 77–104; Giacomo Delledonne, Giuseppe Martinico, and Leonardo Pierdominici, eds., *Il costituzionalismo canadese a 150 anni dalla Confederazione. Riflessioni comparatistiche* (Pisa: Pisa University Press, 2017).

powers, and a high degree of autonomy in fiscal arrangements. Overall, the two subnational entities enjoy a medium degree of autonomy. At the country level, the average autonomy scores, as well as the overall score, reflect the picture at the subnational entity level: medium autonomy in status and powers, high autonomy in fiscal arrangements, and medium autonomy overall.

In terms of constitutional asymmetry, the only dimension in which Québec and Nova Scotia differ is in the status dimension, with Québec having a slightly higher autonomy score than Nova Scotia. As explained in Chapter 2, this derives from the fact that Québec is the only province to which three seats in the Supreme Court are reserved, given that it is the only province with a civil law legal system based on the French codified tradition, and this guarantees knowledge of Québec civil law in the Supreme Court. The other provinces do not enjoy the same autonomy as these two domains, but aside from these minimal (yet politically significant) differences, all the Canadian provinces share the same level of autonomy in the remaining two dimensions of powers and fiscal arrangements. Therefore, the resulting overall score for constitutional asymmetry is extremely low (0.02), rather close to constitutional symmetry.

5.1.2 Indonesia

For the Indonesian case, the two selected subnational entities were Aceh, one of the provinces enjoying special autonomy which has a distinctive ethnocultural identity, and East Kalimantan, an ordinary province which is also one of the richest in terms of resources and assets.[163]

Looking at the subnational autonomy scores, we can see that, in both entities, autonomy is low in status and fiscal arrangements, whereas it is medium in powers. Overall, in both entities, autonomy is low, even though it is close to the 0.34 threshold for medium autonomy. At the country level, the average autonomy scores reflect the situation already depicted at the subnational

163 On asymmetries and decentralisation in Indonesia, see Simon Butt, "Provincial Asymmetry in Indonesia: What Is so 'Special' About It? A Country Study of Constitutional Asymmetry in Indonesia," in *Constitutional Asymmetry in Multinational Federalism*, ed. Patricia Popelier and Maja Sahadžić (Cham, Switzerland: Palgrave Macmillan, 2019), 227–54; Jacques Bertrand, "Indonesia: 'Special Autonomy' for Aceh and Papua," in *Territory and Power in Constitutional Transitions*, ed. George Anderson and Sujit Choudhry (Oxford: Oxford University Press, 2019), 119–39; Anthony Reid, "Indonesia's Post-Revolutionary Aversion to Federalism," in *Federalism in Asia*, ed. Baogang He, Brian Galligan and Takashi Inoguchi (Cheltenham: Edward Elgar, 2007), 144–64.

level: low autonomy in status and fiscal arrangements, medium autonomy in powers, and low autonomy overall.

In terms of constitutional asymmetry, this is only slightly present in status and powers, whereas the fiscal arrangement dimension is fully symmetrical. The difference in status and powers mainly derives from the peculiar position of Aceh within the Indonesian constitutional system, as the Constitution recognises the existence of special provinces at Art. 18B, and the 2014 Law on Regional Autonomy recognises Aceh as a Special Province at Art. 399 thus isolating it (along with the other special provinces)[164] from the rest of the provinces. Moreover, Aceh must be consulted when the central parliament or executive are drafting laws or enacting policies concerning the governance of Aceh, whereas this treatment is not reserved to the other ordinary provinces. In terms of powers, Aceh is a particular case of direct implementation of Islamic law within the province, especially of Islamic criminal law with *shari'a* courts adjudicating Islamic law cases.[165] Finally, Aceh is the only subnational entity in Indonesia which may form a regional party. All other parties must be nationalised.

Despite the significant impact of asymmetry on the rights and freedoms of non-Muslims citizens living in Aceh, the overall constitutional asymmetry score is 0.06, and therefore extremely low. Other than strictly formally, Indonesia is practically symmetrical.

5.1.3 Bosnia and Herzegovina

In Bosnia-Herzegovina, the two selected subnational entities were the Federation of Bosnia-Herzegovina (FBiH), one of the two entities constituting the system, and the Brčko district, an autonomous district established in 1999 after an arbitration process.[166] At the subnational level, Bosnia-Herzegovina is com-

---

164 Aside from Aceh, the other special regions in Indonesia are the provinces of Papua and West Papua, whose special autonomy is entrenched in the 2001 Law on Special Autonomy for Papua Province, and the cities of Yogyakarta and Jakarta (the capital city), whose special autonomy is rooted in historical reasons and respectively entrenched in the 2012 Law on The Special Region of Yogyakarta, and the 2007 Law on the Administration of the Special Region of Jakarta.

165 See Bonifati, "Asymmetries and Mixed Legal Systems," 171–173.

166 On asymmetries and federalism in Bosnia and Herzegovina, see Maja Sahadžić, "Mild Asymmetry and Ethnoterritorial Overlap in Charge of the Consequences of Multinationalism," in *Constitutional Asymmetry in Multinational Federalism*, ed. Patricia Popelier and Maja Sahadžić (Cham: Palgrave Macmillan, 2019), 47–76; Thorsten Gromes, "Federalism as a Means of Peace-Building: The Case of Postwar Bosnia and Herzegovina," *Nationalism and Ethnic Politics* 16, no. 3–4 (2010): 354–74; Soeren Keil, "Federalism as a Tool of Conflict-Resolution: The Case of Bosnia and Herzegovina," *L'Europe En Formation* 363,

posed of two entities, i.e., FBiH and Republika Srpska, enjoying the same level of autonomy. It therefore made little sense to select both of them to assess the presence of constitutional asymmetry, whereas the Brčko district is a distinct tier of government, having its own legislative, executive, and judicial branches, though enjoying less autonomy than the entities.

Looking at the subnational autonomy scores, the Federation of Bosnia-Herzegovina enjoys a high degree of autonomy in status and fiscal arrangements and a medium degree in powers, producing an overall high degree of subnational autonomy. Conversely, in the Brčko district autonomy is medium in status and powers, and high in fiscal arrangements, leading to a medium overall degree of autonomy. At the country level, the situation in terms of average autonomy is similar to the one emerging from Brčko (although with higher values): medium autonomy in status and powers, high autonomy in fiscal arrangements, and an overall medium degree of autonomy.

Constitutional asymmetry is not present in all dimensions, but rather only to a medium degree in status and low degree in powers, while it is absent in fiscal arrangements. Indeed, the highest asymmetry score in status (0.18) derives from the fact that the Brčko district is not directly represented in central institutions (legislative, executive, judiciary), despite having its own institutions at the subnational level. Conversely, the electorate of the Federation of Bosnia-Herzegovina is represented in the central parliament and in the central executive and can veto a law or a decision through "entity voting" or the vital interest veto procedure, whereas the electorate of the Brčko district is not equally entitled to do so.[167] Regarding the power dimensions, Art. XI.1 of the BiH Constitution provides that "four [of the nine] members [of the Constitutional Court] shall be selected by the House of Representatives of the Federa-

no. 1 (2012): 205–18; Soeren Keil, *Multinational Federalism in Bosnia and Herzegovina* (Wey Court East, UK, and Burlington, VT: Ashgate, 2013); Ziatan Meskic and Nezir Pivi, "Federalism in Bosnia and Herzegovina," *Vienna Journal on International Constitutional Law* 5, no. 4 (2011): 597–617; Jens Woelk, "Forced Together, Never Sustainable? Post-Conflict Federalism in Bosnia and Herzegovina," *Kansas Law Review* 71 (2022): 252–74.

167 On "entity voting" and veto powers in Bosnia and Herzegovina and in divided societies, see Allison McCulloch, "The Use and Abuse of Veto Rights in Power-Sharing Systems: Northern Ireland's Petition of Concern in Comparative Perspective," *Government and Opposition* 53, no. 4 (2018): 735–56; Allison McCulloch and Aleksandra Zdeb, "Veto Rights and Vital Interests: Formal and Informal Veto Rules for Minority Representation in Deeply Divided Societies," *Representation* 58, no. 3(2020): 427–42; Maja Sahadžić, "Veto mehanizmi u parlamentima na državnoj i entitetskoj razini u Bosni i Hercegovini," in *Parlamentarizam u Bosni i Hercegovini*, ed. Saša Gavrić (Sarajevo: Sarajevski otvoreni centar/Fondacija Friedrich Ebert , 2012), 293–320.

tion",[168] thus marking the representation of the entity in the BiH Constitutional Court, whereas the Brčko district is not represented.

It should further be noted that representation of the entities in the central level institutions as well as in the Constitutional Court is more closely linked to identity than territory, as the seats of the representatives in the central parliament and central executive, as well as the Constitutional Court judges appointed by the national parliaments of the two entities, are distributed according to the power-sharing principle of parity. In practice, this means that the four judges appointed by the House of Representatives of the Federation are normally two Bosniaks and two Bosniak-Croats, guaranteeing parity between the two constituent peoples cohabiting in the entity. Conversely, the Brčko district does not follow ethnic logic and therefore its equal representation was not included in the power-sharing arrangements which make up the constitutional system.

Overall, the difference between the two subnational autonomy scores is 0.10 and the relative converted score is 0.19, therefore the degree of constitutional asymmetry falls within the interval of low degree, albeit not as low as Canada and Indonesia.

5.1.4 Malaysia

Finally, for the Malaysian case the two analysed subnational entities are Sarawak, the largest entity in size and one of the two entities enjoying a differentiated degree of autonomy within the system (along with Sabah), and Pulau Pinang, the smallest ordinary state in Malaysia.[169]

Looking at the subnational autonomy scores, Sarawak enjoys medium autonomy in status, while low autonomy in powers (despite being at the limit of the interval) and in fiscal arrangements. Overall, the degree of autonomy in Sarawak is medium. In Pulau Pinang, the situation is rather similar. Although the degrees of autonomy are the same across the three dimensions, the scores are considerably lower, especially in the fiscal arrangements

---

168 Constitution of Bosnia and Herzegovina – Art. XX.1(a).

169 On federalism and asymmetry in Malaysia, see William Case, "Semi-Democracy and Minimalist Federalism in Malaysia," in in *Federalism in Asia*, ed. Baogang He, Brian Galligan and Takashi Inoguchi (Cheltenham: Edward Elgar, 2007), 124–143; Asri Salleh, Arnold Puyok, and Toni Paridi Bagang, "Constitutional Asymmetry in Malaysia: A Case Study of Sabah and Sarawak," in *Constitutional Asymmetry in Multinational Federalism*, ed. Patricia Popelier and Maja Sahadžić (Cham, Switzerland: Palgrave Macmillan, 2019), 315–40; Harihar Bhattacharyya, *Federalism in Asia. India, Pakistan, Malaysia, Nepal and Myanmar* (London: Routledge, 2020).

dimension, where the score for Pulau Pinang is 0, indicating that it is normally a domain of the central level. This imbalance creates an overall low degree of subnational autonomy in Pulau Pinang. At the central level, the previous picture is confirmed: medium autonomy in status, low autonomy in powers and fiscal arrangements, and overall a low degree of subnational autonomy.

Constitutional asymmetry is present in all dimensions but to different degrees. As one might expect from the previous assessment on subnational autonomy, asymmetry is low in status and powers, whereas it is medium in fiscal arrangements. Indeed, in the status dimension the only differences concern the fact that the special position of Sarawak within the Malaysian Federation is locked by a *de facto* eternity clause in Art. 161E of the Federal Constitution, a provision that does not extend to any other state. Moreover, Sarawak enjoys wider subnational constitutional autonomy, as it is entitled to make substantial arrangements in constitutional matters such as fundamental rights, identity clauses, and representative structures, whereas ordinary states can only make arrangements regarding the latter. As with the other subnational entities previously analysed, Sarawak is consulted in matters that affect its interests or competences and is represented in the Federal Court through the Chief Judge of the High Court of Sabah and Sarawak. In terms of powers, Sarawak enjoys wider powers than ordinary states, especially concerning economic policies, a domain over which ordinary states have no powers. Finally, in terms of fiscal arrangements, despite having no power to set the base and/or rate of taxes, Sarawak has a unique power to introduce new taxes and set tax reliefs, whereas in ordinary states fiscal autonomy is extremely limited and under the control of the central level.

Overall, the constitutional asymmetry score is 0.13 (and the converted value 0.26), which mainly derives from the high score in the dimension of fiscal arrangements but indicates a low degree of constitutional asymmetry.

5.1.5 Comparative Overview

The four countries displaying a low degree of constitutional asymmetry follow two different paths. In Canada and Bosnia-Herzegovina, at the country level the overall degree of subnational autonomy is medium in status and powers, and high in fiscal arrangements, leading to an average medium degree of subnational autonomy. Conversely, in Indonesia and Malaysia, at the country level the overall degree of subnational autonomy is medium as regards only one dimension (respectively powers and status), while in the remaining two dimensions autonomy is low, leading to an overall low degree of subnational autonomy.

However, as anticipated at the beginning of the paragraph, this parallel is not translated into constitutional asymmetries. Indeed, Canada and Indonesia display extremely low scores of asymmetry in one or two dimensions: in Canada asymmetry is present only in the status dimension (0.03), whereas in Indonesia asymmetry is present in status (0.06) and in powers (0.04). Therefore, in Canada and Indonesia the asymmetry score is significantly lower and close to full symmetry. This could derive from the fact that in these two systems constitutional asymmetries were introduced to address the presence of the traditional civil law legal system in Québec and the specific and localised autonomy claims coming from Aceh in Indonesia. Conversely, in Bosnia-Herzegovina and in Malaysia, the scores of constitutional asymmetry are higher and are present in two or three dimensions. In BiH, constitutional asymmetry is medium in status and low in powers, while in Malaysia it is low in status and powers and medium in fiscal arrangements. This could derive from the fact that in BiH and Malaysia asymmetries were introduced to preserve the integrity of the systems and avoid separatism, holding the system in balance.

5.2 *Low Constitutional Asymmetry "in Action"*

Among the four analysed cases, Indonesia is a rather effective example of the fact that even a formally low degree of asymmetry can have an enormous impact on the rights and freedoms of citizens, and therefore there should always be a closer look at the impact of asymmetries on the system. As already anticipated in Chapter 2, in Indonesia the 2006 Special Autonomy Law first authorised Aceh to implement Islamic law, expressly mentioning criminal law (*jinayat*) in Art. 125(2) and granting wide powers to the Aceh government to regulate the implementation of Islamic law, by issuing *Qanun*. Moreover, Art. 126(1) provides that "Every adherent to Islam in Aceh must adhere to and observe Islamic law", while Art. 126(2) adds that "Every person living in or present in Aceh must respect the application of Islamic law". Even though the same law at Art. 127(2) specifies that the Aceh government is required to respect religious diversity, Islamic criminal law currently also applies to the non-Muslim in Aceh. Indeed, in 2014, the Aceh government issued the *Qanun Jinyat* (the Islamic Criminal Code), raising concerns over violations of human rights standards. Moreover, the enacting of the *Qanun Jinyat* was controversial because in Art. 75 it asserts that its provisions and the imposed precepts prevail over national laws and even international human rights laws. This would of course be in violation of the Indonesian Constitution, protecting human rights in chapter XA from Art. 28 to 28(J).[170]

For its part, Malaysia is a case of "promised" asymmetries, that largely remained unfulfilled. Indeed, the 20-Point and 18-Point Memorandum, as well as the Malaysia Agreement in 1963 set out the potential for strong and intentional asymmetries to include Sabah and Sarawak in the Malaysian federation, against separatist threats. However, the federal government has progressively implemented symmetrisation provisions and retains the upper hand in the regulation of the extent of the differentiated autonomy to Sabah and Sarawak. As such, their legislative and financial autonomy is still subject to the oversight of the federal government, further reducing the space for asymmetry.[171] Therefore, despite their strong potential, constitutional asymmetries remain low in reality due to the strong oversight from the central level.

Then, concerning Bosnia-Herzegovina, it is interesting to notice how sometimes the system is depicted as strongly asymmetrical, even though constitutional asymmetries are rather limited. Indeed, the two entities, i.e., the Federation of Bosnia-Herzegovina and the Republika Srpska, are extremely different in terms of institutional structures, with the former being a decentralised federation, and the latter a centralised and unitary republic. However, when looking at their status, powers, and fiscal arrangements, the two entities are completely symmetrical. Therefore, the "asymmetries" are a product of a radically different implementation of their autonomy at the institutional design level, rather than a different degree of autonomy. Moreover, the power-sharing principle of parity would make it rather difficult to accept asymmetries among constituent peoples, another reason why asymmetries are low in Bosnia-Herzegovina and are only traceable when looking at the differentiated position of the Brčko district within the system.

Finally, even though constitutional asymmetries are almost non-existent in Canada, which is often framed as a symmetrical system,[172] significant asymmetries emerge in two policy sectors (i.e., immigration and manpower train-

170 Specifically, freedom of religion is recognised in Art. 28E(1), "Every person shall be free to choose and to practice the religion of his/her choice [...]", and Art. 28E(2), "Every person shall have the right to the freedom to believe his/her faith (*kepercayaan*), and to express his/her views and thoughts, in accordance with his/her conscience". Moreover, Art. 28I (5) states that "For the purpose of upholding and protecting human rights in accordance with the principle of a democratic and law-based state, the implementation of human rights shall be guaranteed, regulated and set forth in laws and regulations."

171 Salleh, Puyok, and Bagang, "Constitutional Asymmetry in Malaysia," 334–336.

172 Sahadžić, *Asymmetry*, 83.

ing),[173] where Québec has sought to depart from other provinces when elaborating public policies, especially through bilateral agreements.[174] When assessing constitutional asymmetries in Canada, Gagnon and Garon conclude that the cohabitation of two political communities could make asymmetric federalism an important feature in the future developments of Canada as a multinational federation.[175]

6 Concluding Remarks

This chapter provided a comparative overview of the case studies analysed in the research, identifying three groups of divided multi-tiered systems: high, medium, and low degree of constitutional asymmetry. For each case, it was interesting to observe the variations in subnational autonomy at the subnational entity-level and at the country-level, identifying the dimensions where constitutional asymmetry is present. What clearly emerges from this chapter is that, as anticipated, constitutional asymmetries can vary significantly not only among cases but also among the dimensions of autonomy, as they are not necessarily present in all three dimensions but may be concentrated in just one or two dimensions, as is the case in Canada, Indonesia, Bosnia-Herzegovina, and Spain. Conversely, there are cases where constitutional asymmetries are pervasive in all three dimensions, as in Italy, Pakistan, Belgium, and Myanmar. It was also interesting to observe the reality of the implementation of asymmetries, beyond the formal level. Indeed, it is possible to trace a dominant resymmetrisation trend, with constitutional symmetry framed as a synonym for equality. Though an in-depth analysis would be required to properly assess the degree and appreciate the detailed implementation of constitutional asymmetries, this chapter constitutes a first exploration of the complexity of asymmetries in a variety of divided multi-tiered systems, taking primarily an institutional perspective but also recognising the importance of the non-institutional level of implementation.

Furthermore, this book showed how numbers can tell the researcher different things and should be used carefully to serve the purpose of the research, best exemplified by the difference between the asymmetry scores and the converted values of asymmetry. Although similar (i.e., values comprised be-

173 See also David Milne, "Asymmetry in Canada: Past and Present," *Asymmetry Series - IIGR, Queen's University* (2005): 1–8.

174 Gagnon and Garon, "Constitutional and Non-Constitutional Asymmetries," 94–100.

175 Gagnon and Garon, "Constitutional and Non-Constitutional Asymmetries," 101.

tween 0 and 1), they tell us very different things. The asymmetry scores resulting from the subtraction of the subnational autonomy scores give us a qualitative indication on the constitutional system and on the specific dimension of asymmetry. If the overall score is close to 0, it means that the difference in terms of subnational autonomy is minimal, and thus the constitutional system or the specific dimension is almost symmetrical. Indeed, if the subnational autonomy scores were equal, the asymmetry score would be 0 and this would mean that there is no constitutional asymmetry, but, rather, symmetry. Conversely, the higher the asymmetry score, the higher the difference in terms of subnational autonomy, with completely different implications for the constitutional system. If we consider a paradoxical situation in which the asymmetry score was equal to 1, it would mean that the two entities analysed are so diverse in terms of subnational autonomy that they do not belong to the same constitutional system.

As anticipated by Popelier, "the asymmetry spread, in combination with the cohesion scores, will enable us to examine at which point the spread (and in which category) becomes so wide that constitutional asymmetry endangers constitutional stability".[176] Certainly, this was an extreme example to describe the meaning of numbers, but it is helpful to understand why there are no asymmetry scores close to 1 in the analysis provided by this book. As further explained in the rest of the chapter, the highest overall asymmetry score is Iraq (0.48), and the highest score in a dimension of asymmetry is asymmetry in fiscal arrangements in Iraq and Myanmar (0.63), whereas the lowest overall asymmetry score is Canada (0.01) and asymmetry in powers in Indonesia and Malaysia (0.04). The analysis also shows that, in some asymmetrical constitutional systems, some dimensions can be symmetrical, as in Indonesia (i.e., symmetry in fiscal arrangements), or in Canada (asymmetry only in status, and symmetry in powers and fiscal arrangements). This is a further demonstration of the fact that this level of refinement is possible only through the use of standardised indexes and thus the use of quantitative methods, as long as these are interpreted in qualitative terms and with reference to the law in action. Again, the case of low asymmetry in Indonesia and its substantial consequences for the protection of the fundamental rights of minorities is emblematic in this respect.

However, if we want to move from a qualitative and detailed analysis of single cases to a comparison across cases and across dimensions according to degrees of intensity, we cannot rely on the same numbers, as these would

176 Popelier, *Dynamic Federalism*, 85.

not allow for a coherent comparison. As also explained in Chapter 2, the conversion of asymmetry scores through normalisation allows for the identification of degrees and thus rigorous comparison. Moreover, relying on the same classification of degrees of intensity according to the percentiles (0–0.33; 0.34–0.66; 0.67–1) for subnational autonomy and constitutional asymmetry allows comparison of the respective degrees and reflection upon the relationship between the two. However, it is important to remember that if a converted value of asymmetry equals 0, this does not mean constitutional symmetry (as in the case of the original asymmetry score), but simply that it is the minimum value of asymmetry and thus belongs to the lowest extreme of the percentile. Similarly, if the converted value of asymmetry equals 1, this does not mean disintegration of the constitutional system (as in the case of the original asymmetry score), but that it is the maximum value of asymmetry and thus belongs to the highest extreme of the percentile. Therefore, using a conversion of values through normalisation is helpful to compare the degrees of asymmetry across and within cases, but do not give us a precise qualitative indication as the asymmetry scores.

In conclusion, this book helps us to reflect on the use of numbers and empirical methods in comparative legal research, reminding researchers that knowing and acknowledging the different meanings of numbers is crucial for comparative lawyers who want to employ quantitative methods in their research.

Bibliography

Alkadiri, Raad. "Federalism and Iraq's Constitutional Stalemate." *Chatham House Research Paper Middle East and North Africa Programme*, 2020, 1–23.

Anderson, George, and Sujit Choudhry, eds. *Territory and Power in Constitutional Transitions*. Oxford: Oxford University Press, 2019.

Anderson, Paul. "Decentralisation at a Crossroads: Spain, Catalonia and the Territorial Crisis." *Ethnopolitics* 19, no. 4 (2020): 342–55.

Anghie, Antony. *Imperialism, Sovereignty and the Making of International Law*. Cambridge: Cambridge University Press, 2004.

Arban, Erika, and Adriano Dirri. "Aspirational Principles in African Federalism: South Africa, Ethiopia and Nigeria Compared." *African Journal of International and Comparative Law* 29, no. 3 (2021): 362–82.

Bâli, Aslı Ü., and Omar M. Dajani, eds. *Federalism and Decentralization in the Contemporary Middle East and North Africa*. Cambridge: Cambridge University Press, 2023.

Banović, Damir, Saša Gavrić, and Mariña Barreiro. *The Political System of Bosnia and Herzegovina: Institutions – Actors – Processes*. Cham: Springer, 2021.

Baxi, Upendra. "Constitutionalism as a Site of State Formative Practices." *Cardozo Law Review* 21, no. 4 (2000): 1183–1210.

Belser, Eva Maria. "A Failure of State Transformation Rather than a Failure of Federalism? The Case of Iraq." *Ethnopolitics* 19, no. 4 (2020): 383–401.

Benedizione, Ludovica, and Valentina Rita Scotti, eds. *Twenty Years after Dayton. The Constitutional Transition of Bosnia and Herzegovina*. Rome: LUISS University Press, 2016.

Bertrand, Jacques. "Indonesia: 'Special Autonomy' for Aceh and Papua." In *Territory and Power in Constitutional Transitions*, edited by George Anderson and Sujit Choudhry, 119–39. Oxford: Oxford University Press, 2019.

Bhattacharyya, Harihar. *Asymmetric Federalism in India: Ethnicity, Development and Governance*. Cham: Springer Nature Switzerland, 2023.

Bhattacharyya, Harihar. *Federalism in Asia. India, Pakistan, Malaysia, Nepal and Myanmar*. London: Routledge, 2020.

Bhattacharyya, Harihar. "States Reorganization and Accommodation of Ethno-Territorial Cleavages in India." In *Territory and Power in Constitutional Transitions*, edited by George Anderson and Sujit Choudhry, 81–98. Oxford: Oxford University Press, 2019.

Bogaards, Matthijs. "Iraq's Constitution of 2005: The Case Against Consociationalism 'Light.'" *Ethnopolitics* 20, no. 2 (2021): 186–202.

Bognetti, Giovanni. *Diritto costituzionale comparato. Un approccio metodologico*. Modena: Mucchi Editore, 2015.

Bomhoff, Jacco, and Maurice Adams, eds. *Practice and Theory in Comparative Law*. Cambridge: Cambridge University Press, 2012.

Bönnemann, Maxim, and Jung Laura. "Critical Legal Studies and Comparative Constitutional Law." In *Max Planck Encyclopedia of Comparative Constitutional Law*, edited by Rainer Grote, Frauke Lachenmann, and Rüdiger Wolfrum. Oxford University Press, 2017.

Bossacoma Busquets, Pau, and Marc Sanjaume-Calvet. "Asymmetry as a Device for Equal Recognition and Reasonable Accommodation of Majority and Minority Nations." In *Constitutional Asymmetry in Multinational Federalism*, edited by Patricia Popelier and Maja Sahadžić, 429–60. Cham: Palgrave Macmillan, 2019.

Brand, Dirk J. "Asymmetry in Federal Systems – Constitutional Arrangements in South Africa." In *Asymmetries in Constitutional Law*, edited by Francesco Palermo, Karl Kössler, and Carolin Zwilling, 117–32. Bolzano/Bozen: Accademia Europea di Bolzano, 2009.

Breen, Michael G. "Asymmetry or Equality? Ethnic Nationalities in a Bamar-Dominated State." In *Constitutional Asymmetry in Multinational Federalism*, edited by Patricia Popelier and Maja Sahadžić, 341–68. Cham: Palgrave Macmillan, 2019.

Burgess, Michael. *The British Tradition of Federalism.* London: Leicester University Press, 1995.

Bussani, Mauro, and Ugo Mattei, eds. *The Cambridge Companion to Comparative Law.* Cambridge: Cambridge University Press, 2012.

Butt, Simon. "Provincial Asymmetry in Indonesia: What Is so 'Special' About It? A Country Study of Constitutional Asymmetry in Indonesia." In *Constitutional Asymmetry in Multinational Federalism*, edited by Patricia Popelier and Maja Sahadžić, 227–54. Cham, Switzerland: Palgrave Macmillan, 2019.

Cassidy, Julie. "The Legacy of Colonialism." *The American Journal of Comparative Law* 51, no. 2 (2003): 409–56.

Cheikh Anta Babou. "Decolonization or National Liberation: Debating the End of British Colonial Rule in Africa." *The Annals of the American Academy of Political and Social Science* 632, no. 1 (2010): 41–54.

Childs, Peter, and Patrick Williams. *An Introduction to Post-Colonial Theory.* London and New York: Routledge, 1997.

Choudhry, Sujit. "Does the World Need More Canada? The Politics of the Canadian Model in Constitutional Politics and Political Theory." *International Journal of Constitutional Law* 5, no. 4 (2007): 606–38.

Collins, Michael. "Decolonisation and the 'Federal Moment.'" *Diplomacy & Statecraft* 24, no. 1 (2013): 21–40.

Dann, Philipp. "Southern Turn, Northern Implications: Rethinking the Meaning of Colonial Legacies for Comparative Constitutional Studies." *Comparative Constitutional Studies* 1, no. 2 (2023): 174–96.

Dann, Philipp, Michael Riegner, and Maxim Bönnemann, eds. *The Global South and Comparative Constitutional Law.* Oxford: Oxford University Press, 2020.

De Vergottini, Giuseppe. *Comparazione e diritto costituzionale.* Napoli: Editoriale Scientifica, 2018.

De Vergottini, Giuseppe. *Diritto costituzionale comparato.* Milano: Wolters Kluwer, 2022.

De Vergottini, Giuseppe. "Constitutional Law and the Comparative Method." In *Encyclopedia of Contemporary Constitutionalism*, edited by Javier Cremades and Cristina Hermida, 1–42. Cham: Springer International Publishing, 2020.

Delledonne, Giacomo, Giuseppe Martinico, and Leonardo Pierdominici, eds. *Il costituzionalismo canadese a 150 anni dalla Confederazione. Riflessioni comparatistiche.* Pisa: Pisa University Press, 2017.

Dickson, Brice. "Work in Progress." In *Constitutional Asymmetry in Multinational Federalism*, edited by Patricia Popelier and Maja Sahadžić, 461–88. Cham: Palgrave Macmillan, 2019.

Dirri, Adriano. "Asimmetria costituzionale e pluralismo identitario negli Stati federali multinazionali: le (diverse) asimmetrie di Etiopia, Iraq, India." *Rivista Gruppo Di Pisa* 3, no. 2 (2020): 365–85.

Dodge, Toby. "The Failure of Peacebuilding in Iraq: The Role of Consociationalism and Political Settlements." *Journal of Intervention and Statebuilding* 15, no. 4 (2020): 459–75.

Economist Intelligence Unit. "Democracy Index 2023: Age of Conflict." London: Economist Intelligence, 2024.

Erk, Jan. "Aspirational and Representative Constitutional Identity in Africa." *Global Constitutionalism* 12, no. 1 (2023): 154–73.

Erk, Jan. "Federalism and Decentralization in Sub-Saharan Africa: Five Patterns of Evolution." *Regional & Federal Studies* 24, no. 5 (2014): 535–52.

Fasone, Cristina. "Canada as an 'Importer' and as an 'Exporter' of Federal Arrangements: A View from Europe." *DPCE Online* 38, no. 1 (2019): 643–71.

Fessha, Yonatan T., and Biniyam N. Bezabih. "Federation Among Unequals." In *Constitutional Asymmetry in Multinational Federalism*, edited by Patricia Popelier and Maja Sahadžić, 137–62. Cham: Palgrave Macmillan, 2019.

Fessha, Yonatan Tesfaye. *Ethnic Diversity and Federalism: Constitution Making in South Africa and Ethiopia*. Burlington, VT: Ashgate, 2010.

Fiseha, Assefa. "Emergence and Transformation of Territorially Based Cleavages and Constitutional Responses in Ethiopia." In *Territory and Power in Constitutional Transitions*, edited by George Anderson and Sujit Choudhry, 60–80. Oxford: Oxford University Press, 2019.

Fombad, Charles M., ed. *Constitutional Identity and Constitutionalism in Africa*. Oxford: Oxford University Press, 2024.

Gagnon, Alain-G, and Jean-Denis Garon. "Constitutional and Non-Constitutional Asymmetries in the Canada Federation." In *Constitutional Asymmetry in Multinational Federalism*, edited by Patricia Popelier and Maja Sahadžić, 77–104. Cham: Palgrave Macmillan, 2019.

Gagnon, Alain-G., and Guy Laforest. "The Future of Federalism: Lessons from Canada and Quebec." *International Journal* 48, no. 3 (1993): 470–91.

Gambaro, Antonio, and Rodolfo Sacco. *Sistemi giuridici comparati*. Torino: UTET, 2018.

Gebeye, Berihun Adugna. *A Theory of African Constitutionalism*. Oxford: Oxford University Press, 2021.

Gromes, Thorsten. "Federalism as a Means of Peace-Building: The Case of Postwar Bosnia and Herzegovina." *Nationalism and Ethnic Politics* 16, no. 3–4 (December 16, 2010): 354–74.

Häberle, Peter. "Legal Comparison for Constitutional Development: The Relevance of Federalism and Regionalism." In *A World of Second Chambers. Handbook for Constitutional Studies on Bicameralism*, edited by Jörg Luther, Paolo Passaglia, and Rolando Tarchi, 47–64. Milano: Giuffrè, 2006.

Hartmann, Christof. "Limits of Constitutional Reform in Managing African Conflicts." *Ethnopolitics* 15, no. 5 (2016): 523–27.

Hausing, Kham Khan Suan. "Asymmetric Federalism and the Question of Democratic Justice in Northeast India." *India Review* 13, no. 2 (2014): 87–111.

Hausing, Kham Khan Suan. "Autonomy and the Territorial Management of Ethnic Conflicts in Northeast India." *Territory, Politics, Governance* 10, no. 1 (2022): 120–43.

Hirschl, Ran. *Comparative Matters: The Renaissance of Comparative Constitutional Law*. Oxford: Oxford University Press, 2014.

Hirschl, Ran. "Comparative Methodologies." In *The Cambridge Companion to Comparative Constitutional Law*, edited by Roger Masterman and Robert Schütze, 11–39. Cambridge: Cambridge University Press, 2019.

Hirschl, Ran. "The Question of Case Selection in Comparative Constitutional Law." *The American Journal of Comparative Law* 53, no. 1 (2005): 125–56.

Iacovino, Raffaele. "Partial Asymmetry and Federal Construction: Accommodating Diversity in the Canadian Constitution." In *Asymmetric Autonomy and the Settlement of Ethnic Conflicts*, edited by Marc Weller and Katherine Nobbs, 75–96. Philadelphia: University of Pennsylvania Press, 2012.

Jackson, Vicki. "Comparative Constitutional Law: Methodologies." In *The Oxford Handbook of Comparative Constitutional Law*, edited by Michel Rosenfeld and András Sajó, 54–74. Oxford: Oxford University Press, 2012.

Kane, Sean, Joost R Hiltermann, and Raad Alkadiri. "Iraq's Federalism Quandary." *The National Interest*, no. 118 (2012): 20–30.

Keil, Soeren. "Federalism as a Tool of Conflict-Resolution: The Case of Bosnia and Herzegovina." *L'Europe En Formation* 363, no. 1 (2012): 205–18.

Keil, Soeren. *Multinational Federalism in Bosnia and Herzegovina*. Southeast European Studies. Wey Court East, UK and Burlington, VT: Ashgate, 2013.

Kelly, Michael J. "The Kurdish Regional Constitution." *Penn State Law Review* 114, no. 3 (2010): 707–808.

Kendle, John. *Federal Britain*. London: Routledge, 1997.

Khoso, Shahal. "Postcolonial Federalism: A Conceptual Analysis for Tracing State-Formation in the Global South." *Nationalism and Ethnic Politics* 30, no. 4(2024): 488–511.

Kössler, Karl. "Changing Faces of Asymmetry – The Canadian Example." In *Asymmetries in Constitutional Law*, edited by Francesco Palermo, Karl Kössler, and Carolin Zwilling, 133–66. Bolzano/Bozen: Accademia Europea di Bolzano, 2009.

Law, David S., ed. *Constitutionalism in Context*. Cambridge: Cambridge University Press, 2022.

Masterman, Roger, and Robert Schütze, eds. *The Cambridge Companion to Comparative Constitutional Law*. Cambridge: Cambridge University Press, 2019.

Mattei, Ugo. "Three Patterns of Law: Taxonomy and Change in the World's Legal Systems." *The American Journal of Comparative Law* 45, no. 1 (1997): 5–44.

McCulloch, Allison, and Eduardo Wassim Aboultaif. "Territorial and Institutional Settlement in the Global South and Beyond." In *Oxford Research Encyclopedia of International Studies*, 2023.

McGarry, John. "Asymmetric Autonomy in the United Kingdom." In *Asymmetric Autonomy and the Settlement of Ethnic Conflicts*, edited by Marc Weller and Katherine Nobbs, 148–79. Philadelphia: University of Pennsylvania Press, 2012.

McGarry, John, and Brendan O'Leary. "Iraq's Constitution of 2005: Liberal Consociation as Political Prescription." *International Journal of Constitutional Law* 5, no. 4 (2007): 670–98.

Medina Alcoz, Luis. "The Spanish Apprach to Asymmetric Federalism." In *Asymmetries in Constitutional Law*, edited by Francesco Palermo, Karl Kössler, and Carolin Zwilling, 49–62. Bolzano/Bozen: Accademia Europea di Bolzano, 2009.

Merino, Roger. "Constitution-Making in the Andes: A Decolonial Approach to Comparative Constitutional Change." *Rabels Zeitschrift Für Ausländisches Und Internationales Privatrecht* 86, no. 1 (2022): 226–53.

Merino, Roger. "Decolonial Theory and Comparative Law." In *The Cambridge Handbook of Comparative Law*, edited by Mathias Siems and Po Jen Yap, 1st ed., 408–25. Cambridge: Cambridge University Press, 2024.

Meskic, Ziatan, and Nezir Pivi. "Federalism in Bosnia and Herzegovina." *Vienna Journal on International Constitutional Law* 5, no. 4 (2011): 597–617.

Meuwese, Anne, and Mila Versteeg. "Quantitative Methods for Comparative Constitutional Law." In *Practice and Theory of Comparative Law*, edited by Maurice Adams and Jacco Bomhoff, 230–57. Cambridge: Cambridge University Press, 2012.

Michaels, Ralf. "Decolonial Comparative Law: FAQ." In *A Research Agenda for Comparative Law*, edited by Jaakko Husa, 61–86. Cheltenham, UK: Edward Elgar, 2024.

Michaels, Ralf. "The Functional Method of Comparative Law." In *The Oxford Handbook of Comparative Law*, edited by Mathias Reimann and Reinhard Zimmermann, 339–82. Oxford: Oxford University Press, 2006.

Mignolo, Walter D. "Delinking: The Rhetoric of Modernity, the Logic of Coloniality and the Grammar of Decoloniality." *Cultural Studies* 21, no. 2–3 (2007): 449–514.

Monateri, Pier Giorgio, and Mauro Balestrieri. *Quantitative Methods in Comparative Law*. Cheltenham, UK and Northampton, MA: Elgar Publishing, 2023.

O'Leary, Brendan. "Thinking About Asymmetry and Symmetry in the Remaking of Iraq." In *Asymmetric Autonomy and the Settlement of Ethnic Conflicts*, edited by Marc Weller and Katherine Nobbs, 183–212. University of Pennsylvania Press, 2010.

Olivetti, Marco. "Il federalismo asimmetrico belga e le sue recenti evoluzioni." In *Integrazione europea e asimmetrie regionali*, edited by Guerino D'Ignazio, 63–90. Milano: Giuffrè, 2007.

Palermo, Francesco, and Alice Valdesalici. "Irreversibly Different." In *Constitutional Asymmetry in Multinational Federalism*, edited by Patricia Popelier and Maja Sahadžić, 287–314. Cham: Palgrave Macmillan, 2019.

Pandey, Rajendra Kumar. "Accommodating Diversity, Consolidating Nationhood." In *Constitutional Asymmetry in Multinational Federalism*, edited by Patricia Popelier and Maja Sahadžić, 197–226. Cham: Palgrave Macmillan, 2019.

Parolari, Sara. "Asymmetrical Devolutionary Tendencies and Policy-Making in the United Kingdom." In *Asymmetries in Constitutional Law*, edited by Francesco Palermo, Karl Kössler, and Carolin Zwilling, 63–76. Bolzano/Bozen: Accademia Europea di Bolzano, 2009.

Popelier, Patricia. "Asymmetry and Complexity as a Device for Multinational Conflict Management." In *Constitutional Asymmetry in Multinational Federalism*, edited by Patricia Popelier and Maja Sahadžić, 17–46. Cham: Palgrave Macmillan, 2019.

Reimann, Mathias. "The Progress and Failure of Comparative Law in the Second Half of the Twentieth Century." *The American Journal of Comparative Law* 50, no. 4 (2002): 671–700.

Reimann, Mathias, and Reinhard Zimmermann, eds. *The Oxford Handbook of Comparative Law*. Oxford: Oxford University Press, 2019.

Resta, Giorgio. "'So Lonely': Comparative Law and the Quest for Interdisciplinary Legal Education." *International Journal for the Semiotics of Law – Revue Internationale de Sémiotique Juridique* 37, no. 5 (2024): 1569–86.

Rosenfeld, Michel, and András Sajó, eds. *The Oxford Handbook of Comparative Constitutional Law*. 1st ed. Oxford: Oxford University Press, 2012.

Sacco, Rodolfo. "Legal Formants: A Dynamic Approach to Comparative Law (Installment I of II)." *The American Journal of Comparative Law* 39, no. 1 (1991): 1–34.

Sacco, Rodolfo. "Legal Formants: A Dynamic Approach to Comparative Law (Installment II of II)." *The American Journal of Comparative Law* 39, no. 2 (1991): 343–401.

Sahadžić, Maja. "Can Asymmetrical Constitutional Arrangements Provide an Alternative Answer for the Disputed? Bringing Constitutional Asymmetries into Play in the Middle East Peace Process." *Perspectives on Federalism* 12, no. 1 (2020): 3–25.

Sahadžić, Maja. "Mild Asymmetry and Ethnoterritorial Overlap in Charge of the Consequences of Multinationalism." In *Constitutional Asymmetry in Multinational Fed-*

eralism, edited by Patricia Popelier and Maja Sahadžić, 47–76. Cham: Palgrave Macmillan, 2019.

Sahadžić, Maja, Damir Banović, Dražen Barbarić, and Goran Marković, eds. *Citizens, Constitution, Europe. Glossary of Essential Constitutional Concepts in BiH*. Sarajevo: Pravni fakultet Univerziteta, 2023.

Salaymeh, Lena, and Ralf Michaels. "Decolonial Comparative Law: A Conceptual Beginning." *Rabels Zeitschrift Für Ausländisches Und Internationales Privatrecht* 86, no. 1 (2022): 166–88.

Salleh, Asri, Arnold Puyok, and Toni Paridi Bagang. "Constitutional Asymmetry in Malaysia: A Case Study of Sabah and Sarawak." In *Constitutional Asymmetry in Multinational Federalism*, edited by Patricia Popelier and Maja Sahadžić, 315–40. Cham, Switzerland: Palgrave Macmillan, 2019.

Sanjaume-Calvet, Marc, Lesley-Ann Daniels, and Pau Bossacoma Busquets. "Territorial Conflict in the Spotlight: Unveiling Paths to Territorial Clarity." *Publius: The Journal of Federalism* 55, no. 1 (2025): 201-221..

Saunders, Cheryl. "The Use and Misuse of Comparative Constitutional Law." *Indiana Journal of Global Legal Studies* 13, no. 1 (2006): 37–76.

Schacherreiter, Judith. "Postcolonial Theory and Comparative Law: On the Methodological and Epistemological Benefits to Comparative Law through Postcolonial Theory." *Verfassung in Recht Und Übersee* 49, no. 3 (2016): 291–312.

Siems, Mathias. *Comparative Law*. Cambridge: Cambridge University Press, 2022.

Siems, Mathias. "Empirical Methods." In *The Cambridge Handbook of Comparative Law*, edited by Mathias Siems and Po Jen Yap, 157–76. Cambridge: Cambridge University Press, 2024.

Siems, Mathias. "Varieties of Legal Systems: Towards a New Global Taxonomy." *Journal of Institutional Economics* 12, no. 3 (2016): 579–602.

Solnick, Steven L. "Federalism and State-Building: Post-Communist and Post-Colonial Perspectives." In *The Architecture of Democracy*, edited by Andrew Reynolds, 1st ed., 171–205. Oxford University Press Oxford, 2002.

Von Bogdandy, Armin. "Comparative Constitutional Law as a Social Science? A Hegelian Reaction to Ran Hirschl's Comparative Matters." *MPIL Research Paper Series* 09 (2016): 1–15.

Wolff, Stefan. "Cases of Asymmetrical Territorial Autonomy." In *Asymmetric Autonomy and the Settlement of Ethnic Conflicts*, edited by Marc Weller and Katherine Nobbs, 17–47. Philadelphia: University of Pennsylvania Press, 2010.

Zitzke, Emile. "A Decolonial Critique of Private Law and Human Rights." *South African Journal on Human Rights* 34, no. 3 (September 2, 2018): 492–516.

Zitzke, Emile. "Decolonial Comparative Law: Thoughts from South Africa." *Rabels Zeitschrift Für Ausländisches Und Internationales Privatrecht* 86, no. 1 (2022): 189–225.

PART 2

The Role of Constitutional Courts

CHAPTER 4

Courts and the Accommodation of Diversity

1 Introduction

This chapter opens the second part of the book, introducing the role of courts in addressing ethnocultural diversity. Specifically, the chapter examines the relationship between courts and diversity from two different perspectives. The first perspective addresses how constitutional courts deal with internal diversity in their constitutional system, analysing four landmark cases delivered by constitutional courts that played a meaningful role in the accommodation of diversity, such as the 1996 *First Certification Judgment* of the Connotational Court of South Africa, the 2000 *Constituent Peoples'* case of the Constitutional Court of Bosnia-Herzegovina, the 1998 *Reference Re Secession of Québec* of the Supreme Court of Canada, and the 1985 *Shah Bano* case of the Supreme Court of India. The same paragraph addresses how supranational courts addressed issues related to internal diversity and minority rights, reviewing the experience of the International Court of Justice, the European Court of Human Rights, the Inter-American Court of Human Rights, the Badinter Commission, and the African Commission on Human and Peoples' Rights.

Then, the second perspective analysed in the chapter explores how diversity can also be reflected within courts, addressing two peculiar compositions of courts, i.e., the so-called "power-sharing courts", and the "hybrid constitutional courts", comparing courts such as the BiH Constitutional Court, the Constitutional Court of Cyprus, and the Constitutional Court of Kosovo.

Finally, the chapter concludes with a reflection on the use of foreign law by courts to address ethnocultural diversity, recalling the experience of the domestic and supranational courts previously analysed in the chapter, and their relative judicial dialogue.

2 Diversity and Courts

2.1 *Ethnicity and Rights: A Contested Terrain?*

Contemporary constitutionalism is characterised, among other features, by the existence of a system of rights defining the political community, even

 | DOI:10.1163/9789004739109_006

though the catalogue of rights may vary,[1] as well as the degree to which these rights are enforceable through judicial review.[2] Despite these differences, liberal democracies are typically informed by the image of "a consolidated political community of free and equal citizens constituted as such by a system of rights".[3] However, when it comes to divided societies, this conception of the polity may be more complicated. Harvey and Schwartz see at least two reasons why fragmented societies complicate rights-based constitutionalism. First, the standard model puts the individual at the centre of constitutional values, as the goal is to protect the individual against the abuse of public power and such an individualistic perspective may not effectively address the problems which may arise in divided societies. In fact, minority groups may fear that the majority will violate their rights or marginalise their interests. Rights-based constitutionalism registers group-based concerns not as "matters of principle", but as "matters of policy" to be determined by the majority.[4] The second reason revolves around the communitarian meaning of rights-based constitutionalism, as these may define the nature of a political community. In divided societies, this may not necessarily be the case. If it is true that a common framework of rights might have a unifying effect on the polity, it is also true that the same framework could conflict with the recognition of difference.[5]

Relative to these issues, Ghai argued that "human rights now speak to many, often competing, concerns"[6] that need to be reconciled within a framework mediating between individual and collective rights. This had become especially problematic in the aftermath of decolonisation when the imposition of the nation-state-based model in a context of ethnocultural diversity led to the marginalisation of minority groups. In fact, the borders of former colonies were designed to meet the economic and political interests of colonial powers and disregarded the pre-existing polities, often bringing together peoples speaking different languages, and belonging to different faiths and cultures.[7] Moved by the same goal to serve their own interests, colonial powers

1 See Norman Dorsen, et al., eds. *Comparative Constitutionalism. Cases and Materials* (Eagan, Minnesota: West Academic, 2016), 33–39.

2 See Albert HY Chen and Miguel Poiares Maduro, "The Judiciary and Constitutional Review," in *Routledge Handbook of Constitutional Law*, ed. Mark Tushnet, Thomas Fleiner, and Cheryl Saunders (London and New York: Routledge, 2013), 365–411.

3 Colin Harvey and Alex Schwartz, "Introduction," in *Rights in Divided Societies*, ed. Colin Harvey and Alex Schwartz (Oxford and Portland: Hart Publishing, 2012), 1.

4 Harvey and Schwartz, "Introduction," 2.

5 Harvey and Schwartz, "Introduction," 3.

6 Yash Ghai, "Ethnicity and Competing Notions of Rights," in *Rights in Divided Societies*, ed. Colin Harvey and Alex Schwartz (Oxford and Portland: Hart Publishing, 2012), 51.

7 Ghai, "Ethnicity and Competing Notions of Rights," 51–52.

relied on local ethnicities to exercise dominance in the territory and administer the colonies and perpetuated the idea of "tribalism", i.e., that colonised polities were governed by tribes and not by other forms of pre-existing political power.[8] This also resulted in the establishment of disparities and the consolidation of hierarchies among ethnic groups, and even in the "creation" of ethnic groups by colonial administrators.[9] Reflecting on the legacies of colonialism in the African continent, Gilbert observed that "the historical use of ethnic identity to rule and conquer, and the role law played in it, represents a critical legacy of colonisation that impacts on contemporary legal approaches to ethnicity in most African states".[10] Similarly, in India, the dramatic experience of the partition of the Indian subcontinent after the end of colonial rule substantially weakened the claims for group rights, since the establishment of a Muslim-majority Pakistan "eased the path towards a liberal and secular constitution".[11] Moreover, the need for distance from colonial rule meant abandoning the logic of group rights in a corporate sense, especially because such a conception of rights was "an important technique of control during colonial rule".[12] Nonetheless, in other parts of the world, the unfolding of decolonisation led to political claims based on ethnicity that revolved around the legal recognition of culture and religion (such as the recognition of customary laws in civil and family matters), the adoption of special affirmative measures to improve socio-economic conditions, representation in political institutions, and state-support for religious and cultural rights. The denial of these claims had the potential to lead to even more substantial demands, such as "a fundamental re-design of the state or even secession",[13] and were increasingly rooted in international norms on human rights protection.

However, before proceeding with the analysis, it is important to make a clarification in order to avoid a purely Eurocentric perception of human rights and minority rights. In fact, it should be noted that, in the African context, ethnicity did not contribute to the emergence of constitutional and international legal frameworks aimed at protecting minority rights. Conversely, most post-independence African constitutions were much more focused on the

---

8 Jeremie Gilbert, "Constitutionalism, Ethnicity and Minority Rights in Africa: A Legal Appraisal from the Great Lakes Region," *International Journal of Constitutional Law* 11, no. 2 (2013): 428.

9 Gilbert, "Constitutionalism, Ethnicity and Minority Rights in Africa," 429.

10 Ibidem.

11 Ghai, "Ethnicity and Competing Notions of Rights," 63.

12 Ibidem.

13 Ghai, "Ethnicity and Competing Notions of Rights," 55.

principles of sovereignty and non-interference from foreign powers,[14] and thus sought to distance themselves from the category of ethnicity for the sake of the national unity, insofar as recognising minority rights was interpreted as a threat to the process of nation-building. Unsurprisingly, this played an important role in "preventing the development of a strong corpus of constitutional law protecting minority rights".[15] Moreover, the very dichotomy between minority/majority might appear to make "little sense",[16] as most African identities are constructed along a complex interplay of several, cross-cutting facets, including ethnic, tribal, cultural, religious, and national identities. For these reasons, minority rights have often been perceived as a "Western concept" based on Western values, and as such not as universal as they are intended to be. This is also an argument brought forward in the debate on decolonial legal studies, and specifically decolonial human rights law, that has critically discussed whether the principles of "African communitarianism" should be integrated to make the international system on human rights more universal.[17] In this way, the focus would be not only on the individual, but also on the community, thus encompassing the "communitarian approach to rights that is found in the traditional socio-legal systems across Africa".[18] Nevertheless, if decentring Eurocentrism is essential to adopt a truly global perspective, it could also be argued that the contention against a more developed constitutional framework for minority rights in most African countries rests on a distorted understanding of minority rights. In this respect, Gilbert identified three main arguments against minority rights, according to which the recognition of minority rights would threaten national unity, would make little sense since "everyone is a minority", and would create privileges for some groups to the detriment of others. Conversely, the essence of minority rights is precisely the opposite, namely, to ensure that marginalised groups enjoy the same rights and opportunities as dominant groups, thus guaranteeing substantial equality, not creating privileges.

Nonetheless, human rights and ethnicity seems to clash, as the two concepts appear to be conceptualised along opposing lines:

---

14 See A. Bolaji Akinyemi, "The OAU and the Concept of Non-Interference in the Internal Affairs of Member States," *British Yearbook of International Law* 46 (1972): 393.

15 Gilbert, "Constitutionalism, Ethnicity and Minority Rights in Africa," 430.

16 Gilbert, "Constitutionalism, Ethnicity and Minority Rights in Africa," 431.

17 See Emile Zitzke, "A Decolonial Critique of Private Law and Human Rights," *South African Journal on Human Rights* 34, no. 3 (2018): 492–516; Emile Zitzke, "Decolonial Comparative Law: Thoughts from South Africa," *Rabels Zeitschrift Für Ausländisches Und Internationales Privatrecht* 86, no. 1 (2022): 189–225.

18 Gilbert, "Constitutionalism, Ethnicity and Minority Rights in Africa," 432.

> Human rights seek to be colour-blind, aloof from religious or other affiliations; ethnicity makes these affiliations basic to identity and human existence. Human rights empower the individual; ethnicity the group. Human rights are the framework for relations between citizens inter se and between citizens and the state; ethnicity compels attention to and regulation of inter-ethnic relations, and the relations of the group to the state. Human rights aim to be inclusive, ethnicity exclusive.[19]

In this respect, Ghai refers to a "framework of rights" as "the standards and norms of human rights reflected in international instruments and the institutions for the interpretation and enforcement of rights".[20] Such a framework becomes the pillar of the constitutional system, not only in the process of nation-building and negotiation of policies, but also in the settlement of competing claims based on ethnicity by the judiciary, as will emerge in the following section.

2.2 *Constitutional Courts in Divided Societies*

Constitutional courts have played a major role in enforcing constitutional rights and in addressing ethnocultural diversity.[21] In a recent study, Biagi showed the pivotal role played by constitutional courts in constitutional transitions to democracy by comparing three generations of European constitutional courts: the Italian Constitutional Court, the Spanish Constitutional Tribunal, and Constitutional Court of the Czech Republic.[22] Focusing on Italy and Spain, the respective constitutional courts were key actors in moving away from a previous authoritarian past, and in the consolidation of the regional model introduced by newly adopted democratic constitutions. Indeed, the Italian Constitutional Court and the Spanish Constitutional Tribunal im-

---

19 Ghai, "Ethnicity and Competing Notions of Rights," 59.

20 Ghai, "Ethnicity and Competing Notions of Rights," 60.

21 See Bertus De Villiers et al., eds., *Litigating the Rights of Minorities and Indigenous Peoples in Domestic and International Courts* (Leiden and Boston: Brill | Nijhoff, 2021); Francesco Biagi, *Constitution-Building After the Arab Spring: A Comparative Perspective* (Cambridge: Cambridge University Press, 2025), 140–88; Tom Ginsburg and Zachary Elkins, "Ancillary Powers of Constitutional Courts," *Texas Law Review* 87, no. 7 (2009): 1431–1162; Wojciech Sadurski, "Judicial Review and the Protection of Constitutional Rights," *Oxford Journal of Legal Studies* 22, no. 2, (2002): 275–299; Wojciech Sadurski, *Rights Before Courts* (Cham: Springer, 2014); Mattias Kumm, "Constitutional Rights as Principles: On the Structure and Domain of Constitutional Justice," *International Journal of Constitutional Law* 2, no. 3 (2004): 574–596.

22 See Francesco Biagi, *European Constitutional Courts and Transitions to Democracy* (Cambridge: Cambridge University Press, 2020).

printed an unprecedented change in upholding the normativity of the constitution, that had previously been considered a "symbolic text" only[23] and thus had no normative value. As observed by Biagi, "it is mainly thanks to the action of the constitutional judges that in Europe the Constitution was recognised as a legal norm, and in particular as the supreme norm. Indeed, in each of the three generations of courts, these bodies considered the text of the Constitution to be legally binding in its entirety [...]".[24] Thanks to the formulation of constitutional provisions, the adoption of laws aimed at protecting rights, and the general process of internationalisation in constitutional law,[25] constitutional courts also became crucial in safeguarding fundamental rights and freedoms, and this is even more meaningful when it is considered that previous Fascist and Francoist regimes dramatically restricted individual rights.[26] Finally, it is worth mentioning that, in Spain, one of the most sensitive issues in the democratic transition concerned precisely the territorial organisation of the state, and the Spanish Constitutional Tribunal played a unique role in solving the dispute between the central state and the autonomous communities (especially the Basque Country and Catalonia), leading to the stabilisation of the state of autonomies.[27]

Shifting the focus to divided societies, Issacharoff argued that constitutional courts such as the South African and Bosnian-Herzegovinian courts, saw in their constitutional authority a "responsibility to mediate the inherent conflict between democratic self-governance and the risk of majoritarian op-

---

23 Louis Favoreu, "American and European Models of Constitutional Justice," in *Comparative and Private International Law: Essays in Honor of John Henry Merryman on His Seventieth Birthday*, ed. David S. Clark (Berlin: Duncker & Humblot, 1990), 119.

24 Biagi, *European Constitutional Courts and Transitions to Democracy*, 180.

25 On the internationalisation of constitutional law and the relative impact on fundamental rights, see Sergio Bartole, *The Internationalisation of Constitutional Law. A View from the Venice Commission* (Oxford and Portland: Hart Publishing, 2020); Wen-Chen Chang and Jiunn-Rong Yeh, "Internationalization of Constitutional Law," in *The Oxford Handbook of Comparative Constitutional Law*, ed. Michel Rosenfeld and András Sajó (Oxford: Oxford University Press, 2012), 1165 ff; Manuel José Cepeda, "The Internationalization of Constitutional Law: A Note on the Colombian Case," *Verfassung Und Recht in Übersee / Law and Politics in Africa, Asia and Latin America* 41, no. 1 (2008): 61–77; Charles Manga Fombad, "Internationalization of Constitutional Law and Constitutionalism in Africa," *The American Journal of Comparative Law* 60, no. 2 (2012): 439–73; Francesco Palermo, "Internazionalizzazione del diritto costituzionale e costituzionalizzazione del diritto internazionale delle differenze," *European Diversity and Autonomy Papers*, no. 2 (2009): 5–32; Giuseppe Franco Ferrari, *I diritti nel costituzionalismo globale: luci e ombre* (Modena: Mucchi Editore, 2023).

26 Biagi, *European Constitutional Courts and Transitions to Democracy*, 181–185.

27 See Biagi, *European Constitutional Courts and Transitions to Democracy*, 124–130.

pression", helping their divided societies to "move away from the risk of locking in social fractures that would have been present had the immediate majorities held unfettered power".[28] To further exemplify the role played by constitutional courts in divided societies, the rest of this section reviews four landmark cases: the 1996 *First Certification Judgment* of the Constitutional Court of South Africa, the 2000 *Constituent Peoples'* case of the Constitutional Court of Bosnia-Herzegovina, the 1998 *Reference Re Secession of Québec* of the Supreme Court of Canada, and the 1985 *Shah Bano* case of the Supreme Court of India. In these landmark judgments, the respective constitutional/supreme courts of divided multi-tiered systems addressed internal ethnocultural diversity in ways that deeply impacted on the constitutional system and the protection of fundamental rights. Before proceeding with the analysis, it should be clarified that, even though South Africa was not included in the case studies of this book (as it is does not display constitutional asymmetries), the experience of the South African Constitutional Court in the democratic transition after the end of apartheid is too meaningful to be left out of a chapter dedicated to courts and ethnocultural diversity.

2.2.1 The First Certification Judgment

Before addressing the South African judgment, it should first be recalled that the constitution-making process following the democratic transition from apartheid was one of the most complex constitutional democracies ever witnessed.[29] Indeed, the process was characterised by a multitude of actors, through several multi-party fora, such as the Conference for Democratic South Africa (CODESA I and II) and the Multi-Party Negotiating Process (MPNP) that started even before the 1994 elections.[30] The process led to an agreement on some foundational elements of the constitution-making process, including the 1993 Interim Constitution, the establishment of a Constitutional Court, and the 34 fundamental constitutional principles[31] that

28 Issacharoff, "Constitutionalizing Democracy," 1893.

29 Lollini and Palermo, "Comparative Law and the Proceduralization of Constitution-Building Processes," 310.

30 See Veronica Federico, *Sudafrica* (Bologna: Il Mulino, 2009), 43–59; Heinz Klug, *The Constitution of South Africa: A Contextual Analysis* (Oxford and Portland: Hart Publishing, 2010); Donald Horowitz, *A Democratic South Africa? Constitutional Engineering in a Divided Society* (Berkeley: University of California Press, 1992); Nancy L. Clark and William H. Worger, *South Africa: The Rise and Fall of Apartheid*, 2nd ed (Harlow, England and New York: Longman, 2011); Bertus de Villiers, *Democratic Prospects for South Africa* (Cape Town: HSRC Publishers, 1992).

31 See Ghai, "Ethnicity and Competing Nations of Rights," 77–81.

served as binding guiding principles for the subsequently elected constitutional assembly.[32] These principles "contained an amalgam of broad democratic principles consistent with the new international post-cold war consensus on constitutionalism",[33] and were a substantial turning point in terms of the protection and accommodation of diversity. As such, the principles included prohibition of discrimination (III), gender and racial equality in both formal (I) and substantive terms (V), cultural and linguistic diversity (XI), collective rights of self-determination in civil society sectors (XII), the recognition of traditional and customary laws (XIII), and a system of provincial government (XVIII–XXII).

The proposal for a newly established South African Constitutional Court[34] came from the African National Congress (ANC), marking one of the most significant alterations to the prior South African political institutions.[35] Indeed, the South African Constitutional Court played a unprecedented role in counter-majoritarian protection, being entrusted with the power to ensure that the final Constitution was in conformity with the constitutional princi-

---

32 Lollini and Palermo, "Comparative Law and the Proceduralization of Constitution-Building Processes," 310.

33 Heinz Klug, "How the Centre Holds in South Africa: Managing Claims for Regional and Ethnic Autonomy in a Democratic South Africa," in *Autonomy and Ethnicity. Negotiating Competing Claims in Multi-Ethnic States*, ed. Yash Ghai (Cambridge: Cambridge University Press, 2000), 112.

34 On the South African Constitutional Court, see Theunis Roux, "Principle and Pragmatism on the Constitutional Court of South Africa," *International Journal of Constitutional Law* 7, no. 1 (2008): 106–38; James Fowkes, "Constitutional Court of South Africa," in *Max Planck Encyclopedia of Comparative Constitutional Law*, ed. Rainer Grote, Frauke Lachenmann, and Rüdiger Wolfrum (Heidelberg: Max Planck Institute for Comparative Public Law and International law, 2017); Nico Steytler, "The Constitutional Court of South Africa: Reinforcing an Hourglass System of Multi-Level Government," in *Courts in Federal Countries*, ed. Nicholas Aroney and John Kincaid (Toronto: University of Toronto Press, 2017), 328–66; Andrea Lollini, *Constitutionalism and Transitional Justice in South Africa* (New York and Oxford: Berghahn Books, 2011), 63–70; Heinz Klug, "South Africa's Constitutional Court: Enabling Democracy and Promoting Law in the Transition from Apartheid," *Journal of Comparative Law*, 3, no. 2 (2008): 174–93; Elsa Van Huyssteen, "The Constitutional Court and the Redistribution of Power in South Africa: Towards Transformative Constitutionalism," *African Studies* 59, no. 2 (2000): 245–65; Daniel Bonilla Maldonado, *Constitutionalism of the Global South: The Activist Tribunals of India, South Africa, and Colombia* (Cambridge: Cambridge University Press, 2013); Francesco Lucherini, "Il diritto a un'abitazione adeguata in India e Sudafrica. Realtà e potenzialità del dialogo tra le corti," *Diritto Pubblico Comparato ed Europeo*, no. 2 (2020): 427–450.

35 Issacharoff, "Constitutionalizing Democracy," 1871.

ples of democratic governance.[36] This arrangement was intended to satisfy the security interest of parties and was considered an integral part of the peaceful transition to constitutional democracy.[37] In this context, such a counter-majoritarian role was carefully interpreted by the Court in the *First Certification Judgment* in 1996,[38] when it refused to certify the first constitutional text of the final Constitution. In this judgment, the Court directly addressed the counter-majoritarian dilemma, recognising the "problems of justifying the existence of a judicial power to prevent the constitution drafter by a democratically elected Constitutional Assembly from coming into effect".[39] However, the landmark nature of this judgment lies precisely in the interpretation of its role in protecting the values and institutions of constitutionalism and the rule of law, limiting the power of a representative government. Moreover, as argued by Chaskalson and Davis, "the widespread acceptance of the judgment by the political parties reflects the degree to which constitutionalism and the rule of law have become uncontroversial facts of South African political life",[40] soon after the end of the apartheid regime.

Moving to the content of the decision, in the *First Certification Judgment*, the Court found that nine provisions of the constitutional text failed to comply with several fundamental principles, and required the constitutional assembly to re-write some sections according to the 34 fundamental principles.[41] For the purposes of this book, it is worth focusing on the fact that "the court's denial of certification was based to a large extent on the failure to, on balance, grant sufficient powers to the region",[42] which was one of the most politically controversial topics in the constitution-making process. Indeed, a number of the non-compliant provisions concerned local government, and the relative powers and competences (including fiscal arrangements).[43] In particular, Chapter 7 of the constitutional text failed to provide a comprehensive frame-

36 See Matthew Chaskalson and Dennis Davis, "Constitutionalism, the Rule of Law and the First Certification Judgment," *South African Journal on Human Rights* 13, no. 3 (1997): 430–45.

37 Issacharoff, "Constitutionalizing Democracy," 1877.

38 Certification of the Constitution of the Republic of South Africa, 1996 (CCT 23/96) [1996] ZACC 26; 1996 (4) SA 744 (CC); 1996 (10) BCLR 1253 (CC) (6 September 1996).

39 Chaskalson and Davis, "Constitutionalism, the Rule of Law and the First Certification Judgment," 432.

40 Ibidem.

41 For a detailed analysis, see Chaskalson and Davis, "Constitutionalism, the Rule of Law and the First Certification Judgment," 436–444.

42 Klug, "How the Centre Holds in South Africa," 113.

43 *First Certification judgment*, para. 300–301. See Chaskalson and Davis, "Constitutionalism, the Rule of Law and the First Certification Judgment," 437–439. For some references

work for local government, as provided by Constitutional Principle XXIV,[44] to design appropriate legislative procedures, as required by Principle X,[45] or to provide adequate fiscal powers and functions for local government,[46] as required by Principle XXV.[47] In its decision, the Court also enforced Constitutional Principle XVIII(2), ensuring that "the powers and functions of the provinces defined in the Constitution, including the competence of a provincial legislature to adopt a constitution for its province, shall not be substantially less than or substantially inferior to those provided for in this Constitution".[48]

Looking beyond the *First Certification Judgment*, the early case law of the South African Constitutional Court marked a clear discontinuity from the past, striking down previous legislation and reversing official decisions inherited from the apartheid regime. As concluded by Klug, "what might under other circumstances have been perceived as a counter-majoritarian and hence anti-democratic power was instead embraced as the triumph of human rights standards over the legacies of apartheid".[49] Finally, it is further interesting to notice that the process of negotiation that led to the agreement on the first version of the final Constitution witnessed a series of amendments concerning constitutional asymmetries. Specifically, the round of amendments to the Interim Constitution that occurred in March 1994 introduced greater powers to the provinces when drafting their own constitutions, opening space for asym-

---

on the role of South African Constitutional Court in dealing with regionalism-related disputes, see Klug, "How the Centre Holds in South Africa," 108–112.

44 Interim Constitution of South Africa (1993) – Schedule 4 "Constitutional Principles", principle XXIV: "A framework for local government powers, functions and structures shall be set out in the Constitution. The comprehensive powers, functions and other features of local government shall be set out in parliamentary statutes or in provincial legislation or in both."

45 Interim Constitution of South Africa (1993) – Schedule 4 "Constitutional Principles", principle X: "Formal legislative procedures shall be adhered to by legislative organs at all levels of government."

46 It is interesting to notice that, in respect of fiscal powers, "the concern of the Court was that the text allocated local government too much power, not too little" (Chaskalson and Davis, "Constitutionalism, the Rule of Law and the First Certification Judgment," 438).

47 Interim Constitution of South Africa (1993) – Schedule 4 "Constitutional Principles", principle XXV: "The national government and provincial governments shall have fiscal powers and functions which will be defined in the Constitution. The framework for local government referred to in Principle XXIV shall make provision for appropriate fiscal powers and functions for different categories of local government."

48 Interim Constitution of South Africa (1993) – Schedule 4 "Constitutional Principles", principle XVIII(2).

49 Klug, "South Africa's Constitutional Court," 180.

metries.[50] However, these asymmetrical provisions were eventually discarded and in the final Constitution "all the asymmetrical federal features disappeared".[51]

2.2.2 The Constituent Peoples' Case

Concerning Bosnia-Herzegovina,[52] the BiH Constitutional Court's decision on the so-called *Constituent Peoples*,[53] delivered in 2000, is another notable instance of the powerful role played by courts in managing internal diversity. To assess its impact, it is first necessary to trace the different phases of constitutional transition in the aftermath of the Bosnian war.[54] The signing of the Dayton Peace Agreement (DPA) in 1995 paved the way for the start of a peaceful transition, regulating the terms of the ceasefire and encompassing a newly drafted Constitution for Bosnia and Herzegovina. Notably, the BiH Constitution is the Annex IV of the DPA and was introduced to the system without any internal ratification.[55] Thus, the first phase of the constitutional transition in Bosnia and Herzegovina (1995–1997) was characterised by the rigid application of ethnic and territorial separation between the previous belligerent groups, the implementation of the ceasefire and the setting out of the political institutions provided for by the Dayton, which modelled the system along

50 Nico Steytler and Johann Mettler, "Federal Arrangements as a Peacemaking Device During South Africa's Transition to Democracy," *Publius: The Journal of Federalism* 31, no. 4 (2001): 96.

51 Steytler and Mettler, "Federal Arrangements as a Peacemaking Device," 104.

52 The Constitutional Court of Bosnia and Herzegovina will be further analysed in Chapter 4 (paragraph 3.2) and Chapter 5 (paragraphs 2.2 and 3.6).

53 Constitutional Court of Bosnia and Herzegovina, Case U-5/98 III, 1 July 2000. On this decision, see Francesco Palermo, "Bosnia-Erzegovina: la Corte Costituzionale fissa i confini della (nuova) società multietnica," *Diritto Pubblico Comparato ed Europeo* 4 (2000): 1479–89; Samuel Issacharoff, "Constitutionalizing Democracy in Fractured Societies," *Texas Law Review* 82 (2004): 1861–93; Jens Woelk, *La transizione costituzionale della Bosnia ed Erzegovina* (Padova: CEDAM, 2008), 111–122; Sujit Choudhry and Richard Stacey, "Independent of Dependent? Constitutional Courts in Divided Societies," in *Rights in Divided Societies*, ed. Colin Harvey and Alex Schwartz (Oxford and Portland: Hart Publishing, 2012), 97–99; Gavrić et al., *The Political System of Bosnia and Herzegovina*, 24–26; Zlatan Begić and Zlatan Delić, "Constituency of Peoples in the Constitutional System of Bosnia and Herzegovina: Chasing Fair Solutions," *International Journal of Constitutional Law* 11, no. 2 (2013): 447–65; Lidia Bonifati, "The 'Constituent Peoples' Case' and its Enduring Legacy in Bosnia and Herzegovina," in *Comparative Constitutional History. Volume 3: Landmark Judgments*, ed. Francesco Biagi, Justin O. Frosini, and Jason Mazzone (Leiden and Boston: Brill, forthcoming 2026).

54 See Woelk, *La transizione costituzionale.*

55 Woelk, *La transizione costituzionale*, 80.

ethnic lines. However, this was in tension with the dynamic elements provided for by other constitutional provisions. In fact, Art. I of the Constitution states that "Bosnia and Herzegovina shall be a democratic state, which shall operate under the rule of law and with free and democratic elections".[56] Moreover, Art. II states that "the rights and freedoms set forth in the European Convention for the Protection of Human Rights and Fundamental Freedoms and its Protocols shall apply directly in Bosnia and Herzegovina. These shall have priority over all other law".[57] These constitutional principles contrast with the predominant role played by ethnicity within the system,[58] and this tension becomes even more evident when considering the mechanisms for the protection of minority rights aimed at promoting the return of refugees and internally displaced persons to their homes and, thus, the rebuilding of the previous multi-ethnic society.[59]

A new phase of the constitutional transition was triggered by the decisions of the BiH Constitutional Court, among which was the decision in the *Constituent Peoples'* case. These introduced some "constitutional corrections" to the original constitutional design, insofar as, originally, the Dayton Constitution established that the pre-existing sub-state constitutions[60] had to be amended within three months to ensure their conformity with the state Constitution,[61] but at the time of the claim the amendments were still to be made. Among the contested constitutional provisions[62] was the definition in the RS Constitution of the Republika Srpska as the "State of Serb peoples" and the recognition of Serbian as the only official language, and the explicit recognition in the Constitution of the Federation of BiH of only two constituent peoples (Bosniaks and Bosnian-Croats) and of only two official languages. These provisions are emblematic of the fact that "the two subnational constitutions were

---

56 Constitution of Bosnia and Herzegovina – Art. I(2).

57 Constitution of Bosnia and Herzegovina – Art. II(2)

58 Woelk, *La transizione costituzionale*, 104.

59 Ibidem.

60 The Constitution of Republika Srpska was adopted in 1992, upon the declaration of independence from the former Republic of Bosnia and Herzegovina, whereas the Constitution of the Federation of BiH was adopted in 1994, upon the signature of the Washington Agreement (ending the conflict between the Bosniak and Croat warring parties).

61 Constitution of Bosnia and Herzegovina – Art. XII(2).

62 Other contested provisions in the Constitution of the Republika Srpska concerned the preferred relations with "other Serbian states", the explicit support of the Republika Srpska for the Orthodox Church, the limitations to property rights, and provisions on the central bank. In the case of the Constitution of the Federation of BiH, other contested provisions concerned matters related to defence and international relations.

adopted as constitutions of sovereign states, on which was later imposed the common structure of the Constitution of Bosnia and Herzegovina".[63]

The initiative came from the NGO "Serbian Citizen Council", denouncing the discrimination of Serbs in the Federation of Bosnia-Herzegovina and of Bosniaks and Croats in the Republika Srpska, since they were not listed as constituent peoples in the constitution of the respective entity. As a former Bosniak member of the Presidency and thus eligible to pose a request to the Constitutional Court at the time, Alija Izetbegović filed a lawsuit on this matter. The Court passed four individual judgments, declaring several articles of the entity constitutions in breach of the 1995 Dayton Constitution. The decisions were passed by a simple majority, namely by the vote of the three international judges and two Bosniak judges. The Croat and Serb judges voted against the decisions. Thus, the judgment was only possible because the Constitutional Court is one of the few BiH institutions that does not make decisions by consensus, nor does it have veto mechanisms in place.

The first individual judgment decided whether the nature of the border between the entities, i.e., the so-called inter-entity boundary line (IEBL), was a political border between states or an administrative boundary between entities, opting for the latter perspective.[64] The second decision concerned matters related to collective property,[65] and the fourth dealt with many aspects, including language, religion, and defence.[66] The third partial decision concerned precisely the issue of the constituent peoples, and specifically whether the reference to the constituent peoples in the Preamble of the Dayton Constitution[67] should translate into equal status for the three constituent peoples across the entirety of the territory or follow a narrow interpretation, related only to parity in their representation in state institutions.[68] Moreover, the Constitutional Court had to answer affirmatively whether the Preamble of the Constitution, in general, can have normative character, accepting the opinion that some lines of the Preamble have normative content.[69]

63 Woelk, *La transizione costituzionale*, 112.

64 Constitutional Court of Bosnia and Herzegovina, Case U-5/98 I, 30 January 2000.

65 Constitutional Court of Bosnia and Herzegovina, Case U-5/98 II, 19 February 2000.

66 Constitutional Court of Bosnia and Herzegovina, Case U-5/98 IV, 19 August 2000.

67 Constitution of Bosnia and Herzegovina – Preamble: "Bosniacs, Croats, and Serbs, as constituent peoples (along with Others), and citizens of Bosnia and Herzegovina hereby determine that the Constitution of Bosnia and Herzegovina is as follows: [...]".

68 Woelk, *La transizione costituzionale*, 113.

69 On the political and normative nature of constitutional preambles, see Justin O. Frosini, "Constitutional Preambles: More than Just a Narration of History," *University of Illinois Law Review* 2017, no. 2 (2017): 603–28.

In the Court's judgment, the tension between the individual dimension of rights and the collective dimension imposed by the consociational model clearly emerges. To illustrate this, it is sufficient to note that the Court was divided on an ethnic basis. On the one hand, the majority, consisting of the three foreign judges and the two Bosniak judges,[70] argued that the provisions of the subnational constitutions that recognised only majority groups as constituent peoples were not only discriminatory against minorities, but also a practice that went on to perpetuate the ethnic cleansing operations carried out during the 1990s conflict.[71] Furthermore, the majority ruled that ethnic segregation is never to be regarded as a legitimate end, even in those systems where a consociational model is present, and that the protection of individual rights is not a threat to peaceful coexistence between groups, but rather they are just as important as collective rights.[72] On the other hand, the four minority judges (i.e., the two Bosnian-Serb judges and the two Bosnian-Croat judges) favoured the consociational logic over the protection of individual rights.

From its decision, the Constitutional Court derived three general normative principles: the principle of multi-ethnicity; the principle of collective equality of constituent peoples; and the principle of prohibition of *de jure* and *de facto* discrimination.[73] The implementation of these decisions led to the inclusion of Serbs as constituent people in the Federation and of Bosniaks and Croats as constituent peoples in the Republika Srpska. The "Others" (i.e., national minorities) were also recognised as having rights to representation in parliaments and administrative bodies. Through its decisions, the Court intended to conceive of the state as multi-ethnic, and tried to promote the integration and not the segregation of the ethnic groups. These decisions re-defined the principle according to which ethnicity was identified with territory. Thus, the main outcome was that there are three constituent ethnic groups in the entire territory of Bosnia-Herzegovina, ending the discrimination against ethnic groups within the entities.

Finally, it should not be forgotten that, despite its great significance, the Court's decision was only implemented thanks to the exercise of the "Bonn

70 Bosniak judges, as well as their respective political parties, tend to favour an integrated view of the legal system, on the strength of their numerical majority over the other two ethnocultural groups.

71 Choudhry and Stacey, "Independent of Dependent," 98.

72 Ibidem.

73 Saša Gavrić, Damir Banović, and Mariña Barreiro, *The Political System of Bosnia and Herzegovina: Institutions – Actors – Processes* (Sarajevo: Sarajevo Open Center, 2013), 24–26.

powers"[74] by the High Representative, who eventually imposed the necessary amendments on the entity constitutions to force compliance with the decision. Nonetheless, the *Constituent Peoples'* case represented a crucial turning point in the constitutional transition of Bosnia-Herzegovina, as the Court imprinted a multiethnic and multinational direction on the BiH constitutional system, after five years of implementation of the Dayton Peace Agreement that risked cementing ethnic segregation. As noted by Marko, the Constitutional Court prioritised the realisation of the dynamic goal of Dayton, i.e., the rebuilding of the pre-existing multiethnic society.[75]

2.2.3 The Reference Re Secession of Québec

Before delving into the analysis of the landmark decision *Reference Re Secession of Québec*,[76] decided in 1998 by the Canadian Supreme Court, it is first necessary to briefly outline the dynamics of Québec nationalism, and the position of Québec within the Canadian federation. One of the factors that led to the introduction of the federal structure through the 1867 Constitution Act was the need to accommodate internal diversity between the two major linguistic and cultural groups. The province of Québec, mainly populated by francophones, was granted the right to use both French and English in the provincial legislature and in the national parliament and courts[77]. Moreover, as previously analysed in Chapter 2, Québec could retain its civil law system within an otherwise common law system,[78] which later led to a reform of the Supreme Court of Canada in 1985, providing that three of the nine judges must come from Québec (although without any provincial involvement in their appointment) to ensure an adequate knowledge of civil law within the Supreme Court.[79] The 1985 Supreme Court Act occurred soon after the introduction of the Canadian Charter of Rights and Freedoms in 1982, framed by the federal government as a response to the centrifugal forces coming from Québec. In fact, after a first phase of defensive constitutional claims, aimed at

74 See Tim Banning, "The 'Bonn Powers' of the High Representative in Bosnia Herzegovina: Tracing a Legal Figment," *Goettingen Journal of International Law* 6, no. 2 (2014): 259–302.

75 Joseph Marko, "Problems of State- and Nation-Building in Post-Conflict Situations: The Case of Bosnia-Herzegovina," *Vermont Law Review* 30, no. 3 (2006): 532.

76 *Reference Re Secession of Quebec* [1998], 2 S.C.R. 217.

77 Constitution Act 1867, s. 133.

78 Constitution Act 1867, s. 94.

79 See Sujit Choudhry, and Richard Stacey, "Independent or Dependent? Constitutional Courts in Divided Societies," in *Rights in Divided Societies*, ed. Colin Harvey and Alex Schwartz (Oxford and Portland: Hart Publishing, 2012), 105–106.

safeguarding the existing areas of self-government, during the so-called "Quiet Revolution"[80] in the 1960s, "Québec's goals shifted to ethnolinguistic nation-building and an expansion of its jurisdiction over social and economic policy".[81] By adopting the Charter, the federal government brought forward the political goal to contrast Québec nationalism by both "regulating ethno-linguistic nation-building in Québec and constituting a pan-Canadian political community throughout Canada".[82] As observed by Ghai, "the primary aim of the Charter does not seem to have been the strengthening of rights, for they were on the whole well protected under the law", but rather the need to "offer Canadians an identity they could all embrace. That identity was to come from the Bill of Rights".[83] However, the proposal of a Bill of Rights that would have forged a "new" Canadian identity was faced with opposition from several groups that perceived the Charter as excluding their concerns, such as those of other provinces fearing for the original rationale of Canadian federalism, the aboriginal peoples for their right to cultural autonomy, the francophones for their language policies, the new immigrants for their own culture, feminist movements for the need to protection against discrimination and vulnerability, and the English speaking for the possibility of exceptions to the universal character of the Charter.[84]

Against this backdrop, the Canadian Supreme Court played a substantial role in addressing these issues,[85] especially concerning the constitutional relationship of Québec within Canada. It heard for instance a series of language rights cases dealing with the tensions between plurinational accommodation and individual rights.[86] More generally, the Supreme Court interpreted the Charter as guided by the

---

80 See Jeremy Webber, *Reimagining Canada: Language, Culture, Community, and the Canadian Constitution* (Montréal and Kingston: McGill-Queen's University Press, 1994), 44–47.

81 Choudhry, and Stacey, "Independent or Dependent," 107.

82 Ibidem.

83 Ghai, "Ethnicity and Competing Nations of Rights," 66–67.

84 For further references, see Ghai, "Ethnicity and Competing Nations of Rights," 67–71; Sujit Choudhry, "Does the World Need More Canada? The Politics of the Canadian Model in Constitutional Politics and Political Theory," *International Journal of Constitutional Law* 5, no. 4 (2007): 606–38.

85 See Robert Schertzer, "Recognition or Imposition? Federalism, National Minorities, and the Supreme Court of Canada," *Nations and Nationalism* 14, no. 1 (2008): 105–26; G. Alan Tarr, "Subnational Constitutions and Minority Rights: A Perspective on Canadian Provincial Constitutionalism," *Rutgers Law Journal* 40, no. 4 (2009): 767–92.

86 For an analysis of these cases, see Choudhry, and Stacey, "Independent or Dependent," 108–110.

> respect for the inherent dignity of the human person, commitment to social justice and equality, accommodation of a wide variety of beliefs, respect for cultural and group identity, and faith in social and political institutions which enhance the participation of individuals and groups in society.[87]

As mentioned, since the early 1960s, Québec had witnessed increasing nationalist claims from political movements and parties, in two directions: the Quebec Liberal Party advocated for greater powers of the provincial government within a reformed Canadian federation, whereas the Parti Québécois pushed for a sovereign and independent Québec.[88] This is an essential element to understanding the setting of the 1998 *Reference Re Secession*,[89] as the conflict between those supporting continued membership of the federation (i.e., the "federalists") and those supporting a sovereign Québec and the relative shift towards a confederal model (i.e., the "sovereignists") constituted an additional element of (internal) fragmentation and was at the heart of the two referenda in Québec in 1980 and 1995. In both instances, voters preferred the former, though at times by a very narrow majority. This was precisely the case in the 1995 referendum on Québec unilateral secession, which was rejected by 50.58% of voters.[90] Moreover, from a decolonial perspective, the position of the aboriginal peoples living in Québec should not be overlooked as it provides for an additional layer of internal fragmentation. Indeed, they did not share the same aspiration of Québec to become a separate and independent entity, and in the 1995 referendum they overwhelmingly voted against secession. As recalled by Watts, aboriginal peoples claimed that "if Québec separated from Canada they would have the right to separate from Québec to remain within Canada".[91]

---

87 *R v. Oakes* [1986] 1 SCR 103, 136.

88 Ronald L. Watts, "Federalism and Diversity in Canada," in *Autonomy and Ethnicity*, ed. Yash Ghai (Cambridge: Cambridge University Press, 2000), 35.

89 For a detailed analysis of the decision, see Jean-François Gaudreault-DesBiens, "The Quebec Secession Reference and the Judicial Arbitration of Conflicting Narratives About Law, Democracy, and Identity," *Vermont Law Review* 23, no. 4 (1999): 793–844; David P. Haljan, "A Constitutional Duty to Negotiate Amendments: *Reference Re Secession of Quebec*," *International and Comparative Law Quarterly* 48, no. 2 (1999): 447–57.

90 Élections Québec, "1995 referendum on Québec's accession to sovereignty," available at https://www.electionsquebec.qc.ca/en/results-and-statistics/1995-referendum-on-quebecs-accession-to-sovereignty/ (last accessed 10 February 2025).

91 Watts, "Federalism and Diversity in Canada," 38.

In the aftermath of the 1995 referendum, three questions were submitted to the Supreme Court of Canada, concerning the legal authority of Québec, under domestic and international law, to secede from Canada. In its unanimous decision, the Court rejected the right of Québec to unilaterally and unconditionally secede from Canada, both under Canadian constitutional law and under international law (as recognised in Canada).[92] The 1998 decision sparked a lively debate in the academic and political spheres, both inside and outside Canada.[93] Part of the reason is that, despite rejecting Québec's unilateral right to secede, the Court famously held that:

> The Constitution is not a straitjacket. Even a brief review of our constitutional history demonstrates period of momentous and dramatic change. Our democratic institutions necessarily accommodate a continuous process of discussion and evolution, which is reflected in the constitutional right of each participant in the federation to initiate constitutional change.[94]

The Court thus suggested the possibility of a negotiated secession, acknowledging that "the Canadian constitutional order could not be indifferent to a clear expression of a clear majority of Quebecers that they no longer wish to remain in Canada".[95] Similarly, the Court recognised the pivotal importance of four unwritten and underlying constitutional principles, i.e., federalism,[96] democracy,[97] constitutionalism and the rule of law,[98] and the protection of minorities.[99] According to the Court, these principles "give rise to the duty to negotiate",[100] and as such would govern "the conduct of the parties in such negotiations".[101] Nonetheless, the decision left a series of issues unresolved, such as the vagueness around what would constitute a "clear majority" and a

92 Haljan, "A Constitutional Duty to Negotiate Amendments," 447.

93 On the impact of *Reference Re Secession* on other European secessionist contexts, see especially the work by Giuseppe Martinico and Giacomo Delledonne, eds., *The Canadian Contribution to a Comparative Law of Secession* (Cham, Switzerland: Palgrave Macmillan, 2019).

94 *Reference Re Secession of Quebec* [1998], 2 S.C.R. 217, para. 150.

95 *Reference Re Secession of Quebec* [1998], 2 S.C.R. 217, para. 151.

96 *Reference Re Secession of Quebec* [1998], 2 S.C.R. 217, para. 55–60.

97 *Reference Re Secession of Quebec* [1998], 2 S.C.R. 217, para. 61–69.

98 *Reference Re Secession of Quebec* [1998], 2 S.C.R. 217, para. 70–78.

99 *Reference Re Secession of Quebec* [1998], 2 S.C.R. 217, para. 79–82.

100 *Reference Re Secession of Quebec* [1998], 2 S.C.R. 217, para. 90.

101 Ibidem.

"clear question",[102] which was left to political evaluations.[103] As a result, in 2000, the federal Parliament passed the Clarity Act,[104] giving effect to the requirement of clarity. Under the Act, the clarity of the question is to be defined politically by the federal Parliament and, should the Parliament reject the question for lack of clarity, the Act provides that no negotiations will follow. However, at times clarity has been confused with the radicalism of the question, and some scholars have argued that this could be a matter of political expedience.[105] In fact, statistically, the more radical (and clearer) the question on secession was, the less support it gained from Quebecers. Conversely, the vaguer the question, the more popular support it obtained, though not meeting the clarity requirement.

Overall, according to Haljan, "the most interesting feature of the *Reference* opinion is its introduction of an obligation binding constitutional participants to negotiate when one or more wish to initiate constitutional change".[106] However, despite this significant contribution and the positive receipt of this landmark decision, *Reference Re Secession* also drew some criticisms, first and foremost "the Court's approach to the dialectical relation between the juridical realm and the political realm".[107] Gaudreault-DesBiens observed that such a distinction between law and politics not only is inaccurate[108] but also neglects the nature of Canadian constitutional law, and ends up refusing the fact that constitutional law inevitably has an inherent political component, that "always involves policy choices, and always entails a certain degree of judicial creativity".[109] Interestingly, in his analysis, Gaudreault-DesBiens argued that the Court should have been criticised for its interpretation of international law, insofar as it might have had a lack of jurisdiction in respect of the second issue pertaining to international law, and it adopted "a rather simplistic view

---

102 *Reference Re Secession of Quebec* [1998], 2 S.C.R. 217, para. 150: "[…] a *clear majority* vote in Quebec on a *clear question* in favor of secession would confer democratic legitimacy on the secession initiative which all of the other participants in Confederation would have to recognize".

103 On the clarity issue, see also Bossacoma, *Morality and Legality of Secession*, 281–307.

104 An Act to give effect to the requirement for clarity as set out in the opinion of the Supreme Court of Canada in the Quebec Secession Reference, S.C. 2000, c. 26

105 See Stephen Tierney, *Constitutional Referendums. The Theory and Practice of Republican Deliberation* (Oxford: Oxford University Press, 2012), 143.

106 Haljan, "A Constitutional Duty to Negotiate Amendments," 456.

107 Gaudreault-DesBiens, "The Quebec Secession Reference," 839.

108 This appears to be especially true when addressing secession, as suggested by the recent volume by Antoni Abat i Ninet, *Constitutional Law and Politics of Secession* (London and New York: Routledge, 2023).

109 Gaudreault-DesBiens, "The Quebec Secession Reference," 840.

of the contemporary international legal framework governing secessionist claims".[110] Despite these possible weaknesses in the Court's decision, Gaudreault-DesBiens concluded that these "do not vitiate its overall quality",[111] as it "asks the right questions and calls upon all Canadians to reflect on their concept of identity, and their ideas of Canada. Moreover, it invites them not to blind themselves to Canada's intrinsic complexity".[112]

2.2.4 The Shah Bano Case

In the aftermath of the Indian partition in 1947, the Indian Constituent Assembly had to reconcile the need to bring about social reforms with its commitment to protecting minorities.[113] Constitution makers decided to shift from a corporate to a more liberal framework, without forgetting Indian ethnocultural diversity, and at the same time without abandoning the project on nation-building after independence from the British colonial power. This led to the adoption of two sets of instruments, each embodying two different philosophies of rights, i.e., the enforceable Bill of Rights for civil and political rights,[114] and the non-justiciable Directive Principles[115] regulating the measures of social and economic equality.[116] However, the dialectic interaction between the judicially enforceable Bill of Rights and the non-justiciable Directive Principles became a source of tension that had to be addressed by courts, especially when reviewing the validity of legislation deemed to be in breach of rights of property or against the principle of equality and non-discrimination.[117] Ghai observed that, if originally courts were reluctant to develop a coherent interpretation of the supremacy between the Bill of Rights and the Directive Principles, eventually they accepted that they had to harmonise fundamental rights and the Directive Principles.

Focusing on the Bill of Rights, several provisions concern the protection of minority rights, especially freedom of religion or belief[118] as it was a major source of conflict between communities. These include the protection of reli-

110 Gaudreault-DesBiens, "The Quebec Secession Reference," 842.

111 Ibidem.

112 Gaudreault-DesBiens, "The Quebec Secession Reference," 843.

113 Ghai, "Ethnicity and Competing Notions of Rights," 61.

114 Constitution of India – Part III "Fundamental Rights" (Articles 12 to 35).

115 Constitution of India – Part IV "Directive Principles of State Policy" (Articles 36 to 51).

116 Ghai, "Ethnicity and Competing Notions of Rights," 62.

117 Ghai, "Ethnicity and Competing Notions of Rights," 65.

118 Constitution of India – Part III "Fundamental Rights": Art. 25. Freedom of conscience and free profession, practice and propagation of religion; Art. 26. Freedom to manage religious affairs; Art. 27. Freedom as to payment of taxes for promotion of any particular

gious belief and practices, the right of religious groups to manage their religious affairs, also through the owning of property, the right to establish their own educational facilities and to preserve the use of their languages, scripts and cultures. However, these forms of non-territorial autonomy were subject to limitations, especially at the outset of the Indian federal state. One critical point of contention concerned the right of minority groups to maintain their own personal laws,[119] regulating civil and family law matters such as marriage, divorce, and inheritance.[120] The Constituent Assembly originally proposed the adoption of a uniform civil code, deemed necessary to cement a newborn national identity and unity. The proposal was met with considerable resistance from Muslim political leaders and the compromise that was reached in the Assembly was to move such provision to the Directive Principles.[121] In this way, it would have been non-legally binding but would have been a guidance to the state.

On these premises, the personal law system is still in place in India, and its complexity has generated several issues. For instance, Hindu personal laws[122] are applied not only to those Hindus who dissent from the understanding of the Hindu religious doctrine entrenched in the personal laws, but also to reli-

religion; Art. 28. Freedom as to attendance at religious instruction or religious worship in certain educational institutions.

119 Comparatively speaking, the term "personal laws" refers to a subset of private law, generally limited to a list of matters (i.e., family law, inheritance, marriage, divorce). These may be the Hindu, Muslim, Jewish or African customary laws which regulate the life of different communities within the same territory (see for example Rina Verma Williams, *Postcolonial Politics and Personal Laws: Colonial Legal Legacies and the Indian State* (Oxford: Oxford University Press, 2006); Chibli Mallat, "Comparative Law and the Islamic (Middle Eastern) Legal Culture," in *The Oxford Handbook of Comparative Law*, ed. Mathias Reimann, and Reinhard Zimmermann (Oxford: Oxford University Press, 2019), 624–651; Rodolfo Sacco, "The Sub-Saharan Legal Tradition," in *The Cambridge Companion to Comparative Law*, ed. Matteo Bussani, and Ugo Mattei (Cambridge: Cambridge University Press, 2012), 332–335.

120 On the system of personal laws in India, see Farrah Ahmed, "Pluralism and Personal Laws in India," in *Constitutions and Religion*, ed. Susanna Mancini (Cheltenham, UK and Northampton, MA: Edward Elgar Publishing, 2020), 415–32; Farrah Ahmed, *Religious Freedom under the Personal Law System* (Oxford: Oxford University Press, 2015); Williams, *Postcolonial Politics and Personal Laws*.

121 Constitution of India – Part IV "Directive Principles of State Policy": "Art. 44. Uniform civil code for the citizens. –The State shall endeavour to secure for the citizens a uniform civil code throughout the territory of India."

122 The four major laws that constitute the system of Hindu personal laws are the Hindu Marriage Act (1955), the Hindu Succession Act (1956), the Hindu Minority and Guardianship Act (1956), and the Hindu Adoptions and Maintenance Act (1956).

gious minorities such as Sikhs, Buddhists, and Jains.[123] Similarly, Muslim personal laws[124] apply regardless of "peculiarities in belief, orthodoxy or heterodoxy",[125] even though courts "generally apply the law of the sects or 'school' to which at least one of the parties belongs".[126] It should be noted that Indians from the same or different beliefs may choose to be governed by one of the general codes of family law, such as the Special Marriage Act 1954. This would allow them to register their marriage both according to civil and traditional or religious ceremonies. However, if a marriage is first celebrated under a personal law, it cannot be later governed by the Special Marriage Act, which would grant the parties a more secular and equal treatment.[127] The tension between the need to recognise group rights, and thus personal laws based on religious doctrines, and the protection of equality and non-discrimination was at the heart of the landmark decision of the Indian Supreme Court in the *Shah Bano* case.[128] Indeed, in *Shah Bano*,[129] what clashed were the different constitutional approaches to managing diversity in India, based on language policies, affirmative actions, and the regime of personal laws, under the overarching principles of equality and cooperative federalism.[130]

---

123 Ahmed, "Pluralism and Personal Laws in India," 417–418.

124 Muslim personal law in India is mainly regulated by the Muslim Personal Law (Shariat) Application Act, 1937, dealing with marriage, succession, inheritance and charities among Muslims, whereas the Dissolution of Muslim Marriages Act, 1939 regulates the circumstances in which Muslim women can obtain divorce and their rights.

125 Paras Diwan, *Muslim Law in Modern India* (Faridabad: Allahabad Law Agency, 2000), 1.

126 Ahmed, "Pluralism and Personal Laws in India," 418.

127 Ahmed, "Pluralism and Personal Laws in India," 419.

128 *Mohd. Ahmed Khan v. Shah Bano Begum* [1985] 3 S.C.R. 844.

129 On *Shah Bano*, see Zakia Pathak, and Rajeswari Sunder Rajan, "Shahbano," *Signs: Journal of Women in Culture and Society* 14, no. 3 (1989): 558–582; Siobhan Mullally, "Feminism and Multicultural Dilemmas in India: Revisiting the Shah Bano Case," *Oxford Journal of Legal Studies* 24, no. 4 (2004): 671–92; Ummul Fayiza, "From Shah Bano to Shayara Bano (1985–2017): Changing Feminist Positions on the Politics of Muslim Personal Law, Women's Rights and Minority Rights in India," *Journal of Muslim Minority Affairs* 41, no. 1 (2021): 122–140; Narendra Subramanian, "Legal Change and Gender Inequality: Changes in Muslim Family Law in India," *Law & Social Inquiry* 33, no. 03 (2008): 631–72; Sylvia Vatuk, "Islamic Feminism in India: Indian Muslim Women Activists and the Reform of Muslim Personal Law," *Modern Asian Studies* 42, no. 2–3 (2008): 489–518; Sylvia Vatuk, "A Rallying Cry for Muslim Personal Law: The Shah Bano Case and Its Aftermath," in *Islam in South Asia in Practice*, ed. Barbara D. Metcalf (Princeton: Princeton University Press, 2010), 352–368; Katherine Lemons, "Sharia Courts and Muslim Personal Law in India: Intersecting Legal Regimes," *Law & Society Review* 52, no. 3 (2018): 603–29.

130 Nesiah, "Federalism and Diversity in India," 56.

In the *Shah Bano* case, Shah Bano brought about an application for maintenance against her former husband, Mohammed Khan, relying upon section 125 of the 1973 Code of Criminal Procedure. The 1973 Code applied to all Indian citizens, regardless of religion, and was enacted primarily as a safeguard against vagrancy.[131] On his part, Shah Bano's husband argued that his liability to pay maintenance should be determined, not under the general law but rather under Muslim personal law. Indeed, according to such law, the liability of the husband to maintain his divorced wife was limited to *iddat*, i.e., the three-month period following divorce, after which Muslim divorced women could remarry. His position was supported by the All India Muslim Personal Law Board, a statutory body intervening on behalf of Mohammed Khan, that argued that "the courts had no right to interfere with the arrangements made by Muslim communities for the maintenance of divorced Muslim women".[132] The case eventually culminated in an appeal to the Indian Supreme Court and raised the question of how and whether the personal laws of a religious community could be subject to the scrutiny of a general law. Mullally observed how the Supreme Court decided to depart from previous strategies,[133] and engaged in a process of re-interpretation of Islamic *shari'a* to assess whether there was a conflict between the Code of Criminal Procedure and Muslim personal law. What is relevant to notice is that the conclusion of the Court, which recognised an obligation to provide maintenance beyond the *iddat* period, was rooted in its reading of the Quran, contrary to the view of the All India Muslim Personal Law Board and the Shariat Board.[134] According to the Court, maintenance was conceived as a societal obligation to prevent vagrancy and destitution, and divorced women were seen as a segment of society that had traditionally been subject to unjust treatment and in need of special protection.[135] As argued by Mullally, "Hiding behind the discourse of protection, rather than simply asserting the fundamental rights of Muslim women was perhaps a strategy to diffuse further conflict. If this was their strategy, however, it failed".[136]

Not surprisingly, the decision of the Supreme Court generated much controversy. Indeed, the *Shah Bano* case was decided by an exclusively Hindu

131 Siobhan Mullally, "Feminism and Multicultural Dilemmas in India: Revisiting the Shah Bano Case," *Oxford Journal of Legal Studies* 24, no. 4 (2004): 678.

132 Ibidem.

133 Mullally, "Feminism and Multicultural Dilemmas in India," 679.

134 Mullally, "Feminism and Multicultural Dilemmas in India," 680.

135 Ibidem.

136 Ibidem.

court in a context of rising power of the Hindu right, "which used secularism and human rights discourse to silence and disempower minorities",[137] and this decision was interpreted by Muslim communities and political leaders as move to consolidate the supremacy of Hindu identity. The backlash following the *Shah Bano* decision was so powerful that it led to the adoption of a law that eventually reversed the Court's decision and restricted the right to alimony to the *iddat*.[138] However, in *Danial Latifi*, a case that followed the several constitutional challenges to the 1986 law, the Court found that "the duty to secure social justice is shared by all religions, and that homelessness and poverty are universal problems that should be decided within a human rights framework".[139] If the 1986 law was deemed constitutional, the Court held that "the requirement to make fair and reasonable provision for a divorced Muslim woman extended to arrangements for her future well-being".[140] As noted by Mancini and Cohen, "the Court was able to guarantee equal treatment and the non-discrimination of Muslim women, within the framework of Muslim personal law".[141]

2.3 *Supranational Courts and Diversity*

In addition to the pivotal role of domestic constitutional courts in dealing with the challenges deriving from divided societies, it should not be forgotten that supranational judicial bodies have also dealt with crucial cases addressing diversity.

It is undeniable that the international standards for human rights protection were originally formulated in terms of individual rights, rooted in the 1948 Universal Declaration of Human Rights, the 1966 International Covenant on Civil and Political Rights, and the 1966 International Covenant on Economic, Social and Cultural Rights. Moreover, the legally binding treaties that constitute the core of the international standards on human rights[142] deal only par-

137 Susanna Mancini, and Elena L. Cohen, "Gender Justice and Religious Freedom in the Post-Secular Age," in *Constitutions and Religion*, ed. Susanna Mancini (Cheltenham, UK and Northampton, MA: Elgar Publishing, 2020), 358.

138 Muslim Women (Protection of Rights on Divorce) Act, 1986. See also Mullally, "Feminism and Multicultural Dilemmas in India," 681–682.

139 *Danial Latifi & Anr v. Union of India* [2001] Supp. (3) S.C.R. 419.

140 Mullally, "Feminism and Multicultural Dilemmas in India," 684.

141 Mancini and Cohen, "Gender Justice and Religious Freedom in the Post-secular Age," 358.

142 The nine core international human rights instruments are the International Convention on the Elimination of All Forms of Racial Discrimination (1965), the International Covenant on Civil and Political Rights (1966), the International Covenant on Economic, Social

tially with minority rights. However, since the 1990s, the international system on human rights has gradually evolved into a more inclusive system, encompassing a number of non-binding instruments addressing specifically minority and group rights. These include the Declaration on the Rights of Persons Belonging to National or Ethnic, Religious, and Linguistic Minorities[143] and the Declaration on the Rights of Indigenous Peoples (UNDRIP)[144] (at the UN level), and the Lund Recommendations on the Effective Participation of National Minorities in Public Life[145] and the Ljubljana Guidelines on Integration of Diverse Societies[146] (within the framework on the Organisation for Security and Co-operation in Europe). Conversely, the Council of Europe adopted the legally binding European Charter for Regional or Minority Languages (ECRML)[147] and the Framework Convention for the Protection of National Minorities (FCNM),[148] becoming a major standard-setter in the protection of minority rights in Europe.[149] As previously mentioned, the human rights system in the African context has afforded a different attention to minority rights than other regional human rights instruments.[150] However, the African Charter on Human and Peoples' Rights explicitly recognised the communitarian perspective of rights, not only placing the "peoples" alongside "human" rights

---

and Cultural Rights (1966), the Convention on the Elimination of All Forms of Discrimination against Women (1979), the Convention against Torture and Other Cruel, Inhuman or Degrading Treatment or Punishment (1984), the Convention on the Rights of the Child (1989), the International Convention on the Protection of the Rights of All Migrant Workers and Members of Their Families (1990), the International Convention for the Protection of All Persons from Enforced Disappearance (2006), and the Convention on the Rights of Persons with Disabilities (2006).

143 General Assembly resolution 47/135 (1992).

144 General Assembly resolution 61/295 (2007).

145 OSCE High Commissioner on National Minorities (September 1999).

146 OSCE High Commissioner on National Minorities (November 2012).

147 Council of Europe, ETS no. 148 (1992).

148 Council of Europe, ETS no. 157 (1998).

149 For further references on the international standards for minority protection, see Will Kymlicka, "The Internationalization of Minority Rights," in *Constitutional Design for Divided Societies: Integration or Accommodation?*, ed. Sujit Choudhry (Oxford: Oxford University Press, 2008), 111–40; Jane Boulden and Will Kymlicka, *International Approaches to Governing Ethnic Diversity* (Oxford: Oxford University Press, 2015); Joseph Marko, et al., "Legal Standards Setting and Monitoring of Human and Minority Rights Law after 1945," in *Human and Minority Rights Protection by Multiple Diversity Governance. History, Law, Ideology and Politics in European Perspective*, ed. Joseph Marko and Sergiu Constantin (London and New York: Routledge, 2019), 78–91.

150 On the African human rights system and minority rights, see Solomon Dersso, "The African Human Rights System and the Issue of Minorities in Africa," *African Journal of International and Comparative Law* 20, no. 1 (2012): 42–69.

in its title, but also recognising the right of all peoples to be equal (Art. 19)[151] and their right to self-determination (Art. 20), as well as their right to dispose of their wealth and natural resources (Art. 21), their right to development (Art. 22), to peace and security (Art. 23) and to a "general satisfactory environment" (Art. 24). This communitarian approach to rights has also been highlighted by the UN Office of the High Commissioner for Human Rights, describing the African Charter as an international instrument that "combines African values with international norms by not only promoting internationally recognised individual rights, but also by proclaiming collective rights and individual duties".[152]

On these premises, this paragraph briefly reviews three jurisdictions and their respective treatment of diversity issues: the International Court of Justice and claims of self-determination; the European Court of Human Rights and non-discrimination in power-sharing democracies; and the Inter-American Court of Human Rights and the protection of indigenous peoples' rights. Finally, it accounts for the experience of two quasi-judicial international bodies in addressing diversity, i.e., the Badinter Commission and the African Commission on Human and Peoples' Rights.

2.3.1 The International Court of Justice and Self-Determination under International Law

Since the evolution of the international system after WWII, the subject of self-determination has been often discussed before the International Court of Justice (ICJ) in judgments and advisory opinions. In *Namibia*,[153] *Western Sahara*,[154] *East Timor*,[155] and *Wall*,[156] the significance of the principle of self-determination in international law grew significantly, and the ICJ progressively "refined" its interpretation of the principle. In particular, in 1995, in its

151 African Charter on Human and Peoples' Rights – Art. 19: "All peoples shall be equal; they shall enjoy the same respect and shall have the same rights. Nothing shall justify the domination of a people by another."

152 UN Office of the High Commissioner for Human Rights, "Minority Rights under the African Charter on Human and Peoples' Rights," *Pamphlet No. 6 of the UN Guide for Minorities*, 2001.

153 *Legal Consequences for States of the Continued Presence of South Africa in Namibia (South West Africa) notwithstanding Security Council Resolution 276 (1970)*, Advisory Opinion, (1971) ICJ Reports 16.

154 *Western Sahara*, Advisory Opinion, (1975) ICJ Reports 12.

155 *East Timor (Portugal v. Australia)*, Judgment, (1995) ICJ Reports 90.

156 *Legal Consequences of the Construction of a Wall in the Occupied Palestinian Territory*, Advisory Opinion, (2004) ICJ Reports 136.

judgment on *East Timor*,[157] the ICJ built on its previous findings in the *Namibia* and *Western Sahara* advisory opinions, stating that self-determination had an *erga omnes* character and was "one of the essential principles of contemporary international law".[158] Later, in its *Wall* advisory opinion, the Court implicitly attributed to Israel's breach of the principle of self-determination the consequences that would normally flow from a breach of a *ius cogens* norm.[159]

Nevertheless, Sparks argued that the ICJ, despite recognising the significance of self-determination in international law, showed "little awareness of the different norms of self-determination with which it was dealing", and that this "conceptual confusion afflicting self-determination reduced the rigour and analytical values of judicial treatment of its forms".[160] According to the author, this perspective seems to be confirmed especially by the 2010 *Kosovo* advisory opinion,[161] when the ICJ chose to reinterpret the question posed by the UN General Assembly on the legality of Kosovo's unilateral declaration of independence under international law. Indeed, the Court chose to answer whether a prohibition on declarations of independence existed under international law, thus ignoring the secessionist issue at the heart of the opinion.[162] In confirming that declarations of independence are not against international law, the ICJ relied on the traditional neutrality of international law towards these declarations to cast secession as an issue falling outside the legal realm. As highlighted by Sparks, in *Kosovo*, the Court appeared to treat secession as "a fact of which international law will take note if it is successful and will treat as an entirely internal matter if it is not".[163] However, other authors, such as Mancini, argued that the ICJ "implicitly suggests the legitimacy of a democratic and 'gradual' secessionist process, heavily involving regional and/or in-

157 See Tom Sparks, *Self-Determination in the International Legal System* (Oxford and Portland: Hart Publishing, 2023), 145–150.

158 *East Timor* (1995), para. 29.

159 *Wall* (2004), para. 159.

160 Sparks, *Self-Determination in the International Legal System*, 230.

161 *Accordance with International Law of the Unilateral Declaration of Independence in Respect of Kosovo*, Advisory Opinion, (2010) ICJ Reports 403.

162 *Kosovo* Advisory Opinion (2010), para. 56: "The Court is not required by the question it has been asked to take a position on whether international law conferred a positive entitlement on Kosovo unilaterally to declare its independence or, a fortiori, on whether international law generally confers an entitlement on entities situated within a State unilaterally to break away from it. Indeed, it is entirely possible for a particular act – such as a unilateral declaration of independence not to be in violation of international law without necessarily constituting the exercise of a right conferred by it. The Court has been asked for an opinion on the first point, not the second."

163 Sparks, *Self-Determination in the International Legal System*, 231.

ternational authorities".[164] Moreover, Bossacoma observed that, in *Kosovo*, the Court of Justice seemed to outline some requirements for unilateral declaration of independence to be compatible with international law, such as peaceful means, democratic process, and previous unsuccessful attempts at negotiations and agreement.[165]

Finally, in the 2019 *Chagos* advisory opinion,[166] the ICJ had to identify whether colonial self-determination had emerged as a legal norm by the time Chagos detached from Mauritius in 1965. The Court answered positively and relied especially on the 1960 Resolution 1514 (XV) of the UN General Assembly, i.e., the Declaration on the Granting of Independence to Colonial Countries and People.[167] Although the opinion was criticised by some of its members for not going further and recognising colonial self-determination as a *ius cogens* norm, it could be argued that *Chagos* represents a positive development, as the Court established more precisely than in the past "the point in time at which colonial self-determination emerged as a legal norm [...], and it has strongly implied that the norm has in the modern day acquired a peremptory status".[168] Indeed, the ICJ held that colonial self-determination crystallised as a customary rule with the adoption of Resolution 1514 (XV) of the UN General Assembly, finding a "clear relationship between Resolution 1514 (XV) and the process of decolonisation following its adoption".[169]

2.3.2 The European Court of Human Rights and Power-Sharing Democracies

A particularly interesting perspective on the role of supranational courts when addressing ethnocultural diversity is provided by the case law of the European Court of Human Rights (ECtHR),[170] especially in the cases concerning power-sharing constitutional structures in divided societies. One of the most

164 Mancini, "Secession and Self-Determination," 493.

165 Bossacoma, *Morality and Legality of Secession*, 182.

166 *Legal Consequences of the Separation of the Chagos Archipelago from Mauritius in 1965*, Advisory Opinion, (2019) ICJ Reports 95.

167 UN General Assembly, Resolution 1514 (XV), 14 December 1960.

168 Sparks, *Self-Determination in the International Legal System*, 226.

169 *Chagos* (2019), para. 150.

170 The European Court of Human Rights was established in 1959 by the European Convention on Human Rights and is the judicial body competent over the interpretation and application of the Convention and its additional protocols. On the ECtHR case-law on minority rights, see Roberta Medda-Windischer, "The European Court of Human Rights and Minority Rights," *Journal of European Integration* 25, no. 3 (2003): 249–271.

emblematic cases is *Sejdić-Finci v. Bosnia-Herzegovina*,[171] delivered by the ECtHR in 2009, on the discrimination against national minorities running for the highest electoral positions (i.e., the collective Presidency and the second chamber of the Parliamentary Assembly). The two applicants, Dervo Sejdić and Jakob Finci, belonged to the so-called "Others", a residual constitutional category encompassing all those citizens who are not affiliated with one of the three constituent peoples (i.e., Muslim/Bosniaks, Serbs, Croats) recognised by the BiH Constitution.[172] The "Others" might be citizens belonging to religious, national, or ethnic minorities, or having a mixed ethnic background, or simply rejecting the system of ethnic affiliation. Since the BiH Electoral Code requires those standing for election to the Presidency and the House of Peoples to self-declare their affiliation to one of the three constituent peoples to be eligible, the two applicants (respectively of Roma and Jewish origin) were excluded from the electoral competition. The applicants were held to have been discriminated against on the basis of their ethnic origin after claiming the violation of multiple articles of the European Convention on Human Rights (ECHR), more specifically Art. 3 (prohibition of torture), Art. 13 (right to an effective remedy), Art. 14 (prohibition of discrimination), Art. 3 Protocol no. 1 (right to free elections) and Art. 1 Protocol no. 12 (general prohibition of discrimination).

The BiH government justified the differentiated treatment of the two citizens who refused to affiliate to the constituent peoples on the ground that the system of ethnic affiliation guaranteed the peaceful coexistence of ethnocultural communities, as well as the delicate constitutional system designed by the Dayton Peace Agreement. For its part, the ECtHR framed it as a case of ethnic discrimination against vulnerable peoples,[173] and declared the BiH constitutional provisions in breach of Art. 14 ECHR, read in conjunction with Art. 3 Protocol no. 1, and of Art. 1 of Protocol no. 12. Even though the Court ruled with a clear majority, worth mentioning is the dissenting opinion of Judge Bonello, who argued that the Court had no legitimacy in intervening in the national constitutional order, especially an extremely complex and fragile system such as Bosnia-Herzegovina. Moreover, he criticised the Court's failure to take into account the possible consequences of its judgment, namely the potential threat to peace. For these reasons, Bonello concluded that the

171 European Court of Human Rights (Grand Chamber), Case Nos. 27996/06 and 34836/06, *Sejdić and Finci v. Bosnia and Herzegovina*, 22 December 2009.

172 On the constituent peoples in the BiH constitutional system, see also paragraph 2.2.2.

173 Stefan Graziadei, "Democracy v. Human Rights? The Strasbourg Court and the Challenge of Power Sharing," *European Constitutional Law Review* 12, no. 1 (2016): 67.

Court should have granted Bosnia-Herzegovina a wider margin of appreciation.[174]

The decision of the ECtHR provoked multiple reactions and triggered a heated debate about the relationship between consociations and human rights standards.[175] McCrudden and O'Leary provided an insightful critique of the court's decision,[176] arguing that there are two particular rights primarily challenged: the right not to be discriminated against on the basis of particular protected characteristics (such as race or ethnicity), and the dilution of a person's right to participate in the political process on equal terms with others.[177] The authors noted that human rights scholars identify not only specific rights that may be endangered by consociations, but also a more general conflict between consociationalism and the foundations of human rights, since consociations may conflict with the liberal individualist paradigm that underpins contemporary international human rights norms, as observed by Wippmann.[178] However, other scholars, such as Choudhry, argue that consociational peace settlements do include mechanisms of human rights protection, an argument that defenders of liberal consociationalism see as a strong safeguard for liberal values.[179] More generally, McCrudden and O'Leary conclude that "the reasoning presented by the Court to justify its decision is surprisingly sketchy and somewhat ambiguous",[180] since key issues such as the timing, modalities and actors involved in the liberalisation of the BiH constitutional system remain undefined.[181]

Although the ECtHR decision of *Sejdić-Finci* remains unimplemented, it is considered a landmark case for many reasons. First of all, it was the first time that the Strasbourg court found a country's constitution to be in violation of the Convention, and it was also the first time the court applied Protocol no. 12, the ECHR free-standing equality right. Moreover, with *Sejdić-Finci* and subse-

---

174 See the Dissenting opinion of Judge Bonello in *Sejdić and Finci.*

175 See, for example, Christine Bell, "Power-Sharing and Human Rights Law," *The International Journal of Human Rights* 17, no. 2 (2013): 204–37; Caroline A. Hartzell and Matthew Hoddie, *Power Sharing and Democracy in Post–Civil War States. The Art of the Possible* (Cambridge: Cambridge University Press, 2020); David Wippman, "Practical and Legal Constraints on Internal Power Sharing," in *International Law and Ethnic Conflict*, ed. David Wippman (Ithaca, NY: Cornell University Press, 2018), 211–241.

176 See McCrudden, and O'Leary, *Courts and Consociations.*

177 McCrudden, and O'Leary, *Courts and Consociations*, 93–95.

178 Wippmann, "Practical and Legal Constraints on Internal Power Sharing," 232.

179 See Sujit Choudhry, "After the Rights Revolution: Bills of Rights in the Post-Conflict State," *Annual Review of Law and Social Science* 6 (2010): 301–322.

180 McCrudden, and O'Leary, *Courts and Consociations*, 145.

181 McCrudden, and O'Leary, *Courts and Consociations*, 146.

quent related decisions (*Zornić*,[182] *Pilav*,[183] *Baralija*,[184] *Pudarić*[185], *Kovačević*) [186] the Court seemed to move away from its previous case-law regarding consociations. In fact, in *Mathieu-Mohin and Clerfayt*,[187] the Strasbourg court held that "the exclusion of declaratively French-speaking parliamentarians from the Flemish regional parliament did not amount to discrimination".[188] This conclusion was justified by the margin of appreciation granted to states, the peculiarities of the Belgian institutional system, the temporary nature of the arrangement, and the wide majority of French- and Dutch-speaking groups supporting such arrangement.[189] In *Mathieu-Mohin and Clerfayt*, the dissenting judges[190] argued that the system of self-classification was in violation of the Convention rights of French-speaking voters and candidates, discriminating against French-speakers solely on the basis of their language. As observed by Graziadei, prior to *Sejdić-Finci*, the ECtHR took a rather prudent approach in its right to vote and elections jurisprudence, neither imposing specific electoral systems nor demanding that "all votes have equal weight".[191] Moreover, the Court granted states a wider margin of appreciation in the limitation of passive voting rights, compared to the narrower margin in restricting active

182 European Court of Human Rights, Case No. 3681/06, *Zornić v. Bosnia and Herzegovina*, 15 July 2014.

183 European Court of Human Rights, Case No. 41939/07, *Pilav v. Bosnia and Herzegovina*, 9 June 2016.

184 European Court of Human Rights, Case No. 30100/18, *Baralija v. Bosnia and Herzegovina*, 29 October 2019.

185 European Court of Human Rights, Case No. 55799/18, *Pudarić v. Bosnia and Herzegovina*, 8 December 2020.

186 European Court of Human Rights, Case No. 43651/22, *Kovačević v. Bosnia and Herzegovina*, 29 August 2023 (currently under referral to the Grand Chamber). It should be noted that *Kovačević* presents some interesting innovations compared to the previous ones since the applicant claimed the violation of his active (and not passive) right to vote on the ground of both his non-affiliation (as in *Sejdić and Finci* and *Zornić*) to any constituent people and his place of residence (as in *Pilav* and *Pudarić*). For further details, see Lidia Bonifati, "The European Court of Human Rights on Kovačević: Time for Constitutional Change in Bosnia and Herzegovina?" *Diritti Comparati* (4 October 2023), available at https://www.diritticomparati.it/the-european-court-of-human-rights-on-kovacevic-time-for-constitutional-change-in-bosnia-and-herzegovina/ (last accessed 16 February 2025).

187 European Court of Human Rights, Case No. 9267/81, *Mathieu-Mohin and Clerfayt v. Belgium*, 2 March 1987.

188 Graziadei, "Democracy v. Human Rights," 59.

189 Ibidem.

190 Judges Cremona, Bindschedler-Robert, Spielmann, and Valticos.

191 Graziadei, "Democracy v. Human Rights," 60.

voting rights.[192] Graziadei also argued that *Sejdić-Finci* and the subsequent cases "raised human rights protection to a higher but more politically sensitive level",[193] having possible repercussions for other European power-sharing systems.[194]

In conclusion, while state courts in consociations tend to uphold or cautiously extend consociational arrangements,[195] the ECtHR went further and decided on a "first-order challenge",[196] namely those challenges involving the state constitutional and political structure or the rules determining access to the political community, creating the "legitimacy dilemma" recalled by Judge Bonello in his dissenting opinion.[197]

2.3.3 The Inter-American Court of Human Rights and Indigenous Peoples' Rights

Another interesting perspective on supranational courts and minority rights is provided by the case law of the Inter-American Court of Human Rights (IACtHR) and its undeniable role in advancing the rights of indigenous peoples.[198] Established in 1978 after the American Convention on Human Rights

---

192 Ibidem

193 Graziadei, "Democracy v. Human Rights," 63.

194 For a more detailed analysis of the BiH cases' implications, see Graziadei, "Democracy v. Human Rights," 69–72. See also McCrudden, and O'Leary, *Courts and Consociations*, 105–146.

195 See McCrudden, and O'Leary, *Courts and Consociations*, 43–45.

196 Samuel Issacharoff, "Democracy and Collective Decision Making," *International Journal of Constitutional Law* 6, no. 2 (2008): 231.

197 To address this dilemma, Graziadei proposes the "integrative democratic tolerance" approach, reconciling the democracy principle with the protection of fundamental rights (see Graziadei, "Democracy v. Human Rights," 75–83).

198 See Thomas M. Antkowiak, "Rights, Resources, and Rhetoric: Indigenous Peoples and the Inter-American Court," *University of Pennsylvania Journal of International Law* 35, no. 1 (2013): 113–88; Christina Binder, "The Prohibition of Amnesties by the Inter-American Court of Human Rights," *German Law Journal* 12, no. 5 (2011): 1203–30; Isabel Madariaga Cuneo, "The Rights of Indigenous Peoples and the Inter-American Human Rights System," *Arizona Journal of International and Comparative Law* 22, no. 1 (2005): 53–64; Alejandro Fuentes, "Protection of Indigenous Peoples' Traditional Lands and Exploitation of Natural Resources: The Inter-American Court of Human Rights' Safeguards," *International Journal on Minority and Group Rights* 24, no. 3 (2017): 229–53; Jo M. Pasqualucci, "The Evolution of International Indigenous Rights in the Inter-American Human Rights System," *Human Rights Law Review* 6, no. 2 (2006): 281–322; Jo M. Pasqualucci, "International Indigenous Land Rights: A Critique of the Jurisprudence of the Inter-American Court of Human Rights in Light of the United Nations Declaration on the Rights of Indigenous Peoples," *Wisconsin International Law Journal* 27, no. 1 (2009): 51–98; Alexandra Tomaselli and Federica Cittadino, "Land, Consultation and Participa-

(ACHR) entered into force,[199] the IACtHR is one of the two competent bodies, along with the pre-existing Inter-American Commission on Human Rights (IACHR), that oversee the respect of human rights obligations within the Inter-American human rights system.[200] The Court's jurisprudence on indigenous peoples' rights has passed through different phases: the "late-indigenist" period during the 1970s, the increasing interest during the 1980s and 1990s, and the current "evolutionary jurisprudence" phase that started in the early 2000s with the *Awas Tingni* case.[201] In this landmark case, the IACtHR first

---

tion Rights of Indigenous Peoples in the Jurisprudence of the Inter-American Court of Human Rights", in *Litigating the Rights of Minorities and Indigenous Peoples in Domestic and International Courts*, ed. Bertus De Villiers et al. (Leiden and Boston: Brill | Nijhoff, 2021), 149–178.

199 The ACHR was adopted on 22 November 1969 in San José (Costa Rica) and was originally signed by 12 states, but it only entered into force in 1978, when 11 states ratified it in accordance with Art. 74(2) ACHR.

200 The two bodies have different jurisdictions and functions. On the one hand, the IACHR is a permanent body established in 1959, after the adoption of the American Declaration of the Rights and Duties of Man in 1948 by the Organisation of American States (OAS), and as such it has a wide jurisdiction covering all the OAS Member States as well as the 24 Member States that have ratified the ACHR. The Commission meets regularly and has the authority to prepare country reports and monitor the state of human rights protection in state parties, as well as investigate individual complaints about human rights violations. Generally speaking, the ACHR provides that "the main function of the Commission shall be to promote respect for and defence of human rights" (ACHR – Art. 41). On the other hand, the Inter-American Court is the judicial body established by the ACHR to adjudicate over violations of human rights of the American Convention. The jurisdiction of the Court is narrower than the Commission, as Art. 61(1) of the ACHR provides that only the state parties and the Commission have the right to submit cases to the Court. However, the acceptance of the jurisdiction of the Court is not automatic upon ratification of the ACHR, but rather it needs to be recognised by state parties. Moreover, the acceptance of the Court's jurisdiction is not necessarily permanent, as Art. 62(2) of the ACHR provides that state parties may recognise the jurisdiction of the Court "unconditionally, on the condition of reciprocity, for a specified period, or for specific cases." Finally, alongside the Commission and the Court, the Inter-American system of human rights is complemented by additional thematic conventions and protocols, and during the 1990s the Commission established seven thematic Rapporteurships drawing attention to specific human rights issues. For the purposes of this book, and this chapter in particular, it should be recalled that the first to be created was the Rapporteurship on the Rights of Indigenous Peoples in 1990. For further references, see UN Office of the High Commissioner for Human Rights, "Protection of Minority Rights in the Inter-American Human Rights System," *Pamphlet No. 5 of the UN Guide for Minorities*, 2001. For the competences and procedures of the IACHR see also American Convention on Human Rights, Art. 33–51.

201 Inter-American Court of Human Rights, *Mayagna (Sumo) Awas Tingni Community v. Nicaragua*, 31 August 2001.

gave an "evolutionary interpretation" of human rights in a case about a violation of land rights of indigenous peoples.[202] Moreover, in *Awas Tingni*, the Court recognised that indigenous peoples enjoy a collective right to land within the general right to property entrenched in Art. 21 of the ACHR.[203] Such an evolutionary approach was confirmed in several subsequent cases,[204] in which the Court further stated that "human rights treaties are living instruments, the interpretation of which must evolve over time and reflect current living conditions".[205] Interestingly, at the time, the Court gave this interpretation in the absence of a specific norm on indigenous peoples' rights, as the American Declaration on the Rights of Indigenous Peoples was adopted only in 2016 (although non-binding).[206]

Two recent cases have built upon the Court's evolutionary jurisprudence, especially concerning the right of indigenous peoples to land, participation, and consultation, in the light of the American Convention. The first case is *People of Sarayaku v. Ecuador* (2012), in which the Court determined that:

> Given this intrinsic connection that indigenous and tribal peoples have with their territory, the protection of property rights and the use and enjoyment thereof is necessary to ensure their survival.[207]

Moreover, the Court found that four fundamental indigenous rights, i.e., the right to culture or cultural identity, consultation, participation, and land, are interdependent. Indeed, the spiritual connection between indigenous peoples and their land is an essential component of their cultural identity, that needs to be respected and protected, including through their right to consulta-

202 *Awas Tingni* (2001), para. 148.

203 American Convention on Human Rights – Art. 21: "(1) Everyone has the right to the use and enjoyment of his property. The law may subordinate such use and enjoyment to the interest of society. (2) No one shall be deprived of his property except upon payment of just compensation, for reasons of public utility or social interest, and in the cases and according to the forms established by law. (3) Usury and any other form of exploitation of man by man shall be prohibited by law."

204 See Alejandro Fuentes, "Judicial Interpretation and Indigenous Peoples' Rights to Land, Participation and Consultation. The Inter-American Court of Human Rights' Approach," *International Journal on Minority and Group Rights* 23 (2015): 39–79.

205 Inter-American Court of Human Rights, *Kichwa Indigenous People of Sarayaku v. Ecuador*, 27 June 2012, para. 161.

206 Tomaselli and Cittadino, "Land, Consultation and Participation Rights of Indigenous Peoples," 149.

207 *People of Sarayaku v. Ecuador* (2012), para. 146.

tion.[208] Similarly, their right to consultation is a fundamental guarantee of their right to participation and their relative exercise, especially in decision-making processes that involve indigenous peoples' interests and rights.[209] A final innovative element of *People of Sarayaku v. Ecuador* is that the Court went beyond even the ACHR and concluded that the right to consultation is a principle of international law.[210]

A few years later, in *Kaliña and Lokono Peoples v. Suriname*,[211] the Court recognised the collective legal personality of indigenous peoples as "both an autonomous right and a necessary step to ensure the enjoyment of other rights, including the right to land".[212] Indeed, the Court not only highlighted the importance of the demarcation of indigenous territories but also identified the survival of indigenous peoples "as an important element to strike the right balance between national restrictions and the enjoyment of indigenous property rights".[213] It is even more interesting to note that the Court stated that the parameter of survival must be used also by national authorities when decisions in respect of the balance of rights are delegated to them.

A final point worth making is that the IACtHR in its jurisprudence on indigenous peoples' rights made wide use not only of its previous case law, but also of the case law of the Inter-American Commission, having a wider jurisdiction over states that do not recognise the jurisdiction of the Court (e.g., Canada, Belize, USA). Moreover, the Court relied extensively on international human rights treaties, from those protecting economic and cultural rights (ICCPR and ICESCR), to indigenous peoples' rights (i.e., the ILO Convention no. 169[214] and the UNDRIP), and even to international biodiversity law.[215] However, as noted by Tomaselli and Cittadino, the IACtHR innovative jurisprudence is not sufficient to protect the fundamental rights of indigenous peoples and to solve the power imbalance they continue to face.[216]

208 *People of Sarayaku v. Ecuador* (2012), para. 159.

209 *People of Sarayaku v. Ecuador* (2012), para. 160.

210 *People of Sarayaku v. Ecuador* (2012), para. 164.

211 Inter-American Court of Human Rights, *Kaliña and Lokono Peoples v. Suriname*, 25 November 2015.

212 Tomaselli and Cittadino, "Land, Consultation and Participation Rights of Indigenous Peoples," 174.

213 Ibidem.

214 International Labour Organisation, Indigenous and Tribal Peoples Convention (No. 169), 1989.

215 Tomaselli and Cittadino, "Land, Consultation and Participation Rights of Indigenous Peoples," 175.

216 Tomaselli and Cittadino, "Land, Consultation and Participation Rights of Indigenous Peoples," 175–176.

2.3.4 The Relevance of Quasi-judicial Bodies

Before concluding this paragraph, it should be noted that the accommodation of internal diversity, and specifically self-determination, has also been addressed by "quasi-judicial" bodies, such as the Arbitration Commission of the Conference on Yugoslavia (the so-called "Badinter Commission") and the African Commission on Human and Peoples' Rights. Although these are (or were) not full courts, they have produced important opinions and decisions when dealing with self-determination, especially in times of conflict.

2.3.4.1 *The Badinter Commission*

Starting with the Badinter Commission,[217] this was established as a court of arbitration within the context of the 1991 Peace Conference on Yugoslavia initiated by the European Community and its Member States in the aftermath of the dissolution of the Yugoslavian federation. Indeed, the Peace Conference was guided by the fundamental principles that "any change in internal and international borders by force is not acceptable and that any solution should guarantee the rights of peoples and minorities in all the Republics".[218] With such principles in mind, the mandate of the Court was to provide assistance and guidance to the Conference on questions of international law such as self-determination, state succession, and the protection of human rights and minorities. Originally, the Court would have been composed of five members: two unanimously nominated by the federal Presidency of Yugoslavia, and three by the European Community. However, due to internal disagreements in the Yugoslavian presidency, eventually all five members were nominated by the European Community. In its first composition (in 1991), the Court was composed of Robert Badinter (former president of the French *Conseil Constitutionnel*), Aldo Corasaniti (president of the Italian Constitutional Court), Roman Herzog (president of the German Federal Constitutional Court), Irène Pétry (president of the Belgian Court of Arbitration), and Francisco

217 On the Badinter Commission, see Malgosia Fitzmaurice, "Badinter Commission (for the Former Yugoslavia)," *Max Planck Encyclopedias of International Law* (June 2019); Alain Pellet, "The Opinions of the Badinter Arbitration Committee. A Second Breath for the Self-Determination of Peoples," *European Journal of International Law* 3 (1992): 178–185; Michla Pomerance, "The Badinter Commission: The Use and Misuse of the International Court of Justice's Jurisprudence," *Michigan Journal of International Law* 20, no. 1 (1998): 31–58; Peter Radan, "The Badinter Arbitration Commission and the Partition of Yugoslavia," *Nationalities Papers* 25, no. 3 (1997): 537–557; Steve Terrett, *The Dissolution of Yugoslavia and the Badinter Arbitration Commission* (London and New York: Routledge, 2017).

218 Declaration on Yugoslavia, Press Release 77/91, 1.

Tomas y Valiente (president of the Spanish Constitutional Tribunal).[219] Two years after it was first established, the Badinter Commission was reconstituted[220] and its composition changed, with five permanent members: three members appointed by the Council of Ministers of the European Community from the judges of the constitutional courts of the Member States, a fourth member appointed by the President of the International Court of Justice, and a fifth member selected from the judges of the European Court of Human Rights. Therefore, the second composition of the Commission was Robert Badinter, Roman Herzog, Francesco Paolo Casavola (president of the Constitutional Court of Italy), Elisabeth Palm (judge of the ECtHR), and José María Ruda (former president of the ICJ). Moreover, in contentious proceedings, it was provided that the parties could appoint *ad hoc* members.[221]

Despite the fact that its mandate was rather vague, the Badinter Commission issued 15 Opinions on a variety of statehood-related aspects.[222] For the purposes of this chapter, it is important to briefly review the opinions on self-determination, i.e., Opinions 2 and 3, that were sought by the federal Yugoslavian presidency on the right to self-determination of the Serbian population in Croatia and Bosnia-Herzegovina, and whether this impacted on its borders under international law. In Opinion 2, the Commission stated that, although the Serbian population within BiH and Croatia were minorities, this did not entitle them to any right to external self-determination, and thus to change the existing borders, but it treated them as minorities with the right to internal self-determination. What is also interesting to note is that, in Opinion 2, the Badinter Commission outlined a very extensive notion of minority rights, to the point of arguing that these rights have achieved the status of *ius cogens* norms of international law.[223] Moreover, in Opinion 3, the Badinter Commission broke new ground by recognising the application of the principle of *uti possidetis* outside the colonial context, holding that "where one or more of the republics become an independent state, the former internal boundaries become frontiers protected by international law".[224]

219 Fitzmaurice, "Badinter Commission."

220 Work Programme of the Conference [1992] 31 ILM 1534, 1536.

221 Fitzmaurice, "Badinter Commission."

222 The Badinter Commission's Opinions can be grouped into different categories: opinions relating to statehood (Opinions 1, 8–11), Opinions relating to self-determination and the frontiers of the new states (Opinions 2 and 3), opinions relating to the application of the EC declaration on recognition of new states (Opinions 4–7), and opinions relating to the question of state succession (Opinions 9, 11–15).

223 Fitzmaurice, "Badinter Commission."

224 Fitzmaurice, "Badinter Commission."

Finally, it should be recalled that the Commission issued a series of opinions on state recognition, among which Opinion 4 concerned the international recognition of Bosnia-Herzegovina as an independent state. In this Opinion, the Commission refused to grant BiH such recognition given the lack of referendum clearly demonstrating the will of the people to be an independent state. For Bosnia-Herzegovina, the holding of a referendum under international supervision constituted an additional requirement to those already entrenched in the Declaration on the "Guidelines on the recognition of the new states in Eastern Europe and in the Soviet Union" adopted in 1991, providing for respect for the principles of democracy, human rights, and the rule of law, as well as the guarantee of respect of the rights of ethnic and national minorities.[225] Although often criticised for its lack of clarity and inconsistencies among opinions, it is undeniable that the Opinions of the Badinter Commission represent a significant contribution to the development of critical legal issues in international law, especially concerning statehood and state succession.

2.3.4.2 *The African Commission on Human and Peoples' Rights*

Moving now to the work of the African Commission on Human and Peoples' Rights (ACHPR), this operates as a quasi-judicial body entitled to interpret the African Charter on Human and Peoples' Rights, and to submit cases to the African Court on Human and Peoples' Rights.[226] Established in 1987, the African Commission is one of several bodies in the African human rights system, alongside the African Committee of Experts on the Rights and Welfare of the Child, the African Court on Human and Peoples' Rights (ACtHPR), the ECOWAS Community Court of Justice, and the East African Court of Justice

225 Extraordinary EPC Ministerial Meeting, "Declaration on the "Guidelines on the recognition of the new states in Eastern Europe and in the Soviet Union" (Brussels, 16 December 1991).

226 On the African Commission and its relationship with the African Court, see Ali Badawi, "The Future Relationship between the African Court and the African Commission," *African Human Rights Law Journal* 2, no. 2 (2002): 252–60; Gina Bekker, "The African Court on Human and Peoples' Rights: Safeguarding the Interests of African States," *Journal of African Law* 51, no. 1 (2007): 151–72; Tom Gerald Daly and Micha Wiebusch, "The African Court on Human and Peoples' Rights: Mapping Resistance against a Young Court," *International Journal of Law in Context* 14, no. 2 (2018): 294–313; Rachel Murray, "A Comparison between the African and European Courts of Human Rights," *African Human Rights Law Journal* 2, no. 2 (2002): 195–222; Rachel Murray, *The African Commission on Human and Peoples' Rights and International Law* (Oxford and Portland: Hart Publishing, 2000); Makau Mutua, "The African Human Rights Court: A Two-Legged Stool?," *Human Rights Quarterly* 21, no. 2 (1999): 342–63.

(EACJ).[227] As previously mentioned, the African Charter does not explicitly mention "minorities" but refers to the "peoples". Nonetheless, it became an established practice of the African Commission to rely on the articles protecting the rights of the peoples when addressing minority issues, with the only limitation that, should such rights also apply to minorities, "such group could not ordinarily exercise peoples' rights in a manner that would infringe the right of others and undermine national unity and territorial integrity of states".[228]

For the purposes of this chapter, the 1995 decision by the African Commission in *Katangese Peoples' Congress v. Zaire*[229] should be recalled, which followed a communication brought by the Katangese Peoples' Congress against Zaire in 1992.[230] In the aftermath of the independence of the Democratic Republic of Congo (DRC) from Belgian colonial power in the early 1960s, the region of Katanga sought independence from the new republic but eventually failed and returned to the control of the DRC with the assistance of the UN peacekeeping mission ONUC.[231] Their secessionist aspirations returned in the early 1990s, when the secessionist movement *Katangese Peoples' Congress* filed a suit before the African Commission claiming the breach of the previously recalled Art. 20 of the African Charter, providing the inalienable right of peoples to self-determination:

> All peoples shall have the right to existence. They shall have the unquestionable and inalienable right to self-determination. They shall freely determine their political status and shall pursue their economic and social development according to the policy they have freely chosen. (2) Colonized or oppressed peoples shall have the right to free themselves

227 From 2005 to 2012, the human rights system also included the Tribunal of the Southern African Development Community (SADC). Moreover, at the 2004 African Union Summit, the Heads of State and Government decided on a merger between the African Court of Human and Peoples' Rights and the African Court of Justice (intended to be the highest judicial body of the African Union, but which never came into force), to form a new court, i.e., the African Court of Justice and Human Rights (ACJHR). Although the protocol for the establishment of the ACJHR was signed in 2008, as of 18 June 2020 only eight countries (Angola, Benin, Burkina Faso, Congo, Gambia, Libya, Liberia, Mali) ratified the protocol, out of the 15 necessary for the Court to come into force (see Protocol on the Statute of the African Court of Justice and Human Rights, Status list).

228 Dersso, "The African Human Rights System," 48.

229 African Commission on Human and Peoples' Rights, *Katangese Peoples' Congress v. Zaire*, communication no. 75/92 (1995).

230 From 1971 to 1997, Zaire was the name of the now known Democratic Republic of Congo.

231 See Sparks, *Self-Determination in the International Legal System*, 150.

> from the bonds of domination by resorting to any means recognized by the international community. (3) All peoples shall have the right to the assistance of the State Parties to the present Charter in their liberation struggle against foreign domination, be it political, economic or cultural.[232]

In the communication, the Congress requested its recognition as a liberation movement entitled to the support of state parties in the achievement of independence for Katanga, the recognition of the independence of Katanga, and support in securing the evacuation of Zaire from Katanga.[233] In its decision, the African Commission argued that there had been no allegations of human rights violations against the Katangese, and thus the claim concerned the alleged denial of self-determination.[234] Then, the Commission sought to clarify the ambiguities around the definition of "peoples" and "self-determination", as the wording of Art. 20(1) of the African Charter is rather vague. Despite recognising such a right, the African Commission argued that the issue was not the self-determination of "the Zaireans as a people"[235] but of the Katangese in particular, and it did not find any evidence to suggest that the Katangese consisted of one or more ethnic groups. What is interesting to notice is that the African Commission sought to strike a balance between (internal) self-determination, such as federalism and other forms of self-government, and the principles of sovereignty and territorial integrity, holding that "self-determination may be exercised in [...] any other form of relations that accords with the wishes of the people but fully cognisant of the other recognised principles such as sovereignty and territorial integrity".[236] Moreover, the Commission clarified that it was bound to uphold the sovereignty and territorial integrity of Zaire, as it was part of the Organisation of the African Union and a state party of the African Charter.[237] As a result, the African Commission concluded that:

> In the absence of concrete evidence of violations of human rights to the point that the territorial integrity of Zaire should be called to question and in the absence of evidence that the people of Katanga are denied

232 African Charter on Human and Peoples' Rights – Art. 20.
233 *Katangese Peoples' Congress v. Zaire*, para. 1.
234 *Katangese Peoples' Congress v. Zaire*, para. 2.
235 *Katangese Peoples' Congress v. Zaire*, para. 3.
236 *Katangese Peoples' Congress v. Zaire*, para. 4.
237 *Katangese Peoples' Congress v. Zaire*, para. 5.

> the right to participate in government as guaranteed by Article 13(1) of the African Charter, the Commission holds the view that Katanga is obliged to exercise a variant of self-determination that is compatible with the sovereignty and territorial integrity of Zaire.[238]

Therefore, the Commission recognised Katanga's right to internal self-determination and to political participation in the government of Zaire under Art. 13(1) of the African Charter. Although not clearly stated by the Commission, Sparks suggested that with this decision the African Commission also seemed to imply that, if these rights and forms of internal self-determination were to be denied, "secession may be lawful when employed as a final resort to remedy abuses".[239]

3 Diversity within Courts

If the previous paragraph addressed how courts have dealt with the accommodation of internal ethnocultural diversity, this paragraph assesses what happens when such diversity enters the composition of the courts. Specifically, the following sections explore two peculiar configurations of courts, i.e., the so-called "power-sharing courts" and "hybrid constitutional courts".

3.1 *Power-Sharing Courts*

The "power sharing courts" can be defined as those courts where judge selection and decision-making is corrected to address ethnocultural cleavages in divided societies.[240] More precisely, Graziadei argued that given the function of apex courts is "as fora of arbitration between different constituent communities in divided polities, their composition, organisation and decision-making rules reflect the principle of consociational democracy".[241] Power-sharing courts can be further distinguished between strong and weak courts. In strong power-sharing courts, judges are appointed on a parity (and not proportional) basis, in order to equally represent the constitutive ethnocultural identities. This may entail, for example, parity in terms of language requirements, as in the Belgian Constitutional Court. As such, their function is "to be an external

---

238 *Katangese Peoples' Congress v. Zaire*, para. 6.

239 Sparks, *Self-Determination in the International Legal System*, 152.

240 See Stefan Graziadei, "Power Sharing Courts," *Contemporary Southeastern Europe* 3, no. 2 (2016): 66–105.

241 Graziadei, "Power Sharing Courts," 99.

forum for conflict resolution, allowing that political conflict on divisive issues is deflated through judicialization" and "no decision is possible against the judges who are expression of one constitutive nation acting collectively".[242] Moreover, in strong-power sharing courts, the allocation of the highest office is shared among constitutive communities. Instances of strong power-sharing courts are the Belgian Constitutional Court, the BiH Constitutional Court, the Constitutional Court of Cyprus, as well as the former constitutional courts in Yugoslavia and Czechoslovakia. Conversely, weak power-sharing courts "reflect the salient cleavages in the population on proportional and not paritarian basis".[243] In this respect, their function is to be an independent tribunal, resolving disputes on competences among tiers of government, and identity conflicts. However, their legitimacy as power-sharing courts is limited insofar as "their composition is determined by the majority nation",[244] and there is no consensus requirement to reach a decision. Overall, "weak power-sharing courts are judicial bodies with some form of recognition of minority representation in their composition".[245] The apex courts in Kosovo, North Macedonia, and Canada are examples of weak power-sharing courts. Generally speaking, Graziadei identified four main characteristics of power-sharing courts: (i) judges are selected on the basis of their ethnic or linguistic background,[246] (ii) their main function is to act as arbiters in salient inter-community conflicts in deeply divided societies;[247] (iii) they may have to take decisions by consensus, though providing tie-breaking mechanisms;[248] and (iv) the highest posts (i.e., presidency and vice-presidency) are distributed between communities, on a rotation basis.[249]

Certainly, power-sharing courts have attracted several critiques, that closely resemble those moved against the consociational model, not least because they share some core features of power sharing (i.e., parity, cross-community mechanisms, rotation of highest offices).[250] The most fundamental criticism is their illegal, undemocratic, and unmeritocratic characteristics, but another set of sceptical opinions concern their compatibility with the principles of judicial independence and concerns about their lack of internal

242 Graziadei, "Power Sharing Courts," 77.
243 Graziadei, "Power Sharing Courts," 78.
244 Ibidem.
245 Ibidem.
246 Graziadei, "Power Sharing Courts," 79–84.
247 Graziadei, "Power Sharing Courts," 84–86.
248 Graziadei, "Power Sharing Courts," 86–87.
249 Graziadei, "Power Sharing Courts," 90–91.
250 Graziadei, "Power Sharing Courts," 99.

diversity, given that only politically salient communities are included.[251] However, Graziadei observed that "the most convincing defence of power-sharing courts is that their function justifies their composition"[252] and that in divided societies it is essential for the legitimacy of courts that these are an expression of the different constituent communities, and not only of the majority.[253] After all, as argued by Graziadei:

> Just as consociational democracy is not the antithesis to but merely a different form of democracy, power sharing courts are not illegal or illegitimate, but represent a different way of organising judicial institutions adapted to the specific circumstances of deeply divided polities.[254]

3.2 *Hybrid Constitutional Courts*

A further configuration of constitutional court available to address internal diversity in multinational systems has been introduced in the process of conflict resolution, namely the so-called "hybrid" courts.[255] Such courts, in fact, are composed of both domestic and foreign judges: the former promote the domestic legitimacy of the court, while the latter are placed to ensure impartiality and balancing between groups.[256] Although hybrid constitutional courts have found limited space in the literature, they represent a topic of extreme interest in comparative constitutional law.[257] Indeed, it was precisely the use of the comparative method that made it possible for Dixon and Jackson to formulate the three currently existing models (sometimes overlapping) of hybrid constitutional courts: (i) courts in which the presence of foreign judges is intended to reinforce the court's reputation and independence; (ii) courts in very small jurisdictions, in which the hybrid character is intended to

251 Graziadei, "Power Sharing Courts," 93–96.
252 Graziadei, "Power Sharing Courts," 96.
253 Graziadei, "Power Sharing Courts," 96–98.
254 Graziadei, "Power Sharing Courts," 100.
255 This section draws on a comparative study on hybrid constitutional courts in multinational systems previously published in Italian in Lidia Bonifati, "Le 'corti ibride' negli ordinamenti multinazionali: una prospettiva comparata," *DPCE Online* 66, Special Issue no. 2 (2024): 1119–1137.
256 Alex Schwartz, "International Judges on Constitutional Courts: Cautionary Evidence from Post-Conflict Bosnia," *Law & Social Inquiry* 44, no. 1 (2017): 2.
257 See Rosalind Dixon and Vicki Jackson, "Hybrid Constitutional Courts: Foreign Judges on National Constitutional Courts," *Columbia Journal of Transnational Law*, no. 57 (2018): 283–356; Anna Dziedzic and Simon N.M. Young, eds., *The Cambridge Handbook of Foreign Judges on Domestic Courts* (Cambridge: Cambridge University Press, 2023).

support their capacity and independence; and (iii) courts that are operating in contexts of democratic transition and power sharing between different previously conflicting groups.[258] The authors also identify three courts exemplifying such models, respectively, the Hong Kong Court of Final Appeal, the Court of Appeal and Supreme Court of Fiji, and the Constitutional Court of Bosnia and Herzegovina.[259] In addition to the classification of hybrid courts, the comparative study carried out by Dixon and Jackson also allowed for the identification of a number of advantages and disadvantages that can result from the appointment of foreign judges in domestic jurisdictions. In terms of advantages, the presence of foreign judges may lead to a form of constitutional engagement through the sharing of the knowledge of judges from outside the domestic jurisdiction, increased impartiality and independence of individual judges and the court as a whole, and the creation of possible channels for increased awareness and sensitisation of foreign governments, international and non-governmental organisations, regarding possible unconstitutional practices by domestic governments or possible positive developments in the rule of law.[260] These positive aspects are contrasted, however, with a number of potential disadvantages. Foreign judges may not have sufficient knowledge of the context in which they find themselves to fully play their role, they may not be perceived as impartial and independent but as the bearers of specific foreign interests (and thus of a particular interpretation of constitutional disputes), and, finally, they may slow down the process of democratic development such that their presence is no longer necessary and the court could be composed only of domestic judges.[261] How the positives and negatives interact with each other and balance each out other depends largely on specific factors related to the context in which these courts operate. These include, for example, the motivations behind the appointment of foreign judges,[262] the individual profiles of these judges, the length of their term of office, and the manner of appointment.[263]

---

258 Rosalind Dixon and Vicki Jackson, "Hybrid Constitutional Courts: Foreign Judges on National Constitutional Courts," *Columbia Journal of Transnational Law* 57 (2018): 293.

259 Dixon and Jackson, "Hybrid Constitutional Courts," 292.

260 Dixon and Jackson, "Hybrid Constitutional Courts," 289–290.

261 Dixon and Jackson, "Hybrid Constitutional Courts," 290.

262 For a more in-depth analysis of the underlying motivations for choosing foreign judges in domestic courts, see Dixon and Jackson, "Hybrid Constitutional Courts," 326–331, as well as Anna Dziedzic, "An Introduction to Foreign Judges on Domestic Courts," in *The Cambridge Handbook of Foreign Judges on Domestic Courts*, ed. Anna Dziedzic and Simon N.M. Young (Cambridge: Cambridge University Press, 2023), 11–14.

263 Ibidem.

Another important comparative study that is worth recalling is the one recently conducted by Dziedzic and Young, who further explored the presence of foreign judges in domestic courts without limiting themselves to constitutional courts.[264] It is particularly interesting to notice how Dziedzic also reflects upon some defining issues, beginning with what allows judges to be identified as "foreign." Indeed, the concept of "foreign" is relative, complex and changing and does not only denote non-membership of the domestic system in which the judge is called upon to operate.[265] Specifically, two general criteria are identified that qualify a judge as foreign, namely citizenship and the place of one's professional training, and it should be observed that the interplay between these two elements contribute to blurring the concept of "foreign".[266] In some contexts, for example, while judges do not have to be citizens of the system, it is also a requirement that they come from countries where the same legal system applies. The case of the Hong Kong Court of Final Appeal, where foreign judges are chosen from judges who are not citizens of Hong Kong but come from other common law jurisdictions[267] is emblematic. Moreover, the qualification of a judge as "foreign" is further complicated by the increasing mobility of judges resulting from the processes of globalisation, supranational integration and cross-border cooperation.[268] Despite this, Dziedzic points out that "jurisdictional and state borders still matter, and laws and judges are still closely tied to domestic polities".[269]

As anticipated, the hybrid character of a court may be a configuration specifically designed for those societies crossed by deep ethnocultural divisions to avoid identity-based judgments. In such contexts, foreign judges are expected to be decisive if the rest of the court adopts polarised positions.[270] Despite the pressing nature of the "post-conflict dilemma"[271] to which hybrid courts are called to respond, legal doctrine has observed how the presence of foreign judges tends to be "ambiguous".[272] In particular, a recent study by Schwartz has shown that the assumption of impartiality of foreign judges seems to be

264 See Anna Dziedzic and Simon N.M. Young, eds., *The Cambridge Handbook of Foreign Judges on Domestic Courts* (Cambridge: Cambridge University Press, 2023).
265 Dziedzic, "An Introduction," 3–5.
266 Dziedzic, "An Introduction," 4.
267 Dziedzic, "An Introduction," 5.
268 Dziedzic, "An Introduction," 6.
269 Ibidem.
270 Schwartz, "International Judges," 2.
271 Ibidem.
272 Schwartz, "International Judges," 25.

flawed and that they do not necessarily prove decisive in split decisions.[273] Conversely, the inevitable tendency to side with one side or another can potentially undermine the Court's counterbalancing role and damage its authority.[274] In addition, Schwartz argues that over-reliance on the international community "to enforce controversial decisions purchases short-term results at the expense of the sort of incremental activism that constitutional courts typically use to build authority over time".[275] Moreover, it is possible to question the adverse effects that the presence of foreign judges can generate on the legitimacy and effectiveness of the courts. In particular, Dziedzic notes how sometimes the appointment of foreign judges can be used instrumentally to cover distorted motives. In some contexts, for example, this could serve to perpetuate a colonial attitude, to control the development of legal systems previously subject to colonial powers.[276] Another adverse effect relates to the possibility of political pressure on such courts, as foreign judges often have shorter terms of office than domestic judges and for that reason are perceived by authoritarian regimes as a "less dangerous" and more easily subject to political interference.[277]

It is also worth briefly recalling some factors that make the adoption of a hybrid model in court composition more likely. As mentioned above, it has been observed that small jurisdictions in particular often resort to the appointment of foreign judges to domestic courts to make up for the lack of a sufficient number of local judges to meet the needs of the judicial system, as is the case in many jurisdictions in the Pacific and Caribbean countries.[278] Another element that is interesting to note is that the majority of the jurisdictions analysed by the literature have a common law system.[279] Without suggesting any causal link between the presence of foreign judges and common law systems, Dziedzic notes that this finding could be due to the central role played by the judge in common law systems, as well as the British colonial experience, which saw the former colonies maintain the practice of appointing judges from the United Kingdom or other Commonwealth countries.[280]

---

273 Schwartz, "International Judges," 26.

274 Ibidem.

275 Ibidem.

276 Dziedzic, "An Introduction," 14.

277 This, for example, is the case in the Gambia, where the appointment of foreign judges was preferred over domestic judges so that the government could exercise forms of control over the judiciary (see Dziedzic, "An Introduction," 15).

278 Dziedzic, "An Introduction," 16.

279 Ibidem.

280 Dziedzic, "An Introduction," 16–17.

Finally, the involvement of the international community is certainly a factor that should not be underestimated, as some jurisdictions are particularly susceptible to the influence of international actors due to their own colonial past, geopolitical dynamics, or international intervention to resolve internal conflicts.[281] Critics of the hybrid model often argue that the presence of foreign judges goes against the sovereignty of the state,[282] echoing disputes over the use of foreign law by domestic courts.[283] In Rwanda, for example, the possibility of a hybrid court dealing with war crimes related to the Rwandan genocide was ruled out on the grounds that this would constitute "breach of the sovereignty of the Rwandese people".[284] As much as there remains a strong symbolic and potentially controversial value behind the appointment of foreign judges, Dziedzic notes that foreign judges are appointed with full respect for state sovereignty, either by specialised bodies or by Parliament.[285]

Focusing on those jurisdictions that have introduced hybrid courts because of their multinational nature, it should be noted that there is only one hybrid constitutional court currently operating in a divided society, i.e., the Constitutional Court of Bosnia and Herzegovina, whereas in the past hybrid courts were also introduced in Cyprus and Kosovo. In these two latter contexts, the hybrid nature of constitutional courts was an integral part of the respective conflict resolution processes but was interpreted as a transitional arrangement, to be abandoned at a later stage. Starting with the experience of the Cypriot hybrid court,[286] this was limited in time and, more importantly, was

---

281 Dziedzic, "An Introduction," 17.

282 On this point see for example Joseph Marko, "Foreign Judges: A European Perspective," in *Hong Kong's Court of Final Appeal: The Development of the Law in China's Hong Kong*, ed. Simon N.M. Young and Yash Ghai (Cambridge: Cambridge University Press, 2014), 637–65.

283 Unable to elaborate on this point here, see, among many others, Giuseppe de Vergottini, *Oltre il dialogo tra corti* (Bologna: Il Mulino, 2010); Gábor Halmai, "The Use of Foreign Law in Constitutional Interpretation," in *The Oxford Handbook of Comparative Constitutional Law*, ed. András Sajó and Michel Rosenfeld (Oxford: Oxford University Press, 2012), 1328–48; Giuseppe Franco Ferrari, ed., *Judicial Cosmopolitanism: The Use of Foreign Law in Contemporary Constitutional Systems* (Leiden and Boston: Brill | Nijhoff, 2020); Francesco Biagi, "Foreign Law in Constitutional Interpretation," in *Max Planck Encyclopedia of Comparative Constitutional Law*, ed. Rainer Grote, Frauke Lachenmann, and Rüdiger Wolfrum (Oxford: Oxford University Press, 2021), 1–18.

284 Gérard Prunier, *Africa's World War: Congo, the Rwandan Genocide, and the Making of a Continental Catastrophe* (Oxford: Oxford University Press, 2009), 12.

285 Dziedzic, "An Introduction," 17–18, 21–22.

286 On the Cypriot constitutional system and in particular the experience of the Supreme Constitutional Court, see Christella Yakinthou, *Political Settlements and Ethnically Divided Societies: Consociationalism and Cyprus* (Cham: Palgrave, 2009); Hubert Faust-

abandoned not at the completion of a transition, but because of a deep constitutional crisis. The hybrid nature of the court was one of the elements introduced by the consociational model of the 1960 Constitution to regulate internal divisions between the Greek and Turkish communities. Until 1964, when the consociational experiment failed, the Supreme Constitutional Court of Cyprus consisted of a Greek Cypriot judge, a Turkish Cypriot judge, and a "neutral" foreign judge, who filled the role of the President of the Court and was to cast the deciding vote if the other two judges took opposing positions.[287] Schwartz notes how despite this composition, or perhaps because of it, the Court was actually ineffective in dealing with the series of constitutional conflicts that resulted in the crisis that led to the failure of the power-sharing institutions in 1964.[288] In particular, the crisis originated from the resignation in 1963 of the Court's President, German Judge Ernst Forsthoff, and the subsequent resignation of Turkish officials from public office. The same happened in the lower courts, effectively making it impossible for the court system to function.[289] The crisis was resolved following the adoption of Law 33/64[290] on the state of necessity and the *Ibrahim* decision[291] of the newly established Supreme Court, which took over the previous functions of the High Court

mann and Andrekos Varnava, eds., *Reunifying Cyprus: The Annan Plan and Beyond* (London: Bloomsbury, 2009); Marise Cremona and Nikos Skoutaris, "Speaking of the De... rogations: Accommodating a Solution of the Cyprus Issue within the Union Legal Order," *Journal of Balkan and Near Eastern Studies* 11, no. 4 (2009): 381–395; John McGarry, "Centripetalism, Consociationalism and Cyprus: The Adoptability Question," in *Power-Sharing: Empirical and Normative Challenges*, ed. Allison McCulloch and John McGarry (London and New York: Routledge, 2017), 16–35; Feargal Cochrane, Neophytos Loizides, and Thibaud Bodson, *Mediating Power-Sharing: Devolution and Consociationalism in Deeply Divided Societies* (London and New York: Routledge, 2018), 80–104; Constantinos Kombos, "Idiosyncratic Constitutional Review in Cyprus: (Re-)Design, Survival and Kelsen," *ICL Journal* 14, no. 4 (2020: 473–496; James Milligan, "Power-Sharing as a Means of Conflict Resolution: A Comparative Analysis of the Peace Processes in Northern Ireland and Cyprus," *IFF Paper Online* 40 (2023): 1–33; Costantinos Kombos and Athena Herodotou, "The Supreme Court of Cyprus: The Centre of Gravity Within the Separation of Powers," in *Constitutional Review in Western Europe. Judicial-Legislative Relations in Comparative Perspective*, ed. Kálmán Pócza (London and New York: Routledge, 2024), 77–107.

287 Schwartz, "International Judges," 3; Kombos, "Idiosyncratic Constitutional Review," 481–488.

288 Schwartz, "International Judges," 3.

289 Kombos, "Idiosyncratic Constitutional Review," 481.

290 Law 33/64, Administration of Justice (Miscellaneous Provisions) Law.

291 Supreme Court of Cyprus, Appeals Nos. 2729, 2734, 2735, *The Attorney-General of the Republic v. Ibrahim* (Nov. 10, 1964).

and the Supreme Constitutional Court.[292] This evolution of the Court, as noted by Kombos, meant not only that it was composed only of Greek Cypriot judges, but also a shift from a centralised to a diffuse model of constitutionality review.[293] A proposed reform of the Court,[294] including the 2004 Annan Plan for the reunification of Cyprus that was never implemented, stipulated that foreign Supreme Court judges should not only not be Cypriot citizens, but not even Turkish, Greek, or British.[295] This was supposed to make a court otherwise subject to the influences of the plurality of political forces in the system, domestic and international, fully impartial.

Conversely, regarding the Kosovo experience,[296] the Constitutional Court was established in 2009 following Kosovo's declaration of independence. The original composition provided for the presence of three foreign judges appointed by the International Civilian Representative (ICR) after consultation with the President of the European Court of Human Rights.[297] Although the article in the Constitution that provided for the presence of the three foreign

292 Kombos, "Idiosyncratic Constitutional Review," 481–482, 488–493.

293 Kombos, "Idiosyncratic Constitutional Review," 482–483, 489. On the different models of constitutional review, see also Chapter 5, paragraph 2.1.

294 On this point, see also Kombos, "Idiosyncratic Constitutional Review," 493–495.

295 See Dziedzic, "An Introduction," 12; Faustmann and Varnava, *Reunifying Cyprus*, 33, 77, 102.

296 On the international character of the Kosovo Constitutional Court, see Constance Grewe and Michael Riegner, "Internationalized Constitutionalism in Ethnically Divided Societies: Bosnia-Herzegovina and Kosovo Compared," *Max Planck Yearbook of United Nations Law Online* 15, no. 1 (2011): 1–64; Enver Hasani, "The Role of the Constitutional Court in the Development of the Rule of Law in Kosovo," *Review of Central and East European Law* 43, no. 3 (2018): 274–313; Enver Hasani, Oren Doli, and Fisnik Korenica, "Individual Complaint Mechanism as a Means to Protecting Fundamental Human Rights and Freedoms: The Case of the Constitutional Court of Kosovo," *European Yearbook of Human Rights* (2012): 383–400; Enver Hasani and Fisnik Korenica, "'Two Courts' for *One Constitution*: Fragmentation of Constitutional Review in the Law of the Kosovo Specialist Chambers in The Hague," *German Law Journal* 24, no. 2 (2023): 385–401; Andrea Lorenzo Capussela, "A Critique of Kosovo's Internationalized Constitutional Court," *European Diversity and Autonomy Papers* 2 (2014): 5–40; Laura A. Dickinson, "The Relationship between Hybrid Courts and International Courts: The Case of Kosovo," *New England Law Review* 37, no. 4 (2002): 1059–72; Constance Grewe, "Foreign Judges in the Constitutional Courts of Bosnia-Herzegovina and Kosovo. 'Mission Impossible'?," in *The Cambridge Handbook of Foreign Judges on Domestic Courts*, ed. Anna Dziedzic and Simon N.M. Young (Cambridge University Press, 2023), 103–23; Roberto Toniatti, "The Principle of Reflective Judiciary in Divided Societies: Challenges and Opportunities in the Western Balkans," *Rivista Di Diritti Comparati*, no. 3 (2023): 1–43.

297 Constitution of Kosovo – Art. 152(4) "Temporary Composition of the Constitutional Court".

judges was repealed in 2012, the judges selected under that provision remained in office thereafter according to an agreement between the European authorities and the President of Kosovo, who renewed their mandate initially until 2016 and then until 2018.[298] Regarding the impact of foreign judges on the Kosovo Constitutional Court, Grewe draws a substantially negative conclusion. The author notes how the foreign judges did not take a consistent approach, confirmed by the fact that they voted unanimously only occasionally. According to Grewe, foreign judges in the Kosovar Court did not feel invested with a real mission, unlike what happened, as we shall see, in the Constitutional Court of Bosnia and Herzegovina.[299] It is also true that the two contexts, although sharing some common elements, are not perfectly overlapping. In Kosovo there is a clearly dominant group, the Albanian, against a numerically small Serbian minority, and the Kosovo Constitution, unlike the BiH Constitution, recognises the existence of only one people, the Kosovo people, enshrining the principle of multi-ethnicity, with no one group benefiting from a special status over the others.[300] This is also reflected in the composition of the Court, which did not (and still does not) provide for the appointment of national judges on an ethnic basis. Therefore, Grewe argues that foreign judges in Kosovo have not contributed to the Court's legitimacy and have not had a decisive impact on constitutional jurisprudence.[301]

Regarding the case of Bosnia and Herzegovina, it is necessary to point out that originally in the constitutional system, in addition to the Constitutional Court, there were two other judicial bodies in which foreign judges were present, namely the Human Rights Chamber (until 2002) and the Court of Bosnia and Herzegovina (until 2007).[302] Notably, in the Human Rights Chamber the presence of foreign judges was preponderant compared to domestic judges, in a ratio of eight to six.[303] It is equally significant to notice that both courts, along with the Constitutional Court, have jurisdiction over the protection of human rights and the rule of law, so their presence was functional in ensuring

298 Hasani, "The Role of the Constitutional Court," 292–293.

299 Grewe, "Foreign Judges," 122.

300 Grewe, "Foreign Judges," 106.

301 Grewe, "Foreign Judges," 122.

302 As for the Court of Bosnia and Herzegovina, foreign judges sat in the chamber dealing with war crimes and organised crime, as well as at the appellate level. Initially, the ratio of judges was two foreign judges and fronted by one domestic judge, while later the ratio was reversed in favour of domestic judges. For more details on the functioning of the Court, see David Re, "The Court of Bosnia and Herzegovina" *Bar News* (Summer 2008/2009): 32–34.

303 Gavrić et al., *The Political System of Bosnia and Herzegovina*, 47–48.

the application of international human rights standards and the European Convention on Human Rights.[304] With regard specifically to the Constitutional Court of Bosnia and Herzegovina,[305] this is provided for in Art. VI of the Constitution and consists of nine judges, three of whom are appointed by the President of the European Court of Human Rights after consultation with the collective Presidency. The Constitution further specifies that foreign judges may not be citizens of Bosnia and Herzegovina or neighbouring states.[306] As noted by Dziedzic, this reinforces a conception of national citizenship whereby national identity goes beyond state borders, making judges from neighbouring jurisdictions not fully impartial in identity-based disputes.[307] The other six judges are appointed by the parliamentary assemblies of the sub-state entities: four by the House of Representatives of the Federation of Bosniaks and Herzegovina (the Bosniak and Bosnian-Croat majority entity) and two by the National Assembly of Republika Srpska (the Bosnian-Serb majority entity).[308] Although there is no explicit provision for any ethnic allocation of judges, the practice is that the judges appointed by the Federation are two Bosniaks and two Bosnian-Croat judges, while the two judges appointed by Republika Srpska are two Bosnian-Serb judges. The Constitution stipulates that the Constitutional Court has exclusive jurisdiction over con-

304 Cfr. Dziedzic, "An Introduction," 13.

305 On the Constitutional Court of Bosnia and Herzegovina, see Joseph Marko, "Five Years of Constitutional Jurisprudence in Bosnia and Herzegovina: A First Balance," *European Diversity and Autonomy Papers* 7 (2004): 5–39; Alex Schwartz and Melanie Janelle Murchison, "Judicial Impartiality and Independence in Divided Societies: An Empirical Analysis of the Constitutional Court of Bosnia-Herzegovina," *Law & Society Review* 50, no. 4 (2016): 821–55; Dawn Walsh, "Constitutional Courts as Arbiters of Post-Conflict Territorial Self-Government: Bosnia and Macedonia," *Regional & Federal Studies* 29, no. 1 (2019): 67–90; Harun Išerić, "The Role of the Constitutional Court of Bosnia and Herzegovina in Profiling Cooperative Federalism in a Multinational State," in *Ethnic Diversity, Plural Democracy and Human Dignity*, ed. Mario Krešić et al. (Cham: Springer International Publishing, 2022), 153–83; Edin Skrebo, "La Corte Costituzionale della Bosnia ed Erzegovina fissa i limiti alla modifica del riparto di competenze tra Stato centrale ed entità federali," *DPCE Online*, no. 4 (2022): 2353–65; Laura Montanari, "La composizione della Corte Costituzionale della Bosnia ed Erzegovina tra influenza del fattore etnico e garanzie internazionali," in *Le corti costituzionali: composizione, indipendenza, legittimazione* ed. Marina Calamo Specchia (Torino: Giappichelli Editore, 2011), 113–35.

306 Constitution of Bosnia and Herzegovina – Art. VI(1)b.

307 It is worth noting that in other contexts the position is the opposite. In Kuwait, Qatar and the United Arab Emirates, the appointment of foreign judges to domestic courts is granted only to judges who are nationals of other Arab countries, indicating a commonality of identity based on language, religion and legal traditions (see Dziedzic, "An Introduction," 4).

308 Constitution of Bosnia and Herzegovina – Art. VI(1)a.

flicts between the two entities, between entities and the central state, and between state institutions, as well as constitutional review.[309] Access to the Court is limited to members of the collective Presidency, the President of the Council of Ministers, the President and Vice-President of both chambers of the BiH parliamentary assembly, a quarter of the members of each chamber of the BiH parliament, and a quarter of each chamber of the parliaments of the entities.[310] Turning now to the Court's work and the role it has played in the evolution of the BiH legal system, it is crucial to recall that the Constitutional Court assumed a decisive role in the constitutional transition of Bosnia and Herzegovina.[311] Indeed, after an initial phase of strict implementation of the constitutional model imposed by the 1995 Dayton Accords, which provided for the introduction of a complex political and territorial architecture, through a series of corrective decisions the Court initiated a new phase of the transition, aimed at relaxing some of the original rigidities. In this phase, the Court took on the role of a true "systemic court",[312] ruling on disputes concerning ethnic symbols (e.g., toponymy, flags, coats of arms), the composition and powers of political institutions, so-called vital interests and the use of the veto power,[313] and individual appeals on alleged violations of human rights and the right of return of refugees.[314]

Aside from the already analysed *Constituent Peoples'* case, another interesting case, from a few years later, is the so-called *Place Names* case which concerned two laws adopted by the Parliamentary Assembly of Republika Srpska, under which some towns were to be renamed to indicate their Serbian origin.[315] Unlike in the previous case, the Court was unanimous in recognising the unconstitutionality of the two laws, as they implied the superiority of

309 Constitution of Bosnia and Herzegovina – Art. VI(3)a-c.

310 Constitution of Bosnia and Herzegovina – Art. VI(3)a.

311 On the stages of constitutional transition, see in particular Woelk, *La transizione costituzionale.*

312 Woelk, *La transizione costituzionale*, 110.

313 The consociational model introduced by the Dayton Accords stipulates that the groups recognised by the Constitution (Bosniaks, Bosnian-Croats, and Bosnian-Serbs) have the right to exercise veto power if they feel that the vital interests of their groups have been violated or are in danger of being violated (Constitution of Bosnia and Herzegovina – Art. IV(3)e & Art. V(2)d).

314 After the end of the work of the Human Rights Commission (formerly called the Human Rights Chamber), the relevant powers were transferred to the Constitutional Court in 2004.

315 Constitutional Court of Bosnia and Herzegovina, Case U-44/01, 27 February 2004. On the *Place Names* case, see David Feldman, "Renaming Cities in Bosnia and Herzegovina," *International Journal of Constitutional Law* 3, no. 4 (2005): 649–62.

Serbian identity over the others and discouraged members of the other two communities from settling in the "renamed" towns or returning to them as required by the provisions of the Dayton Accords on the return of refugees.[316] Thus, through these two rulings, the Constitutional Court clearly redefined the multi-ethnic nature of Bosnian society, demonstrating that the ethnic (and thus collective) character must be brought within the limits set by individual rights.[317] However, there were cases in which the Court was unable to let individual rights prevail over collective rights, as occurred in the appeals that preceded the previously analysed decision of the Strasbourg Court *Sejdić and Finci v. Bosnia and Herzegovina*.[318] On this occasion, the Constitutional Court rejected the claims of the plaintiffs, both of whom belonged to the "Others" category provided for in the Constitution gathering national minorities, who claimed to have been discriminated against because of their ethnic origin. In one of the three cases that came before the Court, the judges were unanimous in declaring the case inadmissible,[319] while in the other two cases, two judges (including the foreign judge Constance Grewe) expressed their dissenting opinion.[320] In the Court's opinion, the constitutional provisions that prevented citizens who did not identify with one of the three constituent peoples from running for the collective presidency and the second chamber of the state parliament were justified when considered in the overall context in which Bosnia and Herzegovina found itself, in which a delicate peaceful balance had been achieved through the Dayton Accords. The Court also referred to an earlier Strasbourg Court ruling, *Mathieu-Mohin and Clerfayt v. Belgium*,[321] in which the restrictions imposed on the election of the presidency had been considered legitimate and instrumental to maintaining a peaceful dialogue between the language communities. The Court's different attitude to the two cases from the early 2000s can be explained if one considers that the cases concerning electoral legislation concerned the heart of the BiH consociational system (i.e., the composition of state political offices), as

316 Choudhry and Stacey, "Independent of Dependent," 99–100.

317 Choudhry and Stacey, "Independent of Dependent," 100.

318 European Court of Human Rights, Cases 27996/06 and 34836/06, *Sejdić and Finci v. Bosnia and Herzegovina*, 22 December 2009. On the *Sejdić and Finci* judgment, see paragraph 2.3.2.

319 Constitutional Court of Bosnia and Herzegovina, Case U-5/04, 31 March 31 2006.

320 Constitutional Court of Bosnia and Herzegovina, Case U-13/05, 26 May 2006 and Case AP-2678/06, 29 September 2006. In both decisions, the dissenting judges were foreign judge Constance Grewe and Court President Seada Palavric.

321 European Court of Human Rights, Case 9267/81, *Mathieu-Mohin and Clerfayt v. Belgium*, 2 March 1987.

opposed to the case of constituent peoples and city names.[322] Finally, it is necessary to note that the presence of foreign judges has presented the Constitutional Court with significant problems in respect of its rulings and, consequently, its authority. For example, in 2010 the Court had declared unconstitutional certain sections of the state election legislation and the Statute of the City of Mostar, requiring their amendment. However, the ruling was not implemented until 2020, leaving the city of Mostar without a democratically elected mayor for 12 years.[323] Similarly, in 2015, the Court declared unconstitutional a law of Republika Srpska establishing a "national holiday" on January 9, the same day on which the Serbian entity declared its independence from the Republic of Bosnia and Herzegovina in 1992, on the grounds that such a holiday would discriminate against non-Serb citizens.[324] Despite the fact that this ruling prevented such celebration, the authorities of Republika Srpska openly violated the ban and events have taken place regularly since – including in January 2025.[325] As also noted recently by the Strasbourg Court, non-compliance with Constitutional Court rulings further threatens respect for the principles of the rule of law.[326]

In seeking to draw some concluding thoughts on the presence of foreign judges in domestic courts, it is useful to start from the observation that in most of the cases analysed by the doctrine these are transitional and not permanent solutions. This choice may be linked to peacebuilding processes aimed at reinforcing the principles of the rule of law and rebuilding institutions at the end of a conflict, as occurred in Kosovo or East Timor.[327] Once the specific needs that led to the appointment of foreign judges have been met, their presence is gradually abandoned. Although this trend has been further confirmed by the processes of decolonisation, which has seen a gradual increase in the appointment of national judges rather than judges from the former colonial powers, Dziedzic notes how the hybrid model may become increasingly common in

322 Choudhry and Stacey, "Independent of Dependent," 101.

323 Constitutional Court of Bosnia and Herzegovina, Case U-9/09, 26 November 2010.

324 Constitutional Court of Bosnia and Herzegovina, Case U-3/13, 26 November 2015, on the case see Mirha Karahodžić, "Bosnian Constitutional Court: Unconstitutionality of the 'Day of the Republic': Judgment of 26 November 2015, U 3/13," *ICL Journal* 11, no. 1 (2017): 153–61.

325 Azem Kurtic, "Bosnian Serbs Celebrate Banned Holiday With Massive Parade," *Balkan Insight* (9 January 2025), available at https://balkaninsight.com/2025/01/09/bosnian-serbs-celebrate-banned-holiday-with-massive-parade/ (last accessed 14 August 2025).

326 European Court of Human Rights, Case 30100/28, *Baralija v. Bosnia and Herzegovina*, 29 October 2019.

327 Dziedzic, "An Introduction," 11.

the future, fully reflecting the complex nature of "emerging forms of legal pluralism".[328] With regard specifically to the case of Bosnia and Herzegovina, it is worth noting that the authorities in Republika Srpska, in order to disregard the decisions of the Constitutional Court, have challenged its legitimacy by instrumentally relying on the very presence of foreign judges, who are accused of not being impartial and siding with the Bosniak judges.[329] One of the most recent examples of this dynamic concerns the adoption of a property law by the National Assembly of Republika Srpska, which took place after it was first declared unconstitutional by the Constitutional Court and later suspended by the High Representative, another essential figure called upon to enforce the terms of the Dayton Accords including through the use of broad powers.[330] In this case, despite the fact that the Constitutional Court again ruled on the law and confirmed its unconstitutionality, the Parliament of Republika Srpska proceeded anyway with the publication of the law in its Official Gazette. As a result of this case, the Parliament of the Serb entity adopted a law openly stating that it does not recognise the authority of the Constitutional Court in Republika Srpska because of the presence of foreign judges, which made the Court effectively illegitimate.[331] Despite the seemingly temporary nature of this law, this is yet another attack on the authority of the Constitutional Court, as well as on the principles of the rule of law. Thus, the Bosnian case perfectly exemplifies the trade-off between advantages and disadvantages of hybrid constitutional courts as identified by Dixon and Jackson.[332] Indeed, while it is true that the hybrid nature of the Court was necessary and functional

328 Dziedzic, "An Introduction," 30.

329 Lidia Bonifati, "Constitutional Design and the Seeds of Degradation in Divided Societies: The Case of Bosnia and Herzegovina," *European Constitutional Law Review* 19, no. 2 (2023): 246.

330 The High Representative enjoys so-called "Bonn powers," through which he can compel the adoption of certain laws and remove public officials from office. These powers were used particularly in the early stages of the constitutional transition and then gradually limited due to their broad scope, although recently the current High Representative has made extensive use of them, not without controversy (on this point see Tim Banning, "The 'Bonn Powers' of the High Representative in Bosnia Herzegovina: Tracing a Legal Figment," *Goettingen Journal of International Law* 6, no. 2 (2014): 259–302; Dariusz Kalan, "Bosnia's Peace Envoy is Caught in a Political Tug of War," *Foreign Policy* (24 February 2023), available at https://foreignpolicy.com/2023/02/24/bosnia-christian-schmidt-peace-envoy-constitution-changes/ (last access 21 March 2025).

331 Azem Kurtic, "Bosnia's Serb Entity Passes Law Rejecting Constitutional Court's Authority," *Balkan Insight* (28 June 2023), available at https://balkaninsight.com/2023/06/28/bosnias-serb-entity-passes-law-rejecting-constitutional-courts-authority/ (last access 21 March 2025).

332 Dixon and Jackson, "Hybrid Constitutional Courts", 353–356.

to ensure the proper application of the Dayton Accords and the Constitution, as well as the European Convention on Human Rights, it is also true that the presence of foreign judges (as well as the High Representative) continues to be increasingly controversial, especially in terms of legitimacy. Therefore, a rethinking of the composition of the Court, abandoning its current hybrid nature, would be necessary.[333] Despite the urgent nature of this reform, it is part of a complex political-institutional framework, in which carrying out fundamental reforms that would lead to an evolution of the legal system (especially with a view to European integration)[334] is regularly halted by vetoes of ethnonationalist parties, which are unwilling to abandon a model that guarantees them broad power.[335] Therefore, as long as its composition is not changed, the Constitutional Court of Bosnia and Herzegovina continues to remain a unique case in the comparative landscape, with all the critical issues this entails.

4 Courts and the Use of Foreign Law to Address Internal Diversity

Before ending this chapter, a final remark on the role of courts in the accommodation of diversity concerns the use that courts have made of foreign law in such decisions. Since the end of the Second World War, courts have increasingly engaged in dialogue with each other, at a national and supranational level, encouraging references to foreign law in their understanding and interpretation of constitutional law and principles,[336] and engaging in comparison at two separate moments: in the process of reasoning (comparative reasoning) and at the moment of decision (comparative judgment).[337] If it is true that the trend toward judicial dialogue has increased, it should not be forgotten that not all constitutional courts rely on comparative analyses in the same way and

333 On this point see, in particular, Stefan Graziadei, "Six Models for Reforming the Selection of Judges to the BiH Constitutional Court," *Center for Southeast European Studies Working Papers* 14 (2016): 1–38; Bonifati, "Le 'corti ibride' negli ordinamenti multinazionali", 1133–1136.

334 It should be mentioned that the reform of the Constitutional Court, especially with regard to the presence of foreign judges, is among the 14 key priorities identified by the European Commission for Bosnia and Herzegovina to join the European Union (see European Commission, "Commission Opinion on Bosnia and Herzegovina's Application for Membership of the European Union," 2019).

335 On this point, see Jens Woelk, "Forced Together, Never Sustainable? Post-Conflict Federalism in Bosnia and Herzegovina," *Kansas Law Review* 71 (2022): 252–74.

336 See de Vergottini, "Constitutional Law and the Comparative Method," 25–32.

337 See de Vergottini, "Constitutional Law and the Comparative Method," 29.

with the same intensity. In fact, there are exceptional cases, such as the Constitutional Court of South Africa,[338] which have developed an interpretative practice strongly oriented towards comparison based on a specific constitutional provision,[339] or the Supreme Courts of Canada, Israel, and Brazil, which often made use of foreign law while deciding on cases concerning fundamental rights (e.g., discrimination on the ground of sexual orientation, or freedom of expression).[340] On the other hand, there are instances such as the US Supreme Court, which have traditionally opposed the use of comparison in constitutional adjudication, deeming the reference to foreign law as highly problematic.[341] Then, in an intermediate position, there are courts that are receptive to foreign law despite not explicitly incorporating it in their *ratio decidendi*, such as the French *Conseil Constitutionnel* and the Italian Constitutional Court.[342] Finally, the "comparative courts" of excellence tend to be supranational courts, such as the European Court of Human Rights and the Court of Justice of the European Union, which make use of comparison while referring to the law of their Member States.[343]

338 See Angelo Rinella and Valentina Cardinale, "The Comparative Tool-Kit of the Constitutional Court of South Africa," in *Judicial Cosmopolitanism*, ed. Giuseppe Franco Ferrari (Leiden and Boston: Brill, 2019), 217–259; Andrea Lollini, "Legal Argumentation Based on Foreign Law. An Example from Case Law of the South African Constitutional Court," *Utrecht Law Review* 3, no. 1 (2007): 60–74.

339 Art. 35.1 of the Interim Constitution included explicit authorisation of the use of comparison (especially in the interpretation of the Bill of Rights). Although with a less explicit formulation, Art. 39 of the current Constitution provides for the use of foreign law, and the South African Constitutional Court has continuously operated in such direction (a systematic analysis of the extra-systemic parameters adopted by the South African Constitutional Court when engaging in comparison is provided by Andrea Lollini, "From Import to Export? Some Signs of the External Circulation of South African Constitutional Jurisprudence," in *The Quest for Constitutionalism*, ed. Hugh Corder and Veronica Federico (London and New York: Routledge, 2016), 253–266.

340 See de Vergottini, "Constitutional Law and the Comparative Method," 26–27.

341 On this issue, the arguments against comparison by former Justice Scalia in *Lawrence v. Texas* are well-known in the debate within the USSC and in the academic and political spheres. Although, it should be noted that Hirschl argues that the attitude of the Court towards comparison is less antagonistic than in the past, and that the Court has "hesitantly joined the comparative reference trend", although in an a-systematic, result-driven fashion (see Hirschl, "Comparative Methodologies", 21). For other arguments in favour of comparative analyses in the US constitutional system, see Mark Tushnet, "The Possibilities of Comparative Constitutional Law," *The Yale Law Journal* 108, no. 6 (1999): 1225–1309.

342 See de Vergottini, "Constitutional Law and the Comparative Method," 28.

343 For more on courts and the comparative method, see de Vergottini, *Oltre il dialogo tra le corti*; Michal Bobek, *Comparative Reasoning in European Supreme Courts* (Oxford: Ox-

For the purpose of this chapter, it is fascinating to consider how domestic and supranational courts have referred to other courts in their case law on minority rights and the accommodation of internal ethnocultural diversity. As anticipated, perhaps the most notable example of a constitutional court extensively relying on foreign law is the Constitutional Court of South Africa. The South African case is exceptional insofar as it is the Constitution itself that entitles the Court to "consider foreign law" when interpreting the Bill of Rights to "promote the values that underlie an open and democratic society based on human dignity, equality and freedom".[344] As argued by Lollini, this constitutional provision led to a "wide use of foreign jurisprudence and legislation, as well as extra-systemic parameters, that have formed the basis for models of legal argumentation, the balancing of general principles and literal interpretation".[345] Another experience that can be recalled is the case of the Constitutional Court of Bosnia-Herzegovina, that in the *Constituent Peoples'* case made great use of comparative law in its argumentative phase.[346] As has already been discussed, *Reference Re Secession of Québec* had a wide-ranging impact outside the Canadian federation and has been recalled in several jurisdictions, becoming a sort of lodestar in how internal diversity should be interpreted in democratic, cooperative, and negotiated terms. Specifically, in the *Constituent Peoples'* case, the BiH Constitutional Court explicitly recalled the reasoning of the Canadian Supreme Court in *Reference Re Secession* to justify the normative nature of constitutional principles guiding the constitutional system,[347] concluding that

> [The] constitutional commitment [to pluralism, fair procedures, peaceful relations following from the text of the Constitution], legally binding on all public authorities, cannot be isolated from other elements of the Constitution, in particular the ethnic structures, and must therefore be

---

ford University Press, 2013); Christopher McCrudden, "Using Comparative Reasoning in Human Rights Adjudication: The Court of Justice of the European Union and the European Court of Human Rights Compared," in *Cambridge Yearbook of European Legal Studies*, ed. Catherine Barnard, vol. 15 (Cambridge: Cambridge University Press, 2015), 383–415.

344 Constitution of South Africa – Art. 39.

345 Andrea Lollini, "Legal Argumentation Based on Foreign Law: An Example from Case Law of the South African Constitutional Court," *Utrecht Law Review* 3, no. 1 (2007): 60.

346 See Laura Montanari, "The Use of Comparative and International Law by the Constitutional Court of Bosnia and Herzegovina," in *Judicial Cosmopolitanism*, ed. Giuseppe Franco Ferrari (Leiden and Boston: Brill | Nijhoff, 2019), 708–44.

347 *Constituent Peoples'* case, paras. 23, 54 and 55.

> interpreted by reference to the structure of the Constitution as a whole (see Canadian Supreme Court "Reference Re Secession of Quebec" (1998), 2.S.C.R., para 50).[348]

The justification of the normative nature of the principles contained in the Preamble of the BiH Constitution was also supported by reference to another landmark decision, i.e., the 1971 *Grande Décision* of the French *Conseil Constitutionnel*,[349] that had been invoked by the applicant's representative to uphold the normative and binding nature of the constitutional preamble.[350]

Moreover, it should be noted that courts have often relied on foreign law to justify the distinction between federal states and other forms of territorial decentralisation to manage increasing tensions between territorial-based ethnocultural communities. Again, the BiH Constitutional Court implicitly recalled the constitutional arrangements in other federal states to argue that the two BiH entities are not sovereign states, but subnational entities.[351] Similarly, the South African Constitutional Court referred to the US federal model and the US Supreme Court decision in *New York v. United States*[352] to clarify that "unlike their counterparts in the United States of America, the provinces in South Africa are not sovereign states".[353] However, the fact that these courts adopted notable "comparative judgments" does not mean that these were accepted as a legitimate use of comparative law by every member of the court. Specifically, in the dissenting opinion of the minority judges in the *Constituent Peoples'* case, Judge Miljko argued that the reference to other federal states (i.e., Canada, Switzerland, Belgium) could not form part of the *ratio decidendi*, as they often represent specific situations and are thus incomparable.[354]

---

348 *Constituent Peoples'* case, para. 54.

349 Conseil Constitutionnel, Decision no. 71–44 DC (16 July 1971). For more on this landmark judgment, see Justin O. Frosini, "The Legal Value of Constitutional Preambles and the Significance of the *Grande Décision* of the *Conseil Constitutionnel* of 1971," in *Comparative Constitutional History. Volume 3: Landmark Judgments*, ed. Francesco Biagi, Justin O. Frosini, and Jason Mazzone (Leiden and Boston: Brill, forthcoming 2026); Louis Favoreu, and Loïc Philip, *Les grandes décisions du Conseil constitutionnel* (Paris: Dalloz, 2007).

350 *Constituent Peoples'* case, para. 57.

351 *Constituent Peoples'* case, paras. 28–30.

352 Supreme Court of the United States, *New York v. United Stated*, 505 US144 (1992).

353 Constitutional Court of South Africa, *Ex Parte Speaker of the National Assembly: In Re Dispute Concerning the Constitutionality of Certain Provisions of the National Education Policy Bill 83 of 1995*, 1996 (3) SA 289 (CC), para. 23.

354 *Constituent Peoples'* case, Separate Opinion of Judge Zvonko Miljko, 48.

Finally, what is further interesting to notice is that decisions by supranational courts on the accommodation of diversity have the power to inspire other regions of the world. This is perfectly exemplified by the African Commission on Human and Peoples' Rights' decision in *Endorois Welfare Council v. Kenya*.[355] In fact, in several paragraphs[356] the African Commission extensively referenced previous cases on indigenous peoples' rights as decided by the Inter-American Court of Human Rights,[357] as well as some judgments of the European Court of Human Rights on property rights,[358] minority rights,[359] and proportional limitation of rights.[360]

5 Concluding Remarks

This chapter sought to review how (constitutional and supranational) courts have addressed internal ethnocultural diversity across a variety of dimensions, such as internal self-determination, the protection of fundamental rights of minorities, and the principle of equality in divided societies. As has emerged from the cases analysed in the previous pages, courts have often had to address ethnocultural diversity in their case-law and to strike a balance between individual and collective rights in deeply divided consti-

355 African Commission on Human and Peoples' Rights, *Centre for Minority Rights Development (Kenya) and Minority Rights Group (on behalf of Endorois Welfare Council) v. Kenya*, decision on communication no. 276/03 (2010).

356 See especially paras. 190, 192, 198, 207, 208 on the decisions, whereas in para. 94 the African Commission reports the applicants' reference to other courts that recognised the violations of indigenous property rights "stemming from colonial seizure of land, such as when modern states rely on domestic legal title inherited from colonial authorities" (para. 94). In particular, the applicants relied on the Judicial Committee of the Privy Council, *Amodu Tijani v. Secretary, Southern Nigeria*, 2 AC 399 (1921), Supreme Court of Canada, *Calder et al v. Attorney-General of British Columbia*, 34 D.L.R. (3d) 145 (1973), High Court of Australia, *Mabo v. Queensland*, 107 A.L.R. 1 (1992), and Constitutional Court of South Africa, *Alexkor Ltd v. Richtersveld Community*, CCT 19/03 (2003).

357 See Inter-American Court of Human Rights, *Mayagna (Sumo) Awas Tingni Community v. Nicaragua*, 31 August 2001; Inter-American Court of Human Rights, *Saramaka People v. Suriname*, 28 November 2007; Inter-American Court of Human Rights, *Case of the Moiwana Community v. Suriname*, Serie C No. 124, 15 June 2005.

358 European Court of Human Rights, *Doğan and Others v. Turkey*, Case Nos. 8803–8811/02, 8813/02 and 8815–8819/02, 18 November 2004.

359 European Court of Human Rights, *Connors v. United Kingdom*, Case No. 66746/01, 27 August 2004.

360 European Court of Human Rights, *Handyside v. United Kingdom*, Case No. 5493/72, Series A.24, 7 December 1976.

tutional systems. This was shown through the review of several paradigmatic cases of national constitutional courts in divided multi-tiered systems, namely the Constitutional Court of South Africa, the Constitutional Court of Bosnia-Herzegovina, the Supreme Court of Canada and the Supreme Court of India. In these cases, constitutional courts generally supported an integrated and multi-ethnic interpretation of their constitutional systems to protect the rights of minority groups and ensure equality, despite at times attracting criticisms as in the Indian and BiH cases. Moreover, the case law of international and supranational courts shows how the issue of diversity governance has expanded beyond national borders. This is especially relevant if we consider the cases related to the self-determination of peoples, as in the case law of the ICJ, the Badinter Commission and the ACHPR, and the guarantee of collective rights, as in the case law of the ECtHR and the IACtHR. Interestingly, the chapter also showed how both domestic and supranational courts often found inspiration in each other's decisions. This emerged rather clearly in the decision of the BiH Constitutional Court in the *Constituent Peoples'* case, recalling the Canadian *Reference Re Secession of Québec*, and in the case law of the African Commission of Human and Peoples' Rights, which made extensive reference to previous decisions of the two regional human rights systems, i.e., the Inter-American Court of Human Rights and the European Court of Human Rights.

Moreover, an added value of this chapter was a reflexive understanding of diversity *within* courts, addressing two peculiar compositions of courts. The first was the so-called power-sharing courts, where the ethnocultural diversity of the constitutional systems finds a translation not only in the political institutions but also in the composition of apex courts. This configuration is detectable in Belgium and Bosnia-Herzegovina, and (unsurprisingly) it tends to attract the same criticisms as power-sharing democracies, i.e., its illegitimate and undemocratic nature. Then, the so-called hybrid constitutional courts are those courts where domestic judges sit alongside foreign or international judges, to ensure a balance between national legitimation and impartiality. These have often been introduced into post-conflict societies and the paradigmatic case in this respect is, again, the Constitutional Court of Bosnia-Herzegovina, where three of the nine judges are appointed by the European Court of Human Rights after consultation with the BiH collective Presidency. The hybrid composition of the Court has been at the centre of several crises and is one of the reasons behind the current crisis of legitimacy of the Court.

Overall, this chapter intended to show that courts are an essential element when dealing with the governance of internal ethnocultural diversity, and this provides a solid background for the final chapter on the role of courts in reshaping the degree of constitutional asymmetry.

Bibliography

Ahmed, Farrah. "Pluralism and Personal Laws in India." In *Constitutions and Religion*, edited by Susanna Mancini, 415–32. Cheltenham, UK and Northampton, MA: Edward Elgar Publishing, 2020.

Ahmed, Farrah. *Religious Freedom under the Personal Law System*. Oxford: Oxford University Press, 2015.

Antkowiak, Thomas M. "Rights, Resources, and Rhetoric: Indigenous Peoples and the Inter-American Court." *University of Pennsylvania Journal of International Law* 35, no. 1 (2013): 113–88.

Badawi, Ali. "The Future Relationship between the African Court and the African Commission." *African Human Rights Law Journal* 2, no. 2 (2002): 252–60.

Bekker, Gina. "The African Court on Human and Peoples' Rights: Safeguarding the Interests of African States." *Journal of African Law* 51, no. 1 (2007): 151–72.

Biagi, Francesco. *European Constitutional Courts and Transitions to Democracy*. Cambridge: Cambridge University Press, 2020.

Biagi, Francesco. "Foreign Law in Constitutional Interpretation." In *Max Planck Encyclopedia of Comparative Constitutional Law*, edited by Rainer Grote, Frauke Lachenmann, and Rüdiger Wolfrum, 1–18. Oxford: Oxford University Press, 2021.

Binder, Christina. "The Prohibition of Amnesties by the Inter-American Court of Human Rights." *German Law Journal* 12, no. 5 (2011): 1203–30.

Bonifati, Lidia. "Constitutional Design and the Seeds of Degradation in Divided Societies: The Case of Bosnia-Herzegovina." *European Constitutional Law Review* 19, no. 2 (2023): 223–48.

Bonifati, Lidia. "Le 'corti ibride' negli ordinamenti multinazionali: una prospettiva comparata." *DPCE Online* 66, Special Issue no. 2 (2024): 1119–1137.

Capussela, Andrea Lorenzo. "A Critique of Kosovo's Internationalized Constitutional Court." *European Diversity and Autonomy Papers* 2 (2014): 5–40.

Chaskalson, Matthew, and Dennis Davis. "Constitutionalism, the Rule of Law and the First Certification Judgment." *South African Journal on Human Rights* 13, no. 3 (1997): 430–45.

Choudhry, Sujit. "Does the World Need More Canada? The Politics of the Canadian Model in Constitutional Politics and Political Theory." *International Journal of Constitutional Law* 5, no. 4 (2007): 606–38.

Cuneo, Isabel Madariaga. "The Rights of Indigenous Peoples and the Inter-American Human Rights System." *Arizona Journal of International and Comparative Law* 22, no. 1 (2005): 53–64.

Daly, Tom Gerald, and Micha Wiebusch. "The African Court on Human and Peoples' Rights: Mapping Resistance against a Young Court." *International Journal of Law in Context* 14, no. 2 (2018): 294–313.

De Villiers, Bertus, Joseph Marko, Francesco Palermo, and Sergiu Constantin, eds. *Litigating the Rights of Minorities and Indigenous Peoples in Domestic and International Courts.* Leiden and Boston: Brill | Nijhoff, 2021.

Dersso, Solomon. "The African Human Rights System and the Issue of Minorities in Africa." *African Journal of International and Comparative Law* 20, no. 1 (2012): 42–69.

Dickinson, Laura A. "The Relationship between Hybrid Courts and International Courts: The Case of Kosovo." *New England Law Review* 37, no. 4 (2002): 1059–72.

Dixon, Rosalind, and Vicki Jackson. "Hybrid Constitutional Courts: Foreign Judges on National Constitutional Courts." *Columbia Journal of Transnational Law*, no. 57 (2018): 283–356.

Dziedzic, Anna, and Simon N. M. Young, eds. *The Cambridge Handbook of Foreign Judges on Domestic Courts.* Cambridge: Cambridge University Press, 2023.

Eno, Robert Wundeh. "The Jurisdiction of the African Court on Human and Peoples' Rights." *African Human Rights Law Journal* 2, no. 2 (2002): 223–33.

Fowkes, James. "Constitutional Court of South Africa." In *Max Planck Encyclopedia of Comparative Constitutional Law*, edited by Rainer Grote, Frauke Lachenmann, and Rüdiger Wolfrum. Heidelberg: Max Planck Institute for Comparative Public Law and International Law, 2017.

Fuentes, Alejandro. "Protection of Indigenous Peoples' Traditional Lands and Exploitation of Natural Resources: The Inter-American Court of Human Rights' Safeguards." *International Journal on Minority and Group Rights* 24, no. 3 (2017): 229–53.

Gaudreault-DesBiens, Jean-François. "The Quebec Secession Reference and the Judicial Arbitration of Conflicting Narratives About Law, Democracy, and Identity." *Vermont Law Review* 23, no. 4 (1999): 793–844.

Ghai, Yash. *Autonomy and Ethnicity. Negotiating Competing Claims in Multi-Ethnic States.* Cambridge: Cambridge University Press, 2000.

Ghai, Yash. "Ethnicity and Competing Notions of Rights." In *Rights in Divided Societies*, edited by Colin Harvey and Alex Schwartz, 51–84. Oxford and Portland: Hart Publishing, 2012.

Ghai, Yash. "Universalism and Relativism: Human Rights as a Framework for Negotiating Interethnic Claims." *Cardozo Law Review* 21, no. 4 (2000): 1095–1140.

Gilbert, Jeremie. "Constitutionalism, Ethnicity and Minority Rights in Africa: A Legal Appraisal from the Great Lakes Region." *International Journal of Constitutional Law* 11, no. 2 (2013): 414–37.

Ginsburg, Tom, and Zachary Elkins. "Ancillary Powers of Constitutional Courts." *Texas Law Review* 87, no. 7 (2009): 1431–62.

Graziadei, Stefan. "Democracy v. Human Rights? The Strasbourg Court and the Challenge of Power Sharing." *European Constitutional Law Review* 12, no. 1 (2016): 54–84.

Graziadei, Stefan. "Power Sharing Courts." *Contemporary Southeastern Europe* 3, no. 2 (2016): 66–105.

Graziadei, Stefan. "Six Models for Reforming the Selection of Judges to the BiH Constitutional Court." *Center for Southeast European Studies Working Papers* 14 (2016): 1–38.

Graziadei, Stefan. "The Strasbourg Court and Challenges to the Constitutional Architecture of Post-Conflict Federalism in Bosnia-Herzegovina and Beyond." *Review of Central and East European Law* 42, no. 2–3 (2017).

Grewe, Constance. "Foreign Judges in the Constitutional Courts of Bosnia-Herzegovina and Kosovo. 'Mission Impossible'?" In *The Cambridge Handbook of Foreign Judges on Domestic Courts*, edited by Anna Dziedzic and Simon N. M. Young, 1st ed., 103–23. Cambridge: Cambridge University Press, 2023.

Grewe, Constance, and Michael Riegner. "Internationalized Constitutionalism in Ethnically Divided Societies: Bosnia-Herzegovina and Kosovo Compared." *Max Planck Yearbook of United Nations Law Online* 15, no. 1 (2011): 1–64.

Haljan, David P. "A Constitutional Duty to Negotiate Amendments: *Reference Re Secession of Quebec*." *International and Comparative Law Quarterly* 48, no. 2 (1999): 447–57.

Harvey, Colin J., and Alex Schwartz, eds. *Rights in Divided Societies*. Oxford and Portland: Hart Publishing, 2012.

Hasani, Enver. "The Role of the Constitutional Court in the Development of the Rule of Law in Kosovo." *Review of Central and East European Law* 43, no. 3 (2018): 274–313.

Hasani, Enver, Oren Doli, and Fisnik Korenica. "Individual Complaint Mechanism as a Means to Protecting Fundamental Human Rights and Freedoms: The Case of the Constitutional Court of Kosovo." *European Yearbook of Human Rights*, 2012, 383–400.

Hasani, Enver, and Fisnik Korenica. "'Two Courts' for *One Constitution*: Fragmentation of Constitutional Review in the Law of the Kosovo Specialist Chambers in The Hague." *German Law Journal* 24, no. 2 (2023): 385–401.

Išerić, Harun. "The Role of the Constitutional Court of Bosnia and Herzegovina in Profiling Cooperative Federalism in a Multinational State." In *Ethnic Diversity, Plural Democracy and Human Dignity*, edited by Mario Krešić, Damir Banović,

Alberto Carrio Sampedro, and Jānis Pleps, 153–83. Cham: Springer International Publishing, 2022.

Issacharoff, Samuel. "Constitutionalizing Democracy in Fractured Societies." *Texas Law Review* 82 (2004): 1861–93.

Karahodžić, Mirha. "Bosnian Constitutional Court: Unconstitutionality of the 'Day of the Republic': Judgment of 26 November 2015, U 3/13." *ICL Journal* 11, no. 1 (2017): 153–61.

Klug, Heinz. "How the Centre Holds: Managing Claims for Regional and Ethnic Autonomy in a Democratic South Africa." In *Autonomy and Ethnicity. Negotiating Competing Claims in Multi-Ethnic States*, edited by Yash Ghai, 99–121. Cambridge: Cambridge University Press, 2000.

Klug, Heinz. "South Africa's Constitutional Court: Enabling Democracy and Promoting Law in the Transition from Apartheid." *Journal of Comparative Law*, 3, no. 2 (2008): 174–93.

Kombos, Constantinos. "Idiosyncratic Constitutional Review in Cyprus: (Re-)Design, Survival and Kelsen." *ICL Journal* 14, no. 4 (2021): 473–96.

Korenica, Fisnik. "'Advise and Rule' or 'Rule by Advising': The Changing Nature of the Advisory Jurisdiction of the Constitutional Court of Kosovo." *German Law Journal* 21, no. 8 (2020): 1570–85.

Langa, Pius. "Transformative Constitutionalism." *Stellenbosch Law Review* 3 (2006): 351–60.

Lemons, Katherine. "Sharia Courts and Muslim Personal Law in India: Intersecting Legal Regimes." *Law & Society Review* 52, no. 3 (2018): 603–29.

Lollini, Andrea. "Legal Argumentation Based on Foreign Law. An Example from Case Law of the South African Constitutional Court." *Utrecht Law Review* 3, no. 1 (2007): 60–74.

Lollini, Andrea, and Francesco Palermo. "Comparative Law and the Proceduralization of Constitution-Building Processes." In *Facets and Practices of State-Building*, edited by Julia Raue and Patrick Sutter, 301–26. Leiden and Boston: Brill | Nijhoff, 2009.

Mancini, Susanna, ed. *Constitutions and Religion*. Cheltenham, UK and Northampton, MA: Elgar Publishing, 2020.

Martinico, Giuseppe, and Giacomo Delledonne, eds. *The Canadian Contribution to a Comparative Law of Secession*. Cham, Switzerland: Palgrave Macmillan, 2019.

McCrudden, Christopher, and Brendan O'Leary. *Courts and Consociations: Human Rights versus Power Sharing*. Oxford: Oxford University Press, 2013.

Montanari, Laura. "La complessa soluzione istituzionale adottata in Bosnia ed Erzegovina: finalità ed effetti nel passare del tempo." *European Diversity and Autonomy Papers* 2 (2019): 6–27.

Montanari, Laura. "La composizione della Corte costituzionale della Bosnia ed Erzegovina tra influenza del fattore etnico e garanzie internazionali." In *Le Corti costituzionali: composizione, indipendenza, legittimazione*, edited by Marina Calamo Specchia, 113–35. Torino: Giappichelli Editore, 2011.

Montanari, Laura. "The Use of Comparative and International Law by the Constitutional Court of Bosnia and Herzegovina." In *Judicial Cosmopolitanism*, edited by Giuseppe Franco Ferrari, 708–44. Leiden and Boston: Brill | Nijhoff, 2019.

Mukherjee, Gaurav. "Transformative Constitutionalism." In *Max Planck Encyclopedia of Comparative Constitutional Law*, edited by Rainer Grote, Frauke Lachenmann, and Rüdiger Wolfrum. Heidelberg: Max Planck Institute for Comparative Public Law and International Law, 2023.

Mullally, Siobhan. "Feminism and Multicultural Dilemmas in India: Revisiting the Shah Bano Case." *Oxford Journal of Legal Studies* 24, no. 4 (2004): 671–92.

Murray, Rachel. "A Comparison between the African and European Courts of Human Rights." *African Human Rights Law Journal* 2, no. 2 (2002): 195–222.

Mutua, Makau. "The African Human Rights Court: A Two-Legged Stool?" *Human Rights Quarterly* 21, no. 2 (1999): 342–63.

Nesiah, Vasuji. "Federalism and Diversity in India." In *Autonomy and Ethnicity. Negotiating Competing Claims in Multi-Ethnic States*, edited by Yash Ghai, 53–76. Cambridge: Cambridge University Press, 2000.

Palermo, Francesco. "Bosnia-Erzegovina: la Corte Costituzionale fissa i confini della (nuova) società multietnica." *Diritto Pubblico Comparato ed Europeo* 4 (2000): 1479–89.

Palermo, Francesco. "Internazionalizzazione del diritto costituzionale e costituzionalizzazione del diritto internazionale delle differenze." *European Diversity and Autonomy Papers*, no. 2 (2009): 5–32.

Pasqualucci, J. M. "The Evolution of International Indigenous Rights in the Inter-American Human Rights System." *Human Rights Law Review* 6, no. 2 (2006): 281–322.

Pasqualucci, Jo M. "International Indigenous Land Rights: A Critique of the Jurisprudence of the Inter-American Court of Human Rights in Light of the United Nations Declaration on the Rights of Indigenous Peoples." *Wisconsin International Law Journal* 27, no. 1 (2009): 51–98.

Raulston, Elizebeth. "(Un)Justifiable: A Comparison of Electoral Discrimination Jurisprudence at the European Court of Human Rights and the Constitutional Court of Bosnia and Herzegovina." *American University International Law Review* 28, no. 2 (2013): 669–706.

Roux, Theunis. "Principle and Pragmatism on the Constitutional Court of South Africa." *International Journal of Constitutional Law* 7, no. 1 (2008): 106–38.

Schertzer, Robert. "Recognition or Imposition? Federalism, National Minorities, and the Supreme Court of Canada." *Nations and Nationalism* 14, no. 1 (2008): 105–26.

Schwartz, Alex. "International Judges on Constitutional Courts: Cautionary Evidence from Post-Conflict Bosnia." *Law & Social Inquiry* 44, no. 1 (2019): 1–30.

Schwartz, Alex, and Melanie Janelle Murchison. "Judicial Impartiality and Independence in Divided Societies: An Empirical Analysis of the Constitutional Court of Bosnia-Herzegovina." *Law & Society Review* 50, no. 4 (2016): 821–55.

Sparks, Tom. *Self-Determination in the International Legal System: Whose Claim, to What Right?* Oxford and Portland: Hart Publishing, 2023.

Steytler, Nico. "The Constitutional Court of South Africa: Reinforcing an Hourglass System of Multi-Level Government." In *Courts in Federal Countries*, edited by Nicholas Theodore Aroney and John Kincaid, 328–66. Toronto: University of Toronto Press, 2017.

Subramanian, Narendra. "Legal Change and Gender Inequality: Changes in Muslim Family Law in India." *Law & Social Inquiry* 33, no. 03 (2008): 631–72.

Tahiri, Xhafer. "Judicial Activism or Constitutional Interpretation?: An Analysis of the Workings of the Constitutional Court of Kosovo." *European Public Law* 23, no. 1 (2017): 147–64.

Tarr, G Alan. "Subnational Constitutions and Minority Rights: A Perspective on Canadian Provincial Constitutionalism." *Rutgers Law Journal* 40, no. 4 (2009): 767–92.

Toniatti, Roberto. "The Principle of Reflective Judiciary in Divided Societies: Challenges and Opportunities in the Western Balkans." *Rivista di Diritti Comparati*, no. 3 (2023): 1–43.

Van Huyssteen, Elsa. "The Constitutional Court and the Redistribution of Power in South Africa: Towards Transformative Constitutionalism." *African Studies* 59, no. 2 (2000): 245–65.

Vatuk, Sylvia. "Islamic Feminism in India: Indian Muslim Women Activists and the Reform of Muslim Personal Law." *Modern Asian Studies* 42, no. 2–3 (2008): 489–518.

Watts, Ronald L. "Federalism and Diversity in Canada." In *Autonomy and Ethnicity. Negotiating Competing Claims in Multi-Ethnic States*, edited by Yash Ghai, 29–52. Cambridge: Cambridge University Press, 2000.

Williams, Rina Verma. *Postcolonial Politics and Personal Laws: Colonial Legal Legacies and the Indian State.* Oxford: Oxford University Press, 2006.

Woelk, Jens, ed. "Jurisdiction and Pluralisms: Judicial Functions and Organisation in Federal Systems." *Perspective on Federalism* 12, no. 2 (2020).

CHAPTER 5

Constitutional Courts, Federalism, and Asymmetries

1 Introduction

Having addressed the role of constitutional courts in the accommodation of diversity in the previous chapter, this final chapter focuses specifically on the role played by courts in the 12 case studies.

This is achieved by progressively analysing three aspects. First, the chapter reviews the models of judicial review in the 12 case studies, exploring whether these adopted the centralised or decentralised model of judicial review, and assessing whether the model of judicial review is linked to the nature of legal system as often argued in the literature.

Second, the analysis shifts to those courts that have developed a rich federalism-related jurisprudence, highlighting whether they adopted a centralist or federalist behaviour, i.e., strengthening the centre or favouring self-government. Since not all courts have developed such a rich jurisprudence, the chapter focuses on the Canadian Supreme Court, the Belgian Constitutional Court, the Spanish Constitutional Tribunal, the Indian Supreme Court, the Italian Constitutional Court, and the Constitutional Court of Bosnia and Herzegovina.

Finally, having completed the previous two steps, the chapter focuses on the role played by apex courts in addressing asymmetries. Among the 12 case studies, only five courts have addressed cases related to asymmetries in their case law: the Indian Supreme Court, the Italian Constitutional Court, the Spanish Constitutional Tribunal, and the Indonesian Supreme and Constitutional Courts. As further explained, Indonesia is a rather interesting case, insofar as the apex courts did not develop a rich federalism-related jurisprudence, but did address asymmetries in a series of decisions that proved to have a significant impact on the constitutional system and on the protection of fundamental rights. The constitutional case law of each court is analysed relying on the same conceptualisation of asymmetries, i.e., along the three dimensions of status, powers, and fiscal arrangements, to enable a coherent comparison.

 | DOI:10.1163/9789004739109_007

2 Constitutional Adjudication in Multi-tiered Systems

The role of courts in federal systems is deeply rooted in classic federal theory. As Dicey famously stated, "federalism [...] means legalism – the predominance of the judiciary in the constitution – a prevalence of a spirit of legality among the people".[1] With this statement, Dicey identified courts, and their authority in federal systems as guardians of the constitution, to be not only a defining characteristic of federations, but also a weakness.[2] In recent decades, federal scholarship has reframed its attitude towards courts in federal systems and, according to Watts, courts have become a main feature of federal states, such that they are included in institutional definitions of federations.[3] Courts, and especially constitutional courts, are no longer seen as a weakness, but as an essential component of federalism, as they are "umpires in disputes among the levels of government, [...] whose principal purpose is to protect the supremacy of the (federal) constitution within the legal order".[4] For the purposes of this research, it is relevant to recall what judicial body is entitled to review central and subnational legislation, as well as to resolve disputes among tiers of government, since this can have a significant impact on federal dynamics, including constitutional asymmetry.

2.1 *Federalism and the Archetypical Models of Judicial Review*

As observed in the literature, constitutional courts are a common feature of almost all federal systems.[5] The link between courts and federalism, as well as the central role played by courts in federal systems, is further strengthened by the fact that both models of judicial review originated in two federal states.[6]

1 Albert V. Dicey, *Introduction to the Study of the Law of the Constitution*, 3rd ed. (London: Macmillan, 1889), 163.

2 Palermo and Kössler, *Comparative Federalism*, 266.

3 Watts, *Comparing Federal Systems*, 7.

4 Palermo and Kössler, *Comparative Federalism*, 266.

5 Palermo and Kössler, *Comparative Federalism*, 266–267.

6 For some references on the different models of judicial review, see Hans Kelsen, "Judicial Review of Legislation: A Comparative Study of the Austrian and the American Constitution," *The Journal of Politics* 4, no. 2 (1942): 183–200; Mauro Cappelletti and John Clarke Adams, "Judicial Review of Legislation: European Antecedents and Adaptations," *Harvard Law Review* 79, no. 6 (1966): 1207–24; Mauro Cappelletti, *Judicial Review in the Contemporary World* (Indianapolis: Bobbs-Merrill, 1971); Allan Randolph Brewer-Carias, *Judicial Review in Comparative Law* (Cambridge: Cambridge University Press, 1989); Louis Favoreu, "Constitutional Review in Europe," in *Constitutionalism and Rights: The Influence of the United States Constitution*, by Louis Henkin and Albert J. Rosenthal (New York: Columbia University Press, 1990), 38–62; Víctor Ferres Comella, "The Rise of Specialized Constitutional Courts," ed. Tom

The first model of judicial review was established by the landmark case *Marbury v. Madison*[7] in 1803, marking the "victory for the Federalists advocating a strong national government, [...] and the birth of judicial control of constitutionality".[8] After *Marbury*, constitutional review in the US entailed that the supremacy of the federal constitution, and of the relative distribution of powers among tiers of government, would be judicially safeguarded and restored. However, as noted by Palermo and Kössler, in some instances, the US Supreme Court (USSC) has refrained from reviewing federal laws, explicitly referring to the "theory of political safeguards of federalism".[9] According to this theory, only the two political branches of government should enforce the constitutional limits of federal powers, and not the courts. Although it has now lost its influence and in more recent judgments the USSC has reintroduced judicial review of federal powers,[10] the theory of political safeguards of federalism had given rise to a seminal ruling in 1985,[11] where the US Supreme Court overruled a previous decision[12] by announcing that "it would no longer examine the constitutionality of federal legislation that threatened to violate the sovereignty of the states".[13] Going back to the US model of judicial review,

---

Ginsburg and Rosalind Dixon (Cheltenham, UK and Northampton, MA: Edward Elgar, 2011), 265–77; Alec Stone Sweet, "Constitutional Courts," in *The Oxford Handbook of Comparative Constitutional Law*, ed. Michel Rosenfeld and András Sajó (Oxford: Oxford University Press, 2012), 816–30; Albert HY Chen and Miguel Poiares Maduro, "The Judiciary and Constitutional Review," in *Routledge Handbook of Constitutional Law*, ed. Mark Tushnet, Thomas Fleiner, and Cheryl Saunders (London and New York: Routledge, 2013), 97–109; Arianna Vedaschi, "La giustizia costituzionale," in *Diritto costituzionale comparato*, ed. Paolo Carrozza, Alfonso Di Giovine, Giuseppe Franco Ferrari (Bari: Laterza, 2014), 1087–1136; Tom Ginsburg and Mila Versteeg, "Why Do Countries Adopt Constitutional Review?," *Journal of Law, Economics, & Organization* 30, no. 3 (2014): 587–622; Cheryl Saunders, "Courts with Constitutional Jurisdiction," in *The Cambridge Companion to Comparative Constitutional Law*, ed. Roger Masterman and Robert Schütze (Cambridge: Cambridge University Press, 2019), 414–40; Giuseppe de Vergottini, *Diritto costituzionale comparato* (Milano: Wolters Kluwer, 2022), 298–310.

7 Marbury v. Madison, 5 U.S. 137 (1803).

8 Palermo and Kössler, *Comparative Federalism*, 272.

9 Palermo and Kössler, *Comparative Federalism*, 273. For more on the political safeguards of federalism, see Herbert Wechsler, "The Political Safeguards of Federalism: The Role of the States in the Composition and Selection of the National Government," *Columbia Law Review* 54, no. 4 (1954): 543–60.

10 Palermo and Kössler, *Comparative Federalism*, 273.

11 *Garcia v. San Antonio Metropolitan Transit Authority*, 469 U.S. 528 (1985).

12 *National League of Cities v. Usery*, 426 U.S. 833 (1976).

13 John C. Yoo, "The Judicial Safeguards of Federalism," *Southern California Law Review* 70 (1996): 1311.

Marbury v. Madison framed a decentralised (or diffused) control of constitutionality, entrusting the ordinary courts with the authority to conduct judicial review, thus seeing such authority as "inherent to judicial power".[14] The US model is also defined as a concrete review of legislation, since it requires judicial review to be related to enacted laws and pending cases. This also means that in the US model judicial review is incidental to the decision of a concrete case (i.e., *incidenter*).

Conversely, in another federal state on the other side of the Atlantic (i.e., Austria), a second model of constitutional review originated. The 1920 Austrian Constitution, drafted mainly by Hans Kelsen,[15] framed a centralised control of constitutionality, through a specialised constitutional court, that is "located 'outside of' the regular court system rather than 'on top of' it",[16] as in the case of the US Supreme Court. The establishment of a specialised court was not the only innovation of the Austrian model. Indeed, this model entailed an abstract (and not concrete) review of legal norms, "regardless of its relevance in a specific court case",[17] and thus before such legislation has been enacted. Furthermore, the Austrian model envisaged a *principaliter* review, where the control of constitutionality is "the only matter at stake"[18] and a decision may be requested by a *Land* government regarding federal laws, and vice versa by the federal government concerning a *Land* law. It should be noted that the Austrian model evolved over time, and only a few years later, in 1929, the Austrian Constitution adopted some elements of the decentralised model, specifically features of concrete and incidental review, according to which the Administrative Court and the Supreme Court, as appeal courts, are obligated to halt their proceedings where there are even mere doubts regarding the constitutionality of the norms they would have to apply, and refer such matters to the Constitutional Court.[19] Finally, if it is true that the Austrian model evolved and combined features of abstract and concrete review, it should be noted that the same is not true for the US model, which ruled out abstract review and remained uncontaminated.[20] A further point of contact

14 Palermo and Kössler, *Comparative Federalism*, 274.

15 See, among many, Hans Kelsen, "Judicial Review of Legislation: A Comparative Study of the Austrian and the American Constitution," *The Journal of Politics* 4, no. 2 (1942): 183–200.

16 Palermo and Kössler, *Comparative Federalism*, 267.

17 Palermo and Kössler, *Comparative Federalism*, 274.

18 Ibidem.

19 Ibidem.

20 Ibidem.

between the two models concerns the validity of the courts' decisions. In the Austrian model, the decisions of constitutional courts have *erga omnes* validity, whereas in the US model they concern only the parties involved in the case (i.e., *inter partes*). However, since the US is a common law system, through the principle of *stare decisis*, the decisions of the US Supreme Court as the final appeal court end up having the same *erga omnes* effect typical of the Austrian model.

As mentioned, the two models of constitutional review, and their hybridisation,[21] have been adopted in many federal systems across the globe.[22] One determining factor, but not the only one, in the diffusion of the two archetypes appears to be the legal system.[23] Within the case studies analysed in this book, Belgium, Bosnia, and Herzegovina, Italy, and Spain belong to the civil law tradition, whereas Canada, and the United Kingdom share an overall predominance of the common law tradition, with the exception of two specific parts of the territory, i.e., Québec in Canada and Scotland in the UK, where there is a mixed common-civil law system. The remaining cases are mixed legal systems,[24] perfectly depicting the complexity of the legacies of

21 For example, the German, Italian and Spanish systems draw from both the US and Austrian models which has given rise to an autonomous *tertium genus* of constitutional review, combining the incidental control typical of the diffused model with the establishment of specialised constitutional courts typical of the centralised model. More specifically, in such systems, whenever ordinary judges have a well-founded conviction (in the case of Germany) or a mere doubt (in the case of Italy) of unconstitutionality, they have to suspend the proceedings and refer the question to the only judicial body entrusted with the power to review the constitutionality of legislation, i.e., the Constitutional Court. Such a hybrid model allows not only for concrete, incidental control, but also for abstract, principal control, especially for what concerns conflicts over allocation of powers between the central government and the subnational entities. Indeed, federal and subnational authorities can challenge acts and legislation deemed interfering with their competences (see Vedaschi, "La giustizia costituzionale," 1111–1115).

22 For an overview of the factors influencing the impact of judicial decisions on federal systems, see Palermo and Kössler, *Comparative Federalism*, 267–272; Nicholas Aroney, and John Kincaid, "Introduction", in *Courts in Federal Countries*, ed. Nicholas Aroney and John Kincaid (Toronto: University of Toronto Press, 2017), 6; Thomas Hueglin and Alan Fenna, *Comparative Federalism. A Systematic Inquiry* (Torondo: Broadview Press, 2006), 275.

23 Palermo and Kössler, *Comparative Federalism*, 274.

24 On mixed legal systems, see Esin Örücü, "What Is a Mixed Legal System: Exclusion or Expansion?," *Journal of Comparative Law* 3, no. 1 (2008): 34–52; Valentine Vernon Palmer, "Mixed Legal Systems ... and the Myth of Pure Laws," *Louisiana Law Review* 67, no. 4 (2007): 1205–18; Valentine Vernon Palmer, "Two Rival Theories of Mixed Legal Systems," *Journal of Comparative Law* 3, no. 1 (2008): 7–33; Valentine Vernon Palmer, "Mixed Legal

colonialism,[25] resulting in hybridisations among legal systems and consequently among models of judicial review. Specifically, these are all constitutional systems in the Global South and, in a number of these, it is possible to observe the full or partial application of Islamic *shari'a*, among other legal traditions: in India we notice a combination of common law, customary law, and Islamic *shari'a* (applied only in personal status issues); in Indonesia of civil law, customary law, and Islamic *shari'a* (applied in full in only one subnational entity, i.e., Aceh); in Iraq of civil law, and Islamic *shari'a* (applied in full); and in Pakistan of common law and Islamic *shari'a* (applied in full).[26] Finally, Myanmar displays a mixed legal system of common law and customary law.

2.2 *Federalism and Constitutional Review in the Civil Law Systems*

For what concerns the models of judicial review, the link between the legal system and the model of constitutional review is clear in the civil law systems, with Belgium,[27] Bosnia and Herzegovina,[28] Italy,[29] and Spain[30] all

---

Systems," ed. Mauro Bussani and Ugo Mattei (Cambridge: Cambridge University Press, 2012), 368–83; Daniel Visser, "Cultural Forces in the Making of Mixed Legal Systems," *Tulane Law Review* 78, no. 1 & 2 (2003): 41–78; Kenneth G.C. Reid, "The Idea of Mixed Legal Systems," *Tulane Law Review* 78, no. 1 & 2 (2003): 5–40; Jacques Du Plessis, "Comparative Law and the Study of Mixed Legal Systems," in *The Oxford Handbook of Comparative Law*, ed. Mathias Reimann and Reinhard Zimmermann (Oxford: Oxford University Press, 2019), 474–501; Valentine Vernon Palmer, Mohamed Y. Mattar, and Anna Koppel, eds., *Mixed Legal Systems, East and West* (Wey Court East, UK and Burlington, VT: Ashgate, 2015).

25 See M.B. Hooker, *Legal Pluralism: An Introduction to Colonial and New-Colonial Laws* (Oxford: Oxford University Press, 1975); Daniel Bonilla Maldonado, *Legal Barbarians. Identity, Modern Comparative Law and the Global South* (Cambridge: Cambridge University Press, 2021); Christian R. Burset, *An Empire of Laws: Legal Pluralism in British Colonial Policy* (New Haven and London: Yale University Press, 2023). For further discussion see Chapter 2, paragraph 2.3 on asymmetries, mixed legal systems, and the legacies of colonialism.

26 See Palmer, "Mixed Legal Systems," 379–382; University of Ottawa, "JuriGlobe – Alphabetical Index of the Political Entities and Corresponding Legal Systems", available at http://www.juriglobe.ca/eng/sys-juri/index-alpha.php (last accessed 20 February 2024).

27 On the Constitutional Court of Belgium, see Christian Behrendt, "The Belgian Constitutional Court," in *The Max Planck Handbooks in European Public Law*, ed. Armin von Bogdandy, Peter Huber, and Christoph Grabenwarter (Oxford: Oxford University Press, 2020), 71–118; Patricia Popelier and Koen Lemmens, *The Constitution of Belgium. A Contextual Analysis* (Oxford and Portland: Hart Publishing, 2015), 192–2012; Patricia Popelier, "The Belgian Constitutional Court: Guardian of Consensus Democracy or Venue for Deliberation?" in *Liberae Cogitationes. Liber Amicorum M Bossuyt*, ed. Andr Alen et al. (Antwerp: Intersentia, 2013), 499–513; Patricia Popelier and Samantha Bielen, "How

adopting the Austrian, centralised model of constitutional review – designing specialised constitutional courts in their respective constitutions[31] and entrusting constitutional courts with the power to review the constitutionality of national and subnational laws as well as to decide on disputes between

---

Courts Decide Federalism Disputes: Legal Merit, Attitudinal Effects, and Strategic Considerations in the Jurisprudence of the Belgian Constitutional Court," *Publius: The Journal of Federalism* 49, no. 4 (2019): 1–30; Patricia Popelier and Laura Martens, "The Belgian Constitutional Court: Navigating Between Constitutional Rights and Consociational Politics," in *Constitutional Review in Western Europe. Judicial-Legislative Relations in Comparative Perspective*, ed. Kálmán Pócza (London and New York: Routledge, 2024), 52–76.

28 On the Constitutional Court of Bosnia and Herzegovina, see paragraph 3.6, whereas on the model of constitutional review adopted in BiH, see Bojan Vlaški and Joseph Marko, "Constitutional Court(s) and Constitutional Review," in *Citizens, Constitution, Europe. Glossary of Essential Constitutional Concepts in BiH*, ed. Maja Sahadžić et al. (Sarajevo: Pravni fakultet Univerziteta, 2023), 321–330.

29 On the Italian Constitutional Court, see Enzo Cheli, *Il giudice delle leggi. La Corte Costituzionale nella dinamica dei poteri* (Bologna: Il Mulino, 1999); Elisabetta Lamarque, *Corte Costituzionale e giudici nell'Italia repubblicana* (Rome: GLF Editori Laterza, 2012); Elena Malfatti, Saulle Panizza, and Roberto Romboli, *Giustizia costituzionale* (Torino: Giappichelli, 2016); Vittoria Barsotti, et al., *Italian Constitutional Justice in Global Context* (Oxford: Oxford University Press, 2016); Antonio Ruggeri and Antonino Spadaro, *Lineamenti di giustizia costituzionale* (Torino: Giappichelli, 2019); Raffaele Bifulco and Davide Paris, "The Italian Constitutional Court," in *The Max Planck Handbooks in European Public Law*, ed. Peter Huber, Armin von Bogdandy, and Christoph Grabenwarter (Oxford: Oxford University Press, 2020), 447–504; Steven Gow Calabresi, *The History and Growth of Judicial Review, Volume 2: The G-20 Civil Law Countries*, 1st ed. (Oxford and New York: Oxford University Press, 2021), 133–156; Diletta Tega, "The Italian Constitutional Court in Its Context: A Narrative," *European Constitutional Law Review* 17, no. 3 (2021): 369–393; Diletta Tega et al., *Italian Constitutional Law in the European Context* (Milano: Wolters Kluwer, 2023), 71–80.

30 On the Spanish Constitutional Tribunal, see Mark D. Eibert, "The Spanish Constitutional Tribunal in Theory and Practice," *Stanford Journal of International Law* 18, no. 2 (Summer 1982): 435–470; Juan Luis Requejo Pagés, "The Spanish Constitutional Tribunal," in *The Max Planck Handbooks in European Public Law*, ed. Armin von Bogdandy, Peter Huber, and Christoph Grabenwarter (Oxford: Oxford University Press, 2020), 719–778; Victor Ferreres Comella, "The Spanish Constitutional Court: Time for Reforms," *Journal of Comparative Law* 3, no. 2 (2008): 22–38; Victor Ferreres Comella. "The Spanish Constitutional Court Confronts Catalonia's 'Right to Decide' (Comment on the Judgment 42/2014)," *European Constitutional Law Review* 10, no. 3 (2014): 571–90; Enrique Guillen Lopez, "Judicial Review in Spain: The Constitutional Court," *Loyola of Los Angeles Law Review* 41, no. 2 (2008): 529–562; Joan-Josep Vallbé, "The Spanish Constitutional Court: The Judicial Politics of Constitutional Review and Interpretation," in *Constitutional Review in Western Europe. Judicial-Legislative Relations in Comparative Perspective*, ed. Kálmán Pócza (London and New York: Routledge, 2024), 241–263.

31 Constitution of Belgium – Art. 142; Constitution of Bosnia and Herzegovina – Art. VI; Constitution of Italy – Art. 134–137; Constitution of Spain – Art. 159–165.

different tiers of government.[32] In this respect, it is interesting to note that, at the time of its establishment in the 1980s, the sole mandate of the Constitutional Court of Belgium was precisely to resolve disputes over allocation of powers between the federal level and subnational entities. It later evolved into a more traditional constitutional court ensuring the protection of fundamental rights, and now only a limited percentage of the Court's final judgments concern disputes over allocation of powers.[33] What is further interesting is that, concerning the review of national and subnational laws, in the Spanish and Italian systems some asymmetries exist between the two tiers, to the benefit of the central government.[34] For example, in Spain, if the national government challenges an act of an autonomous community, that question translates into suspension of the act, whereas the same rule does not apply in the opposite case of an autonomous community challenging a state law.[35]

Conversely, the Italian Constitution provides that the central government can challenge the constitutional legitimacy of regional legislation within 60 days of its publication if it is deemed that such legislation exceeds the competences of the region, and that a region may do the same regarding legislation enacted both by the central government and by other region(s) if it is deemed that these infringe upon its competence.[36] However, if a region can only challenge legislation that interferes with its own competences, the central government may challenge regional laws when these exceed regional competences in a rather broader sense, to the point that, as noted by D'Amico, "any breach of the constitution could justify a challenge".[37] Indeed, this was held by the Italian Constitutional Court in its decision 274/2003, in which the Court concluded that, after the 2001 constitutional reform, the state has the power to challenge regional laws "by deducing the violation of any constitutional parameter".[38] This was derived from the fact that the 2001 reform *de*

32 Constitution of Belgium – Art. 142; Constitution of Bosnia and Herzegovina – Art. VI(3)a; Constitution of Italy – Art. 134; Constitution of Spain – Art. 161(1).

33 Popelier and Bielen, "How Courts Decide Federalism Disputes," 6.

34 Palermo and Kössler, *Comparative Federalism*, 275.

35 Specifically, Art. 161(2) of the Spanish Constitution provides that "the Court must either ratify or lift the suspension, as the case may be, within a period of not more than five months."

36 Constitution of Italy – Art. 127.

37 Marilisa D'Amico, "Constitutional Court," in *Constitutional Law in Italy*, ed. Valerio Onida et al. (Alphen aan den Rijn: Kluwer Law International, 2013), 212.

38 Italian Constitutional Court, decision 274/2003, 8 July 2003.

facto identified the state as the subject entitled to ensure the unitary nature of the Republic. According to the Court, this is provided for not only by the "indivisible" nature of the Republic (Art. 5 Const.), but also by the repeated "unitary request" entailed in the respect for the Constitution, international and European obligations, for the limits to legislative powers and competences (Art. 117(1) Const.), and for the economic and legal unity of the legal system (Art. 120(2) Const.). The 274/2003 decision is extremely helpful in grasping the impact of constitutional courts on the dynamics between tiers of government, which will be assessed later in the chapter.[39]

Finally, concerning the BiH Constitutional Court, it should be noted that the Constitution of Bosnia and Herzegovina outlined a centralised review of constitutionality primarily of the abstract type, identifying as holders of the principal remedy the members of the collective Presidency, the President of the Council of Ministers, the President and Vice-President of both chambers of the state Parliament, a quarter of the members of each chamber of the state Parliament, and a quarter of each chamber of the entity Parliaments.[40] The Court has exclusive jurisdiction over disputes on competences between the entities, between the entities and the central state, or between state institutions,[41] and assesses the constitutionality of the entities' constitutions or laws, as well as of state legislation.[42] The Constitution also provides for the possibility of incidental control by the lower courts;[43] however, Vlaški and Marko note that such concrete control is actually very weak.[44] In fact, the parties can only propose (and not request) that the lower courts refer a question of constitutionality to the Constitutional Court, and cannot require them to stop the proceedings to refer the decision to the Court. Finally, it is worth noting that the Court acts as an appellate jurisdiction in cases involving serious violations of human rights and fundamental freedoms, opening a space for individual appeals.[45]

39 See paragraph 3.5 of this chapter.

40 Constitution of Bosnia and Herzegovina – Art. VI(3)a.

41 Constitution of Bosnia and Herzegovina – Art. VI(3)a.

42 Constitution of Bosnia and Herzegovina – Art. VI(3)c.

43 Constitution of Bosnia and Herzegovina – Art. VI(3)c.

44 Bojan Vlaški, and Joseph Marko, "Constitutional Court(s) and Constitutional Review," in *Citizens, Constitution, Europe*, ed. Maja Sahadžić et al. (Sarajevo: Pravni fakultet Univerziteta, 2023), 327.

45 See Nedžad Smailagić, Joseph Marko, and Maja Sahadžić, "The Constitutional Court of Bosnia and Herzegovina. Individual Complaints," in *Citizens, Constitution, Europe*, ed. Maja Sahadžić et al. (Sarajevo: Pravni fakultet Univerziteta, 2023), 331–335.

2.3 *Federalism and Judicial Review in the Common Law Systems*

Of the two case studies following the common law tradition, Canada[46] adopted the US, decentralised model of judicial review.[47] As in the US, the Canadian Constitution does not explicitly recognise judicial review, and it was the Judicial Committee of the Privy Council (JCPC) that "successfully claimed the review power from the outset",[48] even though, as observed by Russell, this was "based more on imperialism than on constitutionalism".[49] Indeed, the conformity of legislation with the 1867 Constitution Act (i.e., the British North America Act) would need "to be judicially enforced because it was an imperial statute".[50] Indeed, Aroney and Kincaid noted that the Privy Council first developed the "pith and substance" doctrine,[51] later adopted in other common-law systems such as Australia and India,[52] in interpreting "federal arrangements and constitutions within the British Empire, including in Canada and Northern Ireland".[53] It should be further observed that judicial review in Canada, from 1867 to 1982, initially emerged and later developed as a result of the decisions by the JCPC concerning federalism and separation of powers, even after the Canadian Supreme Court replaced the JCPC in 1949 as court of final appeal. After the 1982 Constitution Act, the Canadian Supreme Court

46 On judicial review in Canada, see Steven Gow Calabresi, *The History and Growth of Judicial Review, Volume 1: The G-20 Common Law Countries and Israel*, 1st ed. (Oxford and New York: Oxford University Press, 2021), 183–228; Alan C. Cairns, "The Judicial Committee and Its Critics," *Canadian Journal of Political Science* 4, no. 3 (1971): 301–45; Jennifer Smith, "The Origins of Judicial Review in Canada," *Canadian Journal of Political Science* 16, no. 1 (1983): 115–134; T.A. Cromwell, "Aspects of Constitutional Judicial Review in Canada," *South Carolina Law Review* 46, no. 5 (1995): 1027–1042; J.A.C. Grant, "Judicial Review in Canada: Procedural Aspects," *Canadian Bar Review* 42, no. 2 (1964): 195–224.

47 See Palermo and Kössler, *Comparative Federalism*, 275.

48 Ibidem.

49 Peter H. Russell, *The Judiciary in Canada: The Third Branch of Government* (Toronto: McGraw-Hill Ryerson, 1987), 93.

50 Palermo and Kössler, *Comparative Federalism*, 276.

51 On the pith and substance doctrine in Canada, see Eugénie Brouillet and Bruce Ryder, "Key Doctrines in Canadian Legal Federalism," in *The Oxford Handbook of the Canadian Constitution*, ed. Peter Oliver, Patrick Macklem, and Nathalie Des Rosiers (Oxford: Oxford University Press, 2017), 421–26.

52 See Tony Blackshield, "Working the Metaphor: The Contrasting Use of 'Pith and Substance' in Indian and Australian Law," *Journal of the Indian Law Institute* 50, no. 4 (2008): 518–56.

53 Nicholas Aroney and John Kincaid, "Comparative Observations and Conclusions," In *Courts in Federal Countries*, ed. Nicholas Aroney and John Kincaid (Toronto: University of Toronto Press, 2017), 509.

started "vigorously enforcing"[54] the Canadian Charter of Fundamental Rights and Freedoms, as well as continuing to umpire disputes on federalism and separation of powers.

Regarding the United Kingdom,[55] Palermo and Kössler note that it is a case that "defies any clear categorisation",[56] due to the absence of a written constitution. As a result, political and legal disputes have centred around the common law judicial review of legislation enacted by the devolved parliaments. The judicial body entitled to review devolved legislation and resolve disputes between tiers of government is the UK Supreme Court (UKSC) that since 2009 has functioned as the successor to the Appellate Committee of the House of Lords. As an appellate body, the UKSC hears appeals from all parts of the UK (except for criminal appeals from Scotland)[57] and adjudicates conflicts of competences between the central and subnational tiers of government.[58] In five of the seven cases on competence disputes heard by the UKSC, the Court ruled that the devolved legislatures did have competence over the impugned law.[59] Moreover, despite its recent establishment, the role of the UK Supreme Court proved to be of great significance during the Brexit process from the very beginning.[60] In the first and most notorious

54 Calabresi, *The History and Growth of Judicial Review*, 183.

55 On judicial review in the United Kingdom, see Steven Gow Calabresi, *The History and Growth of Judicial Review, Volume 1: The G-20 Common Law Countries and Israel*, 1st ed. (Oxford and New York: Oxford University Press, 2021), 363–390; Alessandro Torre, "La Corte Suprema, probabile Corte Costituzionale del Regno Unito? Osservazioni su dieci anni di giurisdizione," *Materiali per una storia della cultura giuridica*, no. 1 (2020), 5–25.

56 Palermo and Kössler, *Comparative Federalism*, 277.

57 Brice Dickson, "Work in Progress. A Country Study on Constitutional Asymmetry in the United Kingdom," in *Constitutional Asymmetry in Multinational Federalism*, ed. Patricia Popelier and Maja Sahadžić (Cham: Palgrave MacMillan, 2019), 476.

58 Dickson, "Work in Progress," 476–478.

59 *Whaley v. Lord Advocate* [2007] UKHL 53, [2008] SC 107; *Martin v. HM Advocate* [2010] UKSC 10, [2010] SLT 412; *Christian Institute v. Lord Advocate* [2016] UKSC 51, [2017] SC 29; *Attorney General v. National Assembly for Wales Commission* [2012] UKSC 53, [2012] 1 AC 792; *In Re Agricultural Sector (Wales) Bill* [2014] UKSC 43, [2014] 1 WLR 2622. The two cases where the UKSC found that there was no devolved legislative competence are the *UK Withdrawal from the EU (Legal Continuity) (Scotland) Bill* [2018] UKSC 64, and *In Re Recovery of Medical Costs for Asbestos Wales) Bill* [2015] UKSC 3.

60 For further references, see David Feldman, "Pulling a Trigger or Starting a Journey? Brexit in the Supreme Court," *The Cambridge Law Journal* 76, no. 2 (2017): 217–223; Alison L. Young, "The Constitutional Implications of Brexit," *European Public Law* 23, no. 4 (2017): 757–786; Gordon Anthony, "Sovereignty, Consent, and Constitution: The Northern Ireland References," in *The UK Constitution After Miller: Brexit and Beyond*, ed. Mark Elliott, Jack Williams, and Allison Young (London: Hart Publishing, 2018), 181–201; Stephen Tierney, "Parliament and the Brexit Process: The Battle for Constitutional Suprem-

case (i.e., *Miller*),[61] the Court was asked to decide whether the UK government could trigger Art. 50 TEU without prior approval from the UK Parliament and without the involvement of the devolved legislatures. In *Miller*, the UKSC found that the UK government should have sought the approval of the UK Parliament, but, at the same time, the Westminster Parliament was not constitutionally required to obtain the consent of the devolved legislatures. Therefore, in the *Miller* case, the UKSC ended up reducing the autonomy of the devolved entities to the benefit of the central level by depriving them of the right to consent, thus confirming that "even though the UK comprises four different 'nations' the reality is that the union's Parliament can alone decide what is best for the nation as a whole".[62]

2.4 *Federalism and Judicial Review in the Mixed Legal Systems*

The link between legal system and judicial review appears to hold true also in mixed legal systems, since in India, Malaysia, and Pakistan, the partial presence of a common law tradition (legacy of British colonialism) contributed to the adoption of the US model of judicial review,[63] whereas in Indonesia and Iraq the civil law tradition led to the adoption of a (rather weak) centralised model of constitutional review.[64]

Starting from the three constitutional systems that display a decentralised model, in India, the Constitution provides that the Supreme Court has "original jurisdiction" in any dispute among tiers of government (i.e., union-state and interstate disputes) regarding the distribution of powers.[65] Over time, the

---

acy in the United Kingdom," *Notre Dame Journal of International & Comparative Law* 12, no. 1 (2022): 1–21.

61 *R (Miller) v. Secretary of State for Exiting the EU* [2017] UKSC 5, [2018] AC 61.

62 Dickson, "Work in Progress," 478.

63 Constitution of India – Art. 13, 32, 136, 142, and 226; Constitution of Malaysia – Art. 4, and 128; Constitution of Pakistan – Art. 8, 184, and 199. For some references on judicial review in India, Malaysia, and Pakistan, see Steven Gow Calabresi, *The History and Growth of Judicial Review, Volume 1: The G-20 Common Law Countries and Israel* (Oxford and New York: Oxford University Press, 2021), 263–310; Yvonne Tew, "On the Uneven Journey to Constitutional Redemption: The Malaysian Judiciary and Constitutional Politics," *Washington International Law Journal* 25, no. 3 (2016): 673–696; Ayesha A Malik, "Judicial Review and the Rule of Law in Pakistan," *Asian Journal of Comparative Law* 18, no. 3 (2023): 291–302.

64 Constitution of Indonesia – Art. 24C; Constitution of Iraq – Art. 93. For some references on constitutional review in Indonesia and Iraq, see Steven Gow Calabresi, *The History and Growth of Judicial Review, Volume 2: The G-20 Civil Law Countries* (Oxford and New York: Oxford University Press, 2021), 251–266; Oday Talal Mahmood, "A New Basis for Judicial Review in Iraq," *Arab Law Quarterly* 37, no. 1–2 (2020): 43–79.

65 Constitution of India – Art. 131.

jurisprudence of the Supreme Court (as well as states' High Courts) proved to be crucial to developing the guiding principles of adjudication in federalism-related disputes, such as the "pith and substance" and the "colourable legislation" doctrines on the interpretation of the distribution of legislative and other powers between the union and the states.[66] Moreover, it should not be forgotten that the Supreme Court included the principles of federalism in the unique "basic structure" doctrine[67] that developed starting from the *Keshavananda Bharati* case in 1973,[68] thus entrenching federalism in the unamendable core of the Indian Constitution.[69] Conversely, in Pakistan, even though the Constitution grants the same original jurisdiction to the Federal Supreme Court to resolve intergovernmental disputes,[70] the apex Court deals primarily with cases related to the protection of fundamental rights and the rule of law, equality, access to justice, fair trial, transparency, and good governance.[71] It should be noted that the Federal Supreme Court has recognised federalism to be a "salient feature"[72] of the Constitution of Pakistan, along with other founding principles such as parliamentary democracy, the independence of the judiciary, and Islamic provisions.[73] However, the Pakistani Supreme Court has not developed judicial doctrines comparable to those of its Indian counterpart, and federalism jurisprudence is extremely limited. Overall, the Supreme Court appears not to be a major player in the federal dynamics in

66 See Manish Tewari and Rekha Saxena, "The Supreme Court of India: The Rise of Judicial Power and the Protection of Federalism," in *Courts in Federal Countries: Federalist or Unitarist,* ed. Nicholas Aroney and John Kincaid (Toronto: University of Toronto Press, 2017), 244–254.

67 On the basic structure doctrine, see Sudhir Krishnaswamy, *Democracy and Constitutionalism in India: A Study on the Basic Structure Doctrine* (Oxford: Oxford University Press, 2010); Virendra Kumar, "Basic Structure of the Indian Constitution: Doctrine of Constitutionally Controlled Governance [From Kesavananda Bharati to IR Coelho]," *Journal of the Indian Law Institute* 49, no. 3 (2007): 365–398.

68 *Kesavananda Bharati Sripadagalvaru & Ors. v. State of Kerala & Anr.* (1973) 4 SCC 225; AIR 1973 SC 1461.

69 Tewari and Saxena, "The Supreme Court of India," 252; Palermo and Kössler, *Comparative Federalism*, 41.

70 Constitution of Pakistan – Art. 184(1).

71 See Malik, "Judicial Review and the Rule of Law in Pakistan."

72 See Matthew J. Nelson, "Indian Basic Structure Jurisprudence in the Islamic Republic of Pakistan: Reconfiguring the Constitutional Politics of Religion," *Asian Journal of Comparative Law* 13, no. 2 (2018): 333–357.

73 See *Mahmood Khan Achakzai v. Federation of Pakistan,* PLD 1997 SC 426; *Syed Zafar Ali Shah v. General Pervez Musharraf,* PLD 2001 SC 869; *Pakistan Lawyers Forum v. Federation of Pakistan,* PLD 2005 SC 719; *Dr. Mubashir Hassan v. Federation of Pakistan,* PLD 2000 SC 869.

Pakistan.[74] Finally, in Malaysia, the judicial body entitled to review the constitutionality of federal and subnational legislation is the Federal Court,[75] and, similarly to Pakistan, the Court jurisprudence has primarily dealt with the protection and interpretation of constitutional rights, and not federalism.[76]

Moving to those mixed legal systems that have adopted a centralised model of constitutional review, in Indonesia there are two judicial bodies that have the power to resolve disputes between the central and subnational levels, namely the Supreme Court[77] and the Constitutional Court.[78] The Constitutional Court can review the constitutionality of central legislation to assess its compliance with the Indonesian Constitution, but not of subnational legislation.[79] The constitutionality of subnational legislation can be reviewed only by the Supreme Court, which has broad powers to review secondary legislation and ensure its compliance with national legislation.[80] Despite these powers and its unique position in reviewing subnational legislation, the case law of the Indonesian Supreme Court is particularly poor, raising considerable doubts about its reliability when dealing with disputes between the central and subnational levels.[81] For its part, the Constitutional Court is considered to be reasonably professional and has played a significant role in defining the relative areas of jurisdiction between the central and subnational levels.[82] Then, in Iraq, the 2005 Constitution provides that the Federal Supreme

---

74 On federalism in Pakistan and its criticisms, see Katharine Adeney, "Democracy and Federalism in Pakistan," in *Federalism in Asia*, ed. Baogang He, Brian Galligan, and Takashi Inoguchi (Northampton: Edward Elgar, 2007), 101–124; Katharine Adeney, "A Step Towards Inclusive Federalism in Pakistan? The Politics of the 18th Amendment," *Publius: The Journal of Federalism* 42, no. 4 (2012): 539–565; Mahendra Prasad Singh, and Veena Kukreja, *Federalism in South Asia* (London and New York: Routledge, 2014); Harihar Bhattacharyya, *Federalism in Asia* (London and New York: Routledge, 2021).

75 Constitution of Malaysia – Art. 128.

76 See Tew, "On the Uneven Journey to Constitutional Redemption"; Björn Dressel, and Tomoo Inoue, "Politics and the Federal Court of Malaysia, 1960–2018: An Empirical Investigation," *Asian Journal of Law and Society* 9, no. 1 (2022): 26–58.

77 See Tim Lindsey and Simon Butt, *Indonesian Law* (Oxford: Oxford University Press, 2018), 148–153.

78 See Lindsey and Butt, *Indonesian Law*, 157–166.

79 Constitution of Indonesia – Art. 24C.

80 Constitution of Indonesia – Art. 24A.

81 Simon Butt, "Provincial Asymmetry in Indonesia: What is so "Special" About it? A Country Study on Constitutional Asymmetry in Indonesia," in *Constitutional Asymmetry in Multinational Federalism*, ed. Patricia Popelier and Maja Sahadžić (Cham: Palgrave Macmillan, 2019), 243.

82 For further references to the Supreme Court and the Constitutional Court of Indonesia, see Lindsey and Butt, *Indonesian Law*, 91–93, 100–109.

Court has exclusive jurisdiction over reviewing the constitutionality of federal and subnational laws, as well as in settling disputes over different tiers of government.[83] However, the role of the Iraqi Federal Supreme Court has proved to be problematic. For instance, it has often declared itself to be incompetent to examine the constitutionality of judicial decisions from the Kurdistan Region,[84] and delivered contradictory judgments on the competence of governorates to raise taxes.[85] Overall, the Iraqi Federal Supreme Court is not yet an integrated actor in the federal system, thus does not contribute to the stability and development of the system, especially concerning the relations between the federal and Kurdish governments.[86]

Moreover, it is interesting to note that one mixed legal system, i.e., Myanmar, appears to contradict the link between legal system and model of judicial review since, despite the presence of both common law and customary law, it seems to have introduced a centralised model of constitutional review after the adoption of the 2008 Constitution and the establishment of the Constitutional Tribunal in 2011.[87] Indeed, the power of constitutional review of (national and subnational) legislation, as well as of dispute resolution among levels of government is provided for by Art. 46 of the 2008 Constitution and entrusted to the Constitutional Tribunal. Specifically, the Constitution ap-

83 Constitution of Iraq – Art. 93(1–5).

84 See Iraqi Federal Supreme Court, Decisions No. 32 of 4 May 2011, No. 12 of 4 June 2012 and No. 48 of 10 August 2015.

85 See Bawar Bammarny, "Federalism and Decentralisation in Iraq. A Country Study of Constitutional Asymmetry in Iraq," in *Constitutional Asymmetry and Multinational Federation*, ed. Patricia Popelier and Maja Sahadžić (Cham: Palgrave MacMillan, 2019), 279.

86 See Bammarny, "Federalism and Decentralisation in Iraq," 277–281; Alex Danilovich, *Iraqi Federalism and the Kurds: Learning to Live Together* (London and New York: Routledge, 2014).

87 Constitution of Myanmar – Art. 46, 323, 325 and 326; on constitutional review in Myanmar, see Melissa Crouch, "Rediscovering 'Law' in Myanmar: A Review of Scholarship on the Legal System of Myanmar," *Pacific Rim Law & Policy Journal* 23, no. 3 (2014): 543–578; Melissa Crouch, "Judiciary," in *Routledge Handbook of Contemporary Myanmar*, ed. Adam Simpson, Nicholas Farrelly, and Ian Holliday (London and New York: Routledge, 2017), 248–256; Melissa Crouch, "Dictators, Democrats, and Constitutional Dialogue: Myanmar's Constitutional Tribunal," *International Journal of Constitutional Law* 16, no. 2 (2018): 421–446; Andrew Harding, "The Short and Turbulent History of Myanmar Constitutional Tribunal," in *Constitutional Courts in Asia*, ed. Albert H. Y. Chen and Andrew Harding (Cambridge: Cambridge University Press, 2018), 270–288; Cho Mar Htay, May Hsu Hlaing, and Kyi Kyi Khin, "Implementation of Constitutional Review in Myanmar," in *Implementation of Constitutional Review. Challenges And Development Trends*, ed. Rom Mukhiit and Rentsenkhorloo Anar (Ulaanbaatar, Mongolia: Constitutional Court of Mongolia, 2022), 287–314.

pears to have introduced a hybrid system of constitutional review, that resembles the European-American models combining diffuse and centralised review. On the one hand, Art. 323 of the Constitution provides for concrete, incidental control, according to which in any case heard by an ordinary court where a dispute arises over the contradiction of a legislative provision with the Constitution, such Court has to suspend the proceedings and refer the question to the Constitutional Tribunal.[88] On the other hand, Art. 324 of the Constitution introduced the possibility of abstract, principal control, according to which the governmental authorities of the federal state and of the subnational entities have the right to submit a request to the Constitutional Tribunal in case they question an infringement of their competences or demand constitutional interpretation of a legislative provision.[89] The case of Myanmar is particularly interesting since the Constitutional Tribunal operates in a former authoritarian regime, where the military still retains substantial powers in a peculiar condition defined by Crouch as "military-led constitutionalism",[90] and thus it is strongly influenced by internal political factors and pressures, undermining its legitimacy. Moreover, concerning the deviation of Myanmar from the link between legal system and model of judicial review, Crouch observed that "the structure of the Tribunal as a civil law model in a common law system and as a forum for elite political dialogue inaccessible to individuals has attracted much criticism",[91] negatively impacting on the popular image of the Tribunal, as well as on its authority.

Finally, as already anticipated in the previous pages, it should not be forgotten that in these mixed legal systems, common/civil law coexist with other legal traditions, i.e., customary laws[92] and religious laws.[93] If we rely on Mat-

88 Constitution of Myanmar – Art. 323.

89 Constitution of Myanmar – Art. 324.

90 Crouch, "Dictators, Democrats, and Constitutional Dialogue," 421.

91 Crouch, "Dictators, Democrats, and Constitutional Dialogue," 445.

92 On customary and traditional law in Sub-Saharan Africa, see Salvatore Mancuso, *African Law(s): Comparative Insights on the African Lawscape* (Leiden and Boston: Brill, 2024); Berihun Adugna Gebeye, *A Theory of Africa Constitutionalism* (Oxford: Oxford University Press, 2021); T.W. Bennet, "Comparative Law and African Customary Law," in *The Oxford Handbook of Comparative Law*, ed. Mathias Reimann, and Reinhard Zimmermann (Oxford: Oxford University Press, 2019), 652–680; Rodolfo Sacco, *Il diritto africano* (Torino: Giappichelli, 1995).

93 For some references on Islamic legal tradition, see Mohammad Hashim Kamali, *Principles of Islamic Jurisprudence* (Cambridge: Cambridge University Press, 1991); Wael B. Hallaq, *A History of Islamic Legal Theories*, (Cambridge: Cambridge University Press, 1999); Yasin Dutton, *The Origins of Islamic Law* (London: Routledge, 1999); Wael B. Hallaq, *Shari'a: Theory, Practice and Transformation* (Cambridge: Cambridge Univer-

tei's proposal of classification of legal families, this would suggest that these systems follow the "rule of traditional law", where "where the separation between law and religious and/or philosophical tradition has not taken place".[94] This contrasts with the previously analysed systems, that follow the "rule of professional law" dominant the Western legal tradition, where the legal arena is clearly distinguished by the traditional and political arenas, and the legal process is largely secularised.[95] Therefore, it is important to acknowledge that the 12 constitutional systems analysed in this book have different understanding of the law, and this can also be translated in different understandings of asymmetry.[96]

2.5 *Between Models of Constitutional Review*

A final observation related to the link between federalism and constitutional review concerns a particular ethnic federal state, i.e., Ethiopia. Even though Ethiopia is not among the cases analysed in this book,[97] it is worth recalling its experience because it adopted a unique model of constitutional review, falling outside (or between) the traditional models of constitutional review, based on either political[98] or judicial control. As a result, the Ethiopian Constitution

---

sity Press, 2009); Khaled Abou El Fadl, et al., eds., *Routledge Handbook of Islamic Law* (London and New York: Routledge, 2019); Khaled Abou El Fadl, "The Islamic Legal Tradition," in *The Cambridge Companion to Comparative Law*, ed. Matteo Bussani, and Ugo Mattei (Cambridge: Cambridge University Press, 2012), 295–312; Abdullahi Ahmed An-Na'im, "Islam, Sharia and Comparative Constitutionalism," in *Constitutions and Religion*, ed. Susanna Mancini (Cheltenham and Northampton: Elgar Publishing, 2020), 172–183; Luca Mezzetti, *Diritto islamico* (Torino: Giappichelli, 2022).

94 Ugo Mattei, "Three Patterns of Law: Taxonomy and Change in the World's Legal Systems," *The American Journal of Comparative Law* 45, no. 1 (1997): 35–40.

95 Mattei, "Three Patterns of Law," 23–27.

96 On the overlap between different conceptualisations of legal systems, see Giuseppe Franco Ferrari, "Sistemi giuridici: origine e diffusione," in *Atlante di diritto pubblico comparato*, ed. Giuseppe Franco Ferrari (Torino: UTET giuridica, 2023), 1–24.

97 Despite being of great interest, Ethiopia was not selected as a case study because of its formal constitutional symmetry. On the peculiar nature of symmetry and asymmetry in the Ethiopian federation, see Yonatan T. Fessha and Biniyam N. Bezabih, "Federation Among Unequals," in *Constitutional Asymmetry in Multinational Federalism*, ed. Patricia Popelier and Maja Sahadžić (Cham: Palgrave Macmillan, 2019), 137–62.

98 By political control, we mean a model of constitutional review based on the control over the constitutionality of legal norms by political bodies. The classic example of political control is the French *Conseil Constitutionnel*, a political body composed of nine members appointed by the President of the Republic, by the President of the National Assembly, and by the President of the Senate, and integrated by former Presidents of the Republic. The *Conseil* adopts jurisdictional procedures to preventively assess the constitutionality of laws and parliamentary procedures, prior to their promulgation. The French model is

entrusts the House of the Federation (i.e., the second chamber of the federal Parliament) with authority over all constitutional disputes.[99] Art. 82 of the Constitution provides for the establishment of an advisory body, i.e., the Council of Constitutional Inquiry (CCI), composed of eleven members comprising the President and Vice-President of the Federal Supreme Court, six legal experts appointed by the President upon recommendation of the House of People's Representative (i.e., the lower chamber of the federal Parliament), and three members appointed by the House of the Federation from among its members.[100] The Council thus appears to be a body composed of both legal experts and political representatives. The CCI has the function of investigating constitutional disputes, then submitting them with recommendations to the House of Federation for final decision.[101] It should be further noted that the disputes can be submitted to the CCI by "any court or interested party",[102] and if the Council finds no need for constitutional interpretation, the interested parties can appeal directly to the House of the Federation if dissatisfied with the CCI's decision.[103] Moreover, the House of the Federation has the liberty to accept or reject the recommendations made by the

rooted in the doctrine of parliamentary sovereignty, according to which it would not be imaginable to entrust a non-parliamentary body, and specifically courts, with the power to invalidate a law adopted by the parliament. For further references on the French model, see Massimo Cavino, *Lezioni di giustizia costituzionale francese* (Napoli: Editoriale Scientifica, 2014); Henry Roussillon and Pierre Esplugas-Labatut, *Le Conseil Constitutionnel* (Paris: Dalloz, 2015); Guillaume Drago, *Contentieux Constitutionnel Français* (Paris: Dalloz, 2020); Steven Gow Calabresi, *The History and Growth of Judicial Review, Volume 2: The G-20 Civil Law Countries*, 1st ed. (Oxford and New York: Oxford University Press, 2021), 157–187; Jouanjan, Olivier, "Constitutional Justice in France," in *The Max Planck Handbooks in European Public Law: Volume III: Constitutional Adjudication: Institutions*, ed. Armin von Bogdandy, Peter Huber, and Christoph Grabenwarter (Oxford: Oxford University Press, 2020), 223–278; Servane Le Dû, "The French Constitutional Council: The Gradual Emergence of a Co-legislator?" in *Constitutional Review in Western Europe. Judicial-Legislative Relations in Comparative Perspective*, ed. Kálmán Pócza (London and New York: Routledge, 2024), 108–140. It should be noted that constitutional review based on political control has also been adopted in socialist countries, where the *Presidium* of the parliamentary assembly would be entitled to rule over the constitutionality of the same laws that the assembly had adopted (this was the case, for examples, of the 1977 USSR Constitution, the 1965 Constitution of Romania; the 1972 Hungarian Constitution, and the 1978 Constitution of the Peoples' Republic of China. On the socialist experience, see de Vergottini, *Diritto costituzionale comparato*, 301).

99 Constitution of Ethiopia – Art. 83(1).

100 Constitution of Ethiopia – Art. 83(2).

101 Constitution of Ethiopia – Art. 84(1).

102 Constitution of Ethiopia – Art. 84(2).

103 Constitution of Ethiopia – Art. 84(3)a.

Council, further reducing its role in the system of constitutional adjudication. Finally, it is interesting to mention the object of the constitutional disputes referred by the Council of Constitutional Inquiry to the House of the Federation. Indeed, the majority of cases involved land and property related disputes, with the remaining concerned with family matters or labour-related issues, and these required the CCI to rely only on the Bill of Rights. However, as observed by Fessha and Ayele, "the disputes and the opinions issued by the CCI have no discernible relation to the division of powers between the federal and state governments".[104]

3 Constitutional Courts between Centralist and Federalist Behaviour

Acting as arbiters of constitutional disputes concerning the distribution of powers and competences among levels of government, constitutional courts' decisions might steer the constitutional system in a more centralist or decentralist direction.[105] A number of comparative and in-depth studies have been conducted in order to explore the factors leading to a centralist or decentralist attitude of courts,[106] although interest in the courts' behaviour in multinational federal systems has remained limited.[107]

Adopting a comparative approach, Aroney and Kincaid were able to derive some general trends concerning the behaviour of constitutional and supreme

104 Yonatan T. Fessha, and Zemelak Ayele, "Giving 'Shape and Texture' to a Federal System? Ethiopia's Courts and its Unusual Umpire," in *Federalism and the Courts in Africa*, ed. Yonatan T. Fessha and Karl Kössler (London and New York: Routledge, 2020), 63.

105 Aroney, and Kincaid, "Introduction", 4.

106 See for example Hans-Peter Schneider, Jutta Kramer, Beniamino Caravita di Toritto, eds., *Judge-Made Federalism? The Role of Courts in Federal Systems* (Baden-Baden: Nomos, 2008); Nicholas Aroney and John Kincaid, eds., *Courts in Federal Countries* (Toronto: University of Toronto Press, 2017); Patricia Popelier, "The Constitutional Court's Impact on Federalism in Belgium: a Weakening of the Centralization Theory," in *Jahrbuch des Föderalismus 2020: Föderalismus, Subsidiarität und Regionen in Europa*, ed. Europäischen Zentrum für Föderalismus-Forschung Tübingen (EZFF) (Baden-Baden: Nomos Verlagsgesellschaft mbH & Co. KG, 2020), 67–92; Patricia Popelier and Samantha Bielen, "How Courts Decide Federalism Disputes: Legal Merit, Attitudinal Effects, and Strategic Considerations in the Jurisprudence of the Belgian Constitutional Court," *Publius: The Journal of Federalism* 49, no. 4 (2018): 587–616; Patricia Popelier, "Federalism Disputes and the Behavior of Courts: Explaining Variations in Federal Courts' Support for Centralization," *Publius: The Journal of Federalism* 47, no. 1 (2016): 27–48.

107 See Robert Schertzer, "Federal Arbiters as Facilitators: Towards an Integrated Federal and Judicial Theory for Diverse States," *International Journal of Constitutional Law* 15, no. 1 (2017): 110–136.

courts in a selection of federal systems.[108] The authors observed that, overall, centralising trends tend to prevail, and the judicial decisions of constitutional or supreme courts generally expand the powers of the federal government.[109] This is the case for the US Supreme Court, the Canadian Supreme Court, the Australian High Court, the Supreme Court of Nigeria, and the Brazilian Supreme Federal Court. Some courts appear to have been more federalist in the past and more centralist in recent times, such as the Indian Supreme Court and the Spanish Constitutional Tribunal. Conversely, other courts display a more balanced attitude, such as the German Federal Constitutional Court, the Belgian Constitutional Court, and the Mexican Supreme Court of Justice of the Nation. Among the possible explanatory factors of courts' federalist or unitarist behaviour, Aroney and Kincaid listed historical developments, a single or plural constitutive authority, the constitutional and institutional structure of the federal system, the legal traditions, the selection process and appointment procedures of judges, the court system and relative jurisdiction, and the role of political parties.[110]

According to Popelier, many institutional features may influence the behaviour of courts in federalism disputes, such as the extent of subnational representation in federal policymaking, the degree of integration of the party system, the role of states in the appointment of judges and the composition of the court, the extent of decentralisation in the federal system, and the devolutionary and multinational nature of the federation.[111] Even though Popelier did not find conclusive evidence for any of the several hypotheses tested on eleven federations, it is still worth mentioning the trends she identified. Concerning the factors that might explain a more centralist stance, what emerges is that a low representation of the constituent units in the selection of judges or in the composition of the courts seems to play a significant role in the courts' support for centralisation. Conversely, a weak representation of subnational governments at the federal level, a low gradient of centralisation, or a context of devolution or multinationalism seem to encourage a non-centralist stance.[112] With specific reference to this last factor, Popelier's hypothesis is that "courts will be more likely to take a non-centralist stance if they operate

108 The constitutional systems analysed in the volume are Australia, Belgium, Brazil, Canada, Ethiopia, Germany, India, Mexico, Nigeria, South Africa, Spain, Switzerland, and the United States.

109 Aroney and Kincaid, "Comparative Observations and Conclusions," 483–486.

110 See Aroney and Kincaid, "Comparative Observations and Conclusions," 494–534.

111 See Popelier, "Federalism Disputes and the Behavior of Courts," 34–43.

112 Popelier, "Federalism Disputes and the Behavior of Courts," 44.

in a devolutionary and multinational federal system".[113] Even though subsequent analysis of the case studies does not confirm the hypothesis, there still are some elements of interest. For example, it is found that courts tend to allow for a non-centralist outcome only when the stability of the system is not at stake. Popelier concludes that we might expect that courts in multinational systems tend to be generally "balanced", whereas they are more centralist when threats to the integrity and stability of the system (e.g., secession claims) are present.[114]

Since the goal of this study is to examine the role of courts in divided multi-tiered systems, the following sections explore the attitude of constitutional (or supreme) courts toward territorial self-government. As explained in the previous paragraph, not all courts in the selected case studies developed a rich jurisprudence and interpretative doctrines on federalism-related issues. For this reason, the following sections focus only on those courts that have developed a significant federalism jurisprudence, thus allowing an understanding of how courts can affect federal dynamics through constitutional adjudication in divided multi-tiered systems. A further interesting perspective that future research might address concerns the relationship between central and subnational courts in divided multi-tiered systems. This relationship is the so-called "judicial federalism"[115] and has attracted only limited attention in the federal and legal scholarship, that has so far focused on traditional federations such as the US and Australia.[116]

3.1 *The Canadian Supreme Court: Centralist Umpire or Federal Facilitator?*

Given the difficulty in amending the Canadian Constitution, the Supreme Court played a pivotal role in adapting the Constitution to new societal changes and maintaining a federal balance between tiers of government.[117]

---

113 Popelier, "Federalism Disputes and the Behavior of Courts," 43.

114 Ibidem.

115 According to Gordon, judicial federalism can be framed along three dimensions: institutional (i.e., the existence of a separate system of central and subnational courts); jurisdictional (i.e., the distribution of judicial power between the central and subnational courts); and jurisprudential (i.e., the sources of law binding on the central and subnational courts) (see Jeffrey Steven Gordon, "Comparative Judicial Federalism," *International Journal of Constitutional Law* 21, no. 4 (2023): 976–1010).

116 For more on judicial federalism, see Erin F. Delaney, "Judicial Federalism in Comparative Perspective," In *Federalism and the Courts in Africa*, ed. Yonathan T. Fessha and Karl Kössler (London and New York: Routledge, 2020), 15–28).

117 See Watts, "Federalism and Diversity in Canada," 45–47.

However, Brouillet observed that in Canada there is no unanimous view on whether the attitude of the Supreme Court is centralising or decentralising.[118] Indeed, the dual nature of Canadian federalism, based on two competing views on the development of the Canadian federation,[119] has been partly reflected in the Supreme Court jurisprudence. In Canada (outside Québec), the predominant view of federalism is based on its territorial and mono-national nature and the general understanding is that the federation emerged as a result of an imperial act designing a highly centralised federation. Conversely, in Québec, Canadian federalism is perceived as a genuine federative regime guaranteeing protection for the autonomy of each tier of government, and the pluri-national view of the country is reinforced by the conviction that the federation "stems from a pact among the three original territories and between separate national communities, which was then ratified by the British authorities".[120] Generally speaking, a consensus exists that the Canadian constitutional system is based on federative principles requiring a division of powers among autonomous and coordinated tiers of government. In this respect, the Canadian Supreme Court referred to federalism as a guiding principle not only in the interpretation and application of constitutional provisions, but also in filling any gaps.[121] In its jurisprudence, the Supreme Court has recognised the autonomy of tiers of government as the core of federalism and stressed the need to preserve a balance between the respective powers.[122] Nevertheless, Brouillet argued that the Supreme Court's case law tended to favour the federal government, thus displaying an overall centralist attitude.[123]

One fundamental aspect in the federalism jurisprudence of the Canadian Supreme Court concerns the distribution of powers and competences among tiers of government. It should be recalled that in its early case law, the JCPC interpreted the competences of each tier of government rather

118 Eugénie Brouillet, "The Supreme Court of Canada: The Concept of Cooperative Federalism and Its Effect on the Balance of Power," in *Courts in Federal Countries*, ed. Nicholas Aroney and John Kincaid (Toronto: University of Toronto Press, 2017), 150.

119 For further references, see François Rocher, "La dynamique Québec-Canada of le refus de l'idéal fédéral," In *Le fédéralisme canadien contemporain*, ed. Alain-G. Gagnon (Montréal: University of Montréal Press, 2006), 93–146.

120 Brouillet, "The Supreme Court of Canada," 150.

121 Brouillet, "The Supreme Court of Canada," 151.

122 See for instance *Reference Re Secession of Québec*, [1998] 2 SCR 217; *Reference Re Securities Act*, [2011] 3 SCR 837; *Reference Re Assisted Human Reproduction Act*, [2010] 3 SCR 457; *Canadian Western Bank v. Alberta*, [2007] 2 SCR 3.

123 Brouillet, "The Supreme Court of Canada," 152.

strictly (along a dual conception of federalism) and regarded provincial powers as being "plenary and ample".[124] Unsurprisingly, provinces interpreted the Court's attitude as "an effective safeguard against centralisation efforts".[125] Later on, the Supreme Court became more generous to the federal government, relying on the paramountcy of federal laws in cases of conflict between federal and subnational laws. Indeed, the principle of efficiency has predominantly guided the Supreme Court jurisprudence at the expense of regional autonomy and diversity,[126] often broadening the scope of central federal powers.[127] For example, the Court has expanded the powers of the federal government and of the federal parliament, allowing them to legislate in fields such as trade and commerce, unemployment insurance, and criminal law.[128]

Despite this centralising attitude to the interpretation of exclusive competences, the Supreme Court has more recently limited the cases of antinomies between federal and subnational laws to "scenarios of operational incompatibility in which the observances of one rule would entail the violation of the other".[129] In this way, the Court also restricted the scope of federal paramountcy and the intrusion of the central government into provincial powers. Regarding emergency powers, the constitutional jurisprudence has "consistently recognised the federal power to deal with emergencies", also allowing the federal parliament to legislate in those areas under the exclusive jurisdiction of the provinces (although only temporarily).[130] However, the Supreme Court stated that the powers of disallowance (i.e., the power of the federal government to annul subnational legislation) has "fallen into disuse",[131] and that it is up to the courts to decide whether subnational legislation is *ultra vires*. Therefore, throughout its jurisprudence, it is not possible to observe a clear and definite trend in favour of the central government or in favour of the provincial entities. Indeed, if it is true that the Supreme Court generally ex-

---

124 *Hodge v. The Queen* (Ont) [1883] 9 AC 117 (JCPC).

125 Karl Kössler, "The Role of Constitutional Judges in Protecting Territorial Self-Government," in *Defensive Federalism. Protecting Territorial Minorities from the "Tyranny of the Majority,"* ed. Ferran Requejo and Marc Sanjaume-Calvet (London: Routledge, 2022), 157.

126 See Jean Leclair, "The Supreme Court's Understanding of Federalism: Efficiency at the Expense of Diversity," *Queen's Law Journal* 28 (2003): 411–453.

127 Brouillet, "The Supreme Court of Canada," 154.

128 Ibidem.

129 Kössler, "The Role of Constitutional Judges," 158.

130 Brouillet, "The Supreme Court of Canada," 155.

131 *Re: Objection by Québec to a Resolution to Amend the Constitution*, [1982] 2 SCR 793.

panded federal powers, it is also true that the Court played an important role in protecting self-government.

Besides the allocation of competences, the Supreme Court has also had to rule on fundamental questions related to the federal and multinational nature of Canada. The first two cases concerned Canada's patriation of full sovereignty from the United Kingdom, and the relative impact of former Prime Minister Pierre Trudeau's project on the powers of provinces. The proposal to insert an amendment formula and a charter of fundamental rights and freedoms in the Constitution would have potentially given the provinces a say in the constitutional amendment process, but at the same time it would have limited their powers by reference to the charter of rights.[132] In 1981, in *Re: Resolution to Amend the Constitution*,[133] the Supreme Court ruled that the federal government could legally proceed with the request of patriation, thereby altering the powers of the provinces, even though the majority of provinces were not in favour. Indeed, initially, Trudeau's project was opposed by eight of the ten provinces. However, the Court also concluded that, if the federal Parliament were to act without the consent of the provinces, it would have violated a constitutional convention that required the federal legislature to obtain "a substantial degree of provincial consent".[134] According to this interpretation, the Supreme Court "recognised the principle of equal autonomy of the orders of government but confined its effects to the conventional dimension of constitutional law".[135]

The following year, the government of Québec raised a question of constitutionality concerning the existence of a constitutional convention requiring the federal authority to obtain consent from Québec for constitutional amendments that would have affected its powers or status. The Court of Appeal of Québec answered in the negative, and the decision was upheld by the Supreme Court a few months after the amendment came into force. In *Re: Objection by Québec to a Resolution to Amend the Constitution*,[136] the Supreme Court put an end to the claim that Québec had a *de facto* veto power over amendments affecting its powers or status within the Federation, as well as retiring the idea that the Canadian federation was founded on the basis of an agreement by two equal peoples.[137] Indeed, the Court concluded that the Qué-

132 Brouillet, "The Supreme Court of Canada," 160.
133 *Re: Resolution to Amend the Constitution*, [1981] 1 SCR 733.
134 *Re: Resolution to Amend the Constitution*, [1981] 1 SCR 733, 905.
135 Brouillet, "The Supreme Court of Canada," 161.
136 *Re: Objection by Québec to a Resolution to Amend the Constitution*, [1982] 2 SCR 793.
137 Brouillet, "The Supreme Court of Canada," 161.

bec government failed to show that political actors in previous cases of constitutional amendment felt an obligation to obtain Québec's consent. As a result of this decision, the Constitution Act, 1982 lacks political legitimacy in Québec, since it never formally consented to the act.[138]

Finally, the previously analysed decision on *Reference Re Secession of Quebec* should be recalled,[139] when the Court listed federalism among the guiding principles underlying the Canadian Constitution, along with democracy, constitutionalism and the rule of law, and the protection of minorities. Specifically, the Supreme Court relied on the principles of federalism and democracy "to reconcile the considerations of legality and legitimacy by creating a constitutional obligation to negotiate".[140] In this way, neither side could invoke these principles to act unilaterally in seceding or in ignoring the intention to secede. According to Schertzer, *Reference Re Secession* marked the shift of the Canadian Supreme Court from federal arbiter to facilitator, presenting "the federation as a dynamic system with the judiciary occupying an important position as a facilitator of negotiation over the association".[141] Schertzer further argued that the Canadian Supreme Court also appeared to adopt a similar dynamic understanding of the federal system in following decisions. For instance, in *Canadian Western Bank*,[142] the Supreme Court stressed the need for negotiation given the overlapping jurisdictions in the system and the importance of balancing the "legitimate diversity of regional experimentation" and "the need for national unity".[143] Moreover, in the same decision, the Court also held that the goal of federal arbitration should be to "facilitate, not undermine [...] cooperative federalism".[144] Scherzter's perspective on the Canadian Supreme Court reinforces the idea that the scholarly debate in Canada has not yet found an answer to whether constitutional judges have contributed to maintaining a balance between tiers of government or rather showed a centralist attitude.[145] Overall, Brouillet observed that the Canadian Supreme Court's trend towards centralisation could reflect the "natural propensity of all democratic societies to strengthen the centre".[146] However, he critically

138 See Gil Remillard, "The Constitution Act, 1982: An Unfinished Compromise," *The American Journal of Comparative Law* 32, no. 2 (1984): 269–281.

139 See Chapter 4, paragraph 2.2.3.

140 Brouillet, "The Supreme Court of Canada," 162.

141 Schertzer, "Federal Arbiters as Facilitators," 133.

142 *Canadian Western Bank v. Alberta*, [2007] 2 SCR 3.

143 *Canadian Western Bank*, 24.

144 *Canadian Western Bank*, 24.

145 Kössler, "The Role of Constitutional Judges," 167.

146 Brouillet, "The Supreme Court of Canada," 163.

concluded that a centralist attitude would contrast with a crucial aspect in a diverse constitutional system such as Canada, namely the necessity of balancing the power between the central and subnational levels.

3.2 *The Belgian Constitutional Court: A Balanced Court*

As the judicial body entitled to resolve disputes between federal and subnational entities, the Belgian Constitutional Court secured an "equilibrium" between tiers of government,[147] and is often referred to as a "balanced" court, delivering centralist as well as decentralist decisions.[148] In a recent empirical study, Popelier and Bielen found that the Court's behaviour depends on a multiplicity of factors, and that the probability of a centralist outcome increases when the defending party is the federal government, compared to when it is the subnational government, and vice versa.[149] Moreover, their study showed that legal merits play a role in this dynamic and that each state reform decreased the probability of a centralist outcome, given the progressive decentralisation process that has occurred in Belgium over recent decades.

In particular, the Belgian Constitutional Court has had a significant impact on protecting self-government and resolving issues related to the division of powers.[150] Indeed, the Court has interpreted extensively the exclusive competences of subnational entities by granting them plenary powers.[151] Conversely, the Court has interpreted federal competences narrowly in order to maintain the subnational entities' powers.[152] The Belgian Constitutional Court has also preserved exclusivity, recognising the inevitability of concurrency of powers given the complexity of competences allocation, and reading a proportionality principle into the distribution of powers.[153] As a result, the federal Parliament was obliged to open intergovernmental cooperation when regulating

147 See Patrick Peeters and Jens Mosselmans, "The Constitutional Court of Belgium: Safeguard of the Autonomy of the Communities and Regions," in *Courts in Federal Countries*, ed. Nicholas Aroney and John Kincaid (Toronto: University of Toronto Press, 2017), 69–101.

148 Patricia Popelier and Samantha Bielen, "How Courts Decide Federalism Disputes: Legal Merit, Attitudinal Effects, and Strategic Considerations in the Jurisprudence of the Belgian Constitutional Court," *Publius: The Journal of Federalism* 49, no. 4 (2019): 26

149 See Popelier and Bielen, "How Courts Decide Federalism Disputes," 26–28.

150 For a complete review, see Peeters and Mosselmans, "The Constitutional Court of Belgium," 91–100.

151 See Belgian Constitutional Court, Judgement No. 25, 26 June 1986.

152 See Belgian Constitutional Court, Judgement No. 172, 22 November 2006.

153 Kössler, "The Role of Constitutional Judges," 159.

certain issues and to refrain from making the exercise of subnational competences difficult.[154]

Overall, the Constitutional Court has played a major role as a "safeguard of the autonomy of the communities and regions",[155] supporting a broad interpretation of community and regional powers and reinforcing their spheres of competence through the "double aspect doctrine".[156] However, the Court has managed to ensure the necessary cohesion of the constitutional system, introducing the notion of "economic and monetary union" as a general limitation to the powers of subnational entities. Indeed, in 1988, the Court ruled that an economic and monetary union limits the powers of regions to impose taxes, and that regions must exercise their powers without hindering the free movement of persons, good, services, and capital between the central and subnational entities.[157]

3.3 *The Spanish Constitutional Tribunal: A Polarising Centralist*

Given the open model designed by the 1978 Spanish Constitution, the Spanish Constitutional Tribunal was a fundamental actor in the construction of the state of autonomies.[158] Specifically, the interpretation of the constitutional provision related to the distribution of powers and competences between the central level and the autonomous communities has been carried out through hundreds of decisions of the Constitutional Tribunal. Therefore, as observed by Casanas Adam, "it is impossible to understand the functioning of the state of autonomies without taking the Court's case law into consideration".[159] Especially at the outset of the Spanish regional system, a large number of challenges were brought by the central state as well as the autonomous communities, due to the openness of constitutional provisions and political strategies of the central government and political parties. Traditionally, the challenges concerned primarily the vertical relationship between the state and the autonomous communities, and not the horizontal relations between subnational entities; these have been very limited and have not had a comparable effect on the development of the state of autonomies.[160]

154 Belgian Constitutional Court, Judgement No. 132, 14 July 2004.

155 Peeters and Mosselmans, "The Constitutional Court of Belgium," 102.

156 See Belgian Constitutional Court, Judgement No. 168/2011, 10 November 2011.

157 See Belgian Constitutional Court, Judgement No. 47, 25 February 1988.

158 Elisenda Casanas Adam, "The Constitutional Court of Spain: From System Balancer to Polarizing Centralist," in *Courts in Federal Countries*, ed. Nicholas Aroney and John Kincaid (Toronto: University of Toronto Press, 2017), 386.

159 Casanas Adam, "The Constitutional Court of Spain," 387.

160 Ibidem.

The regional system has evolved from a decentralised system towards an increasingly centralised one. Indeed, centralising legislation has set out extensive functional and substantive competences of the state, limiting the territorial self-government of autonomous communities.[161] Casanas Adam argued that the Spanish Constitutional Tribunal significantly contributed to this centralisation process, validating the legislation adopted by the state parliament and consolidating a centralised interpretation of the constitutional provisions on territorial organisation.[162] However, in some cases, the Court defended territorial self-government, limiting the centralising tendencies of the state, and for this reason the constitutional case-law was regarded as fairly balanced.[163] For instance, the Court defended territorial self-government by invalidating the resymmetrisation legislation enacted by the state parliament (the so-called LOAPA, further analysed in the following paragraph),[164] allowing for the maintenance of historical civil law institutions,[165] accepting their international activity and EU relations, validating the Catalan language policy, and impeding the central state from using their funding to invade areas of competences of the autonomous communities.[166] In its early jurisprudence, the Spanish Constitutional Tribunal also developed a series of interpretative principles and criteria for resolving disputes between tiers of government. In particular, the Court did not rely extensively on the "prevalence clause" but mostly on the "principle of competence",[167] as well as on the principles of "irrenounceability", "unavailability", and "specificity".[168] Moreover, the Constitutional Tribunal argued that a general principle of collaboration between tiers is implied in the system.[169]

The turning point in the constitutional case law, as well as in the public perception of the Court, was provided by two controversial decisions delivered after the wave of reform of autonomy statutes in the early 2000s: the 2007 decision on the Valencian Statute,[170] and the 2010 decision on the Catalan

161 Casanas Adam, "The Constitutional Court of Spain," 387.
162 Ibidem.
163 Casanas Adam, "The Constitutional Court of Spain," 388.
164 Spanish Constitutional Tribunal, decision 76/1983.
165 Spanish Constitutional Tribunal, decision 88/1993.
166 See Spanish Constitutional Tribunal, decisions 153/1989; 165/1994; 82, 83, 84/1986; 337/1994, and 175/1985.
167 Spanish Constitutional Tribunal, decision 163/1995.
168 Spanish Constitutional Tribunal, decisions 87/1993 and 71/1982.
169 Spanish Constitutional Tribunal, decision 18/1982.
170 Spanish Constitutional Tribunal, decision 247/2007.

Statute.[171] Since the latter decision had dramatic implications for the asymmetrical arrangements, it will be analysed in the following paragraph dedicated to constitutional courts and constitutional asymmetries. Conversely, the decision 247/2007 on the Valencian Statute is helpful in understanding the Court's conception of the territorial organisation of the state. Indeed, in its judgment, the Spanish Constitutional Tribunal identified five fundamental principles on which the state relies: (i) autonomy and unity; (II) solidarity between the state and the autonomous communities, and among autonomous communities; (III) equality of citizens, ensuring common basic conditions in the exercise of rights across the territory; (iv) loyalty to the Constitution; and (v) general public interest as a requirement for all decisions adopted by the different tiers of government.[172] In the 2007 decision, as already declared in decision 4/1981, the Court reiterated that national sovereignty belongs to the Spanish people and is not the result of an agreement between historical territories, but a provision emanating from constituent power having binding force.[173]

Moreover, the Court defined in detail the functional and substantive content of the exclusive competences of the state, thus delimiting the scope of intervention of the autonomous communities, and allowing for an expansive interpretation of the central state competences with the so-called "horizontal clause".[174] The Court had already adopted a restrictive approach towards autonomous communities in the past, stating that exclusivity does not imply that autonomous communities have full functions in respect of a particular matter[175] and that the term "exclusive" was not to be interpreted in absolute terms when used in a statute of autonomy.[176] For what concerns the "horizontal clause",[177] the two central competences are the provision on the planning of economic activity[178] and the guarantees of equality among Spanish citizens in the exercise of rights.[179]

An important element to consider is the use that the central government made of the Court in orienting the development of the state of autonomies. Indeed, following the 2010 decision on the Catalan Statute of Autonomy and

171 Spanish Constitutional Tribunal, decision 31/2010.
172 Casanas Adam, "The Constitutional Court of Spain," 389–390.
173 See Spanish Constitutional Tribunal, decision 4/1981.
174 Casanas Adam, "The Constitutional Court of Spain," 391.
175 Spanish Constitutional Tribunal, decision 56/1986.
176 Spanish Constitutional Tribunal, decision 3/1981.
177 For more details, see Casanas Adam, "The Constitutional Court of Spain," 391–392.
178 Spanish Constitutional Tribunal, decisions 125/1984, 95/1986, and 76/1991.
179 Spanish Constitutional Tribunal, decisions 61/1997, and 164/2001.

the consequent re-activation of the pro-independence movement in Catalonia, the Spanish government "used the Constitutional Tribunal to block different legal avenues of the Catalan authorities",[180] stifling the consultation process in Catalonia and placing even more responsibilities on the Court to face critical political (and legal) issues.[181] The Spanish government even resorted to emergency measures, and adopted legislation giving more powers to the Constitutional Tribunal, allowing the Court to impose sanctions and suspend public authorities not complying with its decisions.[182] The central government eventually triggered Art. 155(1) of the Spanish Constitution[183] on the day the "Declaration of Independence" was ratified by the Catalan Parliament in 2017. Through the provisions entrenched in Art. 155(1), the Spanish government suspended the Catalan executive, dissolved its parliament, and called for new regional elections. What is relevant to note is that the Constitutional Tribunal confirmed the lawfulness of the extraordinary measures and the invocation of Art. 155(1). Specifically, the Court recalled Catalonia's reluctance to comply with the Court's previous judgments and emphasised that this constitutional provision allows only for temporary measures and "no definite suspension of autonomy", adding that the use of Art. 155 is limited to "cases in which it is evident that it is the only possible way to restore the constitutional order".[184]

Overall, this brief overview of the case law of the Spanish Constitutional Tribunal shows that the Court was initially perceived as fairly balanced, shifting between a more centralist interpretation of the state's competences and defence of the powers of autonomous communities. However, after the wave of Statutes of Autonomy reform in the early 2000s, the Constitutional Tribunal adopted a decisive unitarist attitude, becoming a "polarising centralist"[185] and the "Spanish government's enforcer".[186] This will become even more evident

180 Casanas Adam, "The Constitutional Court of Spain," 401.

181 See Spanish Constitutional Tribunal, decisions 31/2015, 32/2015, 138/2015, and 259/2015.

182 Kössler, "The Role of Constitutional Judges," 166.

183 Constitution of Spain – Art. 155(1): "If a Self-governing Community does not fulfil the obligations imposed upon it by the Constitution or other laws, or acts in a way that is seriously prejudicial to the general interest of Spain, the Government, after having lodged a complaint with the President of the Self-governing Community and failed to receive satisfaction therefore, may, following approval granted by the overall majority of the Senate, take all measures necessary to compel the Community to meet said obligations, or to protect the abovementioned general interest."

184 Spanish Constitutional Tribunal, decisions 89/ 2019 and 90/ 2019.

185 Aroney and Kincaid, "Comparative Observations and Conclusions," 484.

186 Casanas Adam, "The Constitutional Court of Spain," 402.

when analysing decision 31/2010 on the Catalan Statute of Autonomy in the following paragraph.

3.4 *The Indian Supreme Court: Safeguard of Territorial Self-Government*

According to Tewari and Saxena, in India, the judicial interpretation of constitutional provisions has generally been centralising, and constitutional case law has mainly dealt with the protection of fundamental rights rather than the protection of states' rights.[187] This is an important indication of the fact that the relationships between the union and the states have been guided by the spirit of "cooperative federalism," even though cooperation has been translated into an obligation to conform to central directions under strong overriding powers even in non-emergency times.[188] As in the previous cases, the Supreme Court of India, as well as the subnational constitutional courts, played an essential role in interpreting the constitutional provisions relevant to the distribution of powers and union-state relations. In the attempt to reconcile competing claims, and accommodate states' positions within a complex legal framework, the Indian judiciary developed a series of guiding interpretative principles.

One of the most pressing issues concerned the distribution of legislative and other powers between tiers of government. The Indian Constitution introduces exclusive powers of the federal government and of the states, as well as concurrent powers.[189] In the Seventh Schedule, the Constitution assigns subject matters to one of three categories: the Union List, the Concurrent List, and the State List. Relying on this articulated framework, the Supreme Court has protected subnational powers by giving a "broad and plentiful interpretation" to the State List, because otherwise this would "whittle down the power of the State and might jeopardise the federal principle".[190] Conversely, the Court has also relied on the "pith and substance" doctrine to allow intervention into each other's jurisdiction, mostly to the benefit of the federal government.[191] For what concerns concurrent powers, Art. 254 of the Indian Constitution provides that in cases of inconsistency between union and state legislation, the federal legislation has to prevail unless the state legislation

187 Tewari and Saxena, "The Supreme Court of India," 244.

188 Ibidem.

189 See Constitution of India – Art. 246(1–3).

190 Indian Supreme Court, *International Tourist Corporation v. State of Haryana*, 1981 AIR 774.

191 See Indian Supreme Court, *State of Bombay and Ors v. F.N. Balsara*, 1951 AIR 318.

received previous assent from the President of India.[192] On this last issue, the Supreme Court has clarified the cases and modality of presidential assent[193] and further declared that state occupancy of these concurrent fields is valid until they are not occupied by the federal government.[194] Moreover, the Supreme Court has established certain requirements for the invocation of the "national interest" in order to lawfully enact central legislation in concurrent matters.[195]

An interesting aspect to consider is as regards the constitutional interpretation of the provisions on the suspension of territorial self-government. Kössler defined suspension in a negative sense, by invalidating a subnational law, and in a positive sense, by also imposing national legislation in its place.[196] Regarding the former sense, the Supreme Court played a confrontational role vis-à-vis political actors. The Indian Constitution authorises the President of India to give or withhold their assent to a state bill,[197] however this can be exercised by the state governor (i.e., a presidential appointee). Along with the recommendations of the Sarkaria Commission on union-state relations to use this power only in exceptional cases, the Supreme Court further held that this right concerns only the provisions of subnational legislation that were brought to the President's attention, and not the entire law.[198] The Court also limited the attempts to suspend subnational powers in a positive sense. Indeed, another constitutional provision empowers the President of India to impose emergency rule in case of "failure of the constitutional machinery".[199] Acting upon advice of the Council of Ministers, they may thus issue an emergency rule proclamation, and in the 1970s this extremely invasive power started to be abused to remove state governments controlled by the opposition parties. Once again, the Supreme Court protected territorial self-government. If initially the constitutional judges characterised the issue as a "political thicket"[200] to be determined by the federal government, in a later decision the Court introduced several procedural principles for the invocation of this emergency provision and claimed for itself the power to provide

192 See Kössler, "The Role of Constitutional Judges," 161.
193 Indian Supreme Court, *M. Karunanidhi v. Union of India*, 1979 AIR 898.
194 Indian Supreme Court, *Western Coalfi elds v. Special Area Development*, 1982 AIR 697.
195 See Kössler, "The Role of Constitutional Judges," 164.
196 Ibidem.
197 Constitution of India – Art. 201.
198 Indian Supreme Court, *Kaiser- I- Hind (P) Ltd v. National Textile Corporation Maharashtra North Ltd* (2002), 8 SCC 182.
199 Constitution of India – Art. 356.
200 Indian Supreme Court, *State of Rajasthan v. Union of India*, 1977 AIR 1361.

effective remedy in case of unconstitutional proclamation.[201] This strong stance of constitutional judges in defence of territorial self-government against the suspension of subnational powers was also reinforced by later rulings[202] and is considered essential in having reduced central interventionism based on Art. 356.[203] Aside from the distribution of competences, the federalism jurisprudence of the Supreme Court concerns issues such as the use of armed forces in troubled areas,[204] the extra-territorial nature of many states' tax-laws,[205] and treaty-making powers.[206] Overall, the analysis of the federalism jurisprudence of the Indian Supreme Court[207] shows that despite a historical centralising attitude, the Court has also often decisively defended self-government, especially against the abuse of the federal government.[208]

Finally, as already mentioned, the Supreme Court developed the so-called doctrine of the "basic structure" of the Constitution, that has been elaborated on incrementally and included principles such as democratically elected governments, secularism, and federalism as part of the basic constitutional structure, thus limiting the federal and state legislatures in their exercise of amending powers.[209] The basic structure doctrine contributed to the significant role that the Supreme Court and state High Courts played in promoting a "multicultural and federal conception of nationhood and state".[210]

3.5 *The Italian Constitutional Court: The Interpreter of Italian Regionalism*

As in the previous cases, and especially in the Spanish system, the Italian Constitutional Court was an essential actor in supporting the development of the regional model and was determinative in resolving disputes between

---

201 Indian Supreme Court, *SR Bommai v. Union of India*, 1994 AIR 1918.

202 See for example *Rameshwar Prasad v. Union of India*, 2006 AIR 980.

203 Tewari and Saxena, "The Supreme Court of India," 249.

204 Indian Supreme Court, *Naga Peoples' Movement of Human Rights v. Union of India*, 1998 SC 109.

205 Indian Supreme Court, *The Tata Iron & Steel Co. Ltd. v. the State of Bihar*, *AIR* 1958 Sc 452: 1958.

206 See Indian Supreme Court, *Maganbhai v. Union of India, Hidayatullah CJ*, *AIR* 1969, SC: 784; *P.B. Samantha v. Union of India*, *AIR* 1994, Bombay 324.

207 For further references see also Wilfried Swenden and Rekha Saxena, "Policing the Federation: The Supreme Court and Judicial Federalism in India," *Territory, Politics, Governance* 10, no. 1 (2022): 12–31.

208 Tewari and Saxena, "The Supreme Court of India," 252.

209 Tewari and Saxena, "The Supreme Court of India," 252–253.

210 Tewari and Saxena, "The Supreme Court of India," 252.

the central and regional governments.[211] Moreover, in Italian legal doctrine, it is a consolidated opinion that "regionalism and a centralised system of constitutional adjudication are the two most important innovations introduced in the Second Part of the [1947] Constitution".[212] In the analysis of the constitutional adjudication of regional legislation, the 2001 constitutional reform of Title V of the Italian Constitution is a critical turning point. Indeed, before 2001, questions of constitutionality were raised mainly via the incidental method of review and these "occupied a great part of the [Italian Constitutional Court] docket".[213] The 2001 reform dramatically inverted the direction of constitutional review, with an exponential growth of *principaliter* review. This increase peaked in the midst of the 2010 economic crisis, and in 2012 almost 50% of the Court's judgments derived from challenges raised by the state or regions via principal review.[214] Since 2014, the numbers have begun to decrease, and as of 2023 the percentage of *principaliter* proceedings is around 40%.[215]

Delledonne observed that the factors that have led to such a number of *principaliter* reviews are not only related to interpretative uncertainty deriving from the unclear wording of the post-2001 constitutional provisions on the allocation of competences between state and regions (especially of Art. 117 of the Constitution),[216] but also the fact that the legislative implementation of

---

211 See Giacomo Delledonne, "Federalism and Regionalism in Constitutional Adjudication," in *Federalism and Constitutional Law. The Italian Contribution to Comparative Regionalism*, ed. Erika Arban, Giuseppe Martinico and Francesco Palermo (London and New York: Routledge, 2021), 48–64; Laura Ronchetti, "The Judicial Construction of Italian Regionalism," in *Italian Regionalism: Between Unitary Traditions and Federal Processes*, ed. Stelio Mangiameli (Cham: Springer, 2014), 379–404; Sergio Bartole, "Regionalism and Federalism in the Italian Constitutional Experience," in *Autonomy: Applications and Implications*, ed. Markku Suksi (Leiden and Boston: Brill, 1998), 173–193; Roberto Bin, "Corte costituzionale, Regioni e riforme costituzionali," *Le Regioni* 4 (2001): 601–604; Andrea Guazzarotti, "Diritti fondamentali e Regioni: il nuovo Titolo V alla prova della giurisprudenza costituzionale," *Istituzioni del Federalismo* 5 (2008): 599–621; Antonio D'Atena, "Il riparto delle competenze tra Stato e Regioni ed il ruolo della Corte costituzionale," *Italian Papers of Federalism* 57, no. 4 (2015): 787–807.

212 Delledonne, "Federalism and Regionalism in Constitutional Adjudication," 48. See also Antonio D'Atena, "Regione," *Enciclopedia del Diritto* 39 (1988); Giustino D'Orazio, *La genesi della Corte Costituzionale* (Milan: Edizioni di Comunità, 1981).

213 Barsotti, et al., *Italian Constitutional Justice*, 54.

214 Delledonne, "Federalism and Regionalism in Constitutional Adjudication," 51.

215 Italian Constitutional Court, "Annual Report 2023," available at https://www.cortecostituzionale.it/annuario2023/pdf/AnnualReport2023web.pdf (last accessed 23 August 2024).

216 Delledonne, "Federalism and Regionalism in Constitutional Adjudication," 51.

the constitutional reform has been incomplete, particularly concerning the model of "fiscal federalism" provided by Art. 119.[217] Moreover, the limited co-operation among tiers of government due to an unconsolidated system of intergovernmental relations, and the lack of effective regional participation in the state-level lawmaking process has contributed to a frequent resort to principal review to resolve disputes and clarify the allocation of their respective competences. Finally, the political consensus in respect of the 2001 reform was further undermined by two subsequent reform projects (2006 and 2016) that would have significantly affected the regional system, and that created new opportunities for intergovernmental conflicts.[218] Some scholars also argue that the use of *principaliter* review has become strategic, as it allows the regions controlled by the opposition to do what parliamentary minorities are not entitled to do, and thus they challenge controversial state legislation soon after it enters into force.[219]

Through its regionalism jurisprudence, the Italian Constitutional Court was able to develop a series of interpretative criteria that contributed in a decisive way to the functioning of the Italian regional system, especially after the 2001 constitutional reform. Before 2001, in the absence of a supremacy clause, the Court resorted to the "national interest criterion" provided for in the original Art. 117 of the Constitution to resolve disputes between the state and the regions, often in a centralising sense.[220] With the reform of Title v of the Constitution and the relative "disappearance" of the national interest from the constitutional text, the Court referred to the so-called "prevalence criterion" to resolve disputes between levels of government and interpret the intersection of powers and competences.[221] When the Court was unable to clearly identify

217 See Alice Valdesalici, "Financial Relations in the Italian Regional System," in *Federalism and Constitutional Law. The Italian Contribution to Comparative Regionalism*, ed. Erika Arban, Giuseppe Martinico, and Francesco Palermo (London and New York: Routledge, 2021), 82–99.

218 Delledonne, "Federalism and Regionalism in Constitutional Adjudication," 51.

219 See Cfr. Diletta Tega, "Giudizi su conflitti che riguardano diritti. I parametri sostanziali nel giudizio in via principale," *Quaderni Costituzionali* 39, no. 1 (2019): 131–154; Luca Castelli, "Il modello regionale italiano e la prospettiva del regionalismo differenziato," *Istituzioni del Federalismo*, no. 3 (2023): 461–490.

220 See See Roberto Bin, "L'interesse nazionale dopo la riforma: continuità dei problemi, discontinuità della giurisprudenza costituzionale," *Le Regioni*, no. 6 (2001): 1213–1221; Paolo Caretti, "La Corte e la tutela delle esigenze unitarie: dall'interesse nazionale al principio di sussidiarietà," *Le Regioni*, no. 2–3 (2004): 381–389.

221 See Italian Constitutional Court, decisions 50/2005, 51/2005, and 80/2007. On the prevalence criterion, see also Roberto Bin, "I criteri di individuazione delle materie," *Le Regioni*, no. 5 (2006): 889–902.

the prevalence competence, it resorted to a fundamental principle of Italian regionalism, i.e., the principle of loyal cooperation.[222] According to such principle, "the state legislature has to provide for appropriate tools that ensure regional participation and [...] the protection of regional competences".[223] The principle is guided by the objective of maintaining a balance between unity and autonomy when it comes to regulating specific matters and the non-observance of loyal cooperation might lead to the invalidation of the challenged legislation. Concerning regional involvement in state law-making processes, the Italian Constitutional Court in decision 251/2016 held that a stronger regional participation in law-making at the central level was needed, especially when dealing with the regulation of "complex social phenomena".[224] The relevance of the principle of loyal cooperation in the Court's jurisprudence, as well as decision 251/2016, are two instances of how the Court has protected (at least formally) the institutional role of regions as forms of territorial self-government in the Italian multi-tiered system.[225]

Another important indication of this concerns the Constitutional Court's interpretation of "transversal matters", namely those matters that allow the central parliament to enact legislation that applies to the entire territory and overlaps with regional competences.[226] What is interesting to notice is that the Court has interpreted these matters in the light of cooperative regionalism,[227] i.e., not as a legitimation of the central state to intervene "to the detriment of regional competences",[228] but rather as a way to allow regional legislatures to set higher standards.[229] Finally, the attempt of the Italian

222 See Jens Woelk, "Loyal Cooperation: Systemic Principle of Italy's Regionalism?" in *Federalism and Constitutional Law. The Italian Contribution to Comparative Regionalism*, ed. Erika Arban, Giuseppe Martinico, and Francesco Palermo (London and New York: Routledge, 2021), 170–188; Antonia Baraggia, "Il principio di leale collaborazione tra fatto e diritto," *Le Regioni* 6 (2011); 1246–1255.

223 Delledonne, "Federalism and Regionalism in Constitutional Adjudication," 54.

224 Italian Constitutional Court, decision 251/2016.

225 It is worth noting that the scope of the sentence 251/206 was later downsized by the Court's subsequent jurisprudence, in favour of a centralising reading of the dynamics between the centre and the peripheries (see Nicolò Paolo Alessi, "La crisi come risorsa: riflessioni costruttive sui rapporti tra Stato e Regioni in Italia nella prospettiva della differenziazione," in *Le tendenze del decentramento in Europa*, ed. Francesco Palermo, and Sara Parolari (Napoli: Editoriale Scientifica, 2022), 231–267).

226 Delledonne, "Federalism and Regionalism in Constitutional Adjudication," 54.

227 See Filippo Benelli and Roberto Bin, "Prevalenza e 'rimaterializzazione delle materie': scacco matto alle Regioni," *Le Regioni* 37 (2009): 1203–1207.

228 Ibidem.

229 See Italian Constitutional Court, decisions 105/2008, 61/2009, and 7 /2019.

Constitutional Court to imprint dynamism and flexibility on the competences enumerated in Art. 117 should be recalled. Indeed, in decision 303/2003,[230] the Constitutional Court referred to the principle of subsidiarity ex Art. 118(1) and (4) as applying to legislative competences as well as administrative functions.[231]

A further meaningful aspect to consider when assessing the regionalism jurisprudence of the Italian Constitutional Court is its essential contribution to the theoretical foundations of regionalism as a distinct model, to be distinguished from federalism. Indeed, the Court relied on three categories to "set Italian regionalism apart from historic federations":[232] Parliament, people, and sovereignty. In its decision 106/2002, the Constitutional Court stated that the word "Parliament" exclusively indicates state Parliament, and not regional legislatures insofar as "Parliament is the only place where the national political representation is located".[233] Some years later, in judgment 365/2007, the Court rejected the idea that autonomy and sovereignty were both founding characteristics of regionalism. Indeed, from the Court's perspective, autonomy is a distinctive trait of regionalism, whereas sovereignty is one of federalism.[234] Finally, in decision 170/2010, the Constitutional Court, striking down a law of an ordinary region protecting a historic minority language, held that only the state parliament is entitled to identify a national community and the relative minority groups.[235] Recalling Delledonne's words, the Court argued that "the state is better placed to protect diversity

230 Italian Constitutional Court, decision 303/2003. This decision is one of the two so-called "sentenze Mezzanotte", from the name of the Judge Rapporteur, Carlo Mezzanotte, that were particularly meaningful for Italian regionalism. For further references, see Paolo Caretti, "Le sentenze nn. 303/2003 e 14/2004: due letture 'creative' del nuovo Titolo v della Costituzione," *Le Regioni*, no. 4–5 (2008): 807–810; Stelio Mangiameli, "Giurisprudenza costituzionale creativa e costituzione vivente. A proposito delle sentenze n. 303 del 2003 e n. 14 del 2004," *Le Regioni*, no. 4–5 (2008): 825–841.

231 See Giuseppe Martinico, "Federalism, Regionalism, and the Principle of Subsidiarity," in *Federalism and Constitutional Law. The Italian Contribution to Comparative Regionalism*, ed. Erika Arban, Giuseppe Martinico, and Francesco Palermo (London and New York: Routledge, 2021), 189–205; Erika Arban, *Italian Regionalism and the Federal Challenge: Reconciling Economic Regionalism and Solidarity* (Cham: Springer Nature Switzerland, 2023).

232 Delledonne, "Federalism and Regionalism in Constitutional Adjudication," 59.

233 Italian Constitutional Court, decision 106/2002.

234 Italian Constitutional Court, decision 365/2007.

235 Italian Constitutional Court, decision 170/2010.

as well as the reason for common belonging, and to reconcile pluralism with uniformity".[236]

Throughout its activity, the Italian Constitutional Court has been often criticised for its centralising attitude,[237] both before and after the 2001 Constitutional reform. In fact, the use of the national interest criterion prior to 2001 and the subsequent interpretative criteria based on the principle of subsidiarity and loyal cooperation have generally led to a centralising interpretation of legislative powers in favour of the central level, through an extensive interpretation of transversal matters to the advantage of state legislation and a generally deferential attitude towards the central level.[238] This became especially evident during the 2010 economic crisis, when the Court upheld state legislative measures that applied to the regions by relying on a broad interpretation of the "fundamental principles" to be laid down in state legislation according to Art. 117(3), especially concerning the concurrent competence over the "coordination of public finance and taxation system".[239] In those years, as well as during the Covid-19 pandemic, the Court followed a trend "towards a relative weakening of regional autonomy".[240] Overall, Delledonne observed that, despite its mostly fruitful adjudicating activity, "the interpretative activity of the Italian Constitutional Court has mostly been conservative and has somehow slowed down the unleashing of the innovative potential of territorial pluralism".[241]

---

236 Delledonne, "Federalism and Regionalism in Constitutional Adjudication," 60.

237 See Andrea Filippetti, Sandro Rondinella, and Fabrizio Tuzi, "The Italian Constitutional Court and Recentralization Along the Pendulum of Regionalism," *Constitutional Political Economy* (2024): 1–27.

238 Rosanna Tosi, "Il neo-centralismo della Corte costituzionale: dei canili e di altre storie," *Le Regioni* 44 (2016): 619–624.

239 Constitution of Italy – Art. 117(3): Concurring legislation applies to the following subject matters: [...]; coordination of public finance and taxation system; [...]. In the subject matters covered by concurring legislation legislative powers are vested in the Regions, except for the determination of the fundamental principles, which are laid down in State legislation."

240 Delledonne, "Federalism and Regionalism in Constitutional Adjudication," 56; see also Ignazio Spadaro, "Decentramento politico e pandemia: spunti per un 'regionalismo dell'emergenza'," *Rivista AIC* 4 (2022): 146–165; Tania Groppi, "Lo Stato regionale italiano nel XXI secolo, tra globalizzazione e crisi economica," *Federalismi.it* 12, no. 21 (2014): 22–23.

241 Delledonne, "Federalism and Regionalism in Constitutional Adjudication," 56.

3.6 *The Constitutional Court of Bosnia-Herzegovina: Integration or Disintegration?*

As already discussed in the previous chapter, the BiH Constitutional Court played a significant role in imprinting a multi-ethnic direction on the constitutional system during the democratic transition following the 1992–1995 Bosnian war. However, it should not be forgotten that the Constitutional Court also was an important actor in the definition of the BiH federal system. As early as the 2000 *Constituent Peoples'* case, the Court clearly established that the two entities were to be considered as sub-state entities and not sovereign states.[242] The Court therefore seemed to outline a federal and not a confederal structure, as well as reaffirm the supremacy of the BiH Constitution over the constitutions and laws of the two sub-state entities. Throughout the evolution of the system, the Court has gradually reinforced the central level with the aim of rationalising the system and making it more functional.[243] In particular, the Court has relied on the state's exclusive competence over foreign policy in the evaluation of laws adopted under obligations arising from European integration, particularly the Stabilisation and Association Agreements (SAAs), as well as from accession to the Council of Europe.[244] In addition, the Court outlined a number of concurrent competences, imprinting a cooperative direction on an initially dual federalism. In particular, the Constitutional Court recognised the existence of a common framework within which concurrent competences are articulated in important matters, including the protection of human rights and fundamental freedoms.[245]

The reinforcement of the multilevel character of the BiH system is even more relevant when considered from the perspective of European integration, which began in the early 2000s and culminated in its recognition as a candidate country in December 2022. In 2019, the European Commission identified a number of priorities that Bosnia and Herzegovina must address in order to continue the integration process.[246] Among them, priority no. 4 concerns the improvement of the institutional and constitutional framework, in order to ensure legal certainty regarding the distribution of competences between

242 Constitutional Court of Bosnia and Herzegovina, case U-5/98 III (1 July 2000), para. 30.

243 See Išerić, "The Role of the Constitutional Court of Bosnia and Herzegovina," 180–181.

244 Constitutional Court of Bosnia and Herzegovina, case U-6/07 (4 October 2008); Constitutional Court of Bosnia and Herzegovina, case U-17/09 (27 March 2010).

245 Constitutional Court of Bosnia and Herzegovina, case U-1/11 (13 July 2012).

246 European Commission, "Commission Opinion on Bosnia and Herzegovina's application for membership of the European Union" (Brussels, 2019).

the central level and the entities (priority 4.a).[247] In addition, the Commission indicated the need to adopt a clause allowing the central state to exercise powers of the other levels of government to prevent and remedy possible violations of EU law (priority 4.b). In this regard, two cases that came before the Constitutional Court are emblematic of the difficulties that the Court (and the system as a whole) is currently facing. In December 2021, the National Assembly of Republika Srpska adopted a series of decisions that provided for the unilateral transfer of a number of competences from the central state to the entity, including competences related to the armed forces, the taxation system, the Court of Bosnia and Herzegovina, and the High Judicial and Prosecutorial Council (HJPC).[248] These powers had previously been transferred from the entities to the central state in the early 2000s following an agreement between the state and the entities, an option provided for in the Constitution. The decisions were immediately challenged before the Constitutional Court, which declared them unconstitutional in May 2022[249] confirming that entities cannot unilaterally withdraw their consent from an agreement on the transfer of specific powers to the central state. Subsequently, in February 2022, the Republika Srpska adopted a law on property registration, which was declared unconstitutional by the Constitutional Court twice.[250] In both decisions, the Court confirmed that public property falls under the exclusive powers of the central state and not the entities. It should be noted that the Republika Srpska's authorities, when the law was challenged, immediately stated that they would not comply with the Constitutional Court's decision. This actually happened when, after the Court's first decision, the law was published anyway in the entity's official gazette, thus leading to a new challenge and subsequently a new ruling of unconstitutionality in March 2023. Currently, authorities of the Republika Srpska are moving in a similar manner by legislating in other areas that would be under the central state's competences but are being claimed as entity competences, notably with a medical devices law and a justice system law, and some judgments are still pending before the Court.

247 European Commission, "Commission Opinion on Bosnia and Herzegovina's application for membership of the European Union" (Brussels, 2019), 14.

248 See Lidia Bonifati, "Constitutional Design and the Seeds of Degradation in Divided Societies: The Case of Bosnia-Herzegovina," *European Constitutional Law Review* 19, no. 2 (2023): 246–247.

249 Constitutional Court of Bosnia and Herzegovina, Case U-2/22, 16 May 2022.

250 Constitutional Court of Bosnia and Herzegovina, Case U-10/22, 22 September 2022; Constitutional Court of Bosnia and Herzegovina, Case U-5/23, 2 March 2023.

Thus, as much as the Court has played a crucial role in the evolution of BiH federalism in an integrative direction, over time it has experienced a substantial weakening of its authority.[251] As early as 2010 and 2015, the Court saw important rulings disregarded,[252] further undermining the principles of the rule of law. As discussed, in the past two years, the Republika Srpska has repeatedly and openly stated that it would not respect the Court's decisions, going so far as to adopt a decision in June 2023 holding that the Court's authority is not recognised in the entity.[253] Therefore, the Court's efforts at greater internal integration, also with the aim of effective implementation of European norms once the country joins the European Union, have recently generated a disintegrative effect, as the Republika Srpska has used the Court's rulings politically to deny its authority and to advance its own political claims in a secessionist direction.

4 Constitutional Courts and Asymmetries

Having reviewed the role of courts in addressing federalism-related disputes between tiers of government, it is now possible to focus on the impact of courts on constitutional asymmetry. Despite not having found systematic interest in the literature on asymmetric federalism, constitutional case law is a crucial element in the assessment of the degree of constitutional asymmetry in divided multi-tiered systems. Indeed, it can substantially re-shape federal dynamics by protecting asymmetry against symmetrisation legislation, or conversely reduce the degree of asymmetry by upholding central legislation. Since not all the constitutional courts in the case studies analysed in this book have addressed asymmetry-related disputes, the following sections address those courts that did address asymmetries in their respective constitutional systems (i.e., India, Indonesia, Italy, and Spain) and, by doing so, proved to be crucial in re-shaping the federal dynamics. The analysis starts with India, i.e., the system displaying the highest asymmetry score of the four (0.27), then moving to Italy and Spain (respectively 0.19 and 0.17), and finally Indonesia, the system having the lowest score (0.03). In terms of degrees, as analysed in Chapter 3, India,

251 Bonifati, "Constitutional Design and the Seeds of Degradation," 244.

252 Constitutional Court of Bosnia and Herzegovina, Case U-9/09, 26 November 2010; Constitutional Court of Bosnia and Herzegovina, Case U-3/13, 26 November 2015.

253 Azem Kurtic, "Bosnia's Serb Entity Passes Law Rejecting Constitutional Court's Authority," *Balkan Insight* (28 June 2023), available at https://balkaninsight.com/2023/06/28/bosnias-serb-entity-passes-law-rejecting-constitutional-courts-authority/ (last accessed 16 September 2024).

Italy, and Spain fall within the medium degree interval, with the adequate distinctions, as India is at the higher end of the interval (thus could be defined medium/high degree), whereas Italy and Spain are at the lower end of the interval. Unsurprisingly, Indonesia falls within the low degree of asymmetry.

4.1 *The Indian Supreme Court*

When interpreting its role as umpire, the Indian Supreme Court was often criticised as being too active and intrusive in the domains reserved to the legislative and executive. Despite such criticisms, as previously explained, the Supreme Court often defended the rights of the subnational entities, especially in matters related to the destabilising attempts of the central government to weaken state governments.[254] Concerning the role of the Supreme Court in interpreting asymmetries in Indian federalism, a preliminary distinction should be made. Swenden and Saxena have noted that the Court "has been relatively permissive of asymmetry, even where some arrangements appeared to contradict fundamental rights (such as equality)".[255] However, when it comes to the special status of the former state of Jammu and Kashmir,[256] the attitude of the Supreme Court is far less supportive, as also demonstrated by the most recent decision on the abrogation of Art. 370 of the Indian Constitution.

Starting with the judgments confirming asymmetry, some of these dealt with those constitutional asymmetries entrenched in Schedule V and VI of the Indian Constitution. The Schedules aimed to accommodate "the unique socio-cultural characteristics of the life of the indigenous communities or scheduled tribes and ensuring their economic development in sync with the customs and traditions of specific tribes".[257] Specifically, Schedule VI lists a series of special provisions for the tribal areas in the states in the north-east

254 Rajendra Kumar Pandey, "Accommodating Diversity, Consolidating Nationhood. A Country Study of Constitutional Asymmetry in India," in *Constitutional Asymmetry in Multinational Federalism*, ed. Patricia Popelier and Maja Sahadžić (Cham: Palgrave Macmillan, 2019), 219.

255 Swenden and Saxena, "Policing the Federation," 22.

256 See Rouf Ahmad Dar, "Constitutions and Their Foundational Discontents: Studying the Process of Constitution-making in Jammu and Kashmir," *Global Constitutionalism* 12, no. 3 (2023): 543–61; Michael Fliri, "Federalism as a safeguard of national integrity: Trial and error in the case of Jammu and Kashmir," *Diversity Governance Papers*, no. 2 (2022): 5–17; Fozia Nazir Lone, *Historical Title, Self-Determination, and the Kashmir Question: Changing Perspectives in International Law* (Leiden and Boston: Brill | Nijhoff, 2018).

257 Pandey, "Accommodating Diversity, Consolidating Nationhood," 209.

(i.e., Assam, Meghalaya, Tripura, and Mizoram)[258] that Baruah argued were a legacy of colonial times,[259] whereas Schedule V provides for asymmetrical arrangements applicable to tribal areas in states outside the north-east.[260] For instance, in *Mangal Singh*,[261] the Supreme Court upheld inter- and intra-state asymmetries, as long as they conform to democratic norms and the doctrine of the separation of powers. According to such interpretation, Indian states are entitled to a certain degree of autonomy in their internal organisation, provided that they all have a separate executive, legislature, and judiciary. Moreover, in *State of Sikkim*,[262] the Supreme Court allowed for deviations from Art. 13(1) of the Indian Constitution,[263] confirming the continuation of laws enacted prior to their admission to the Union, even if they could be seen as conflicting with fundamental rights.[264] A similar derogation from democratic principles concerns representation in legislative bodies. Indeed, the Court upheld asymmetries in relation to legislative reservations for certain groups,[265] notwithstanding Art. 332(3) of the Constitution.[266] As argued by Swenden and Saxena, "the Supreme Court endorsed a form of asymmetric federalism in conformity with Article 2 of the Constitution according to which Parliament can admit new States into the union 'on terms and conditions as it sees fit'".[267] This reasoning can be seen as underpinning the Court's

---

258 Constitution of India – Schedule VI "Provisions as to the Administration of Tribal Areas in the States of Assam, Meghalaya, Tripura and Mizoram (Articles 244 (2) and 275 (1))."

259 See Sanjib Baruah, *In the Name of the Nation. India and its Northeast* (Redwood City: Stanford University Press, 2020).

260 Constitution of India – Schedule V "Provisions as to the Administration and Control of Scheduled Areas and Scheduled Tribes (Article 244 (1))."

261 Indian Supreme Court, *Mangal Singh v. Union of India*, AIR 1967, SC 944.

262 Indian Supreme Court, *State of Sikkim v. Surendra Prasad Sharma* (1984), 5 SCC 282

263 Constitution of India – Art. 13(1): "All laws in force in the territory of India immediately before the commencement of this Constitution, in so far as they are inconsistent with the provisions of this Part, shall, to the extent of such inconsistency, be void."

264 See Swenden and Saxena, "Policing the Federation," 23; Louise Tillin, "Asymmetric Federalism," in *The Oxford Handbook of the Indian Constitution*, ed. Sujit Choudhry, Madhav Khosla, and Pratap Bhanu Mehta (Oxford: Oxford University Press, 2016), 540–559.

265 Indian Supreme Court, *RC Poudyal v. Union of India* (1994) Supp 1 SCC 324.

266 Constitution of India – Art. 332(3): "The number of seats reserved for the Scheduled Castes or the Scheduled Tribes in the Legislative Assembly of any State under clause (1) shall bear, as nearly as may be, the same proportion to the total number of seats in the Assembly as the population of the Scheduled Castes in the State or of the Scheduled Tribes in the State or part of the State, as the case may be, in respect of which seats are so reserved, bears to the total population of the State."

267 Swenden and Saxena, "Policing the Federation," 23.

decision in *Ewalangki-E-Ryambai*,[268] in which the Court interpreted Schedule VI as a "self-contained code of governance of the tribal areas of Assam", to be considered as separate from "provisions which apply to other constituent States of the Union".[269] However, this appears to deviate from a previous judgment,[270] in which the Court "denounced legal pluralism and stressed the need for the Constitution to be considered a single legal order".[271]

As noted, the Supreme Court's permissive attitude towards asymmetry changes when it comes to special constitutional provisions on the former state of Jammu and Kashmir, entrenched in Art. 370 of the Constitution.[272] Before its accession to the Union in 1947, the territory was a princely state ruled by a Hindu king, but mostly populated by Muslims. As noted by Bhattacharyya, within the state there was hardly any internal territorial integration and Muslims were the majority only in the region of Kashmir, whereas the other two regions, Jammu and Ladakh, were respectively of Hindu and Buddhist majority.[273] Jammu and Kashmir joined as a state by means of an Instrument of Accession that granted extensive powers to the subnational entity, including the unique power to adopt its own subnational constitution.[274] If initially only Art. 1 and Art. 370 of the Constitution also applied to Jammu and Kashmir,[275] over time central governments progressively aimed to reduce the scope of its autonomy, for ideological or security reasons.[276] Specifically, central authorities relied on the "temporary" nature of these constitutional provisions,[277] and on the clauses contained in Art. 370 enabling the President of the Union with the concurrence of the Government of the State to extend the Parliament's powers to matters of the Union and concurrent lists, as well as

---

268 Indian Supreme Court, *Ewalangki-E-Ryambai v. Jaintia Hills District Council* (2006) 4 SCC 748.

269 Indian Supreme Court, *Ewalangki-E-Ryambai v. Jaintia Hills District Council* (2006) 4 SCC 748, 5.

270 Indian Supreme Court, *Pu Myllai Hlycho v. State of Mizoram* (2005) 2 SCC 92.

271 Swenden and Saxena, "Policing the Federation," 24.

272 Constitution of India – Art. 370 "Temporary provisions with respect to the State of Jammu and Kashmir."

273 Harihar Bhattacharyya, "The Current Challenges to Asymmetric Federalism in India in Comparative Perspective," *Perspective on Federalism* 16, no. 1 (2024): 1–25.

274 Until 2019, the state of Jammu and Kashmir was the only Indian state with its own constitution.

275 Constitution of India – Art. 370(1)c: "The provisions of article 1 and of this article shall apply in relation to that State."

276 Swenden and Saxena, "Policing the Federation," 24.

277 See Ritika Kanwar, "Abrogation of Article 370: Impact on Asymmetrical Federalism in India," *Indian Journal of Integrated Research in Law* 2, no. 3 (2022): 4.

to other provisions of the Constitution.[278] Potentially, these clauses could allow the reduction of constitutional asymmetries among states, re-aligning Jammu and Kashmir with the other Indian states.

One of the key issues in the constitutional challenges brought before the Supreme Court concerned precisely the "concurrence of the Government of the State" mentioned in Art. 370. Indeed, initially this was understood as the Constituent Assembly of Jammu and Kashmir, related to the actions undertaken when the Constituent Assembly was still operating. For instance, this was the case with the 1950 and 1954 Presidential Orders, issued before the dissolution of the Constituent Assembly in 1956. The several Presidential Orders that followed its dissolution were often designed as amendments of the 1954 order and were challenged in the Supreme Court shortly after. In 1959, in *Prem Nath Kaul*, the Court initially framed the controversial temporary nature of Art. 370 as confined only to the provisions requiring the consent of the Constituent Assembly.[279] Moreover, in the same decision, the Court ruled that, in the absence of the Constituent Assembly as final arbiter of the provisions extending parliamentary powers to the state, any additions to such powers would be invalid without its recommendation.[280] Nevertheless, in 1970 the Court overturned *Prem Nath Kaul*, insofar as in *Sampath Prakash*[281] the Supreme Court declared that the entirety of Art. 370 was still in operation, including the provisions requiring the Constituent Assembly's consent. Therefore, it was not necessary to contest the legitimacy of the post-dissolution Presidential Orders. The decision in *Sampath Prakash* sparked academic debate over the meaning of this judgment in relation to the temporary or permanent nature of Art. 370. If Swenden and Saxena argued that the fact that the Court declared the article in usage "did not necessarily amount to

278 Constitution of India – Art. 370(1)b: "The power of Parliament to make laws for the said State shall be limited to: (i) those matters in the Union List and the Concurrent List which, in consultation with the Government of the State, are declared by the President to correspond to matters specified in the Instrument of Accession governing the accession of the State to the Dominion of India as the matters with respect to which the Dominion Legislature may make laws for that State; and (ii) such other matters in the said Lists, as, with the concurrence of the Government of the State, the President may by order specify." The article further clarifies that any other provision of the Indian Constitution may apply to the State of Jammu and Kashmir by order of the President, provided that these provisions are issued in consultation and with the concurrence of the government of the state (see Art. 370(1)d).

279 Indian Supreme Court, *Prem Nath Kaul v. State of Jammu and Kashmir* AIR 1959 SC 749.

280 Balu Gopalakrishnan Nair, "Abrogation of Article 370: Can the President Act Without the Recommendation of the Constituent Assembly?" *Indian Law Review* 3, no. 3 (2019): 261.

281 Indian Supreme Court, *Sampath Prakash v. State of Jammu and Kashmir* AIR 1970 SC 1118.

its permanence",[282] Nair[283] and Kanwar[284] interpreted this decision as an implicit inclusion of Art. 370 in the basic structure, thus confirming its permanence. In 1972, in *Mohd. Maqbook Damnoo*,[285] the Supreme Court upheld the right of the state Governor, appointed by the central government, "to substitute for the state government's concurrence to proposed amendments under Article 370".[286] As noted by Tillin, this decision indicates the Court's role in strengthening the President of India as "guardian of the spirit of autonomy",[287] rather than protecting the special status of Jammu and Kashmir from political intervention. Moreover, Khosla observed that, paradoxically, the possibility given by the Court to the President and the Governor to act without the consent of the Constituent Assembly of Jammu and Kashmir or the state's parliament "has given the Union powers vis-à-vis the State of [Jammu and Kashmir] that it does not ordinarily have with respect to the states".[288]

The special status of Jammu and Kashmir became again a prominent issue when, in August 2019, the Union government led by Prime Minister Narendra Modi honoured the Hinduist nationalist party's (BJP) long-standing promise of abrogating Art. 370. Through the issue of a Presidential Order,[289] the federal government made all provisions of the Indian Constitution applicable to the state of Jammu and Kashmir. Unsurprisingly, the dramatic re-design of the status of Jammu and Kashmir was highly criticised and the use of the Presidential Order was much contested. As noted by Kanwar, critics argued that the Presidential Order was a "colourable exercise of power"[290] and an unjustified action, which further did not comply with the mandate provided by Art. 370(3), insofar as the Presidential Order was passed unilaterally by the central authority without the necessary recommendation of the Constituent Assembly. For its part, the government argued that the Presidential Order was a lawful exercise of power, and that the requirements under Art. 370(3) were met since, in the absence of a state parliament that had been suspended due to presidential rule under the already mentioned Art. 356, the necessary rec-

---

282 Swenden and Saxena, "Policing the Federation," 24.
283 Nair, "Abrogation of Article 370," 269.
284 Kanwar, "Abrogation of Article 370," 5.
285 Indian Supreme Court, *Mohd. Maqbook Damnoo v. State of Jammu and Kashmir* (1972) 1 SCC 536.
286 Swenden and Saxena, "Policing the Federation," 24.
287 Tillin, "Asymmetric Federalism," 548.
288 Madhav Khosla, *The Indian Constitution* (Oxford: Oxford University Press, 2012), 76.
289 Constitution (Application to Jammu and Kashmir) Order 2019.
290 Kanwar, "Abrogation of Article 370," 6.

ommendations were taken by the state Governor.[291] Since the Indian Constitution enables the central parliament to create new states after the President has obtained consent from the state parliament,[292] the union legislature passed the 2019 Jammu and Kashmir (Reorganisation) Act, providing for the bifurcation of the state of Jammu and Kashmir into two separate union territories: the Union Territory of Jammu and Kashmir (with a legislative assembly), and the Union Territory of Ladakh (without a legislative assembly). As such, they now enjoy much less autonomy than what was entrenched in Art. 370, and the central authority can exercise better control and administration over the territory.[293] From a procedural (and democratic) point of view, the fact that the abrogation occurred when the central authority had suspended subnational autonomy through the exercise of Art. 356, thus leaving the state without a democratically elected body, is highly problematic. Indeed, Kanwar emphasised that "there was no constitutional body to make the recommendations either under Article 370(3) or under Article 3".[294] In terms of the impact of the abrogation on asymmetry, this led to a profound contraction of constitutional asymmetry in India, and Kanwar rightly observed that post-abrogation "federal asymmetry of the country [...] is being under constant threat with the respect to the special status granted to other states in accordance with the constitutional provisions".[295] Moreover, Bhattacharyya argued that though the reorganisation of the Indian territory is not something new, since it has happened many times since 1947,[296] the fact that Jammu and Kashmir was "the only Muslim majority region of the State bordering with Pakistan carries special significance".[297]

Regarding the role of the Supreme Court in the changing status of Jammu and Kashmir, it should first be noted that, in 2017, the Supreme Court acknowledged the special status of Jammu and Kashmir and appeared to interpret Art. 370 as a permanent feature of the Constitution.[298] In doing so, the

291 Ibidem.

292 See Constitution of India – Art. 3.

293 Kanwar, "Abrogation of Article 370," 2.

294 Kanwar, "Abrogation of Article 370," 6.

295 Kanwar, "Abrogation of Article 370," 8.

296 Before the demotion of Jammu and Kashmir from state to union territory, the latest reorganisation was in 2014 with the creation of the state of Telangana (see Kham Khan Suan Hausing, "Telangana and the Politics of State Formation in India: Recognition and Accommodation in a Multinational Federation," *Regional & Federal Studies* 28, no. 4 (2018): 447–68).

297 Bhattacharyya, "The Current Challenges to Asymmetric Federalism," 4.

298 Indian Supreme Court, *State Bank of India v. Santosh Gupta* (2017) 2 SCC 538.

Court relied on the constitutional provision stating that Art. 370 can be abrogated only with the necessary recommendation of the Constituent Assembly of Jammu and Kashmir.[299] However, in December 2023, when the Supreme Court finally heard the 22 writ petitions challenging the 2019 governmental action, the constitutional bench upheld the governmental decision to abrogate Art. 370.[300] In its *In Re Article 370 of the Constitution*, the Supreme Court eventually framed Art. 370 as temporary and concluded: "The State of Jammu and Kashmir does not retain any element of sovereignty after the execution of the [Instrument of Accession] and the issuance of the Proclamation dated 25 November 1949 by which the Constitution of India was adopted. The State of Jammu and Kashmir does not have 'internal sovereignty' which is distinguishable from the powers and privileges enjoyed by other States in the country. *Article 370 was a feature of asymmetric federalism and not sovereignty*; [...]."[301] Therefore, the much-awaited decision of the Supreme Court, that arrived after it remained pending for four years, was extremely significant insofar as it confirmed the drastic re-design of constitutional asymmetry in India and framed asymmetric federalism as a temporary feature of the Indian Constitution.

For what concerns the future of constitutional asymmetry in India, Pandey argued that "whatsoever constitutional asymmetries are provided in the Indian Constitution, they are designed to be transitional and temporary provisions with the prospects of withering away in future. Thus, presumably the ultimate objective of the Indian Constitution is to make the Indian federation as symmetric as possible".[302] This view is also shared by Kumar, who observed that "the practice of Indian asymmetrical federalism assumes asymmetry as a social fact by keeping it 'temporary' and 'transitional' in the Constitutional provisions (Part XXI) to reach cooperative federalism as a contingent functioning, if not completely symmetrical federalism as its outcome".[303] The cur-

299 Constitution of India – Art. 370(3): "Notwithstanding anything in the foregoing provisions of this article, the President may, by public notification, declare that this article shall cease to be operative or shall be operative only with such exceptions and modifications and from such date as he may specify: Provided that the recommendation of the Constituent Assembly of the State referred to in clause (2) shall be necessary before the President issues such a notification."

300 Indian Supreme Court, *In Re Article 370 of the Constitution* (2023), WP (C) 1013/2019.

301 Indian Supreme Court, *In Re Article 370 of the Constitution* (2023), para. 514(a).

302 Pandey, "Accommodating Diversity, Consolidating Nationhood," 233.

303 Pratyush Kumar, "'Asymmetrical Symmetricalism' of Indian Constitutional Structure and Practice: Note on Govt. of National Capital Territory ('NCT') of Delhi v Union of India," *DPCE Online*, no. 2 (2022): 3038.

rent attitude of the Supreme Court to the abrogation of Art. 370 seems to confirm these symmetrical aspirations of Indian federalism.[304]

4.2 *The Italian Constitutional Court*

Especially in its early jurisprudence, the Italian Constitutional Court often addressed asymmetry-related disputes. This was also due to the fact that originally the Italian regional system was mainly composed of the five special regions and ordinary regions were only set up in the early 1970s. Specifically, the Constitutional Court contributed to defining the principle of "bilateral cooperation"[305] as the "essential and mandatory core of the constitutional principle of specialty"[306] (and thus of asymmetry). According to this principle, the specific rules regulating special regions cannot be reviewed and implemented unilaterally, neither by the central government nor by the special regions and autonomous provinces. Moreover, the fundamental features of specialty, i.e., the principle of negotiation and balanced rules on coexistence in South Tyrol, cannot be revised.[307] As noted by Palermo and Valdesalici, "the untouchable core of the autonomy statutes appears to be connected with a procedural profile,"[308] consisting of those procedures through which the statute and its rules can be amended, in compliance with the principle of bilateral cooperation. The presence of an implicit limit to constitutional review was further confirmed by the Constitutional Court, holding that statute revisions cannot disrupt the basic elements of specialty since these "belong to the essence of the supreme values"[309] on which the system of specialty and the entire constitutional order rely. It should be added that, within these procedural limits, there is one exception to the contents of the autonomy statutes that can be revised. This concerns the autonomy statute of South Tyrol, and the "unmodifiable guarantee of a system of group rights and rules of coexistence".[310] Aside from upholding the principle of bilateral cooperation, the Constitutional Court also drove the settlement of the differentiated system

304 For a particularly critical perspective on the meaning of asymmetrical federalism in India, see Louise Tillin, "United in Diversity? Asymmetry in Indian Federalism," *Publius: The Journal of Federalism* 37, no. 1 (2006): 45–67.

305 See Italian Constitutional Court, decision 213/1998.

306 Francesco Palermo, and Alice Valdesalici, "Irreversibly Different. A Country Study of Constitutional Asymmetry in Italy," in *Constitutional Asymmetry in Multinational Federalism*, ed. Patricia Popelier and Maja Sahadžić (Cham: Palgrave Macmillan, 2019), 292.

307 Ibidem.

308 Ibidem.

309 See Italian Constitutional Court, decisions 1146/1988 and 366/1991.

310 Palermo and Valdesalici, "Irreversibly Different," 293.

of intergovernmental relations for the special regions. Indeed, each special region has a joint body,[311] grounded in the principle of parity and thus composed of an equal number of representatives from the central level and of the region.[312] The joint bodies are a distinct trait of Italian special regions, insofar as they can "negotiate with the central authority, bilaterally and on equal footing, the development of their self-government".[313] These bodies implement the respective autonomy statutes by drafting by-laws that are then submitted to the central government, which later approves them through governmental decrees. It should be noted that these decrees cannot be repealed or amended by-laws, neither of region nor of the central parliament, and they have a special rank in the system of laws. Such special rank means that they have a superior binding force compared to all other governmental decrees, and have a higher position than ordinary legislation, being subordinated only to the Italian Constitution.[314] Originally, this settlement was not provided for in the autonomy statutes and the rationale of the Constitutional Court in framing it was the "need to overcome the majority-minority ration reflected in the law-making procedures at the central level".[315] Moreover, the Court grounded this differentiated system of IGR in the principle of specialty, consistently upholding this principle,[316] and stated that, as sources of laws, the decrees can even integrate autonomy statute provisions, as long as they do not betray the founding aims of the statute within the principle of regional autonomy.[317] Finally, the Constitutional Court upheld the asymmetry in fiscal arrangements according to which special regions are afforded a more extensive taxing power.[318]

After this first phase in which the Court's jurisprudence was generally oriented towards the defence of asymmetry, the revisitation of the distribution of competences between the state and the regions enacted by the 2001 constitutional reform led to a dramatic turning point and to an increase in constitu-

311 For further references on joint bodies, see Nicolò Paolo Alessi, "Joint Bodies – a Key Factor for Successful Autonomous Systems? The Cases of the Italian Special Regions and the Åland Islands," *Journal of Autonomy and Security Studies* 5, no. 1 (2021): 8–25.

312 For South Tyrol, the equal representation of linguistic group is provided by a special commission of six members that are appointed within the regional body.

313 Palermo and Valdesalici, "Irreversibly Different," 296.

314 Ibidem.

315 Ibidem.

316 Italian Constitutional Court, decisions 20/1956, 22/1961, 151/1972, 180/1980, 237/1983, 212/1984, 160/1985.

317 Italian Constitutional Court, decisions 20/1956, 212/1984, 341/2001.

318 Italian Constitutional Court, decision 102/2008.

tional adjudication by the Italian Constitutional Court, as both levels of government sought clarification over their powers and competences. In many instances, the Court justified the expanding role of the central level, regarding it as the "guardian of the national interest",[319] hidden behind new interpretative mechanisms and advocating a centralising reading of competences. This further reduced the asymmetries between special and ordinary regions and became even more evident first during the global economic crisis of the early 2010s and then during the Covid-19 pandemic. Starting from 2010, the principle of bilateral cooperation was put under pressure, when central legislation significantly reduced the financial autonomy of special regions. The austerity measures enacted at the central level were deemed legitimate by the Constitutional Court, justifying a broad interpretation of concurrent powers under Art. 117(3) of the Italian Constitution on the basis of the urgency of the legislative measures.[320] Moreover, according to the Court, in such circumstances the central government is empowered to limit financial transfers and impose the reduction of expenditures.[321] However, the Constitutional Court also held that such power cannot circumvent the principle of bilateral cooperation,[322] thus protecting the fundamental principle underlying the relationship between the central state and the special regions. The tendency to uphold resymmetrisation legislation was also confirmed during the Covid-19 pandemic. Indeed, a particularly significant case concerning asymmetry is judgment 37/2021, when the Court struck down a regional law of a special region, i.e., Aosta Valley, which provided for anti-pandemic measures.[323] In this case, although health is a concurrent power between the state and the regions under Art. 117(3) of the Italian Constitution, the Court framed the anti-pandemic measures as "international prophylaxis", and thus as an exclusive competence of the central state. This decision came in a particularly complex phase of the pandemic and was highly criticised, when a delicate equilibrium between the central and subnational governments had been reached through a renewed impetus of intergovernmental relations, and such a centralising interpretation of competences deeply affected that equilibrium. The brief analysis of these cases appears to show that, in times of change (e.g., the 2001 constitutional reform or

319 Palermo and Valdesalici, "Irreversibly Different," 298.

320 See Italian Constitutional Court, decision 10/2010.

321 See Italian Constitutional Court, decisions 182/2011, 262/2012, 104/2013, 229/2013, 19/2014, and 26/2014.

322 See Italian Constitutional Court, decisions 198/2012 and 199/2012.

323 See Ignazio Spadaro, "Decentramento politico e pandemia: spunti per un 'regionalismo dell'emergenza'," *Rivista AIC* 4 (2022): 146–165.

the 2010s and 2020s emergencies), the Italian Constitutional Court tended towards expanding the competences of the central level, reducing the space for asymmetry.

What makes Italy a particularly interesting and complex case is the presence, at least potentially, of different forms of constitutional asymmetries. Indeed, alongside the original special status envisaged for some territories, a hypothetical implementation of Art. 116(3) of the Constitution would introduce into the legal system a form of "differentiation" that seems to be nothing more than a (further) variation of constitutional asymmetry.[324] As already observed by Palermo and Valdesalici,[325] in Italy, the implementation of "differentiated autonomy" regularly emerges in the political discourse of some political parties and the most recent example of this trend is precisely Law no. 86 of 2024,[326] which has been debated at length by Italian legal scholarship.[327] In this case too, it is significant to recall the position of the Constitu-

324 An interesting perspective on differentiation and asymmetries is provided by Bifulco, although the author proposes a different interpretation, according to which differentiations are to be interpreted as *de facto* asymmetries (i.e. those inevitable differences within any system, federal or otherwise), while asymmetries are to be interpreted as solely *de jure* asymmetries (cfr. Bifulco, "Differenziazioni e asimmetrie," 139–72).

325 Palermo, and Valdesalici, "Irreversibly Different," 308.

326 Law no. 86 of 26 June 2024 "Provisions for the implementation of the differentiated autonomy of Regions with ordinary statute pursuant to article 116, third paragraph of the Constitution".

327 See Marina Calamo Specchia, "L'autonomia differenziata e la solidarietà interterritoriale: spunti di riflessione per una riforma costituzionalmente sostenibile," *Osservatorio Costituzionale*, no. 5 (2023): 1–16; Eleonora Rinaldi, "Some Reflections on the Implementation of Art. 116(3) of the Italian Constitution. Law 86/2024 and Limits to "Differentiated Regionalism," *Rivista di Diritti Comparati*, no. 3 (2024): 34–60. For further references on the Italian doctrine on differentiated regionalism, see Antonio D'Atena, "A proposito della 'clausola di asimmetria' (art. 116 u.c. cost.)," *Rivista AIC*, no. 4 (2020): 313–33; Paolo Giovarruscio, "Il fondamento costituzionale del regionalismo differenziato. Omogeneità e differenziazione," *Istituzioni del Federalismo*, no. 3 (2023): 491–507; Andrea Patroni Griffi, "Regionalismo differenziato," in *Digesto delle discipline pubblicistiche* (Torino: Utet, 2021); Giovanni Tarli Barbieri, "«Il passaggio dall'idea al fatto è sempre penoso». L'autonomia differenziata tra mito e realtà," *Diritti Regionali*, no. 1 (2024): 81–112; Fulvio Cortese, "Regioni e leale cooperazione," *Le Regioni*, no. 1 (2023): 37–54; Giuliana G. Carboni, "L'attuazione dell'art. 116, comma terzo, Cost. e l'illusione del regionalismo competitivo," *Quaderni Costituzionali*, no. 2 (2023): 405–7; Michele Belletti, "Dialogo sulle dinamiche di ricentralizzazione del regionalismo. Quali prospettive?," *Le Regioni*, no. 1 (2024): 73–86; Giulio M. Salerno, "L'autonomia differenziata: problema o prospettiva costituzionale?," *Federalismi.it*, no. 19 (2023): iv–xi. See also the issues 2/2024 and 3/2023 of the journal *Istituzioni del Federalismo*, as well as issue 2/2023 of the journal *Italian Papers on Federalism*, dedicated to differentiated autonomy.

tional Court, which recently expressed its opinion on the law in its judgment 192/2024,[328] already defined by many as a landmark judgment for having rewritten the regional form of state.[329] In this decision, the Court declared that some of the provisions of the law were unconstitutional (but not the law in its entirety) and reiterated that Art. 116(3) "allows for the uniformity of the allocation of competences to be overcome in order to fully realise the potential inherent in Italian regionalism".[330] However, this constitutional provision "cannot be considered as an isolated monad, but must be placed within the overall framework of the Italian form of state […]",[331] in which regionalism is identified by the Court as a fundamental element.

For the purposes of this chapter, two aspects should be considered. On the one hand, it is worth noting that the Court has expressed a "constitutionally systematic and updated vision"[332] of the Italian regional system, based on the "coexistence and dialectic of pluralism and unity"[333] without calling into question the unity and indivisibility of the Republic. According to this interpretation, the main aspects of Law no. 86 of 2024, namely the transfer of entire matters (and not specific functions), the marginalisation of the Parliament in the transfer process and in the determination of the Essential Levels of Performance, and the financial framework that should have supported differentiated autonomy, were considered by the Court to be an expression of a "dual regionalism" (and, as such, divisive). Conversely, Italian regionalism is part of a "cooperative" model,[334] based on the principle of loyal cooperation and on the implementation of constitutional principles and rights, and Art. 116(3) must be traced back to this model.[335] On the other hand, it is interesting to note that the Court recognises that "the differentiation contemplated by Art. 116, third paragraph, of the Constitution, […] can be not a factor of disintegration of national unity and social cohesion, but an instrument at the ser-

328 Italian Constitutional Court, decision 192/2024.

329 See, for example, the comments by Enzo Cheli, "La forma di Stato regionale in una storica sentenza della Corte costituzionale," *Astrid Rassegna*, no. 18 (2024): 1–3; Andrea Morrone, "Lo Stato regionale dopo la sent. n. 192 del 2024," *Giustizia Insieme* (28 January 2025); Antonino Spadaro, "La 'Quadratura del cerchio' … o della sent. cost. n. 192/2024," *Diritti Regionali*, no. 1 (2025): 1–29.

330 Italian Constitutional Court, decision 192/2024, *considerato in diritto*, 4 [English translation by the author].

331 Ibidem.

332 Cheli, "La forma di Stato regionale," 1.

333 Italian Constitutional Court, decision 192/2024 *considerato in diritto*, 4 [English translation by the author].

334 Ibidem.

335 Ibidem.

vice of the common good of society and the protection of the rights of individuals and social groups".[336] Therefore, the Court seems to contemplate possible further spaces of differentiation (and therefore of asymmetry), as long as these are functional to the protection of rights. Moreover, this seems to foster the idea of sustainable asymmetries as a tool for further integration of in federal systems, previously discussed in Chapter 2.[337]

4.3 *The Spanish Constitutional Tribunal*

As already mentioned, in the Spanish constitutional system, the autonomous status of the subnational entities is recognised in the statutes of autonomy of each nationality or region (i.e., the autonomous communities), which have the potential to establish different levels of self-government. The initial asymmetries among autonomous communities (ACs), which saw the Basque Country and Catalonia in a differentiated position from the other later established ACs, was significantly reduced in a symmetrisation process that had already started in the early 1980s with the adoption of the Organic Law for the Harmonisation of the Process of Self-Government (LOAPA)[338] and that continued in the 1990s. In this process, the Spanish Constitutional Tribunal played a pivotal role. Indeed, in a fundamental decision,[339] the Court invalidated a significant part of the LOAPA, that was enacted in 1982 by the state parliament in an attempt to recentralise powers and delay the development of the state of autonomies, pushing in a resymmetrisation direction. In its judgment, the Court ruled that the state government could not unilaterally redefine the distribution of powers via Art. 150(3) of the Spanish Constitution.[340] In fact, the Court interpreted that constitutional provision as an extraordinary measure to be used in very restricted circumstances, and argued that the preservation of the "general interest" could also be achieved through ordinary means, such as ordinary legislation.[341] Relative to asymmetry, the Court "recognised the balance between homogeneity and heterogeneity and thus a certain degree

336 Ibidem.

337 See Chapter 2, paragraph 2.4.

338 *Ley Orgánica de Armonización del Proceso Autonómico* (1982).

339 Spanish Constitutional Tribunal, decision 76/1983.

340 Constitution of Spain – Art. 150(3): "The State may enact laws laying down the necessary principles for harmonising the rulemaking provisions of the Self-governing Communities, even in the case of matters over which jurisdiction has been vested to the latter, where this is necessary in the general interest. It is incumbent upon the Cortes Generales, by overall majority of the members of each House, to evaluate this necessity."

341 Kössler, "The Role of Constitutional Judges," 163.

of asymmetry as a hallmark of the state of the autonomies".[342] However, already at this stage, the Court did not invalidate the organic law completely, and the parts that were upheld proved to be decisive for a more symmetrical distribution of powers among autonomous communities.

Reacting to the central state's tendency towards symmetry, in 2004 and 2005 the Basque Country and Catalonia proposed reforms to their autonomy statutes, to re-establish their original asymmetrical position, also through the introduction of self-determination clauses. However, both sets of proposals failed, with a strong role played by the Constitutional Tribunal. The Basque 2004 proposal was first rejected by the central parliament given that, among other provisions, Art. 1 of the reformed statute would have established a Basque Community that was "freely associated with Spain", claiming a "right to decide".[343] Following the central parliament rejection, the subnational legislative assembly enacted the Law 9/2008, intending to hold a referendum on the "right to decide" of the Basque people about whether to remain an integral part of Spain or to form an independent Basque Community. The Spanish Constitutional Tribunal declared the Basque law unconstitutional in decision 103/2008, upholding the position of the central government. Aside from having struck down a potential source for increasing asymmetry, the Court's decision is also interesting because it consolidated the view of national sovereignty as belonging exclusively to the Spanish people, thus forbidding the call for "a referendum on self-determination or any other issue that would require a constitutional reform".[344] The Court stated that, on substantial constitutional questions such as sovereignty, self-determination, and secession, only the constituent power "through due constitutional procedures can give public and official answers",[345] thus framing such power in terms of procedure and not of political body.

The Catalan case is slightly different. In fact, the process of reform of the 2006 Catalan Statute of Autonomy had been legally completed through parliamentary agreement and ratification through popular referendum. However, many of the amendments introduced by the 2006 Statute of Autonomy were overruled and neutralised by the Spanish Constitutional Tribunal in the highly controversial judgment 31/2010.[346] Until the Catalan decision, the fundamen-

342 Kössler, "The Role of Constitutional Judges," 163.

343 Bossacoma and Sanjaume, "Asymmetry as a Device for Equal Recognition," 442.

344 Bossacoma and Sanjaume, "Asymmetry as a Device for Equal Recognition," 446.

345 Ibidem.

346 See Francesco Biagi, "*Estatut de Catalunya* e la crisi di legittimazione del *Tribunal constitucional*," *Quaderni Costituzionali* 31, no. 1 (2011): 63–87; Jean-Baptiste Harguindéguy,

tal role of the statutes of autonomy in completing the constitutional design of the regional state was generally accepted, and statutes were considered part of the "block of constitutionality".[347] Conversely, in the Catalan decision, the Court disregarded the legal and negotiated nature of the reformed statute and equated statutes to ordinary legislation (i.e., "organic laws"), and as such concluded they are to be finally enacted by the central state parliament. The Spanish Constitutional Tribunal also found the provisions on Catalonia's participation in state and EU institutions to be void of any normative content and to be entirely dependent on the Spanish state legislation. Beyond deactivating most of the core elements of the reformed Statute of Autonomy, the Court ended up re-constructing them "in a way that went against their original meaning and left them with no legal effect".[348] Unsurprisingly, the Court's decision was received with criticism in academic, political, and public spheres. First, the Court was criticised because it deactivated a reformed statute that was legally agreed and passed in both central and subnational parliaments and approved by referendum. Then, the Court never openly explained why it departed from its previous case law, and it was under considerable political pressure to reach a decision on a delicate and divisive matter.[349] The Court itself was divided and could reach a decision only by voting on different blocks on the challenged legal provisions: the first block included the preamble of the statute and the reference to Catalonia as a nation, the second concerned the provisions declared unconstitutional, the third addressed the provisions declared constitutional, and the fourth one regarded the provisions that were "re-construed" to render them constitutional.[350] Among the possible reasons that led the constitutional judges to reach their decision are that some considered the statute to be a threat to national unity, considered that such substantial reform should be carried out through constitutional amendments, and that the political climate was too controversial to introduce such changes without a wider consensus at the central level.[351] In political terms, for those critical of the decision, the Court was influenced by the political forces opposing the wave of reforms, and by bowing to such pressures it departed from its previous case law and adopted a restrictive interpre-

---

Gonzalo Sola Rodríguez, and José Cruz Díaz, "Between Justice and Politics: The Role of the Spanish Constitutional Court in the State of Autonomies," *Territory, Politics, Governance* 8, no. 2(2018): 222–40.

347 Casanas Adam, "The Constitutional Court of Spain," 394.

348 Ibidem.

349 Casanas Adam, "The Constitutional Court of Spain," 396.

350 Casanas Adam, "The Constitutional Court of Spain," 389.

351 See Casanas Adam, "The Constitutional Court of Spain," 388–395.

tation of the role of the autonomous communities and their statutes in the Spanish state of autonomies. Conversely, those supporting the Spanish Constitutional Tribunal argued that the Court was simply being a safeguard of the constitutional model introduced by the 1978 Constitution.

Overall, the decision 31/2010 is said to have played a significant role in reigniting the pro-secession movements already present in Catalonia.[352] Indeed, following the Court's decision, the political climate in Spain and in Catalonia became more confrontational, leading to the adoption of the "Declaration of Sovereignty and the Right to Decide of the People of Catalonia" by the Catalan Parliament,[353] calling for a self-determination referendum. The Declaration was challenged by the Spanish government and the Spanish Constitutional Tribunal later delivered another decision,[354] declaring that, though the "declaration of sovereignty" was incompatible with the Constitution, the "right to decide" could be interpreted as "the expression of a political aspiration susceptible to being defended within the constitutional framework".[355] Moreover, the Court also called for dialogue and cooperation among levels of government, thus taking a first step towards reconsidering its position as mediator in a plurinational state.[356]

In conclusion, these decisions allow us to understand how the Spanish Constitutional Tribunal, after an initial defence of territorial self-government and asymmetry (decision 76/1983), generally upheld the symmetrisation trend brought forward by the central state (decisions 103/2008, and especially 31/2010). After these critical decisions, Bossacoma and Sanjaume concluded that the inevitable diversity deriving from the powers enshrined in the different autonomy statutes became secondary.[357]

4.4 *The Indonesian Courts*

The Indonesian case is particularly interesting because the two judicial bodies entitled to review central and subnational legislation, respectively the Constitutional Court and the Supreme Court, appear to have confirmed the existing asymmetries in the two special provinces of Papua and Aceh, amidst many

352 Bossacoma and Sanjaume, "Asymmetry as a Device for Equal Recognition," 443.

353 Catalan Parliament, Resolution no. 13, 24 January 2013.

354 Spanish Constitutional Tribunal, decision 42/2014 (for more on this decision, see Víctor Ferreres Comella, "The Spanish Constitutional Court Confronts Catalonia's 'Right to Decide' (Comment on the Judgment 42/2014)," *European Constitutional Law Review* 10, no. 3 (2014): 571–90).

355 Casanas Adam, "The Constitutional Court of Spain," 400.

356 Ibidem.

357 Bossacoma and Sanjaume, "Asymmetry as a Device for Equal Recognition," 450.

controversies. Specifically, this section addresses the decisions of the Constitutional Court on the Papuan customary voting system (i.e., *noken*), and an "implicit" decision of the Supreme Court on the Aceh Islamic Criminal Code (i.e., *Quanun Jinayat*).

4.4.1 The Indonesian Constitutional Court

Starting with the Constitutional Court's decisions on customary voting systems, the cases concerned the customary voting system in Papua, generally referred to as *noken* and employed since the 1971 general elections and still used in the majority of Papuan electoral districts.[358] The term *noken* literally refers to a traditional bag made of bark,[359] but is also used to indicate a series of voting practices. Among these, one is the *noken gantung* ("hanging bag"), involving the customary chief instructing the constituent to vote for their candidate by putting their votes in a bag and not in a secret ballot. The goal of this system is to distribute votes to a single candidate or amongst candidates in a proportion determined by the customary chief or agreed upon by the community.[360] The second system is the "Bigman process",[361] under which citizens allow the customary chief to vote on their behalf. This means that voters do not need to physically attend the polling stations and that community leaders agree on how many votes each candidate should get, then send annotated tally forms to election officials in their regional area.[362] Candidates who lost elections in which this voting system had been used challenged the results in the Constitutional Court, since the Court is entitled to decide disputes over the results of general elections.[363] In its jurisprudence, the Constitutional Court has consistently upheld the practice of the traditional *noken* voting system used in the special region of Papua as a legitimate expression of the local customs and as such protected by Art. 18B(2) of the Indonesian Constitution, which provides that the state "recognises and respects the *adat* [customary]

358 Simon Butt, "Indonesia's Constitutional Court and Indonesia's Electoral System," in *Constitutional Courts in Asia*, ed. Albert HY Chen and Andrew Harding (Cambridge: Cambridge University Press, 2018), 236.

359 See Cillian Nolan, "Votes in the Bag? The Noken System and Conflict in Papua," *International Crisis Group* (11 September 2012), available at https://www.crisisgroup.org/asia/south-east-asia/indonesia/votes-bag-noken-system-and-conflict-indonesian-papua (last accessed 27 August 2024).

360 Butt, "Indonesia's Constitutional Court," 236.

361 Butt, "Indonesia's Constitutional Court," 237.

362 Ibidem.

363 Constitution of Indonesia – Art. 24C(1).

law communities and their traditional rights".[364] In the 2009 *Papua* DPD *case*,[365] the Constitutional Court stated that it "can understand and value the cultural values alive in the unique Papua community in running the election by 'community agreement' or 'acclamation'".[366] The Court also added that it accepted the method of collective voting and argued that such a method had already been accepted in previous elections in the Yahukimo county because, if forced to hold elections according to the applicable electoral legislation, there were concerns over a possible re-emergence of conflict in the community. Therefore, also in the *Papua* DPD *case*, the Court believed that "it is best that they are not involved/carried to a system of competition/division within and between groups that could disturb the harmony with which they have been instilled".[367] It should be recalled that constitutional asymmetry in Papua was introduced after decades of conflict between separatist movements and governmental forces. Indeed, Papuan people held that they were culturally and ethnically distinct[368] from other Indonesians and that they never explicitly agreed to join Indonesia,[369] therefore the maintenance of customary laws and practices has been considered an important recognition of subnational identity.

However, though the Court took the decision to uphold asymmetry to avoid conflict, these local voting processes can be highly problematic from a democratic perspective. Specifically, these procedures do not ensure free and fair elections, nor the transparency of the electoral process,[370] and are in tension with Art. 22E(1) of the Constitution, which requires that "general elections shall be conducted in a direct, public, free, secret, honest, and fair manner".[371] Unsurprisingly, when using a voting system based on the placement of votes publicly in a bag and not in a secret ballot, the vote is neither free nor secret.[372] Nevertheless, as observed by Butt, the Constitutional Court "has not sought to openly reconcile Article 22E(1) with recognising these customary voting processes via Article 18B(2)".[373] Moreover, another shortcoming of up-

364 Constitution of Indonesia – Art. 18B(2).

365 Indonesian Constitutional Court, Decision No. 4/PHPU.A-VII/2009.

366 Indonesian Constitutional Court, Decision No. 4/PHPU.A-VII/2009, para 3.24.

367 Ibidem.

368 The ethnic composition of Papua is mainly Melanesian and for much of Indonesian history Papua was known as "Irian" (see Butt, "Provincial Asymmetry in Indonesia," 237).

369 Butt, "Provincial Asymmetry in Indonesia," 228.

370 Butt, "Provincial Asymmetry in Indonesia," 245–246.

371 Constitution of Indonesia – Art. 22E(1).

372 Butt, "Indonesia's Constitutional Court," 238.

373 Butt, "Indonesia's Constitutional Court," 238.

holding the legality of *noken* systems concerns the overall lack of transparency and the high susceptibility to fraud and conspiracy in fixing outcomes, especially between candidates and customary chiefs. This issue was at the heart of the 2013 *Papua gubernatorial election case*,[374] in which the applicant complained that the *noken* electoral process was a "conspiracy between the regional electoral commission and his competitors to ensure his defeat".[375] Even in the best of cases, when fraud does not occur and chiefs act in good faith preferring one candidate over the others for public policy reasons, elections held according to *noken* voting would still lead to skewed results with 100% participation rates (and with 100% of votes for one candidate),[376] whereas generally participation rates in Indonesian general elections are around 75–80%.[377]

4.4.2 The Indonesian Supreme Court

Moving to the case on the Aceh Islamic Criminal Code, this concerns the already discussed *Qanun Jinayat* enacted in 2014 by the Aceh provincial authorities in accordance with Law 11 of 2006 on the autonomous government of Aceh. The applicants challenged the validity of the Islamic Criminal Code before the Supreme Court, arguing that it violated international human rights standards, as well as domestic legislation on human rights protection.[378] Indeed, the *Qanun Jinayat* criminalises various activities involving consenting adults; allows for the imposition of controversial punishments (e.g., caning); makes rape very difficult to prove; and enables the so-called religious police to enforce the *Qanun*.[379] One of the most controversial aspects regards the fact that the Aceh Islamic Criminal Code claims to be superior to national legisla-

374 Indonesian Constitutional Court, Decision No. 14/PHPU.D-XI/2013.

375 Butt, "Indonesia's Constitutional Court," 237.

376 Butt, "Indonesia's Constitutional Court," 238.

377 Since 2004, the lowest turnout in presidential election was in 2014 (69.78%), whereas the highest was in 2019 (81.97%) (see Statista, "Participation rate of the presidential election in Indonesia from 2004 to 2019," (21 February 2024), available at https://www.statista.com/statistics/1452182/indonesia-voters-turnout-of-presidential-election/ (last accessed 27 August 2024)). In the 2024 general elections, the national participation rate was of 81.78% (see Statista, "Participation rate of the national election in Indonesia in March 2024," (25 March 2024), available at: https://www.statista.com/statistics/1452255/indonesia-voters-turnout-of-2024-national-election/ (last accessed 27 August 2024)).

378 On Indonesian human rights legislation, see Lindsey and Butt, *Indonesian Law*, 244–279.

379 For further references on the content of the *Qanun Jinayat*, see Simon Butt, "Religious Conservatism, Islamic Criminal Law and the Judiciary in Indonesia: A Tale of Three Courts," *The Journal of Legal Pluralism and Unofficial Law* 50, no. 3 (2018): 418–420; Lindsey and Butt, *Indonesian Law*, 205–208.

tion, thus expands the scope and application of substantive Islamic criminal law in Aceh (including punishments)[380] to non-Muslim citizens (in some circumstances). In particular, Art. 72 of the *Qanun* states that if an offence is regulated both by the Islamic Criminal Code and the Indonesian Criminal Code, the *Qanun* prevails. Butt observed that Art. 72 could be an indication of the fact that the Aceh legislature "wants the *Qanun*'s broader prohibition on adultery and same-sex intercourse [...] to prevail over the narrower prohibitions in the [Indonesian] Criminal Code".[381] Butt further noted that the provisions of Art. 72 appear to be not only a direct attempt by the Aceh provincial parliament to assert its authority over the central government, but also to assert the authority of Islam over the nation-state, reinforcing a contest between Islam and the state.[382]

From a strictly legal standpoint, it should be noted that the Indonesian Criminal Code does not provide a legal basis for the enactment of the *Qanun*, thus indicating the Aceh parliament's view of *shari'a* as the predominant source of law in general and of the Islamic Criminal Code in particular. Concerning the Islamic Criminal Code's compatibility with international human rights standards, it is interesting to notice that Art. 2 of the *Qanun* lists a series of underlying principles for its implementation, including the protection of human rights.[383] However, the Elucidation to Art. 2(e) frames "protection of human rights" as the "guarantee that the formulation of Islamic offences and punishments will accord with efforts to protect and respect human rights characteristics, honour and dignity, in accordance with the *understanding of Indonesian Muslims communities about human rights*".[384] This limited definition of human rights appears to be in contradiction not only with Indonesian human rights legislation,[385] but also the international obligations deriving from Indonesia's ratification of international human rights trea-

380 Butt, "Religious Conservatism," 418.

381 Butt, "Religious Conservatism," 420. The Indonesian Criminal Code prohibits a married person from having sex with someone who is not their spouse (Art. 284 Criminal Code), whereas the Islamic Criminal Code prohibits any sex between persons who are not married (Art. 33–36). Similarly, the Indonesian Criminal Code does not prohibit all forms of same-sex intercourse (with the only exception of same-sex intercourse with a minor, prohibited under Art. 292), whereas the *Qanun* prohibits even consensual same-sex intercourse, distinguishing between sodomy and lesbian sex and providing for different punishments (Art. 61–64).

382 Butt, "Religious Conservatism," 420. See also Tim Lindsey, *Islam, Law and the State in Southeast Asia. Volume 1: Indonesia* (London: IB Tauris, 2012).

383 Aceh Islamic Criminal Code – Art. 2(e).

384 Aceh Islamic Criminal Code – Elucidation to Art. 2(e).

385 See Law 39 of 1999 on Human Rights.

ties.[386] Finally, the *Qanun* applies also to those non-Muslim citizens who, along with a Muslim, violate the *Qanun* and voluntarily submit to the *Qanun* (Art. 5(b)), as well as to those non-Muslims who commit an offence under the *Qanun* that is not otherwise prohibited by domestic law (Art. 5(c)).[387] As already mentioned, the enactment of the Aceh Islamic Criminal Code was highly controversial, and many international organisations such as Amnesty International and Human Rights Watch warned against violations of human rights standards, including the prohibition on torture and inhuman treatment.[388] In Indonesia, the Institute for Criminal Justice Reform (ICJR) engaged in strategic litigation to challenge the legality of the *Qanun* before the Supreme Court in 2015. The ICJR had a series of compelling arguments: that the use of caning as punishment did not find support in the Indonesian Criminal Code; that national criminal law does not recognise an oath as a determinative form of evidence and that the *Qanun* would allow rapist to use the oath to avoid prosecution; that caning breached not only constitutional provisions and human rights legislation seeking to protect against torture, inhuman or undignified treatments, but also national child protection laws, international obligations, and the recommendations of the UN Human Rights Committee.[389] Moreover, the applicant challenged the Islamic Criminal Code on a technical level, arguing that it violated several provisions of the 2011 Law on Lawmaking requiring the maintenance of the legal order, since it contained inconsistencies and unclear drafting, thus violating the 2011 Law's requirements on clarity. For its part, the Aceh governor responded by emphasising that "all formal enactment procedures had been followed in respect of the *Qanun*",[390] and that the Law 11/2006 on the autonomous government of Aceh overrode the cited national and international legislation on the ground of the principle *lex specialis derogat lege generalis*.[391]

386 See Simon Butt, "The Position of International Law within the Indonesian Legal System," *Emory International Law Review* 28, no. 1 (2014): 1–28.

387 Interestingly, Butt pointed out that "Read literally, Articles 5(b) and 5(c) also appear to lead to a rather strange result. They appear to allow non-Muslims to escape the reach of the Qanun if they commit a Qanun offence together with a Muslim or Muslims, but not if together with one or more non-Muslims, at least if the offence is not otherwise regulated by national law. This cannot have been the intention of drafters, but it seems to be precisely the effect of these provisions" (see Butt, "Religious Conservatism," 421).

388 Butt, "Religious Conservatism," 421.

389 Butt, "Religious Conservatism," 422.

390 Ibidem.

391 Ibidem.

Even though the law "clearly points to a different result",[392] the Supreme Court refused to hear the case for technical reasons, preferring to avoid conflict by declining to make a decision that would have faced substantial opposition in conservative political and public spheres. In its reasoning for not considering the arguments, the Supreme Court referenced Art. 55 of the Constitutional Court Law, requiring the Supreme Court "to stop hearing a review of a lower-level law against a statute if the constitutionality of that statute is being reviewed by the Constitutional Court".[393] The Court could resort to this technicality because, at the time, the Constitutional Court was indeed reviewing the constitutionality of the 2011 Lawmaking Law, and thus it was entitled to stop the proceedings, although the cases of the Supreme Court and that of the Constitutional Court were unrelated.[394] Though technically speaking resorting to Art. 55 was correct, Butt observed that Art. 55 would not have prevented the Supreme Court from hearing the rest of the applicant and respondent's arguments based on violations of human rights legislation and of the Indonesian Criminal Code, which stood independently from the arguments on the Lawmaking Law.[395] Therefore, the Supreme Court ended up upholding the existing asymmetry in Aceh by not hearing the case, and maintaining the *status quo* avoiding a highly probable backlash from Islamists if the *Qanun* had been overturned.[396]

4.5 *Comparative Observations*

Having reviewed the constitutional case-law of courts on asymmetry, it is now possible to compare apex courts' decisions by relying on the same theoretical framework employed to measure constitutional asymmetries in the constitutional systems.[397] This allows not only for a comparison across courts, but also within courts' case law. Indeed, constitutional courts address disputes on constitutional asymmetry with different outcomes, depending on the specific dimension involved.

Starting from the comparison across cases, it is possible to notice that the only court that has addressed all three dimensions of constitutional asymmetry (i.e., status, powers, and fiscal arrangements) in its case law is the Italian

392 Butt, "Religious Conservatism," 404.
393 Butt, "Religious Conservatism," 423.
394 Ibidem.
395 Ibidem.
396 Butt, "Religious Conservatism," 424.
397 See Chapters 2 and 3 for a complete explanation of the method employed to measure constitutional asymmetries and the relative analysis of the results.

Constitutional Court, whereas the other four courts have dealt with disputes related to asymmetries in status and powers. Overall, from the comparative analysis of the constitutional case-law, it appears that courts confirmed the existing asymmetry in status only when this was limited in degree. This is the case in Italy and Indonesia, where constitutional asymmetry in status is low, and perhaps more acceptable since it does not threaten the territorial integrity of the system. Conversely, where asymmetry in status is (potentially) high, apex courts have decided in favour of symmetry, protecting the integrity of the system and strengthening the role of the centre, as happened in Spain. Indeed, the Basque and Catalan reform proposals would have amended their autonomy statutes to restore their previous differentiated positions within the system, potentially introducing a high degree of asymmetry in status. In this case, the Spanish Constitutional Tribunal declared the proposals unconstitutional and thus protected the existing constitutional *status quo* (i.e., symmetry in status). Regarding the Indian case, it should be noted that the Supreme Court's case law on asymmetry in status is different depending on the subnational entity involved. In fact, if asymmetry was consistently upheld in relation to the special provisions for the states of the northeast, when deciding on disputes related to the state of Jammu and Kashmir, the courts generally decided to uphold symmetrisation legislation, thus reducing the degree of asymmetry. In two decisions (in 1959 and 2017), the Supreme Court upheld the existing asymmetry in status for Jammu and Kashmir, but these decisions were then overturned respectively in 1970 and 2023, ultimately confirming the demotion of Jammu and Kashmir from Indian state to union territory. For what regards asymmetry in powers, constitutional courts appear to have consistently upheld existing asymmetry, thus protecting subnational entities from symmetrisation attempts from the central government. The notable exception is Italy, where it is possible to clearly identify a turning point in the case law of the Italian Constitutional Court. Indeed, in times of crisis, i.e., the 2010s economic crisis and the Covid-19 pandemic, the Court steered towards symmetry, upholding the central legislation and reducing the degree of asymmetry in powers for the special regions. The same happened for asymmetry in fiscal arrangements, which were upheld in decision 102/2008 and then contracted in decision 37/2021.

When looking at the asymmetry jurisprudence within cases, the picture is even more nuanced. As mentioned, in India, asymmetry was consistently upheld by the Supreme Court if considered uncontroversial, even though some decisions confirming asymmetry in powers for the states of the north-east, allowing derogations from constitutional fundamental rights, could be considered controversial and legally problematic. Conversely, the Court "simply followed the prevailing political mood"[398] when deciding over Jammu and Kashmir, given the highly controversial nature of the issue especially during the renewed insurgency on the territory in the 1990s. Then, in the Italian case, the Constitutional Court consistently upheld asymmetry in status, before and during times of crisis, considering the principle of specialty as a core element of Italian regionalism. However, in times of crisis, asymmetry in powers and in fiscal arrangements were drastically reduced, favouring a centralised management of emergencies to the detriment of differentiated autonomy. In another regional system, i.e., Spain, the role of the apex court was extremely controversial, since it significantly reduced the space for further constitutional asymmetry, especially in the dimension of status. Finally, Indonesia is a particularly interesting case because the two decisions on constitutional asymmetry upheld critical aspects of the existing asymmetrical arrangements, as they confirmed the constitutionality of the customary voting system in Papua, despite the evident lack of secrecy and transparency, as well as of the Aceh Islamic Criminal Code, despite the highly problematic consequences of the *Qanun Jinayat* on the legal order and on the fundamental rights of non-Muslim citizens, minorities, and vulnerable groups.

Overall, the constitutional case-law analysis appears to confirm that courts are a relevant factor in (a)symmetrisation processes, as they can facilitate or hinder their development.[399] Specifically, the comparison seems to indicate that apex courts tend to reduce medium degrees of constitutional asymmetry, as happened in India, Italy, and Spain (*especially* because of its controversial nature), whereas they confirm low degree asymmetry (*despite* its controversial nature). Furthermore, it appears that decisions have a more substantial and destabilising effect on federal dynamics when dealing with the dimension of status, as happened in Spain with the Basque and Catalan decisions, and in India with the confirmed abrogation of Art. 370 on Jammu and Kashmir. Decisions were also highly criticised when dealing with powers, either by reducing existing asymmetry, as happened in Italy with the contraction of asymmetry in support of central emergency legislation, or by confirming asymmetry, as happened in Indonesia and in India, when decisions allowed derogations from democratic principles and fundamental rights.

---

398 Swenden and Saxena, "Policing the Federation," 28.

399 Patricia Popelier and Maja Sahadžić, "Conclusion. A Country Studies-Based Deliberation on Constitutional Asymmetry in Multi-tiered Multinational Systems," in *Constitutional Asymmetry in Multinational Federalism*, ed. Patricia Popelier and Maja Sahadžić (Cham: Palgrave Macmillan, 2019), 501.

5 Concluding Remarks

This final chapter focused on the role of constitutional courts in the 12 case studies along three steps. First, it reviewed the models of constitutional adjudication adopted in the cases, and the comparative analysis of the constitutional and supreme courts showed that, generally, the link between the model of judicial review and legal system holds true in all case studies but one (i.e., Myanmar). Indeed, the constitutional systems belonging to the civil law tradition, i.e., Belgium, Bosnia and Herzegovina, Italy, and Spain, all adopted a centralised model of constitutional review. Conversely, Canada and the UK, despite the localised presence of mixed jurisdictions in Québec and Scotland, share the predominance of a common law tradition and adopted a decentralised model of judicial review. When it comes to mixed legal systems, the link also holds true depending on the prevalent colonial legacy that shaped the legal system. In the case of India, Malaysia, and Pakistan, British colonialism and the imposition of common law in these systems laid the foundations for the adoption of a decentralised model of judicial review. In Indonesia and Iraq, the presence of civil law through Dutch colonialism (in Indonesia) or French colonialism (in Iraq) led to the adoption of a centralised model of constitutional review, despite being rather weak and at times problematic. The only case contradicting this relationship appears to be Myanmar, which introduced a centralised model of constitutional review despite the presence of common law.

Then, the chapter explored whether the courts that developed a rich federalism-related jurisprudence adopted a centralist or federalist behaviour. Generally speaking, the analysis confirmed the trend previously identified by Aroney and Kincaid, and by Popelier, depicting an overall centralisation trend. Indeed, the analysed courts, although at times maintaining a balance between the centre and self-governments, tend to strengthen the centre and expand the powers of the central level of government. This also had detrimental effects, as in the Spanish case and the reignition of the secessionist movements. A further point that is worth observing relates to the interpretation that courts gave on the form of state when addressing asymmetries in their constitutional systems. This clearly emerges in the Italian and Spanish cases, where the Constitutional Courts often imprinted a unifying and centralising direction to the system rejecting the "federal idea." Although the analytical category of multi-tiered systems contributes to expanding the analysis beyond the formal definitions of federal, regional, devolutionary systems, it is still important to acknowledge the form of state as an important element to take into consideration when addressing asymmetries and the relative interpretation given by courts.

Finally, the chapter focused on those courts that addressed asymmetries in their case law, i.e., India, Indonesia, Italy, and Spain. In these four systems, constitutional or supreme courts played a crucial role in reshaping the degree of asymmetries in their system, often in critical times for political stability and territorial integrity. Overall, the comparative analysis of their constitutional case law showed that courts tend to reduce asymmetries, thus confirming a resymmetrisation trend. This is the case of the Spanish Constitutional Tribunal, the Italian Constitutional Court, and the Indian Supreme Court. Conversely, the Indonesian case appears to be an outlier since the decisions of the Constitutional Court and the Supreme Court confirmed the existing degree of (low) constitutional asymmetry. Therefore, the analysis seems to suggest that apex courts tend to reduce constitutional asymmetry when its degree is medium (i.e., India, Italy, Spain) but confirm it when it is low (i.e., Indonesia), and that apex courts have shown a changing behaviour not only over time but also across dimensions, as in the case of the Italian Constitutional Court.

Overall, this final chapter has confirmed that courts have a significant impact on the degrees of asymmetry and should be consistently integrated in the study of asymmetries. Moreover, it has shown the advantages of relying on the same framework for conceptualising asymmetries, as this allowed for a more refined analysis of the courts' case law as well as a coherent comparison across cases.

Bibliography

Arban, Erika, Giuseppe Martinico, and Francesco Palermo, eds. *Federalism and Constitutional Law: The Italian Contribution to Comparative Regionalism*. London and New York: Routledge, 2021.

Aroney, Nicholas, and John Kincaid, eds. *Courts in Federal Countries: Federalists or Unitarists?* Toronto: University of Toronto Press, 2017.

Baier, Gerald. *Courts and Federalism. Judicial Doctrine in the United States, Australia, and Canada*. New York: Universit of British Columbia Press, 2006.

Behrendt, Christian. "The Belgian Constitutional Court." In *The Max Planck Handbooks in European Public Law*, edited by Armin von Bogdandy, Peter Huber, and Christoph Grabenwarter, 71–118. Oxford: Oxford University Press, 2020.

Beltrán, Miguel, and Daniel Sarmiento. "Making »Un Tribunal Para La Constitución«: A Documentary on the Creation and First Years of the Spanish Constitutional Court (1980–1986)." *Rechtsgeschichte – Legal History* 2021, no. 29 (2021): 187–96.

Biagi, Francesco. "Estatut de Catalunya e la crisi di legittimazione del Tribunal constitucional." *Quaderni Costituzionali* 31, no. 1 (2011): 63–87.

Bifulco, Raffaele, and Davide Paris. "The Italian Constitutional Court." In *The Max Planck Handbooks in European Public Law*, edited by Peter Huber, Armin von Bogdandy, and Christoph Grabenwarter, 447–504. Oxford: Oxford University Press, 2020.

Bonifati, Lidia. "Il regionalismo asimmetrico alla prova delle corti: il caso italiano in prospettiva comparata." *Percorsi Costituzionali*, no. 1 (2024): 197–230.

Brewer-Carias, Allan Randolph. *Judicial Review in Comparative Law*. Cambridge: Cambridge University Press, 1989.

Brouillet, Eugénie, and Bruce Ryder. "Key Doctrines in Canadian Legal Federalism." In *The Oxford Handbook of the Canadian Constitution*, edited by Peter Oliver, Patrick Macklem, and Nathalie Des Rosiers, 415–35. Oxford: Oxford University Press, 2017.

Butt, Simon. "Indonesia's Constitutional Court and Indonesia's Electoral System." In *Constitutional Courts in Asia*, edited by Albert HY Chen and Andrew Harding, 214–39. Cambridge: Cambridge University Press, 2018.

Butt, Simon. "Religious Conservatism, Islamic Criminal Law and the Judiciary in Indonesia: A Tale of Three Courts." *The Journal of Legal Pluralism and Unofficial Law* 50, no. 3 (2018): 402–34.

Calabresi, Steven Gow. *The History and Growth of Judicial Review, Volume 1: The G-20 Common Law Countries and Israel*. 1st ed. Oxford and New York: Oxford University Press, 2021.

Calabresi, Steven Gow. *The History and Growth of Judicial Review, Volume 2: The G-20 Civil Law Countries*. 1st ed. Oxford and New York: Oxford University Press, 2021.

Cappelletti, Mauro. *Judicial Review in the Contemporary World*. Indianapolis: Bobbs-Merrill, 1971.

Cappelletti, Mauro, and John Clarke Adams. "Judicial Review of Legislation: European Antecedents and Adaptations." *Harvard Law Review* 79, no. 6 (1966): 1207–24.

Chen, Albert HY, and Miguel Poiares Maduro. "The Judiciary and Constitutional Review." In *Routledge Handbook of Constitutional Law*, edited by Mark Tushnet, Thomas Fleiner, and Cheryl Saunders, 97–109. London and New York: Routledge, 2013.

Comella, Víctor Ferres. "The Rise of Specialized Constitutional Courts." edited by Tom Ginsburg and Rosalind Dixon, 265–77. Cheltenham, UK and Northampton, MA: Edward Elgar, 2011.

Comella, Víctor Ferres. "The Spanish Constitutional Court Confronts Catalonia's 'Right to Decide' (Comment on the Judgment 42/2014)." *European Constitutional Law Review* 10, no. 3 (2014): 571–90.

Comella, Víctor Ferres. "The Spanish Constitutional Court: Time for Reforms." *Journal of Comparative Law* 3, no. 2 (2008): 22–38.

Crouch, Melissa. “Dictators, Democrats, and Constitutional Dialogue: Myanmar’s Constitutional Tribunal.” *International Journal of Constitutional Law* 16, no. 2 (June 15, 2018): 421–46.

Crouch, Melissa. “Rediscovering ‘Law’ in Myanmar: A Review of Scholarship on the Legal System of Myanmar.” *Pacific Rim Law & Policy Journal* 23, no. 3 (2014): 543–78.

Dar, Rouf Ahmad. “Constitutions and Their Foundational Discontents: Studying the Process of Constitution-Making in Jammu and Kashmir.” *Global Constitutionalism* 12, no. 3 (2023): 543–61.

Dicey, Albert V. *Introduction to the Study of the Law of the Constitution.* III. London and New York: Macmillan, 1889.

Eibert, Mark D. “The Spanish Constitutional Tribunal in Theory and Practice.” *Stanford Journal of International Law* 18, no. 2 (1982): 435–70.

Favoreu, Louis. “Constitutional Review in Europe.” In *Constitutionalism and Rights: The Influence of the United States Constitution*, edited by Louis Henkin and Albert J. Rosenthal, 38–62. New York: Columbia University Press, 1990.

Fessha, Yonatan Tesfaye, and Karl Kössler, eds. *Federalism and the Courts in Africa.* London and New York: Routledge, 2020.

Filippetti, Andrea, Sandro Rondinella, and Fabrizio Tuzi. “The Italian Constitutional Court and Recentralization along the Pendulum of Regionalism.” *Constitutional Political Economy*, 2024, 1–27.

Fliri, Michael. “Federalism as a Safeguard of National Integrity: Trial and Error in the Case of Jammu and Kashmir.” *Diversity Governance Papers*, no. 2 (2022): 5–17.

Ginsburg, Tom, and Mila Versteeg. “Why Do Countries Adopt Constitutional Review?” *Journal of Law, Economics, & Organization* 30, no. 3 (2014): 587–622.

Gordon, Jeffrey Steven. “Comparative Judicial Federalism.” *International Journal of Constitutional Law* 21, no. 4 (2023): 976–1010.

Graziadei, Stefan. “Six Models for Reforming the Selection of Judges to the BiH Constitutional Court.” *Center for Southeast European Studies Working Papers* 14 (2016): 1–38.

Guillen Lopez, Enrique. “Judicial Review in Spain: The Constitutional Court.” *Loyola of Los Angeles Law Review* 41, no. 2 (2008): 529–62.

Haljan, David P. “A Constitutional Duty to Negotiate Amendments: *Reference Re Secession of Quebec*.” *International and Comparative Law Quarterly* 48, no. 2 (1999): 447–57.

Hausing, Kham Khan Suan. “Telangana and the Politics of State Formation in India: Recognition and Accommodation in a Multinational Federation.” *Regional & Federal Studies* 28, no. 4 (2018): 447–68.

Išerić, Harun. “The Role of the Constitutional Court of Bosnia and Herzegovina in Profiling Cooperative Federalism in a Multinational State.” In *Ethnic Diversity, Plural Democracy and Human Dignity*, edited by Mario Krešić, Damir Banović,

Alberto Carrio Sampedro, and Jānis Pleps, 153–83. Ius Gentium: Comparative Perspectives on Law and Justice. Cham: Springer International Publishing, 2022.

Kanwar, Ritika. "Abrogation of Article 370: Impact on Asymmetrical Federalism in India." *Indian Journal of Integrated Research in Law* 2, no. 3 (2022): 1–9.

Kelsen, Hans. "Judicial Review of Legislation: A Comparative Study of the Austrian and the American Constitution." *The Journal of Politics* 4, no. 2 (1942): 183–200.

Kössler, Karl. "The Role of Constitutional Judges in Protecting Territorial Self-Government." In *Defensive Federalism. Protecting Territorial Minorities from the "Tyranny of the Majority,"* edited by Ferran Requejo and Marc Sanjaume-Calvet, 153–75, 1st ed. London: Routledge, 2022.

Kumar, Pratyush. "'Asymmetrical Symmetricalism' of Indian Constitutional Structure and Practice: Note on Govt. of National Capital Territory ('NCT') of Delhi v Union of India." *DPCE Online*, no. 2 (2022): 3027–39.

Lindsey, Tim, and Simon Butt. *Indonesian Law*. Oxford: Oxford University Press, 2018.

Lone, Fozia Nazir. *Historical Title, Self-Determination and the Kashmir Question: Changing Perspectives in International Law*. Leiden and Boston: Brill | Nijhoff, 2018.

Mahmood, Oday Talal. "A New Basis for Judicial Review in Iraq." *Arab Law Quarterly* 37, no. 1–2 (2020): 43–79.

Malik, Ayesha A. "Judicial Review and the Rule of Law in Pakistan." *Asian Journal of Comparative Law* 18, no. 3 (2023): 291–302.

Mukhiit, Rom, and Rentsenkhorloo Anar. *Implementation of Constitutional Review. Challenges and Development Trends*. Ulaanbaatar, Mongolia: Constitutional Court of Mongolia, 2022.

Nair, Balu Gopalakrishnan. "Abrogation of Article 370: Can the President Act Without the Recommendation of the Constituent Assembly?" *Indian Law Review* 3, no. 3 (2019): 254–79.

Pagés, Juan Luis Requejo. "The Spanish Constitutional Tribunal." In *The Max Planck Handbooks in European Public Law*, edited by Armin von Bogdandy, Peter Huber, and Christoph Grabenwarter, 719–78. Oxford: Oxford University Press, 2020.

Palermo, Francesco, and Karl Kössler. *Comparative Federalism: Constitutional Arrangements and Case Law*. London: Hart Publishing, 2017.

Plessis, Jacques du. "Comparative Law and the Study of Mixed Legal Systems." In *The Oxford Handbook of Comparative Law*, edited by Mathias Reimann and Reinhard Zimmermann, 2nd ed., 474–501. Oxford: Oxford University Press, 2019.

Pócza, Kálmán. *Constitutional Review in Western Europe. Judicial-Legislative Relations in Comparative Perspective*. London and New York: Routledge, 2024.

Popelier, Patricia. "Federalism Disputes and the Behavior of Courts: Explaining Variation in Federal Courts' Support for Centralization." *Publius: The Journal of Federalism* 47, no. 1 (2017): 27–48.

Popelier, Patricia. "The Constitutional Court's Impact on Federalism in Belgium: a Weakening of the Centralization Theory." In *Jahrbuch des Föderalismus 2020: Föderalismus, Subsidiarität und Regionen in Europa*, edited by Europäischen Zentrum für Föderalismus-Forschung Tübingen (EZFF), 1st ed., 67–92. Baden-Baden: Nomos Verlagsgesellschaft mbH & Co. KG, 2020.

Popelier, Patricia, and Samantha Bielen. "How Courts Decide Federalism Disputes: Legal Merit, Attitudinal Effects, and Strategic Considerations in the Jurisprudence of the Belgian Constitutional Court." *Publius: The Journal of Federalism* 49, no. 4 (2019): 1–30.

Reid, Kenneth G. C. "The Idea of Mixed Legal Systems." *Tulane Law Review* 78, no. 1 & 2 (2003): 5–40.

Russell, Peter H. *The Judiciary in Canada: The Third Branch of Government*. Toronto: McGraw-Hill Ryerson, 1987.

Saunders, Cheryl. "Courts with Constitutional Jurisdiction." In *The Cambridge Companion to Comparative Constitutional Law*, edited by Roger Masterman and Robert Schütze, 414–40. Cambridge: Cambridge University Press, 2019.

Schertzer, Robert. "Federal Arbiters as Facilitators: Towards an Integrated Federal and Judicial Theory for Diverse States." *International Journal of Constitutional Law* 15, no. 1 (2017): 110–36.

Spadaro, Ignazio. "Decentramento politico e pandemia: spunti per un 'regionalismo dell'emergenza'." *Rivista AIC* 4 (2022): 146–65.

Stone Sweet, Alec. "Constitutional Courts." In *The Oxford Handbook of Comparative Constitutional Law*, edited by Michel Rosenfeld and András Sajó, 816–30. Oxford: Oxford University Press, 2012.

Swenden, Wilfried, and Rekha Saxena. "Policing the Federation: The Supreme Court and Judicial Federalism in India." *Territory, Politics, Governance* 10, no. 1 (2022): 12–31.

Tarr, G Alan. "Subnational Constitutions and Minority Rights: A Perspective on Canadian Provincial Constitutionalism." *Rutgers Law Journal* 40, no. 4 (2009): 767–92.

Tega, Diletta. "The Italian Constitutional Court in Its Context: A Narrative." *European Constitutional Law Review* 17, no. 3 (2021): 369–93.

Tew, Yvonne. "On the Uneven Journey to Constitutional Redemption: The Malaysian Judiciary and Constitutional Politics." *Washington International Law Journal* 25, no. 3 (2016): 673–96.

Tillin, L. "United in Diversity? Asymmetry in Indian Federalism." *Publius: The Journal of Federalism* 37, no. 1 (2006): 45–67.

Vedaschi, Arianna. "La giustizia costituzionale." In *Diritto costituzionale comparato*, edited by Paolo Carrozza, Alfonso Di Giovine, and Giuseppe Franco Ferrari, 1087–1136. Bari: Laterza, 2014.

Visser, Daniel. "Cultural Forces in the Making of Mixed Legal Systems." *Tulane Law Review* 78, no. 1 & 2 (2003): 41–78.

Walsh, Dawn. "Constitutional Courts as Arbiters of Post-Conflict Territorial Self-Government: Bosnia and Macedonia." *Regional & Federal Studies* 29, no. 1 (2019): 67–90.

Wechsler, Herbert. "The Political Safeguards of Federalism: The Role of the States in the Composition and Selection of the National Government." *Columbia Law Review* 54, no. 4 (1954): 543–60.

Woelk, Jens, ed. "Jurisdiction and Pluralisms: Judicial Functions and Organisation in Federal Systems." *Perspectives on Federalism* 12, no. 2 (2020).

Yoo, John C. "The Judicial Safeguards of Federalism." *Southern California Law Review* 70 (1996): 1311–1406.

Comparative Conclusions

1 Core Findings of the Research

This book aimed to explore constitutional asymmetries in divided multi-tiered systems as a dynamic constitutional model to accommodate ethnocultural diversity, through a comparative analysis of 12 case studies from both the Global North and the Global South. Specifically, this research tested two hypotheses, stemming from the research questions, i.e., the impact of constitutional design and the role of constitutional courts in shaping the degree of constitutional asymmetries. The following sections briefly outline the findings of the comparative analysis.

1.1 *The Dynamic Nature of Constitutional Asymmetries*

The first research hypothesis was that there are different degrees of constitutional asymmetries, and as such, they can provide a dynamic constitutional model for the accommodation of ethnocultural diversity in divided multi-tiered systems. The existence of different degrees of constitutional asymmetries has been acknowledged by the literature, but not empirically tested through rigorous comparison. The comparative analysis of the 12 case studies showed that constitutional asymmetries present to different degrees and have been introduced in very different settings, thus empirically confirming the first hypothesis. Specifically, the comparative analysis carried out in Chapter 3 offered a more nuanced picture of constitutional asymmetries in divided multi-tiered systems in both the Global North and the Global South by providing a more comprehensive analysis of the dimensions in which asymmetries may appear. Indeed, the adopted method to measure constitutional asymmetries allowed us to empirically test the hypothesis that constitutional asymmetries can be introduced to different degrees (i.e., low, medium, high degree).

The variety of constitutional solutions adopted by the systems clearly indicates the dynamic nature of constitutional asymmetries, which can provide flexible arrangements tailored to different needs and settings. In fact, the study showed that the presence of constitutional asymmetries does not entail a pre-fixed structure. Rather, constitutional asymmetries can be present in one or two dimensions, such as Canada displaying constitutional asymmetry only in status, Spain only in the fiscal arrangements dimension, or Bosnia-Herzegovina only in status and powers, or else in all three dimensions, such as in Belgium, Pakistan, and India. Furthermore, the study found that the degree of asymmetry varies not only across constitutional systems but also

 | DOI:10.1163/9789004739109_008

within the same system. This means that the degree of asymmetries also varies among the dimensions of asymmetry (i.e., status, powers, and fiscal arrangements). For example, the degree of asymmetry can be medium in powers, while low in status and fiscal arrangements (e.g., Italy), or it can be present only in status, whereas absent in powers and fiscal arrangements (e.g., Canada).

In addition, the book also confirmed what had already been suggested by the literature, i.e., that asymmetrical solutions can be found in integrationist as well as accommodationist constitutional systems.[1] In fact, the comparative analysis showed that constitutional asymmetries are present in constitutional systems more generally associated with the accommodationist/multinational models of constitutional design (e.g., Belgium, Bosnia-Herzegovina), and in those generally associated with the integrationist/liberal model (e.g., the United Kingdom, Malaysia). Moreover, constitutional asymmetries are present in many constitutional systems that, despite defining themselves as unitary systems (or at least, not as federations), introduced asymmetries to deal with deep internal diversity, as happened in Spain, Italy, and Indonesia.

Therefore, it could be argued that the outcome of this research confirms that constitutional asymmetries tend to be a dynamic instrument for managing internal diversity that is much more accepted than the federal institutional structure.[2] However, this book also warned against an excessive idealisation of constitutional asymmetries, as they are not *per se* a solution to all of the challenges that may arise in divided multi-tiered systems. As emerged in the analysis of Myanmar, the introduction of constitutional asymmetries to satisfy the claims of the majority group, to the exclusion of other segments of society, was one of the factors that led to internal conflict. Indeed, to be an effective device for the treatment of diversity, constitutional asymmetries need to be sustainable[3] and accompanied by the development of a strong culture of autonomy.[4] After all, as already noted by Palermo, the process of (re)negotiation of "workable legal solutions [...] is constantly in progress and, given the nature of the issues involved, never completely finished."[5]

---

1 See Choudhry, "Bridging," 32–5.

2 See Wolff, "Cases of Asymmetrical Territorial Autonomy," 24.

3 See Giuseppe Martinico, "Quanto è sostenibile l'integrazione (asimmetrica) sovranazionale. Note di diritto comparato," *Istituzioni del Federalismo* 2 (2018): 287–300.

4 See in particular, the chapters by Roberto Toniatti, Elena D'Orlando, and Francesco Palermo in Roberto Toniatti, *La cultura dell'autonomia: le condizioni pre-giuridiche per un'efficace autonomia regionale* (Trento: Università degli Studi di Trento, 2018).

5 Francesco Palermo, "Accommodating Differences: The Present and Future of the Law of Diversity," *Vermont Law Review* 30 (2006): 432.

1.2 *The Role of Constitutional Courts in Shaping Asymmetries*

The second research hypothesis was that constitutional courts' decisions on constitutional asymmetries tend to reduce the degree of asymmetry. The role of courts has not been systematically explored in the literature on asymmetric federalism and remains an under-developed perspective in the study of asymmetries. This book analysed the constitutional case-law of the five courts that have addressed asymmetries in their jurisprudence, i.e., the Spanish Constitutional Tribunal, the Italian Constitutional Court, the Indian Supreme Court, the Indonesian Supreme Court, and the Indonesian Constitutional Court. The case-law analysis confirmed that constitutional courts tend to reduce the space for asymmetries, thus significantly reshaping the degree of constitutional asymmetry within the system. Specifically, the comparison suggested that apex courts tend to reduce medium degrees of constitutional asymmetry, as happened in India, Italy, and Spain (*because* of its controversial nature), whereas they confirm low-degree asymmetry (*despite* its controversial nature). Moreover, apex courts show a changing behaviour not only over time but also across dimensions. For instance, the Italian Constitutional Court initially consistently upheld asymmetries in all three dimensions, whereas after the 2010s financial crisis, and again during the Covid-19 pandemic, it reduced asymmetries in powers and fiscal arrangements. The research also found that courts might change their attitude depending on the subnational entity involved in the decision. This has been the case with the Indian Supreme Court and its different decisions on asymmetry in status involving Jammu and Kashmir compared to those involving the states in the northeast.

Therefore, the analysis conducted in this book confirms that courts are a relevant factor in (a)symmetrisation processes, as they can facilitate or hinder their development.[6] Specifically, it appears that decisions have a more substantial and destabilising effect on federal dynamics when dealing with the dimension of status. This is what happened in Spain with the Basque and Catalan decisions, and in India with the confirmed abrogation of Art. 370 on Jammu and Kashmir. Decisions have also been highly criticised when dealing with powers, either reducing existing asymmetry, as happened in Italy with the contraction of asymmetry in support of central emergency legislation, or by confirming asymmetry, as happened in Indonesia and India, when decisions allowed derogations from democratic principles and fundamental

---

6 Patricia Popelier and Maja Sahadžić, "Conclusion: A Country Studies-Based Deliberation on Constitutional Asymmetry in Multi-Tiered Multinational Systems," in *Constitutional Asymmetry in Multinational Federalism*, ed. Patricia Popelier and Maja Sahadžić (Cham: Palgrave Macmillan, 2019), 501.

rights. Overall, the research confirmed that constitutional courts have a significant impact on the degree of asymmetry and should be consistently integrated into the study of constitutional asymmetries in divided multi-tiered systems.

2 Innovative Aspects

The book contributes to the literature on constitutional asymmetries by providing some innovative elements. First, the research is placed in the field of comparative constitutional law, contributing to the development of a comparative legal perspective on asymmetries. Traditionally, the study of asymmetries has been the domain of comparative politics, at the expense of comparative constitutional law. However, constitutional law has the potential to play an essential role in addressing the challenges arising from divided societies, especially through constitutional design. In this respect, this book contributes to the academic debate on constitutional design for divided societies from a legal perspective, proposing the introduction of constitutional asymmetries as a dynamic constitutional model to accommodate ethnocultural diversity. Even within the legal field, this book has a decisive focus on divided multi-tiered systems, thus also providing a different research focus than previous works. Indeed, previous comparative legal research studied the topic of constitutional asymmetries from different perspectives: reviewing asymmetries in regional and federal states, but not specifically in divided societies;[7] exploring the link between asymmetry and multinationalism, but not asymmetries as a model to accommodate diversity;[8] and assessing the role of asymmetries in undermining legitimacy and stability in multinational federal systems, but not the dynamic nature of asymmetries and the role of courts.[9]

Second, this book provides a quantitative, and not only qualitative, assessment of asymmetries. This book builds on the pioneering research by Popelier and Sahadžić, framing constitutional asymmetry in qualitative terms, and proposes a more complete framework to comparatively assess constitutional

7 Francesco Palermo, Karl Kössler, and Carolin Zwilling, eds., *Asymmetries in Constitutional Law: Recent Developments in Federal and Regional Systems* (Bolzano/Bozen: Accademia Europea di Bolzano, 2009).

8 Patricia Popelier and Maja Sahadžić, eds., *Constitutional Asymmetry in Multinational Federalism* (Cham: Palgrave Macmillan, 2019).

9 Maja Sahadžić, *Asymmetry, Multinationalism and Constitutional Law: Managing Legitimacy and Stability in Federalist States* (London and New York: Routledge, 2020).

asymmetries, relying on a different methodology and identifying a low, medium, and high degree of asymmetry. By doing so, the book offers an analytical strategy to measure asymmetry across constitutional systems, allowing researchers to replicate the analysis and apply the same methodology to different case studies. Indeed, the book aimed to expand the boundaries of comparative constitutional law scholarship, combining traditional doctrinal analysis with emerging strands of legal research, such as empirical legal studies and decolonial comparative law. Indeed, the research analyses the constitutional frameworks through the employment of standardised indexes in a medium-N universe of case studies across the Global North and the Global South. Measuring constitutional asymmetries allows for a refined and systematic comparison across case studies, which becomes a foundational element in assessing constitutional design and constitutional change, as well as in better framing the impact of constitutional courts on federal dynamics. Moreover, exploring asymmetries not only at the country level, by identifying an overall degree of asymmetry, but also at the subnational entity level, by looking at each dimension of asymmetry, addresses a major criticism of large-N studies in comparative law, namely the reduction of the analysis to mere numbers. The analytical framework provided by this book aims to acknowledge complexity and allow researchers to look more in-depth at the solutions adopted at the central and subnational levels. The adoption of a decolonial approach to the study of constitutional asymmetries significantly expands federal theory. Indeed, this book sought to delink from Eurocentrism and reframe the assumptions behind the traditional constitutional models of treatment of diversity, acknowledging the role played by colonialism and imagining flexible solutions to accommodate pluralism. Moreover, this research adopted a postcolonial perspective by considering the legacies of colonialism and focusing on a variety of constitutional systems across different parts of the world, covering not only the "classical cases" in the literature, which tend to be overwhelmingly in the Western world (such as Canada, Belgium, Italy, Spain, and the UK), but also constitutional systems in Eastern Europe (i.e., Bosnia and Herzegovina), the MENA region (i.e., Iraq), and the South and South-East Asian regions (i.e., India, Indonesia, Malaysia, Myanmar, and Pakistan). In this particular respect, it is interesting to note that no area of the world appears to be clearly associated with the presence of a specific degree of constitutional asymmetry, which can be found to different degrees in all regions. Low asymmetries are present in North America (i.e., Canada), Eastern Europe (i.e., Bosnia-Herzegovina), and South-East Asia (i.e., Indonesia and Malaysia). Medium asymmetries are present in Western Europe (i.e., Spain, Italy, and Belgium) and in South Asia (i.e., Pakistan). High asymmetries are present in

South and South-East Asia (i.e., India and Myanmar), in Western Europe (i.e., the United Kingdom), and in the MENA region (i.e., Iraq).

Finally, this research builds significantly on the previous literature on asymmetries in multi-tiered systems by systematically analysing the role of constitutional courts. The perspective of courts had only been marginal in Popelier and Sahadžić's work, whereas previous legal scholarship focused on de/centralising attitudes of courts and on the role of courts in protecting the fundamental rights of minorities. Conversely, this book systematically addresses the role of courts in addressing asymmetries and shows that the case law of constitutional courts is a crucial element in the assessment of constitutional asymmetries, as they can have a substantial impact on their degree, often in a resymmetrisation trend. The joint analysis of the impact of constitutional design and the role played by constitutional courts provides a significant contribution to the current literature, as these two aspects have never been comparatively addressed together. To achieve this goal, the book relied on the same conceptual framework on constitutional asymmetries, allowing for a coherent assessment of the impact of constitutional design and the role of courts in shaping the degree of constitutional asymmetries in divided multi-tiered systems. The integrated analysis of the impact of these two aspects, i.e., constitutional design and constitutional courts, offers a unique perspective on the complex interaction between constitutional asymmetries as shaped by the law and by the relative interpretation by courts.

3 Limitations of the Study and Further Developments

Certainly, the focus on the constitutional level of analysis, as well as the employment of empirical qualitative methods, was a challenge in complexity management. On the one hand, the interplay between law on the books and law in action is not easy to grasp through standardised indexes and required a deeper look at each constitutional experience. On the other hand, empirical methods *per se* are not sufficient to provide a complex and nuanced analysis but are surely helpful in supporting traditional legal research. Indeed, they offer a useful resource to identify general trends, provide a new explanation, or confirm a hypothesis that may often have been built on the analysis of only a few cases. In this respect, the comparative nature of the research proved to be essential, as it was possible to analyse a variety of constitutional systems and assess the expressions of constitutional asymmetry across different constitutional experiences. Being an exploratory study, further research is needed to fill some of the gaps that are present in this book.

A first limitation of this work is its static nature, as it is a synchronic comparison, only providing a snapshot of the asymmetries currently in place. However, as emerges in the book, constitutional asymmetries are a dynamic phenomenon and vary over time, as visible in Italy, Myanmar, and India. Further research would be needed to explore the evolution of constitutional asymmetries in the case studies, to assess how they changed and whether they followed a resymmetrisation or asymmetrisation trend.

Then, a further substantial limitation of the research concerns the limited analysis of fiscal arrangements in the case studies. As mentioned in Chapter 2, Popelier's indexes of fiscal arrangements are rather complex and comprehensive, including borrowing powers, shared revenues, and conditional grants. The selection of taxing powers had to do with feasibility and can provide a proxy of asymmetry in the dimension of fiscal arrangements. However, it should be remembered that this is an approximation of reality and therefore does not provide a complete picture of asymmetries in the fiscal domain. Further research could engage with the other indexed fiscal arrangements to have a more complete and accurate measure of constitutional asymmetries in the fiscal domain.

Moreover, the analytical strategy provided by this book allows for a possible expansion in the case selection, as other case studies could have been included, such as Finland and Papua New Guinea. These two constitutional systems can be framed as partially divided societies, addressing distinct identity claims within the territory (i.e., the Åland Island in Finland, and the Autonomous Region of Bougainville in Papua New Guinea). These two cases were eventually excluded due to time-restraints but would be extremely interesting to include in further research on constitutional asymmetries in divided multi-tiered systems.

Finally, two additional paths can be explored starting with the book's findings. A first itinerary of comparative research concerns the relationship between a/symmetry and de/centralisation. This is an intersection that has not been widely addressed by the literature, that has focused on either a/symmetry or de/centralisation.[10] This would provide an innovative research perspective, as often the general assumption would be that more asymmetry is

10 See Ferran Requejo and Klaus-Jürgen Nagel, eds., *Federalism Beyond Federations: Asymmetry and Processes of Resymmetrisation in Europe* (Farnham, England: Ashgate, 2011); Paolo Dardanelli et al., "Dynamic De/Centralization in Federations: Comparative Conclusions," *Publius: The Journal of Federalism* 49, no. 1 (2019): 194–219; Paolo Dardanelli et al., "Authoritarianism, Democracy and De/Centralization in Federations: What Connections?," *Regional & Federal Studies* 33, no. 5 (2023): 577–606.

achieved through more decentralisation, as well as more symmetry by more centralisation. However, as discussed in this book, this is not necessarily the case, as the overall resymmetrisation trend can be achieved by either increased centralisation, as happened in Spain, or by increased decentralisation, as happened in Italy. A second research path concerns the conceptualisation of autonomy. In fact, this book chose to focus on the territorial dimension of autonomy, as the primary interest was in constitutional and institutional design. However, it should not be forgotten that autonomy is not limited to its institutional features and is a much broader concept that also includes non-territorial forms of autonomy, such as group autonomy in cultural, linguistic, and religious matters.[11] With this in mind, future research could study asymmetries based on different degrees of non-territorial autonomy,[12] providing a fascinating perspective on asymmetries and refining the understanding of constitutional design for divided societies.

In conclusion, this book can be regarded as a first step, laying the foundations for further exploration of the different tiles that together compose the mosaic of constitutional asymmetries in divided multi-tiered systems.

Bibliography

Alessi, Nicolò Paolo. *A Global Law of Diversity: Evolving Models and Concepts*. London and New York: Routledge, 2024.

Alessi, Nicolò Paolo, and Martina Trettel, eds. *Federalism and the Law of Diversity*. Leiden and Boston: Brill | Nijhoff, 2025.

Malloy, Tove. "Towards a New Paradigm of Minority Law-Making: A Rejoinder to Palermo and Woelk's Law of Diversity." *European Yearbook of Minority Issues Online* 4, no. 1 (2004): 1–28.

Malloy, Tove, and Francesco Palermo, eds. *Minority Accommodation through Territorial and Non-Territorial Autonomy*. Oxford: Oxford University Press, 2015.

Martinico, Giuseppe. "Quanto è sostenibile l'integrazione (asimmetrica) sovranazionale. Note di diritto comparato." *Istituzioni del Federalismo* 2 (2018): 287–300.

Palermo, Francesco. "Accommodating Differences: The Present and Future of the Law of Diversity." *Vermont Law Review* 30 (2006): 431–42.

---

11 See Nicolò Paolo Alessi, *A Global Law of Diversity: Evolving Models and Concepts* (London and New York: Routledge, 2024), 235–238, 266–268.

12 On non-territorial autonomy, see Tove Malloy and Francesco Palermo, eds., *Minority Accommodation through Territorial and Non-Territorial Autonomy* (Oxford: Oxford University Press, 2015).

Toniatti, Roberto. "Asimmetrie regionali, identità culturale e competitività dei territori: i titoli fondativi dell'autonomia speciale e le incognite della revisione costituzionale." In *Il futuro della specialità regionale alla luce della revisione costituzionale*, edited by Francesco Palermo and Sara Parolari, 13–43. Napoli: ESI, 2016.

Toniatti, Roberto. *La cultura dell'autonomia: le condizioni pre-giuridiche per un'efficace autonomia regionale*. Trento: Università degli Studi di Trento, 2018.

Woelk, Jens, and Francesco Palermo. "From Minority Protection to a Law of Diversity? Reflections on the Evolution of Minority Rights." *European Yearbook of Minority Issues Online* 3, no. 1 (2003): 5–13.

Appendices

Appendix 1: Converted Values of Constitutional Asymmetries in the 12 Case Studies

Table 1 shows the converted values for each dimension of asymmetry and overall at the country level in the 12 case studies.[1] As explained in Chapter 2, the conversion has been done through the normalisation of the original asymmetry scores to allow for coherent and rigorous comparison across dimensions and across cases. Percentiles are used to qualify the degrees of asymmetry as low (0.01–0.33), medium (0.34–0.66), and high (0.67–1.00).

TABLE 1 Converted values of constitutional asymmetry for each dimension and overall at the country level in the 12 case studies

Country	Dimension of asymmetry			Overall
	Status	Powers	Fiscal arrangements	
Belgium	0.22	0.44	0.40	0.43
BiH	0.35	0.20	0.00	0.19
Canada	0.06	0.00	0.00	0.00
India	0.33	0.64	0.40	0.55
Indonesia	0.12	0.07	0.00	0.04
Iraq	0.86	0.63	1.00	1.00
Italy	0.20	0.61	0.19	0.38
Malaysia	0.20	0.07	0.40	0.26
Myanmar	0.25	0.14	1.00	0.57
Pakistan	0.53	0.36	0.21	0.40
Spain	0.00	0.00	0.79	0.34
UK	1.00	1.00	0.40	0.94

1 It should be noted that these autonomy and asymmetry scores are based on the data collected in a previous version of this research, where I involved national experts for each case study to validate the results and ensure accuracy. Since then, the data were further elaborated and refined; thus, I take full responsibility for the revised autonomy and asymmetry scores displayed in this book. For further references to the previous data, see Lidia Bonifati, *Comparative Constitutional Design for Divided Societies: A Model to Explain Constitutional Asymmetries*, University of Bologna and University of Antwerp, doctoral thesis, 2023.

The normalisation formula for the conversion of values that has been employed is the following:

$$\textit{converted asymmetry value} = \frac{(\textit{original asymmetry score} - \textit{minimum asymmetry score})}{(\textit{maximum asymmetry score} - \textit{minimum asymmetry score})}$$

Appendix 2: High Constitutional Asymmetry – Subnational Autonomy Scores

Tables 2 and 3 show the detailed composition of subnational autonomy and asymmetry for the cases displaying a high degree of asymmetry, i.e., the United Kingdom and Iraq. For each case, the tables include: the subnational autonomy scores for each subnational entity and for each dimension of autonomy; the overall degree of autonomy for each dimension, for each subnational entity, and overall at the country level; the resulting constitutional asymmetry score for each dimension and overall at the country level; and the converted values of constitutional asymmetry for each dimension and overall at the country level. Percentiles are used to qualify the degrees of subnational autonomy and asymmetry as low (0.01–0.33), medium (0.34–0.66), and high (0.67–1.00).

TABLE 2 Subnational autonomy and constitutional asymmetry scores for the United Kingdom (converted values for comparison)

UNITED KINGDOM					
Dimensions of autonomy	**Autonomy value Northern Ireland**	**Autonomy value England**	**Average autonomy**	**CA score**	**CA converted score**
Status	0.55	0.04	0.30	0.51	1.00
Powers	0.63	0.04	0.34	0.59	1.00
Fiscal arrangements	0.25	0	0.13	0.25	0.40
Overall scores	0.48	0.03	0.26	0.45	0.94
Overall degree	Medium	Low	Low		High

TABLE 3 Subnational autonomy and constitutional asymmetry scores for Iraq (converted values for comparison)

IRAQ					
Dimensions of autonomy	**Autonomy value Kurdistan Region**	**Autonomy value Governorate**	**Average autonomy**	**CA score**	**CA converted score**
Status	0.65	0.21	0.43	0.44	0.86
Powers	0.58	0.21	0.40	0.37	0.63
Fiscal arrangements	0.63	0	0.32	0.63	1.00
Overall scores	0.62	0.14	0.38	0.48	1.00
Overall degree	Medium	Low	Medium		High

Appendix 3: Medium Constitutional Asymmetry – Subnational Autonomy Scores

Tables 4–9 show the detailed composition of subnational autonomy and asymmetry for the cases displaying a medium degree of asymmetry, i.e., India, Myanmar, Spain, Italy, Pakistan, and Belgium. For each case, the table includes: the subnational autonomy scores for each subnational entity and for each dimension of autonomy; the overall degree of autonomy for each dimension, for each subnational entity, and overall at the country level; the resulting constitutional asymmetry score for each dimension and overall at the country level; and the converted values of constitutional asymmetry for each dimension and overall at the country level. Percentiles are used to qualify the degrees of subnational autonomy and asymmetry as low (0.01–0.33), medium (0.34–0.66), and high (0.67–1.00).

TABLE 4 Subnational autonomy and constitutional asymmetry scores for India (converted values for comparison)

INDIA					
Dimensions of autonomy	**Autonomy value Nagaland**	**Autonomy value Chandigarh**	**Average autonomy score**	**CA score**	**CA converted score**
Status	0.26	0.09	0.18	0.17	0.33
Powers	0.52	0.14	0.33	0.38	0.64
Fiscal arrangements	0.25	0.00	0.13	0.25	0.40
Overall score	0.34	0.08	0.21	0.27	0.55
Overall degree	Medium	Low	Low		Medium

TABLE 5 Subnational autonomy and constitutional asymmetry scores for Myanmar (converted values for comparison)

MYANMAR					
Dimensions of autonomy	**Autonomy value Shan state**	**Autonomy value Wa SAD**	**Average autonomy**	**CA score**	**CA converted score**
Status	0.22	0.09	0.16	0.13	0.25
Powers	0.25	0.17	0.21	0.08	0.14
Fiscal arrangements	0.63	0.00	0.32	0.63	1.00
Overall scores	0.37	0.09	0.23	0.28	0.57
Overall degree	Medium	Low	Low		Medium

TABLE 6 Subnational autonomy and constitutional asymmetry scores for Spain (converted values for comparison)

SPAIN					
Dimensions of autonomy	**Autonomy value Basque Country**	**Autonomy value Andalusia**	**Average autonomy**	**CA score**	**CA converted score**
Status	0.26	0.26	0.26	0.00	0.00
Powers	0.43	0.43	0.43	0.00	0.00
Fiscal arrangements	0.75	0.25	0.50	0.50	0.79
Overall scores	0.48	0.31	0.40	0.17	0.34
Overall degree	Medium	Medium	Medium		Medium

TABLE 7 Subnational autonomy and constitutional asymmetry scores for Italy (converted values for comparison)

ITALY					
Dimensions of autonomy	**Autonomy value Aosta Valley**	**Autonomy value Lombardy**	**Average autonomy**	**CA score**	**CA converted score**
Status	0.46	0.35	0.41	0.11	0.20
Powers	0.79	0.43	0.61	0.36	0.61
Fiscal arrangements	0.75	0.63	0.69	0.12	0.19
Overall scores	0.67	0.47	0.57	0.20	0.38
Overall degree	High	Medium	Medium		Medium

TABLE 8 Subnational autonomy and constitutional asymmetry scores for Pakistan (converted values for comparison)

PAKISTAN					
Dimensions of autonomy	**Autonomy value Punjab**	**Autonomy value Gilgit-Baltistan**	**Average autonomy**	**CA score**	**CA converted score**
Status	0.39	0.12	0.26	0.27	0.53
Powers	0.61	0.40	0.51	0.21	0.36
Fiscal arrangements	0.38	0.25	0.32	0.13	0.21
Overall scores	0.46	0.26	0.36	0.20	0.40
Overall degree	Medium	Low	Medium		Medium

TABLE 9 Subnational autonomy and constitutional asymmetry scores for Belgium (converted values for comparison)

BELGIUM					
Dimensions of autonomy	**Autonomy value Flemish Community**	**Autonomy value German Speaking Community**	**Average autonomy**	**CA score**	**CA converted score**
Status	0.58	0.47	0.53	0.11	0.22
Powers	0.96	0.70	0.83	0.26	0.44
Fiscal arrangements	0.75	0.50	0.63	0.25	0.40
Overall scores	0.76	0.56	0.66	0.21	0.43
Overall degree	High	Medium	Medium		Medium

Appendix 4: Low Constitutional Asymmetry – Subnational Autonomy Scores

Tables 10–13 show the detailed composition of subnational autonomy and asymmetry for the cases displaying a low degree of asymmetry, i.e., Canada, Indonesia, Bosnia and Herzegovina, and Malaysia. For each case, the tables include: the subnational autonomy scores for each subnational entity and for each dimension of autonomy; the overall degree of autonomy for each dimension, for each subnational entity, and overall at the country level; the resulting constitutional asymmetry score for each dimension and overall at the country level; and the converted values of constitutional asymmetry for each dimension and overall at the country level. Percentiles are used to qualify the degrees of subnational autonomy and asymmetry as low (0.01–0.33), medium (0.34–0.66), and high (0.67–1.00).

TABLE 10 Subnational autonomy and constitutional asymmetry scores for Canada (converted values for comparison)

CANADA					
Dimensions of autonomy	**Autonomy value Québec**	**Autonomy value Nova Scotia**	**Average autonomy**	**CA score**	**CA converted score**
Status	0.60	0.57	0.59	0.03	0.06
Powers	0.42	0.42	0.42	0.00	0.00
Fiscal arrangements	0.75	0.75	0.75	0.00	0.00
Overall scores	0.59	0.58	0.59	0.01	0.00
Overall degree	Medium	Medium	Medium		Low

TABLE 11 Subnational autonomy and constitutional asymmetry scores for Indonesia (converted values for comparison)

INDONESIA					
Dimensions of autonomy	**Autonomy value Aceh**	**Autonomy value East Kalimantan**	**Average autonomy**	**CA score**	**CA converted score**
Status	0.24	0.18	0.21	0.06	0.12
Powers	0.46	0.42	0.44	0.04	0.07
Fiscal arrangements	0.25	0.25	0.25	0	0.00
Overall scores	0.32	0.28	0.30	0.03	0.04
Overall degree	Low	Low	Low		Low

TABLE 12 Subnational autonomy and constitutional asymmetry scores for Bosnia-Herzegovina (converted values for comparison)

BOSNIA AND HERZEGOVINA					
Dimensions of autonomy	**Autonomy value FBiH**	**Autonomy value Brčko district**	**Average autonomy**	**CA score**	**CA converted score**
Status	0.73	0.55	0.64	0.18	0.35
Powers	0.54	0.42	0.48	0.12	0.20
Fiscal arrangements	0.75	0.75	0.75	0	0.00
Overall scores	0.67	0.57	0.62	0.10	0.19
Overall degree	High	Medium	Medium		Low

TABLE 13 Subnational autonomy and constitutional asymmetry scores for Malaysia (converted values for comparison)

MALAYSIA					
Dimensions of autonomy	**Autonomy value Sarawak**	**Autonomy value Pulau Pinang**	**Average autonomy**	**CA score**	**CA converted score**
Status	0.50	0.40	0.45	0.10	0.20
Powers	0.33	0.29	0.31	0.04	0.07
Fiscal arrangements	0.25	0	0.13	0.25	0.40
Overall scores	0.36	0.23	0.30	0.13	0.26
Overall degree	Medium	Low	Low		Low

Appendix 5: Comparative Overviews

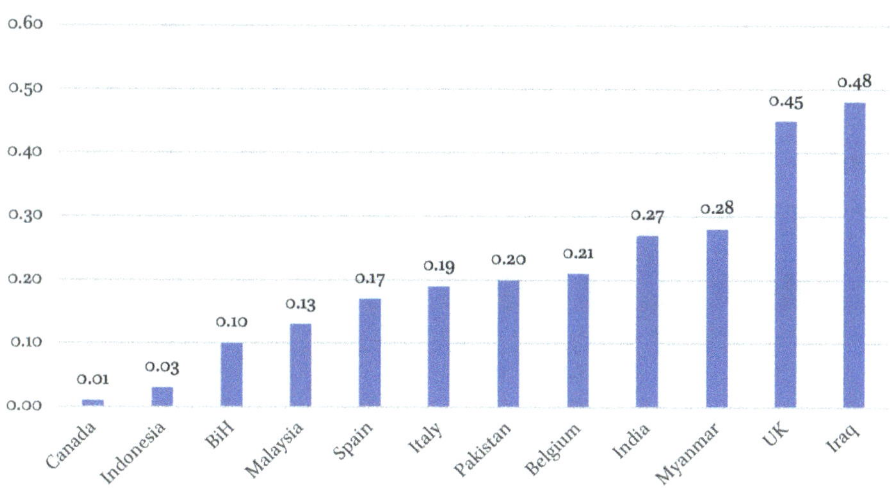

FIGURE 1 Constitutional asymmetry scores for the 12 case studies (average values)

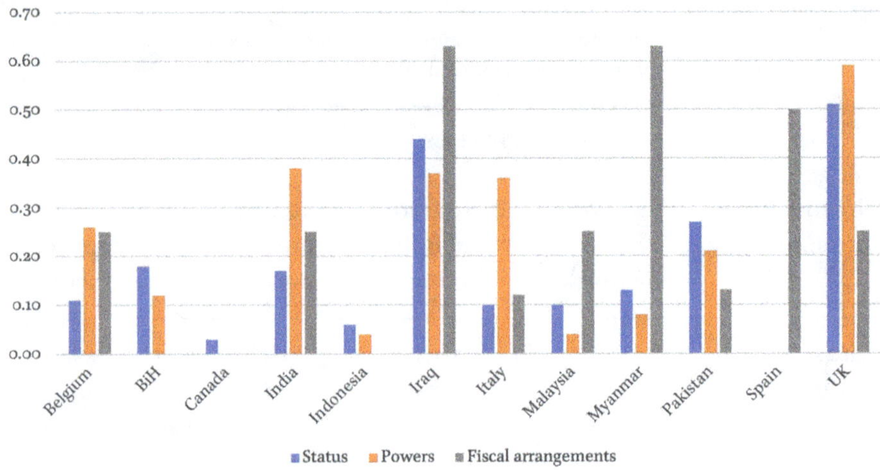

FIGURE 2 Constitutional asymmetry scores for each dimension of asymmetry in the 12 case studies

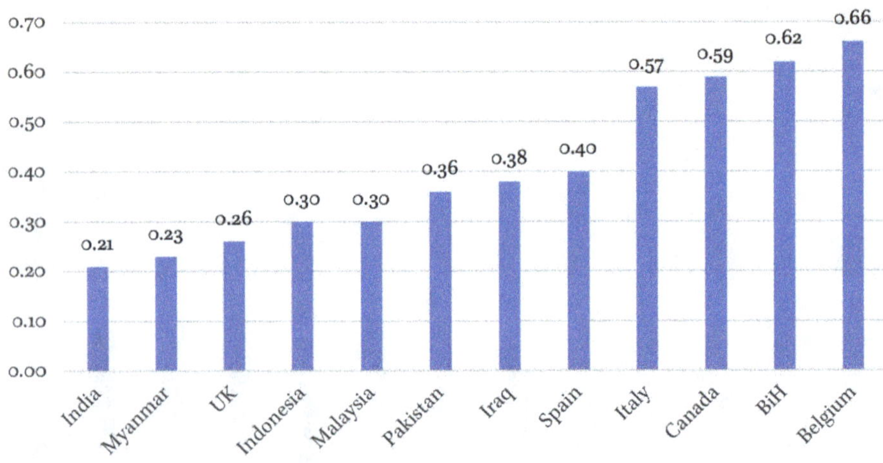

FIGURE 3 Subnational autonomy scores (overall)

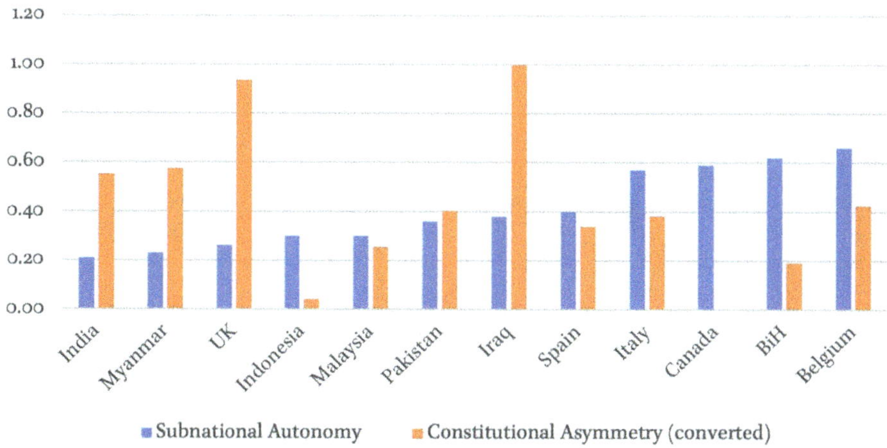

FIGURE 4 Comparison between subnational autonomy and constitutional asymmetry (converted values for degrees intervals)

Index

www.ingramcontent.com/pod-product-compliance
Lightning Source LLC
Chambersburg PA
CBHW071248230926
51849CB00001B/272
* 9 7 8 9 0 0 4 7 3 6 8 7 0 *